THE MANUAL OF
BRANDS AND MARKS

BY MANFRED R. WOLFENSTINE

Edited and with an Introduction by RAMON F. ADAMS

University of Oklahoma Press : Norman

INTERNATIONAL STANDARD BOOK NUMBER: 0–8061–0867–3

LIBRARY OF CONGRESS CATALOG CARD NUMBER: 68–31379

Preface

This is the first complete and serious treatment of the subject of marks and brands for domestic animals. Existing works are written in a humorous vein, are incomplete, dilettante, and few. The primary purpose for writing this manual is to create a comprehensive reference work, so that the origin and history of brands and branding will not be lost to future generations. In order to broaden the reader's understanding of the subject, supplementary discussions of the social, economic, and political factors affecting the use of marks and brands have been included.

Another purpose of this manual is the compilation and standardization of the various elements involved in the design of brands and marks. As is true in the creation of all new designs, the designer must analyze the background and history of the subject matter in order to produce a satisfactory device. This book is intended, therefore, to serve as a guide in the selection of brands, earmarks, and fleshmarks, and in the manufacture of branding irons. A brand properly selected and recorded undoubtedly contributes to the owner's pride in his possessions.

Chapter I traces the history of animal brands from their appearance in Egyptian tombs until the present time. It includes a synopsis of the range cattle industry, with attendant marginal information about the American West. Brands of the famous and infamous are described and illustrated, from those used by George Washington to those of Pancho Villa. Similarities of brands and other graphic symbols—such as marks, merchant seals, chemical signs, heraldic honoraries and charges—are discussed and illustrated. Types of brands and their location on animals are assembled. Of special interest is the first publication of history's first recorded brand, dated *ca.* 2,000 B.C.

Chapter II categorizes for the first time the types of branding irons, tattooing instruments and other tools used for the identification of animals. The application of chemical branding agents has been classified. Branding methods are discussed. Classification of breed registry by type of brand and specie is included. Identification requirements by breed registry associations are listed also.

In Chapter III, criteria for the design of brands are discussed in conjunction with a series of comprehensive alphabets. This chapter examines the aesthetic and functional values of proper design. Illustrations of figures accompanying the text are all-inclusive, planned to aid in the selection of a well-designed brand.

Previously unpublished information contained in Chapter IV pertains to brands exclusively used by various agencies of the U.S. Government, emphasizing the almost-lost brands and systems used by the horse cavalry and by the Department of Indian Affairs. It includes an abstract of all army regulations concerning brands, all of which are now rescinded. Identification of animals relative to disease eradication is discussed in full. Meat brands are described and classified. Illustrations have been arranged to present a panorama of brands used by the federal government.

Chapter V describes brands used by various state agencies. Accompanying illustrations show selected examples of brands applied to state-owned livestock. The subject matter of this chapter provides a sound background for critical comparison by state branding officials.

Chapter VI contains a listing of all known earmarks, wattles, dewlaps, and other marks. It further discusses tattoos applied to poultry, purebred stock, and fur-bearing animals. The monumental number of marks, all illustrated, should be useful in the selection of a functional and distinctive sign of ownership as well as serve in the recognition of the earmarks of famous ranches, past and present.

In Chapter VII text and illustrations describe the brands of all the twenty-one California missions, including items of rare historical value relating to livestock raising during the period when the missions flourished. The subject matter of this chapter is unique, because there is a beginning and an end of California mission brands.

Chapter VIII contains histories of branding laws, applications, fees, inspections, brand books, brand commissions, etc., of all fifty states. The chapter is divided into states employing brand recordation, states with county registration, and states with no compulsory registration. It also contains the first tabulation of all recorded brands in the United States, data of great value to all state branding officials for the study of comparative fees, registration procedures, and legislation.

Chapter IX describes Canadian brand registration procedures, applications, fees, etc., and is subdivided according to provinces. Mentioned also are the uses of Federal and provincial brands and statutes relating to them. The United Kingdom is presented, including abstracts of branding statutes and methods of branding, particularly of sheep. This chapter also contains all known brands used by horse breeders' associations—all described and minutely illustrated. Mexican brands are represented by the brands of famous bull ranches. Hungarian state stud farms are listed, with illustrations of their unusual brands. The last sections deal with branding regulations, including those for elephants, of Thailand.

In order to preserve a measure of continuity, references have been placed at the end of the text. Manuals, circulars, catalogs, and other publications, and references including codes, statutes, laws, ordinances, regulations, and orders are listed in the Bibliography. General works on branding also are included.

MANFRED R. WOLFENSTINE

Seattle, Washington
July 10, 1969

vii

Introduction

Perhaps the best introduction I could provide for this highly technical and valuable book, would be to quote a chapter on this subject from my own book *The Old-Time Cowhand*. Originally written in the cowhand's vernacular, to fit this text it will be put into more sophisticated language. Probably it will give the reader a more condensed and understandable picture of this subject and prepare him for what follows, so we quote:

The language of brands is a special one requiring particular knowledge, both symbolic and useful, and this knowledge marked the genuine cowman more than anything else.

The origin of the brand dates back to antiquity, and there has never been anything to take its place as a permanent mark of ownership. As the cowman says, "A brand's something that won't come off in the wash."

There are many kinds of brands, as well as innumerable forms, and each has a name of its own. They are the cowman's mark of identification—his trade-mark. Branding soon became a systematized business, and brands had to be registered with the proper official of the county, or state, through a written instrument claiming the exclusive right to burn, upon a particular part of an animal, a particular design, and certain specified cuts in the ear, or other skin. If no one else had a claim upon this design, it was formally allowed, and entered into the official brand book.

If a man wished to sell an animal, the buyer could place his own brand upon it. Yet how could this be done without his neighbor becoming suspicious that he had stolen the animal outright? The change was accomplished by what was known as a "vent brand," from the Spanish *venta,* meaning sale. The original owner placed his brand upon another part of the animal, which meant that he had deeded the animal to a new owner, whose brand it also bore. It had the effect of cancelling the ownership brand, thus serving as the acknowledgment of a sale. It was usually placed on the same side of the animal as the original brand. The term "fire out" was sometimes used instead of "vent," but it meant the same process of barring out a brand. "Counter-branding" had the same effect.

When a brand was superseded—by purchase or by discovery that the wrong brand had been placed on a animal or that the brand had been put in the wrong place—the custom was for the brander to burn a bar through the original brand and put his own brand above or below it and also on that part of the animal where it properly belonged, if the correct mark was differently situated. Later in the cattle industry, counterbranding was done by re-peating the undesired brand and placing the new one upon the animal where it belonged, and the use of the bar through the dis-carded brand was discontinued.

With the opening of the cattle trails there came into use an-other brand called the "road brand." This was a special brand of any design for trail herds as a sign of ownership en route. This brand helped the herders avoid mingling their herds with out-side cattle, thereby spiriting off their home range some animals of disinterested ownership.

This type of brand originated in Texas during the trail days, when a law was passed that all cattle driven beyond the northern limits of the state were to be branded by the drover with "a large and plain mark, composed of any mark or device he may choose, which mark shall be branded on the left side of the stock behind the shoulder." With the passing of trail driving, this brand was no longer used.

There was another brand, used only in Texas, called the "coun-ty brand." It consisted of a separate prescribed letter or group of letters for each Texas county, and when used went always, and unlike other brands, upon the animal's neck. This brand was intended to make stealing more difficult, since the rustler would now have to see that his doctored brand was recorded in the same county as the county brand, or alter that mark, too. Trail cattle which had changed ownership often upon their home range and then were driven up the trail to government agencies, at the end of their journey might have their hides thoroughly etched—or, in the language of the cowboy, be "burnt till they looked like a brand book."

Brands are composed of letters, numerals, symbols, monograms, and numerous combinations of each. The reading of brands is an art. To the tenderfoot, brands are so many picture puzzles, and he is almost sure to misread them and be dazed by their queer jumble of lines, letters, and curves. The cowboy, on the other hand, took pride in his ability to call them correctly. He recorded the brand of every animal within his vision, and could see brands from a distance that would be impossible for an unpracticed eye.

Brands have made necessary the coining of a language all their own, and this language, like other languages, follows certain rules. The characters of a brand read from top to bottom, from outside to inside and from left to right. The ability to read these symbols was referred to as "callin' the brands."

It is harder to drive one or two head of cattle than a large herd, and a good cowman avoided driving his stock whenever possible, hence his recourse to branding on the open range. In the early days all branding was done in the open, but later it was regarded with suspicion unless done in the presence of a roundup crew. Cattle branded in the open were said to be "range branded."

"Corral branding" was the branding of stock in a corral. This might not be as picturesque as branding in the open, but it was easier on the men, the cattle, and the horses. Having no herd to hold, every man could take part in the branding. The actual work was done in the same manner as branding in the open, but the steers and dry cows were worked out of the herd before it reached the pens. When the pens were reached, the mother cows were cut outside, where they bawled until the calves were turned out, to relieve their anxiety and receive their sympathy.

Modern ranches now use "chute branding." The animal is run into a narrow chute, a bar is placed in front of the animal and a second dropped behind him so he cannot move. He is then branded through the side railings. A "stamp brand," of the type in use today, is made with a set branding iron which burns the complete brand with one impression.

Traditionally, the regular "calf branding" occurred in the spring, and this was called "ironin' the calf crop," because it was the branding of the season's calves. There were usually at least two "ketch hands" to do the roping, and there was no prettier sight than to watch a smooth roper as he moved into the herd, shaking out his loop and selecting the calf to be dragged to the fire. With a short half-swing of his rope to keep from exciting the animals, he made his cast. His horse turned mechanically and headed for the fire. The roper made a mental note of the earmark and brand of the mother when he roped the calf, and as he approached the "flankers" he called out to the "iron men": "Calf on the string," and the brand of the mother. Usually the cow would follow her calf to the edge of the herd or a little beyond, as her calf was dragged, a protesting bundle of stiffened muscles pulling against the rope. If the boys who were holding the herd did not turn her back, she would sometimes follow her calf all the way and create havoc with man and horse.

The "ketch hand" was not particular how he caught the small spring calves, because they were easily handled. But when he caught a long-aged, or last fall's calf, as a favor to the flankers he would rope it by the hind feet. If he had it in for some flanker, or wanted to see some fun, he would sometimes bring up a big calf roped by the neck and then sit on his horse and laugh as he watched the flankers try to wrestle this calf down.

When the calf arrived at the end of the rope, one flanker would step in and catch the rope with his left hand, halfway between the horse and the calf, letting the rope slide through his hand until the calf was near the fire. Then the man doing the flanking would catch the calf's ear on the opposite side, and slap his hand into the flank on that side. By jerking upward with a pressure of the knees against the calf's side when it took the next jump, the flanker sent the calf's feet outward, and it came down on its side. The side they threw it on depended upon which side was to carry the brand. The rope was freed from its neck or heels early, so the ketch hand could go back for another calf.

After the flankers got the calf stretched on the ground, one sat on the ground behind the animal, with one foot shoving the lower hind leg forward as far as possible, his boot instep wedged in just above the hock. The upper hind leg he held in both hands drawn far back into his lap. The second flanker, back of the calf, rested one knee on its neck, the other on its shoulder, while he held the upper foreleg doubled at the knee, in both hands. He yelled "Calf on the ground!" and the animal was then ready for branding, ear-marking, and other operations. All the calf could do was wriggle a little and bawl plenty. Each set of flankers had their roper, and a good roper could keep them busy. Flanking calves was no vacation.

The "brander," or "iron man," was the one whose immediate duty it was to place the brand on the animal. As soon as the calf was stretched out, he yelled "Hot Iron!" with the name of the brand wanted. The "iron tender," the man who heated and attended to the branding irons, came on the trot from the fire with the branding iron wanted, as it glowed a cherry red. The brander hit the rod against his forearm to jar away the coals and pressed it to the calf's hide. This was called "slappin' a brand on," or "runnin' a brand." It required only a few seconds to mark the ears with a sharp knife and stamp the hot iron on the flesh, but those few seconds were an ordeal of terror to the calf. Usually it bore the knife without a sound, but the sizzling iron caused a doleful wail of agony and fear. When released, the calf strug-

xiii

gled to its clumsy legs and trotted off to seek its mother and sympathy.

The success of the brands depended upon the brander's wisdom in his business. He had to have expert knowledge in order to apply a branding iron properly. If the brand was not burned deep enough it would not peel, and if the iron was too hot it would burn too deep, cook the flesh, blot the brand, and leave a wound that would become infected. If too cold it would leave no brand, only a sore. Yet it had to be hot enough to burn the hair and quickly sear the surface of the hide deep enough to form a scab, which peeled off in time but allowed no hair to grow over it. The iron had to be free from scale and rust in order to make a sharp brand. Very little pressure was necessary to put on a good brand if the iron was at the proper heat. Here are a few "don'ts" the cowman usually kept in mind:

Don't let the iron get too hot; that starts a hair fire, and usually results in a poor brand. Don't use a forge or coal fire; wood is the best fuel for branding fires. Don't use acids or similar humane agents; they leave a scar, not a brand, and often cause a bad sore, and the result is usually unreadable. Don't use a small horse iron on cattle; you never get a readable brand with a small iron. Don't use a thin or burned-up iron; it will cut too deep or make a thin scar which covers over with hair. Don't try to brand a wet or even a damp animal; the brand will scald, leave a blotch, bad sore, or no brand at all. Don't get in a hurry; the cow will wear the brand all her life, and you want it to bring her home. Don't get tenderhearted; the iron must burn deep enough to remove hair and outer layer of skin, and when the iron is lifted the brand should be the color of saddle leather.

It is a good idea to avoid brands with sharp corners or those with narrow spaces between the marks if you want a clean burn. Even with a stamp iron it is hard to put such a brand on an animal that is not lying there like a sleeping baby all the time. The narrow gaps will be burned across and the whole brand will peel, leaving a brand that might be subject to dispute, if not out-right suspicion.

In putting on a brand it is best to rock the iron a little as it is pressed down; in this way some air is let under and it burns more uniformly. Deep branding, especially in the Southwest where the animal's skin is thinner, is apt to cause "warting." It does not necessarily hurt the brand except to make it look ungainly be-cause it causes a scaly growth that sometimes stands up and often causes the animal's tail to get caught on it, when that tail is needed for switching flies.

The hot iron itself was called such names as "iron,"—short for branding iron—"hot stuff," "scorcher," or "cookstove." After a calf was branded it was usually booted toward its anxious moth-er, and branding was spoken of as "burnin' and bootin' 'em," or "burnin' an' trimmin' up calves," and they did get some trim-ming before the work was done.

The "iron tender," or "firetender," was the man who tended the fires and kept the branding irons hot. He had to look to his supply of fuel in advance and see that he had plenty for the work to be done. In the early days, when working in a timberless country he had to depend on cow chips, and it was hard to keep such fires going. His was a hot job, the heat and smoke searing his eyes, but he dared not let his irons get cold until the work was done. Adding fresh fuel, fanning a sickly blaze with his hat while he tried to keep the smoke from his tired eyes, and running to the brander with the irons requested kept him on the jump. Not before the sun shone redly through the smoke was he free to kick the half-burned sticks apart and pour water on them.

Like the rest of the branding crew, he had to know brands and the irons they required. When the brander called for a certain brand the tender had to know which iron to grab. When the brand had been slapped on the calf, he took the iron back to the fire and buried it in the coals to get hot for the next victim of that brand.

THE MANUAL OF BRANDS AND MARKS

The men who cut the earmarks, dewlaps, wattles, and other marks of identification on the animal's anatomy were known as "butchers," or "knifemen," or "cutters." They squatted on their heels, built cigarettes, and sharpened their knives on a little whetstone while the irons were getting hot. They used a cowman's ordinary knife, which they resharpened every time the work slackened a bit. Theirs was a bloody job, for the calves had a way of slinging their heads after they had been earmarked. They not only marked the calves, but also made future steers of the young male animals. They had to know the various earmarks of the brands called, and sometimes each ear had several different marks on it. Working in the dust, the acrid smoke of scorching hair, the blood of cutting operations, and amid the confusion of bawling sufferers and bellowing mothers, they were a sight by the time the work was finished.

The "doctors," or "medicine men," put the finishing touches to the whole operation. They jumped about, as nimble as fleas, with their daubs and pots of tar or other disinfecting dope to smear the wounds of the animals. The "needle man" quickly and expertly used his hypodermic needle to give vaccine and shots for blackleg and other diseases. These medicine men were often smeared with their own concoctions, and smelled like a medicine chest.

Nothing about the work of branding was clean or easy except perhaps the job of the "tally man." He was usually appointed by the roundup captain, and was apt to be an older man, one recently injured, or one not in good physical condition to do heavier work. Above all he was chosen for his honesty, for this position offered many opportunities to falsify the records. Upon his count depended the owner's estimate of the season's profits. If he had some clerical ability, it helped. Although his job was the easiest one of the entire operation, he would rather have been taking an active part in the more strenuous work if he was a real cowman.

Every time a calf slithered to the fire the tally man listened for the flanker's chant of the brand of the animal's mother and its sex. He echoed this call as he set it down in his tally book. As the number of unbranded calves grew smaller, the record in his book grew longer, and as time passed it became more grimy and smudged. At every lax moment he took the opportunity to sharpen a stub pencil which was wearing down steadily. During those period of lull the brander was calling for more calves by yelling "More straw!" but this was music to the tally man's ears, because it gave him a moment to stretch.

Working in a corral full of burned cattle was no job for a weakling, and it had its perilous moments. Anxious mama cows and husky bull calves made branding interesting. When some old cow heard the anguished bawl of her calf and came on the prod, the cowhands had to be alert to keep from getting gored. When the cry "Hook 'em cow!" or "Lookout cowboy!" went up, it was no disgrace to run.

There were a lot of funny things that could happen around a branding fire. Cowhands were always putting up jokes on each other, and since there were usually hands from half a dozen outfits working around the fire, a fellow could never tell what was coming next. When some onery calf kicked a ketch hand in the middle, they laughed so hard they nearly fell off their horses, even if the hand was stretched out cold as a meat hook, with some busted ribs.

And so the work proceeded with a skill that made every move count until the last calf had scampered to its anxious mother. The air was full of smoke, dust, and animal odors; the men were dirty, bloody, with eyes smarting from dust and smoke.

A brand burned deep enough to be permanent was said to be a "fast brand." One not burned deep enough would hair over, and when this happened, in order to read the brand it had to be clipped. This was called "clippin' a brand." "Tally brandin'" was taking an inventory of cattle.

Getting back to the reading of brands, I hope I can give you a few hints along this line. A "boxed brand" is one whose design

xvii

bears framing lines; an "open brand" is a letter or figure not boxed, although the letter "A" with no cross-section is also called an "Open A." A "bench brand" is one resting on a horizontal bracket with its feet downward as a bench, and a "drag brand" is one with a bottom projection that angles downward to some degree. A "flying brand" is one whose letter or figure has wings, and a "forked brand" is one with a V-shaped prong attached to any part of the letter.

Any letter or figure "too tired to stand up," and lying on its side, is called a "lazy brand." One leaning in an oblique position is a "tumbling brand," one with lower designs like feet or legs is a "walking brand," and one with curves at its end or either side is a "running brand." A "rafter brand" is one which has semi-cone-shaped lines above it similar to the roof of a house. A "rocking brand" is one resting upon and connected with a quarter-circle, while a "swinging brand" is one suspended from a quarter-circle. However, when the quarter-circle is separate from the letter or figure, it is read a "quarter-circle."

A letter or figure having one or more enlarged termini is called a "bradded brand"; a "barbed brand" is made with a short projection from some part of it. A straight line is a "bar" if it rests in a horizontal position. If it runs through a part of a letter, it becomes a "cross." If it is perpendicular it is apt to be a "one," or sometimes an "I," but if it leans at an angle it is called a "slash." A brand using this symbol with one leaning one way and the other leaning another is called a "cut and slash." The straight horizontal line, if it is long—like John Chisum's brand, which extended from shoulder to tail—is known as the "fence rail."[1]

The letter "O," if perfectly round is called an "O" or "circle"; but if it is flattened to the least degree it becomes a "mashed O," a "squashed O," or a "goose egg." If only a part of the curved circle is used, it is a "three-quarter circle," "half-circle," or "quar-

[1] John Chisum, the Texas cattle king, is not to be confused with Jesse Chisholm, who laid out the Chisholm Trail by driving his trade wagons down from near Wichita, Kansas, to a place on the Washita River near Fort Cobb.

ter-circle," depending upon the amount used. A circle within a circle is called a "double-circle."

Roman numerals are also used in brands. Such a brand as "IV" is not called "IV," but the "Roman Four." Yet when the numeral "X" is used, it is called after the letter rather than the numeral— "LX" is "LX" brand rather than "Roman Sixty." A "connected brand" is one which combines two or more letters or figures so that they run together in a manner similar to the monogram seen on an Eastern housewife's pillow slips. The "bosal brand" is a stripe burned around an animal's nose; a brand placed on an animal directly in the rear or on the buttocks is called a "butt brand," and to burn a bar or bars across the back of an animal and extending to both sides is a "saddle brand." The "tailbone rafter" is two lines burned on the rump of an animal and meeting at the top of the tailbone.

Every conceivable symbol is used in brands: triangles, bells, pots, kettles, tools, spurs, bits, hearts, and countless others. These are usually easy to read, but there are many that even a cowboy would be at a loss to call correctly, had he not lived in the immediate vicinity and heard its name many times. An odd-looking brand, brought into a district from the outside, and having no letters, numerals, or familiar figures by which it might be called, is dubbed by the cowboy "fluidy mustard." The "whang-doodle" is a brand with a group of interlocking wings with no flying central figure. A brand too complicated to be described with a brief name is called a "fool brand."

Mexican brands are more complicated and perplexing than American brands, and the American cowboy speaking of these intricate Mexican brands did not attempt to translate them, but referred to all of them briefly, but descriptively, as "the map of Mexico," or a "skillet of snakes."

Ranches commonly took their names from the brand burned on their cattle, and owners often lost the identity of their Christian names and were called by their brand. Very often, too, a cowhand working on a ranch was called by its brand, as "Fiddleback Red," to distinguish him from the other redheads of the range and to signify that the one mentioned worked for the "Fiddleback brand."

Cowboys at a branding delighted in giving some brand a new name to see if they could stump the firetender. It developed into quite a game with some of them. When the ketch hand dragged up a calf and called out its mother's brand, the flankers, or brander, called out something entirely different, yet a name that would fit this particular brand. S. Omar Barker gave some good examples of this when he told about a ketch hand calling out "T bench," and the flanker yelling, "Tally one tea party." Or maybe another would sing out, "T at a meetin.'" Wasn't the T sitting on a bench? Or if the brand was a "Quarter-circle jog," he would call "Gimme a jug in the shade." Or if the brand was an "LN" with the N on top of the horizontal part of the L, he would perhaps call it "Sparkin' LN"—wasn't N sitting on L's lap?

Some brands have received a permanent, though unintended, name because no one knew their correct interpretation. The odd brand in Texas which no one seemed to know what to call is now the "Quien sabe." Also, a brand in Wyoming which is really the "Revolving H" is now better known as the "damfino" because when asked its name some cowhand answered, "Damn if I know."

Earmarks are an added means of identification. There were many times when it was hard to read a brand, especially in the winter when the animal's hair was long, and earmarks proved to be quite convenient and could be seen from a distance. Like brands, each mark has a name that forms a part of the cowboy's language.

The "overbit" is a V-shaped mark made by doubling the ear in and cutting a small piece, perhaps an inch, out of the upper part of the ear, an inch in length, and perhaps a third that in depth. The same cut made in the lower side of the ear is an "underbit." When two such triangular cuts are made they are a "double overbit" and "double underbit."

The "seven-overbit" is made by cutting the ear straight down near the tip for about an inch on the top side, then from near the upper base of the ear, making a cut which slopes to meet the straight downward first cut. The "seven-underbit" is made the same way by making the cut on the lower side.

A "crop" is made by cutting about one half of the ear off smoothly, straight from the upper side. Although this can be said to be a "cropped ear," what the cowboy calls a "crop-ear" is an animal with its ears shortened by freezing or sunburn. The "upper half-crop" or "over half-crop" is made by splitting the ear from the tip, midway about halfway back toward the head, and cutting off the upper half. The "lower" or "under half-crop" is made the same way on the underside of the ear.

The "steeple fork" is made by cutting two splits into the ear from the end, back one third and halfway toward the head, and cutting out the middle piece, the splits being about an inch apart. The "split" is made simply by splitting the ear from mid-tip about halfway back toward the head. The "oversplit" is made by making the split from the upper edge of the ear to about the middle; the "undersplit" being the same on the lower side.

The "swallow-fork" is made by hollowing the ear lengthwise, beginning halfway back, and cutting at an angle of forty-five degrees toward the end. The result is a forked notch in the ear. The "swallowtail" is made by trimming the tip of the ear into the form of a bird's flaring tail.

The "overslope" is made by cutting the ear about two-thirds of the way back from the tip straight to the center of the ear at the upper side; the "underslope" is the same cut on the lower side. The "sharp" is made by cutting an under-slope and over-slope on the same ear, giving it a sharp or pointed appearance, sometimes called a "point." The "grub" is a cruel earmark made by cutting the entire ear off smoothly with the head. One of the sayings of the range is "When you see a man grubbin' and sharpin' the ears of his cows, you can bet he's a thief." A man who "grubbed" or "sharped" was looked upon with suspicion, because these marks were resorted to by rustlers to destroy the original earmark, and such marks were unlawful in many states.

The "overhack" is made by simply cutting down an inch on the upper side of the ear, and the "underhack" is the same cut on the lower side. The "over-round" is made by cutting a half-circle from the top of the ear, while the "under-round" is cutting the half-circle from the bottom. The "hole earmark" is made by simply punching a hole in the ear; the "sawtooth" is made by cutting the end of the ear in and out in the shape of the teeth of a saw, while the "saw-set" is made by cropping the ear, then cutting out the center in the shape of a rectangle, and it is sometimes called the "crop and mortice." The "jingle-bob" is an earmark made with a deep slit that leaves the lower half of the ear flopping down—one of the most hideous marks ever devised. The mark was made famous by John Chisum, a pioneer rancher of Lincoln County, New Mexico.

Cattle without earmarks are called "full ears," or "slick ears," and one that has been earmarked is a "stick ear." Earmarks can be used in innumerable combinations.

There are other marks of ownership made with a knife other than those of the ears. The "dewlap" is made on the underside of the neck or brisket by pinching up a quantity of skin and cutting it all, but not entirely off. When healed it leaves a hanging flap of skin. Some were slashed up and called "dewlaps up," others slashed down and called "dewlaps down." The "jug handle" is made by cutting a long slash on the skin of the brisket and not cutting out at either end, so that, when healed, it looks like the handle of a jug.

The "wattle" is made on the neck or jaw of an animal by pinching up a quantity of skin, and cutting it all, but not entirely off. When healed it leaves a hanging flap of skin. The "varruga" is also a wattle, made by cutting a strip of hide down about two inches and letting it hang. "Buds" are made by cutting down a strip of skin on the nose.

As a mark of identification the brand is perfect. It is put on

xxii

in a moment, yet it remains as long as the animal lives, and no matter how far a cow or horse may stray from its home range, identification by the owner, through the brand, is positive. The ability to read brands and earmarks correctly and at a glance ranks almost as high as dexterity with a rope, and higher on a cow ranch than the ability to ride bucking horses.

RAMON F. ADAMS

Dallas, Texas.

Contents

		page
	Preface	v
	Introduction	ix
ONE	History of Brands and Branding	3
TWO	Branding Implements and Methods	42
THREE	Design of Brands	62
FOUR	Federal Government Brands	83
FIVE	State Government Brands	127
SIX	Marks	133
SEVEN	California Mission Brands	157
EIGHT	Brand Registration	162
NINE	Foreign Brands	223
	Miscellany	273
	Glossary	278
	List of Abbreviations	292
	Bibliography	295
	References	305
	Index of Plates and Figures	315
	Plates and Figures	355
	General Index	431

Plates and Figures

beginning on page

I. Egyptian Tomb Paintings (Figs. 1–3)   355
II. Historical Brands (Figs. 4–23)
III. Cattle Trails
IV. Miscellaneous Brands (Figs. 24–49)
V. Similarity of Symbols (Figs. 50–71)
VI. Cadency (Figs. 72–94)
VII. Points and Regions of Cattle (Fig. 95)
VIII. Points and Regions of Horses (Fig. 96)
IX. Points and Regions of Sheep (Fig. 97)
X. Points and Regions of Swine (Fig. 98)
XI. Blotting of Brands (Figs. 99–116)
XII. Types of Running Irons (Figs. 117–123)
XIII. Working Drawing of Stamp Iron
XIV. Rules of Reading Brands (Figs. 124–166)
XV. Brand Dimensions (Figs. 167–179)
XVI. Single and Connected Alphabets (Figs. 180–181)
XVII. Standard and Flying Alphabets (Figs. 182–183)
XVIII. Running and Long Alphabets (Figs. 184–188)
XIX. Hooked and Bradded Alphabets (Figs. 189–190)
XX. Forked and Barbed Alphabets (Figs. 191–192)
XXI. Dragging and Walking Alphabets (Figs. 193–194)
XXII. Swinging and Rocking Alphabets (Figs. 195–196)
XXIII. Crazy and Backward Alphabets (Figs. 197–198)
XXIV. Lazy Down Alphabets (Figs. 200–201)
XXV. Lazy Up Alphabets (Figs. 202–203)
XXVI. Tumbling Alphabets (Figs. 204–205)

XXVII.   Single and Connected Numbers (Figs. 206–207)

XXVIII.   Bars (Figs. 208–243)

XXIX.   Slashes and Triangles (Figs. 244–267)

XXX.   Diamonds (Figs. 268–286)

XXXI.   Boxes (Figs. 287–302)

XXXII.   Circles (Figs. 303–333)

XXXIII.   Common Picture Brands (Figs. 334–369)

XXXIV.   Common Picture Brands (Figs. 370–403)

XXXV.   Army Brands and Branding Irons (Figs. 404–412)

XXXVI.   The West Point Iron (Figs. 413–416)

XXXVII.   U.S. Government Brands (Figs. 417–443)

XXXVIII.   Old Navaho Brands (Figs. 444–461)

XXXIX.   Carcass Brands (Figs. 462–475)

XL.   State Government Brands (Figs. 476–509)

XLI.   Earmarks (Figs. 510–535)

XLII.   Earmarks (Figs. 536–559)

XLIII.   Earmarks (Figs. 560–583)

XLIV.   Earmarks (Figs. 584–607)

XLV.   Earmarks (Figs. 608–635)

XLVI.   Earmarks (Figs. 636–653)

XLVII.   Earmarks (Figs. 654–677)

XLVIII.   Earmarks (Figs. 678–703)

XLIX.   Earmarks (Figs. 704–724)

L.   Earmarks (Figs. 725–746)

LI.   Earmarks (Figs. 747–767)

LII.   Earmarking System for Sheep (Figs. 768–796)

LIII.   Earmarking System for Swine and Goats (Figs. 797–800)

LIV.   Earmarking System for Swine (Figs. 801–824)

LV.   Dewlaps (Figs. 825–831)

LVI.   Dewlaps (Figs. 832–837)

LVII.   Wattles (Figs. 838–848)

LVIII.   Wattles (Figs. 849–854)

LIX.   California Mission Brands (Figs. 855–877)

LX.   Canadian Federal and Provincial Brands
      (Figs. 878–916)
LXI. Scottish Sheep Brands (Figs. 917–961)
LXII. German Horse Brands (Figs. 962–977)
LXIII. German Horse Brands (Figs. 978–989)
LXIV. German Horse Brands (Figs. 990–1,012)
LXV. German Horse Brands (Figs. 1,013–1,029)
LXVI. German Horse Brands (Figs. 1,030–1,048)
LXVII. German Horse Brands (Figs. 1,049–1,069)
LXVIII. German Horse Brands (Figs. 1,070–1,094)
LXIX. German Horse Brands (Figs. 1,095–1,117)
LXX. Mexican Bull Ranch Brands (Figs. 1,118–1,131)
LXXI. Hungarian State Stud Farm Brands
      (Figs. 1,132–1,137)
LXXII. Lewis and Clark Branding Iron
LXXIII. Perspective View of Lewis and Clark
      Branding Iron
LXXIV. An Example of Cryo-branding

THE MANUAL OF
BRANDS AND MARKS

ONE

History of Brands and Branding

The practice of branding as exercised by the Egyptians was very similar to current practices and methods. Temple and royal herds were branded, as were privately owned herds of distinguished individuals. Egyptian branding practices are mostly recorded by paintings, and Mesopotamian practices, by text. There are records of several branding scenes painted on the walls of tombs. These tomb paintings are relatively well preserved and have been documented. Paintings depicting branding are found in the following tombs:

1. Tomb of Enti, at Deshashah. Old Kingdom (2780–2280 B.C.). There is supporting evidence that wall paintings existed depicting branding of cattle.

2. Tomb of Manufer, at Saqqâra. Old Kingdom (2780–2280 B.C.). Evidence uncovered also affirms that branding of cattle was depicted by a painting in this tomb.

3. Tomb of Khemuheted, Tomb No. 3, at Beni Hassan. The tomb dates back to 1900 B.C. and was constructed during the Twelfth Dynasty (2000–1785 B.C.) of the Middle Kingdom (2100–1700 B.C.). The painting in the tomb depicts an Egyptian cowboy leading a spotted ox by a rope. The ox carries a bell suspended from the neck by a rope collar consisting of six coils. On the left thigh, the ox is branded with the first recorded boxed brand, about a foot square with hieroglyphics. This brand is translated as having the inscription: "Royal Agriculture Administration, 43." The last line of pictographs refers to the number of the herd or the number of the animal (Figs. 1 and 5).

4. Tomb of Userhet, Tomb No. 56, at Shekh abd el Gurna.

3

This tomb is the burial place of a royal scribe and dates to King Amenophis II (1488–1422 B.C.), Eighteenth Dynasty of the New Kingdom (1570–1349 B.C.). On the left side wall of the transversal chamber a roundup is depicted in three tiers of pictures. The roundup is taking place in a yard full of trees and bushes and shows cowboys roping the cattle. The lower picture shows a brander applying the stamp iron to the left shoulder of an animal. There are also tally men keeping records, facing away from the branding and toward the master and the owner of the cattle.

5. Tomb of Nebamun, Tomb No. 90, at Thebes. This tomb is the burial place of an officer of King Thutmosis IV (1422–1411 B.C.) of the Eighteenth Dynasty, New Kingdom (1570–1349 B.C.). The painting on the north side of the west wall depicts branding scenes and shows a forced-fed ox, bound with piggin' strings, all four feet together, being branded on the right shoulder. Next to the ox is the iron man heating up another iron over a container filled with coal. The handles on the branding irons are about six inches long and are of essentially the same construction as the ones being used four thousand years later (Figs. 2 and 3).

6. In Mesopotamia, temple, royal, and privately owned sheep, goats, and cattle were branded. This was accomplished by fire brands, as was done in Egypt, or by dye brands on the fleece. The dyes were of different colors. There is one text which describes a chaotic situation after an unusually heavy rain: The dye-brands had been washed off by the rain, and the owners of the sheep could no longer distinguish their animals from those of their neighbors. Another text states that the herd owned by the temple of the goddess Ishtar was branded with a star. The star was the sign of the goddess Ishtar, the Near Eastern equivalent of the Greek goddess Aphrodite.

In the Dark Ages (400–1400 A.D.) it is reported that horses were branded in England in the eighth century, and on the Con-

4

tinent, animals were seared with the Crossed Hammers of Solingen, Germany (Fig. 4). During the Hundred Years' War at the Battle of Crécy-en-Ponthieu, northern France, in 1346, horses of the victorious English yeomen and aristocrats were branded with the Broad Arrow (Fig. 6). This brand is called the British Imperial brand.

The era from 1500 to 1600 is known as the Age of Exploration. In 1519 Captain General Designate Hernán Cortés landed in Mexico and, after subjugating the natives, settled down to ranching. His brand, Three Latin Crosses, represents the first brand in the Western Hemisphere (Fig. 7).

All American cattle, horses, and mules are of foreign ancestry. They were brought to the Western Hemisphere by Spanish explorers and settlers. The first cattle were introduced into the United States at a place near Douglas, Arizona. The shipper of the first cattle to arrive was Gregorio Villalobos. He landed six heifers and one young bull, all of Andalusian ancestry, at Vera Cruz from Santo Domingo. In 1530, Álvar Núñez Cabeza de Vaca and three companions, Dorantes, Maldonado, and Estevan (an "Arab Negro from Azamor"), were the first Europeans to approach the Great Plains. They did not venture into the Great Plains, but they did touch the periphery of this region and saw the buffalo. Cabeza de Vaca's brand was the Head of a Cow (Fig. 8).

The first expedition ever made by white men into the Great Plains was made by Don Francisco Vasquez de Coronado and his army in 1541. Coronado and his men, searching for gold and other treasures, were accompanied by a train of a thousand horses, five hundred cows, and more than five hundred rams and ewes. The cattle were branded.

During the Colonial Period (1600–1821), settlers in the Colonies began branding and marking their animals. This practice was undoubtedly a continuation of the custom as practiced in Europe. It appears that horn branding was extensively practiced, and that all brands were registered. Among the earliest re-

5

corded brands in Richmond County, Staten Island, New York, were the Heart brand of Justice John Veghte in 1739 (Fig. 13); the brand of William Maclane in 1721 (Fig. 9); and the brand of Henry Holland in 1760 (Fig. 11). In California, the first missions were established in 1769, and each mission had at least one brand (see Chapter VII, "California Mission Brands"). In the Southwest, Spanish Governor of Texas Don Pedro de Barrios Junco granted a brand to a militiaman, Don Nicolas Saez, in 1742 (Fig. 14). The first Anglo-Saxon cattle baron was Stephen F. Austin (1793–1835) and his Old Spanish brand was registered in Brazoria County, Texas (Fig. 12). Co-operative arrangements in the 1850's required Mormons to assign one out of each ten lambs to the church. For flocks so acquired, the bishops of the several "stakes" were responsible. As these sheep often grazed along with privately owned flocks, church ownership was indicated by branding the animals with a cross.

From 1821 to 1913 the region of the Great Plains presented a formidable obstacle to the pioneering American. The frontier was practically stationary in the vicinity of the ninety-eighth meridian for a period lasting approximately from 1840 to 1885. During the westward movement of progress, the frontier jumped across the Great Plains and was established along the Pacific slope. Only with the advent of new discoveries and inventions was the farmer able to enter the Great Plains.

At that time, the frontier was reduced by forward movements from the East and by retrograde movements from the West. During the process of solving problems of water, fencing, and other agricultural necessities, the cattle kingdom was born in the Plains country. When the Industrial Revolution at last furnished the means for fully developing the Plains, it also caused the almost total destruction of the new and genuinely original culture born in the Plains.

The phenomenon known as the Cattle Kingdom (1821–1906) had its origin in a region offering almost perfect climatic and topographical conditions for the raising of cattle. This region,

6

shaped in the form of a diamond, was bounded by San Antonio, Old Indianola, Brownsville, and Laredo. From this home range of the cattle industry, cattle drives and sales were irregular and of little consequence. In 1832, Richard H. Chisholm recorded his brand in Gonzales County, Texas. This brand is the first recorded in Texas (Fig. 16). In 1849, a ranchman of Live Oak County found the country overrun with wild and unbranded cattle. He also noted that old branding irons were lying about the prairies in large numbers and that people living nearby did not even recognize the brand. The Civil War temporarily arrested the development of the industry and cattle became more numerous and less valuable at the beginning of the conflict.

The purpose of Texas cattlemen in driving their herds to the north was to find a market for them, even though railheads were twelve to fifteen hundred miles away. There was an expansion period of the cattle industry from 1866 to 1873, but the year 1866 itself was a disastrous one for the Texas drovers, who were beset by robbery, theft, floggings, and worst of all, by the fear of Northern cattlemen that their cattle would be contaminated by the Spanish fever tick (Texas fever) of the Texans' cattle.

In order to provide a market where a Southern drover and a Northern buyer could meet to transact business undisturbed by outlaws and thieves, the first of the cow towns was established at Abilene, Kansas, in 1867. The site was selected because of its excellent grass, water resources, and potential capability to hold large numbers of cattle. From 1866 to 1880 nearly five million head of cattle were shipped from Abilene. At the close of the sixties, herds of considerable size also existed in the northern section of the High Plains and in the adjoining mountain valleys. These herds were accumulated from the stock of gold seekers, emigrants, from herds from California and Oregon, and from the work animals of freighting companies. Good profits were realized by supplying military posts, mining camps, and section crews.

1871 marked the greatest cattle drive. From Texas to Kansas

7

alone, 700,000 head were shipped. However, market conditions were unfavorable that year. In 1872, even with an improved market, demands for a better grade of beef were made. As a consequence, Northern ranchers did better than Southern ranchers because their herds were of an improved stock and fattened with corn. From this time on, Texas cattle were shipped north to be fattened. This situation marked another phase of the industry.

In 1873 the first panic known to the range cattleman occurred with resultant heavy financial losses. Two conditions became clearly apparent to the Southern cattleman: scrub stock could no longer be marketed for the range in the North; and good beef or good animals which could be fattened must henceforth be delivered. In 1876 the cattle industry was recovering from the panic of three years before, and from this year until 1885 was the boom period of the cattle industry. During this time it steadily expanded. The range was still open and free grass available. Many herds were shipped from Texas to Arizona, New Mexico, Indian Territory, and Colorado. In 1873, 400,000 head; in 1874, 165,000 head; and in 1875, 150,000 head were shipped from Texas.

Financial conditions favorable to investment, the decrease in numbers of Indians in the Great Plains, the growing population of the East, the extension of railroads, and the fear that free ranges would not last much longer resulted in Easterners, Englishmen, Scotsmen, Canadians, and Australians flocking to the Great Plains to become ranchers. Under these conditions, prices began to rise. From 1880 to 1885 the demand for stocking cattle on Northern ranges reached the extreme limits of available supply. Many Texas cattle were sold to Northern cattlemen for stocking their ranges in the vicinity of Ogallala, Nebraska. Since the demand was so great, even cattle from adjoining agricultural states were shipped to the West. At the same time, promoters seized the opportunity to harvest fortunes from speculations. Range rights, obtained under various Federal land acts were sold in Europe. The winter of 1880–81 was a severe one for

8

northern ranges, and stockmen incurred severe losses, particularly in Montana. Over-stocking of the ranges had so reduced the grass area that the drought in 1883 brought disaster to Texas cattlemen. In 1884 prices began to fall. The remaining free grass was rapidly going under fence, and range rights were found to be fictitious. In 1885 the boom collapsed—speculators and genuine cattlemen suffered alike.

This decline lasted until 1893. The period from 1885 to 1890 was dark indeed to the range cattleman. Prices continued to decline and conditions became so serious that a Senate committee was appointed to examine all the aspects of meat production. Enormous losses were also sustained from the blizzard in the winter of 1886–87, when 85 per cent of the cattle perished in the Northwest. This catastrophe demonstrated to the cattleman that to depend on the open range and the grass crop alone was a fatal mistake. The future of the industry depended on the capability of hay production to carry herds through the winter.

Cattle raising had ceased to be a frontier industry and it had fallen victim to overexpansion. The small operator found it increasingly difficult to stay in business as, somehow or other, his cattle disappeared. If he maintained his herd, he became the object of suspicion as a possible rustler. His influence in the community waned as the influence of owners of large companies waxed. Outfit after outfit became part of a company with offices in New York, Boston, or Edinburgh.

Nevertheless, wire fences continued to creep westward. Cattlemen, realizing the precariousness of their situation, began to buy and to lease all the land they could acquire. The land fenced included their own, non-leasable government land, leased land, or even the land of homesteading farmers. Cattlemen were now divided into two hostile camps: the free-grass men versus the big pasture (fenced range or wire) men. The free-grass men were still clinging to the idea of continued open range, or were not able to fence. A third party was the farmer (granger, nestor, nester, sod buster) hated by both the free-grass and fenced-

9

range men, because he, too, fenced and enclosed the water. From this period on, ranching had to be operated under a system of fenced pastures, improvement of stock, and more thorough methods of ranching. Water problems were solved by well, windmill, or tank, and railroads were used for transportation. The calamity of 1885 converted ranching from an adventure into as sound a business as farming or manufacturing. Yet the romance of that old type of ranching still persists.

By 1887 the grangers had arrived in force in western Nebraska, and by 1888 Wyoming ranchers were feeling the full impact of this invasion. Granger influence at the county seats grew, and it became next to impossible to obtain convictions for violations of the stock laws. Populism began to appear in the form of anti-stock agitation. Disgruntled farmers, complaining of no rain, low prices, and high freight charges and interest rates began a campaign against the big corporations and money power. Grangers sitting on grand juries boasted of never indicting an accused rustler. Grangers also took to shooting range cattle. The repeal of the pre-emption and timber culture laws, and the modification of the Desert Land Act appeared to them to be the result of influence by the big corporations. Matters became serious and erupted in the Johnson County War (April 6–April 13, 1892). Members of the Wyoming Stock Growers' Association and a band of hired Texas hands attempted to invade the range and to rout rustlers, small cattlemen, and sympathetic county officials who were in the process of laying out independent round-up districts. The invaders were halted by units of the United States Cavalry before they could engage in a fight with the armed population of Buffalo, Wyoming.

By 1890, four types of holdings were distinguishable on the northern ranges: the unirrigated farm, limited to favorable localities until the development of dry farming; the unirrigated stock ranch, depending upon natural hay-lands and open range; the irrigated farm raising crops other than forage; and the irrigated stock ranch—irrigation carried on solely for the purpose of increasing the forage crop on natural pasture lands.

In 1893 the line of the Great Northern railroad was completed across the northern counties of Montana, but settlement along the line was slow. In 1902 settlers' dogs were making it increasingly difficult for old range outfits to operate. This condition, as well as other causes, brought about the termination of many of their operations, even though movement of stock to the northern ranges had furnished more business than the railroads could handle. In 1904 the remaining northern ranges had been overstocked, and the heavy winter losses which followed made continuation of the range-cattle system impossible. The Montana range still remained, but the big stockmen had been compelled to withdraw and the homesteaders were not sufficiently settled to operate on a scale big enough to offset withdrawal of the large herds. Thus the range cattlemen disappeared, with the last roundups on the northern ranges conducted in Wyoming in 1904 and in Montana in 1906.

The reason that the Cattle Kingdom was identified as the center of the cattle industry lies not in the number of cattle involved, but rather in the methods employed to manage them. In 1880 the entire United States had 39,675,333 head of cattle. Of this number, the sixteen Western states and territories accounted for 12,612,089 head, or 34 per cent of the total. But the East managed cattle in an unspectacular fashion compared to the colorful methods employed in the West. For example, a thousand Eastern farms with a total of ten head each, including cows and calves, accounted for 10,000 head and worked them in a very incidental agricultural manner. A single Western ranch, covering as many acres as a thousand Eastern farms and with an equal 10,000 head, managed them in a very distinct manner. There were roundups, rodeos, branding days with the air filled with the smell of seared hair and hide, boots and broad-brimmed hats, jingling spurs and horses, camp cooks and wranglers. This was a culture all its own, promulgating its own law—the Code of the West. This culture found ways and means to solve its own problems. Where the Easterner represented conventions, the plainsman represented innovations; where one carried the law in books and walked, the other rode on horseback with the law tucked in his holster. By 1876 the Cattle Kingdom had spread over the entire Plains area and all over the glassland not occupied by farms, including all or portions of twelve states: Western Texas, Oklahoma, Kansas, Nebraska, North Dakota, South Dakota, Montana, Wyoming, Nevada, Utah, Colorado, and New Mexico. The rate of expansion had no parallel in its growth in American history. When the Industrial Revolution at last furnished the means to fully develop the Plains, it also caused the almost total destruction of this new and distinct culture.

A combination of two developments interrupted the ways of the cattleman. The first incident was the enactment of the Homestead Act of 1862. Under the provisions of this Act, settlers on a public domain could acquire a homestead for a nominal fee, but had to live on that property five years before obtaining title thereto. As yet, the ranchman owned no grass or land, but merely the cattle and the camps. Range rights, recognized by his neighbors, but not yet by law, meant a right to the water he had claimed and a right to the adjoining range. If a ranchman claimed both sides of the stream, his recognized range included the land drained by the stream within the limits of his water frontage. If he possessed only one side of the stream, his range extended only in that direction. Consequently, divides became the boundaries in the range country. Upstream and downstream boundaries were not so easily determined. By an act of the Texas Legislature (Laws of Texas, Sess. 12, 1866), the principle of the accustomed range was recognized. It provided that driving stock from its accustomed range, unless proven that such stock definitely belonged to the drover, was a misdemeanor and punishable by fine and imprisonment. This range situation of the accustomed range prevailed from 1867 to 1880. However, when

12

individual cattle companies claimed range rights over a territory as large as several Eastern states combined, clearly this
situation could no longer endure.

The second development to interrupt the ways of the cattleman was the invention of barbed wire. The advent of this inno-
vation was an important factor contributing to the decline of
the Cattle Kingdom. By its use, it converted the open, free range
into the big pasture country. It caused the cattle trail to become
a crooked lane and forced the cattleman to use the railroad. It
also caused bloodshed and fence-cutter wars in Texas, Wyoming,
and New Mexico. Legislatures of Western states enacted laws
making it a felony to cut wires, but also requiring fencers to
leave necessary gates, and prohibiting the enclosure of small
land owners and the enclosing of public lands. Fencing of the
public domain was prosecuted under the Enclosure Act of 1885,
but a new scheme was devised by ranchmen to circumvent the
law. From the public domain, railroads were granted alternate
sections of land, like squares in a checkerboard. In 1884 land
sales by the railroads in the cattle country began to mount. Because of the checkerboard arrangement of the railroad sections,
the purchaser of fifty sections of railroad property, by merely
fencing his outside sections, gained control of up to forty alternate government sections. Barbed wire principalities were created by running the wire four inches inside the boundary of the
purchased section to within four inches of the intersection with
the government section. Then the fencer went across the point
of intersection of his own two and the government two sections
and started again four inches from the point of intersection and
four inches from the boundary of his own section. This left a gap
of only eight inches. By proceeding in such manner, the fencer
could claim that the public domain was not legally fenced; but
for all practical purposes it was.

Along with the development of barbed wire, the windmill
enabled the rancher to further partition his land into a system
of pastures—summer, winter, bull, range cattle, blooded stock,

13

and others—by sinking wells in different parts of his land to provide water. Now the ranch was cross fenced, with each pasture having its own independent water supply lifted from the well by the windmill.

As the settlers arrived, the ranchman subdivided the fenced pastures and relinquished them to the farmers. They turned under the precious grass and turned over the soil. In some places water was applied by artificial means, either pumped by windmills or from the river. After the drought, when the majority of the farmers left, artificial irrigation permitted a few to remain.

By the time the first Anglo-Saxon settlers reached Texas, the woods were full of Spanish black cattle, mustang cattle (strays), and *cimarrones* (wild cattle). These settlers brought with them their own cattle, of Missouri, Kentucky, and Tennessee strains. In time, all the strains mixed and the result was the longhorn. From the time of the Texas revolution until the Civil War, cattle just grew wild, multiplying at a rapid rate. These cattle were hard and tough as a result of their fight for survival. Longhorns yielded little beef and the small quantity they did produce was coarse and stringy. They yielded even less milk, but longhorns had the ability to survive. This domesticated-animal-run-wild was never found in herds, although a few cows and their calves associated for mutual protection. Bulls were almost always found alone. The Spanish black cattle were the direct descendants of the large herds raised by the Moors on the Andalusian plains. This Andalusian strain also provides the great, black bulls for the bull rings.

Longhorns were of light carcass with long legs, sloping ribs, thin rumps and loins, and disproportionately large bellies. In color they were nondescript—yellow, red, brown, brindle, gruya (mouse colored), white, cream, dun, black, and often had an iron-grey stripe along the back. This stripe, called a lobo (wolf) stripe, was the distinguishing mark of wild cattle, horses, or burros. An animal splotched with a multitude of colors was called

14

a paint, one with a stripe down its back, a lineback. In performance they were almost as tough as the bison they replaced, and
to work with them was sometimes a dangerous task, because the
spread of horns reached six or seven feet. These horns, having an
average spread of four or five feet, arched gently forward generally, but sometimes grew in other directions—such as, for example, a shape like the handle-bar of a bicycle.

The longhorn dominated the range until the late nineteenth
century, when Durham and Hereford stock was crossed, resulting in a crossbred type of range animal which proved to be a
good forager and beef producer. Other successful experiments
include the Texas Brahma, a crossbreed of the longhorn, Brahma,
and Hereford. The Hereford became the standard breed of range
cattle, however, because of a better type of carcass and a general
adaptability to range conditions.

The roundup which originated in the mountains of Kentucky,
Tennessee, North Carolina, Virginia, and West Virginia cannot
be classified with the roundups of the West in magnitude. In
1866 Texas cattle owners began to claim possession of their long-
neglected stock by staging cow-hunts, the primitive forerunners
of the spectacular Western roundup, covering four or five thousand square miles during the 1870–80 decade, the height of the
Cattle Kingdom.

At a meeting of the stockgrowers' association, a foreman (captain) and an assistant foreman were selected who had absolute
authority in the co-operative undertaking. Roundup districts
were established by the association or by counties to include all
ranges. Some point in the district was designated as rendezvous,
where the men gathered with their remudas. The chuck wagon
was usually furnished by the largest outfit. After the camp had
been established, riders diverged fanwise from it and drove the
stock toward the center of the circle, the roundup ground. There
the assembled stock became the roundup herd. After all stock
had been gathered on a particular range and assembled into the

15

roundup herd, the cattleman whose range was being worked made the first cut, cutting out cows with unbranded calves, called the cow-and-calf-cut. Next the stray men (reps) were sent in to cut out stock belonging to their respective outfits. These cattle were held in the stray cut. The calves might be branded when the cut was made or by the owner at a later date. After the first range was completely cleaned up, the owner of that range held his stock, while the day herd (stray herd) was driven to the next range. From the first day, there were as many herds of cattle as there were owners, and the longer the operation progressed, the larger the herd became.

There were two roundups each year. The spring roundup, the more important, was called the calf roundup because it was then that calves were branded. The fall roundup, about September, caught all the summer calves and strays that had been missed during the spring roundup.

Ownership of a calf was based on the fact that it would follow its mother, and no matter how large the herd is, a cow will know her own calf. In case the mother had died or the two had been forcibly kept apart, it was assumed that a maverick calf found on the range in the spring was the property of the man who owned the range and whose cattle were accustomed to graze thereon. This was the basis for the doctrine of the accustomed range in settling ownership problems. It was possible to make mavericks by separating calves from the herd and holding them for a while, until they no longer could find and follow their mothers. Mavericks could also be made by slitting the calf's tongue so that it was not able to suckle and would soon stop following its mother. An act of the Texas Legislature (Laws of Texas, 1866, Sess. 11, pp. 187–88) provided penalties for branding mavericks with an unrecorded brand or altering any existing brand. In Wyoming Territory (Laws of Wyoming Territory, 1884, Sess. 8, pp. 148–52), the maverick was defined and directions promulgated for its disposal. By law, the foreman of the roundup was instructed to take all mavericks and offer them for auction later, branding them with the brand of the purchaser and the brand of the Association. In 1884, the foreman was required to brand mavericks with brand "M" on the side of the neck. This was the official brand of the Association. By this method, the Wyoming Stock Growers' Association made the maverick the property of the Territory, with the Association as trustee.

A method of altering brands by blotting was sometimes successfully used by rustlers. The brand artist (brand worker, brand burner) used the original brand as the basic design and developed from that a design that was totally different and hard to recognize as being superimposed on the old one. When running on a brand, care has to be exercised not to burn the old brand too deeply, because its ridge can form a healing scar only once. Consequently, the old brand may be touched with the branding iron only very lightly. To effectively blend the old and the new brand, a wet sack or blanket can be placed over the old scar and a hot iron run over it. This procedure causes scalding of the old ridge and makes it peel off, together with the scabs of the new brand. As this is a rather difficult process, it is seldom used. A worked brand may be detected only when the superimposed new brand has not healed and peeled off, and by feeling along the new brand for the outline of the old brand. Definite proof of blotting may also be obtained after killing and skinning the animal. The underside of the hide will show up the old brand very plainly.

The easiest way to alter the design of a brand is by adding bars, circles etc., and by extending existing lines. Adding a bar to the Bar T brand will result in the Curry Comb brand (Figs. 99 and 100). Add two circles to the Circle brand, and the result is a Chain brand (Figs. 105 and 106). By adding a bar to the Circle brand, a Buckle brand will result (Figs. 107 and 108). By extending the numerals in the Eleven Quarter Circle brand, the Rocking Chair brand is formed (Figs. 101 and 102); extending lines and curves of the Bar S brand results in the Forty Eight brand (Figs. 109 and 110).

17

The most famous example of blotting is the working of the XIT into the Star Cross brand. This brand was applied to the left side of the animal and extended to its flank. Because the skin of the animal was stretched during the application of the brand, upon release the hide around the flank bearing the T retracted to its normal position, thereby causing the left end of the top bar of the T to raise slightly. The brand artists projected this line and added lines to form a star. With the addition of another bar, the altered brand read Star Cross (Figs. 103 and 104).

Cattle drives began in 1846 and came to an end in 1890. Drives were for the purpose of meeting the rail-heads for shipments East and for distribution of stock on the northern ranges. The movement northward was progressing steadily when the Civil War interrupted its course. After the end of the war, when Texas had surplus cattle and the North was prospering, the drives were resumed with renewed impetus.

When the drives had reached considerable proportions, a law was enacted by the Texas Legislature (Laws of Texas, 1871, Sess. 12, p. 119), requiring that all persons purchasing cattle for driving to market across the northern limits of the state were to use a road brand: "A large and plain mark, composed of any mark or device he may choose, which mark shall be branded on the left side of the back behind the shoulder."

The cattle in the herd usually had been procured from various cattlemen and consequently were branded with many different designs, and the road brand served as a means of identification for one specific drive. After a drover had contracted to deliver a herd at a certain destination, stock was cut out at the roundup and turned over to the trail foreman. In addition to the trail boss, a cowboy for every 175 head of cattle was selected. The riders at the head of the herd were designated pointmen, farther back were the swing riders, then the flank men, and bringing up the rear, the drag men. Men always worked in pairs on opposite sides of the herd. There were also the chuck wagon with the

18

cook and the wrangler with a remuda of from eight to ten horses for each rider. The only natural obstacles in the direction of the drive were the rivers, which could be waded ordinarily. Drives had to be timed to take into consideration thawing of snow and spring rains, which could make the rivers unfordable, and also the most opportune time for foraging.

The cattle drives originating from Texas were by no means the first time that cattle were trail markers. Cattle have accompanied man since the early explorations, but always incidental to his movements and needs. The Texas cattle trails, however, represent the first time that man had to move because the cattle had to move. It presented a spectacle magnificent and unequaled in this country or anywhere else in the world.

Exact locations of particular trails are somewhat indeterminate. The trails themselves resemble at their origin a network of small feeders converging on the main trail. At the northern end, the main trail diverges into numerous small branches leading to different destinations. The first herds after the Civil War were driven over uncharted ways to the western part of Missouri, the ultimate destination being St. Louis. Trails were usually named after the town of origin or terminus, or the cattleman who blazed the trail. Beyond Kansas, trails were known only as the Montana Trail or the Wyoming Trail, without any other specific designation.

Although the exact route and precise name of any particular cattle trail may be extremely vague indeed, four major trails are recognizable. The direction of all the cattle trails is essentially from south to north, running more or less parallel. As the railroads extended westward, so did the trails (Pl. III).

The Sedalia and Baxter Springs Trail (1866 and later) was also known as the Shawnee Trail. With two forks originating near San Antonio and Corpus Christi and joining at Lockhart, it continued northward through Fort Worth to the Red River at Denison. There the trail split again. The eastern fork, the Old Shawnee Trail, continued northeasterly through Fort Smith, Ar-

19

kansas, to Sedalia, Missouri. The western fork, the Middle or West Shawnee Trail, continued northward to Baxter Springs, Kansas.

The Abilene Trail (1867–71) originated near San Antonio and pursued a northward course, crossed the Red River at Red River Station, and entered the Nations, or Indian Territory, now Oklahoma. Thence it continued northward to Elm Springs and Waurika, crossed the Washita River, continued in a northerly direction and crossed the South Canadian River at Silver City; thence northward through Yukon, crossed the Cimarron River at Dover, continued northward through Hennessey, Enid, and Pond Creek, and crossed into Kansas at Caldwell; thence northerly to Abilene. The northern portion of the trail, from Red River Station, is also known as the Chisholm Trail.

The Dodge City Trail (1876–84) was also known as the Western Trail, Fort Griffin–Fort Dodge Trail, and Fort Dodge Trail. It originated near Laredo, led northward through Bandera, Concho, Clyde, and Griffin, crossed the Red River at Doan's Store, and continued northward to Dodge City, Kansas, and Ogallala, Nebraska.

The Goodnight Trail (1866 and later) was also known as the Goodnight-Loving Trail and Pecos Trail. It originated at Fort Concho, now San Angelo, thence ran westward, crossing the Pecos River at Horsehead Crossing, thence northward through Fort Sumner, New Mexico, to Colorado, Wyoming, and Nebraska. There were several branches leading west.

The Ellsworth and Newton Trail (1871–75) was a branch of the Abilene Trail. It veered off in an easterly direction from the Abilene Trail at Elm Spring and continued northward to Newton and Ellsworth, Kansas. It was also known as the West Chisholm Trail.

The Elm Spring–Dodge City Trail was another branch of the Abilene Trail. It turned off in a westerly direction from the Abilene Trail at Elm Spring and continued to Dodge City.

The National Cattle and Horse Growers' Association assembled in convention in St. Louis on November 19, 1884, and passed a resolution urging Congress to establish a National Cattle Trail from Texas to the northern ranges. It was proposed that a strip of the public domain, six miles wide, be set aside as a permanent quarantine ground over which southern cattle could move unobstructed to the northern areas. It was to extend from the Red River to the Canadian border. The Montana and Wyoming delegations bitterly opposed this resolution for fear of overcrowding their ranges. The desires of the southern cattlemen could not be realized for the following reasons: existence of the Kansas quarantine laws, the western farmers, and the crowded conditions on the northern ranges.

As soon as it became evident that money could be made by driving cattle to railheads, the cattle thief appeared. He began his operation by recording a brand with the clerk of one county, purchasing a small herd, and applying his brand. Thus established on a small scale, he began picking up mavericks and branding them with his brand. He would cut out cattle ranging in the vicinity, alter their brands, and when such altered brands were healed, run these cattle in with his own herd.

The stockmen of Limestone, McLennan, Falls, Hill, and Navarro counties (Texas) organized the first protective association in 1868, and hired stock detectives. Drovers driving cattle northward were often careless about picking up local cattle along the trail. A detective force gradually was scattered all over the ranges, surveillant of everyone engaged in the range cattle industry, especially of strangers owning small herds, since that was the way the cattle thief usually started. Antagonism by small ranchers against the absentee capitalist members of the Wyoming Stock Growers' Association began to grow rapidly, in revolt against their methods and control, which always worked to the advantage of the large cattle growers.

In order to prevent the cattle rustler from realizing a profit on his stolen property, whether at a railhead, Indian reservation, community, or other market, an inspection service was formed.

21

The prerequisites for a stock inspector were honesty and a prolific knowledge of brands. Inspectors were employed by stock growers' associations and stationed at chief loading points within the Territory or at exterior points. The Wyoming Association maintained interior inspection at the Pine Ridge and Rosebud Indian Agencies, and exterior inspection at Miles City, St. Paul, Chicago, Clinton, Council Bluffs, and Pacific Junction. By arrangements with associations of other states and territories, expenses of exterior inspection were shared. In addition to identifying rustlers' stock, inspection proved valuable by assuring that the owner of stray animals, which were bound to be included in making up a large shipment, would be properly reimbursed by the commission merchant, through the inspector. The inspector, in turn, sent the money for the strays to the home office of his association, which notified the owner and forwarded the money for the animals.

The "Cowboy Legislature," as the 1885 session of the Montana Legislature was called, created a board of stock commissioners with power to appoint inspectors and detectives. The cost of this service was to be met by a two-mill levy on all cattle, horses, and mules. The bill was amended so that only counties in which the range cattle industry was paramount could levy the tax (Laws of Montana Territory, 1885, Sess. 14, pp. 91–95).

Cattle from Texas, particularly from the southern section of the state, were recognized as being infected with "Texas fever" as soon as the drives began. Adjacent states and territories enacted legislation in order to combat the danger of infecting local herds. It was found that cattle outside Texas or those driven north in the late fall or early spring were free from the disease. The legislation passed either prohibited entry of Texas cattle during the spring and summer, or established quarantine for cattle arriving during this period. Kansas was the first Territory to enact such legislation (Laws of Kansas Territory, 1859, Sess. 5, p. 622). Similar laws were passed by Missouri, Colorado, Nebraska, and Dakota. Neither Montana nor Wyoming took action, since it was felt that the intermediate states acted as a sufficient buffer to prevent introduction of the disease. The quarantine law of Missouri was challenged and was held unconstitutional by the United States Supreme Court because it constituted a usurpation of the power of Congress to regulate commerce among the states. It was ruled that in order for the state to exercise its police power within its jurisdiction, it must provide for expert inspection (Railroad v. Husen, 95 U. S. 465, October, 1877). The decision of the Supreme Court resulted in legislation providing for a system of inspections by government-employed veterinarians; in Kansas in 1882–84, Wyoming, 1882, Nebraska, 1885, Colorado, 1885, and Montana, 1885.

The weakness of individual state and territorial attempts to control animal diseases was apparent. The British Government issued a quasi embargo on American cattle after it was discovered that a shipload of diseased cattle had been sent to England. Consequently, the Treasury Cattle Commission was created in 1882. A bill was finally passed and approved by the President on May 29, 1884, creating within the Department of Agriculture the Bureau of Animal Industry, headed by a competent veterinarian and a clerical force not to exceed twenty people. The B. A. I. was permitted to promulgate rules and regulations for the control of animal diseases.

The scare from pleuro-pneumonia and Texas fever was hardly allayed when the public grew uneasy about the kind of meat being issued from packing houses. In 1890, the action of European governments prohibiting importation of meat gave impetus to a move to place the responsibility for meat inspection within the Bureau of Animal Industry. A further extension of federal inspection was established by passage of The Pure Foods and Drugs Act of 1906.

By taking out land under all federal acts—Pre-emption, Homestead, Timber Culture, and Desert Land—and by living and lying, a cattleman could accumulate enough land for a stock

23

ranch. Innumerable frauds were perpetrated with the enactment of the federal land laws, partly because interpretation of their provisions was made by the personnel of field offices. Nine hundred and sixty acres might be obtained through the following process:

One hundred and sixty acres under the Homestead Act by residing thereon for five years and cultivating the same.

One hundred and sixty acres under the Timber Culture Act by planting forty acres with trees (nuts, slips, or cuttings). Congress, of course, could not legislate the necessary rain.

Six hundred and forty acres under the Desert Land Act by paying down 25 cents an acre and by paying $1 an acre more at time of final entry.

The Pre-emption Acts were laws enacted in the sixties giving citizens the right of purchase before others, under certain conditions, of a portion of land not exceeding a quarter section (160 acres) of public land. The Homestead Act, passed in 1862, authorized the sale of public lands in parcels of a quarter section to settlers. By the Timber Culture Act of 1873 (17 U. S. Stats 605), a settler could obtain an additional 160 acres provided he planted 40 acres of it with trees. The Desert Land Act of 1877 (19 U. S. Stats 377), provided for the sale of a parcel of the public domain consisting of a section (640 acres) at $1.25 an acre; 25 cents at entry and the balance when final proof was made. The other condition was irrigation of the entire section within three years. This Act was amended in 1890, and the acreage was reduced to 320 acres. Under the provisions of the Enclosures Act of 1885, the fencing of any part of the public domain was made subject to prosecution.

As noted above, the invention of barbed wire aided in opening up the prairies of the Great Plains because of its economy and the protection it gave to grazing herds. The use of barbed wire, along with the development of the windmill, made the 160-acre homestead possible. Barbed wire enabled the farmer to stake

24

out his homestead with cheap fencing. The Plains area was immediately recognized as the principal market for the wire, and the barbed wire industry grew to immense proportions accordingly. Two types of barbed wire were invented almost simultaneously. On November 24, 1874, an application for a patent for Joseph F. Glidden, a farmer in De Kalb, Illinois, was allowed—Patent No. 157,124. The patent is described as: "A twisted fence wire having the transverse spur wire D bent at its middle portion about one of the strands of A of said fence-wire, and clamped in position and place by the other wire Z, twisted upon its fellow, substantially as specified . . . ." (Fig. 15). The other successful barbed wire was allowed as a patent on August 31, 1875, issued to Jacob Haish of Illinois (Fig. 18).

The need for a mechanical device to raise water from fifty to two hundred feet as fast and in as great a quantity as possible assured the the adoption of the windmill. After its development, it fulfilled all requirements and made it practical to fence the land into small areas and to cut the ranges into smaller pastures. The windmill was generally introduced into the Great Plains by the railroads, cattlemen, and farmers, the latter making entry into the arid regions in the last two decades of the nineteenth century. Large-scale manufacture of windmills in the United States dates to about 1873.

Because local governments were either too weak, too corrupt, or located too distant for effective action, cattlemen found it necessary to band together for the protection of their property from Indians, thieves, wild animals, or disease. Thus was the reason for the creation of cattlemen's associations. Several of the historical associations are listed below.

1. National Association. Three days before the market disaster of 1873, the Livestockmen's National Association was founded at Kansas City with J. G. McCoy as Secretary. In the subsequent general confusion, the organization quietly disappeared. A second attempt to organize a national association was made when the

National Cattle and Horse Growers' Association was founded at St. Louis in 1884. Again, after the collapse of the cattle market in 1886, this organization also disappeared.

2. Wyoming Stock Grazers' Association, founded in 1871.

3. Colorado Stock Growers' Association, organized January 19, 1872.

4. South Colorado Association, organized in 1872.

5. Stock Association of Laramie County, founded November 29, 1873. This organization became the Wyoming Stock Growers' Association March 29, 1879.

6. Montana Stock Growers' Association, organized January 23, 1879.

7. Eastern Montana Live Stock Association, founded in October, 1883.

8. Cattle Raisers' Association of Texas, organized in 1877, combined from the Stock Growers' Association of Northwest Texas and the South Texas Association.

9. Stock Growers' Association, constitution adopted November 3, 1867. In 1876 it became the Colorado Cattle Growers' Association in order to be distinct from the sheepmen.

10. Stock Growers' Association of Northwest Texas, founded in 1877.

11. South Texas Association.

12. Panhandle & Southwest Stock Raisers' Association.

13. Texas and Southwest Cattle Raisers' Association, combined from the Cattle Raisers' Association of Texas and the Panhandle and Southwest Stock Raisers' Association.

14. Southwest Cattle Growers' Association, established in 1882.

15. Western Central Kansas Stock Association, founded in the spring of 1883.

Owners of stock brands are of a variety of professions and come from all walks of life. Ownership of a brand does not necessarily mean that any livestock whatsoever is owned by the owner of the brand. Below are compiled a few selected brands which demonstrate the variety of famous and infamous people and corporations—presidents and princes, labor leaders and railroad companies—engaged in the livestock industry.

President George Washington used the brand GW (Fig. 24). Regarding the branding irons used by him, the following entries in documents have been recorded:

1. Invoice (dated December 20, 1765) from Robert Cary and Co., London, to Colonel Washington, states: "1 Brand Mark GW for branding the horns of cattle . . . . 9.6."

2. Diaries, Volume I, page 216, November 1, 1765, contains four entries prescribing the branding of cattle for the different units of his Mount Vernon farm.

Cattle at Doeg Run: "branded on ye buttock GW."

Cattle at the Mill: "branded on right shoulder GW."

Cattle at the Neck: "branded on the right buttock GW."

Cattle at the Muddy Hole: "branded on the left shoulder GW."

3. Ledger A, page 365a, contains an entry on branding irons. However, the branding irons referred to may have been either for use on animals or for the branding of barrels.

"Jan. 1, 1772—To cash paid Mr. Cunningham of Alexandria for branding irons etc. from Philadelphia . . . . 3–16–10."

Theodore Roosevelt started to use cattle brands on his Elkhorn Ranch in the Little Missouri Country of Montana in 1883. These brands, the Triangle and the Elkhorn (Figs. 27 and 28), were registered immediately upon establishment of the Board of Livestock Commissioners, Territory of Montana, in July of 1884. Roosevelt also used the Maltese Cross (Fig. 26). He helped to organize the Little Missouri River Stockmen's Association and served as captain in one of its first roundups.

The brand DDE is recorded by the state of Nevada in the name of Dwight D. Eisenhower, Gettysburg. This brand is applied to the left hip of cattle and the left thigh of horses (Fig. 25).

Former President Lyndon B. Johnson, the owner of the LBJ Ranch located near Johnson City, Texas, has brand JO recorded in the Record of Marks and Brands of Blanco County, Texas, in Volume 4, page 161. The date of current registration is December 14, 1960. Location of the brand as stated in the Certificate of Registration of Marks and Brands is the left hip for cattle and the left shoulder for horses. There are no earmarks recorded for Lyndon B. Johnson, neither is the place of residence indicated for the then vice-president-elect (Fig. 24a).

The greatest and most famous American ranch, the King Ranch, used several different brands prior to adopting the current Running W. Brand HK was recorded in the name of Henrietta M. King, March 20, 1859, in Nueces County, state of Texas (Fig. 19). The R Arrow (Ere Flecha) brand and the Rancho brand were recorded in the name of Richard King, June 27, 1859, in Nueces County, state of Texas (Figs. 20 and 21). Richard King and James Wallworth registered their brand with Nueces County, state of Texas, June 27, 1859 (Fig. 22). The R Arrow brand was evidently quite susceptible to infection caused by screwworm, and possibly this condition caused Richard King to register his Running W horse and cattle brand, along with brand K applied to the left cheek of all animals, and earmarks—right ear cut off and left ear hole and split—with Nueces County, state of Texas, February 9, 1869 (Fig. 23). The King Ranch extends across nearly a million acres and is still owned by descendants of Captain Richard King. The ranch has developed the first new breed of beef cattle in North America, the Santa Gertrudis. Two of its racing thoroughbreds, Assault and Middleground, have won the Kentucky Derby. The ranch is also famous for its Quarter Horses.

Don Luis Terrazas, who died in 1923, was the owner of the greatest cattle ranch of all time. His estates extended from Ciudad Juárez, Chihuahua, across the Río Grande from El Paso, Texas, to Chihuahua, a distance of 235 miles, or approximately 6.2 million acres. There were five magnificent haciendas located on the properties and life there was imbued with genuine grandeur. During the 1880's, Don Luis owned more than 400,000 cattle. He used the brand illustrated by Fig. 17.

The XIT Ranch was once the largest fenced ranch in the world. It spread across three million acres, an area almost as large as the state of Connecticut. Situated in the Texas Pan-

28

handle, the ranch extended into nine counties. The state of Texas gave the land in payment for the building of the present Capitol in Austin. The XIT has since been broken up into smaller ranches and sold. The XIT brand was designed by Ab Blocker about 1885 (Fig. 103).

Another great American ranch was the Matador Ranch in West Texas. A pioneer cowman, Henry H. Campbell, and a Chicago banker, A. M. Britton, established the ranch in 1879. In 1882 they sold the 861,000-acre ranch to a company of Scots who retained it until 1951. The Matador V brand, started by John Dawson, was sold to Campbell and Britton in 1879 (Fig. 49).

From Scout's Rest Ranch, near North Platte, Nebraska, (owned by William F. Cody, "Buffalo Bill"), a draft of horses was started for Sheridan, Wyoming, on an expedition that gave Colonel Cody's Wyoming ranch its TE brand and name. At Deadwood, some horses were bought from Cody's friend, Mike Russell, and a string of five hundred horses were trailed over the Big Horn Mountains to the TE Ranch near Meetseetse, Wyoming. Because it was easier to buy the brand of Russell's horses than to rebrand several hundred animals, the TE brand became attached to Buffalo Bill (Fig. 31).

As Edward, Prince of Wales, the Duke of Windsor used the Three Feathers brand on his Canadian ranch. This brand was applied to the right shoulder of horses (Fig. 30). The Three Feathers are a simplification of the three drooping ostrich plumes from the coat of arms of the Prince of Wales. Brand Circle EP is applied to the right ribs of cattle. It is recorded in the Alberta Brand Book, 1954, under the name of "Duke of Windsor, c/o Canadian Colonization Assc., 112 C.P.R. station, Calgary" (Fig. 29). The same brand is applied to the left shoulder of horses. Since Canadian brand books list cattle and horse brands separately, the horse brand is listed, oddly enough, under "Windsor, Duke of, Calgary."

The Deathhead brand was used by the outlaw Pancho Villa, and it is probably one of the most ornate ever designed. It is

29

generally believed that this brand has never been successfully duplicated (Fig. 10).

Dave Beck, the former president of the International Brotherhood of Teamsters, in conjunction with associates Baker and Gessert, had a brand recorded for his Lazy Valley Ranch, Seattle, with the Washington State Recorder of Brands (Fig. 36). This brand is applied to the left shoulder of cattle.

The Yomba Shoshone Indian tribe has the brand YT recorded with the State of Nevada. It is applied to the left ribs of cattle (Fig. 32).

The Union Pacific Railroad Company's brand UP is recorded with the state of Idaho in the name of the Union Pacific Railroad Company at Salt Lake City, Utah, and may be applied anywhere on sheep (Fig. 34). Brand SV is recorded with the state of Idaho in the name of the company at Sun Valley, Idaho. It is applied on the left hip of cattle and on the left shoulder of horses (Fig. 35).

All the larger packing companies have brands recorded for their own herds, usually in several states. The brands used by Armour and Company are a case in point. The brands shown in Figures 42, 43, and 44 demonstrate a functional stylization of the abbreviation A.C. Brands recorded in Washington are applied to the right shoulder of cattle (Fig. 42); the left hip of cattle (Fig. 45); and the right neck of cattle (Fig. 46). In Nevada, the illustrated brand is applied to the left ribs of cattle (Fig. 43). The recorded brand in Idaho is applied to the left shoulder of cattle (Fig. 45).

The Cudahy Packing Company's brand, the Bar C, is recorded in the state of Idaho and applied to the left shoulder of cattle (Fig. 33).

The following brands are all recorded in Idaho for Swift and Company. Figure 37, applied to the left hip of cattle; Figure 38, left shoulder of cattle; and Figure 39, left shoulder and left hip of cattle. Brand 9 Double Bar and brand F9 (Figs. 40 and 41, respectively) are applied to the right neck of cattle and are recorded in Washington.

In 1946, the Thoroughbred Racing Protective Bureau (TRPB) established a standard method of identification for racing horses which has been adopted by horse owners. Under this system, a set of numbers and a code letter are tattooed on the upper lip of each registered thoroughbred in order to discourage forgery. The lip is then photographed. So far this system has made substitution of race horses impossible (Fig. 47).

Designs of animal brands have been developed and rules established in a process very similar to the science of heraldry. Because of the functional aspects and the severe limitations of application, brands seem to be crudely executed compared to the elegantly emblazoned achievements of arms. Nonetheless, both brands and heraldic devices belong to the same greater classification to which trade marks, bale seals, merchant marks and other means of identification belong. Inasmuch as the conditions of application are entirely different for brands and for coats of arms, a well-seared brand is as much a manifestation of good craftsmanship as a well-emblazoned shield or other supplementary insignia on a coat of arms. The act of properly impressing a sizzling iron on a tied and living animal on a hot and dusty range is certainly different from delineating in the comfort of a room. In order to produce an easily legible brand, the design of the brand itself must allow for the limitations of the branding surface and the means of application. The need for a brand that would not blotch and consideration for the imperfections of the iron influenced the design of brands, making them more functional and eliminating refinements such as are found in the presentation of arms. Despite such practical streamlining, brands retain much of the heraldic character, with occasional variations in terminology.

The bend sinister is a somewhat unusual heraldic ordinary, or emblem, and generally—but not always—denotes illegitimacy

31

(Fig. 50). When the bend is removed from its shield, it becomes a slash, a common component of a brand (Fig. 51). An ordinary such as a chevron becomes a rafter (Figs. 52 and 53), but the ordinary of a cross remains a cross (Figs. 54 and 55). A subordinary such as the lozenge becomes a diamond (Figs. 56 and 57). Charges such as a mullet become rowels; or a fish naiant becomes just a plain fish (Figs. 58 and 59).

Early cattle barons proudly exhibited their brands in a manner similar to the custom of European nobility in displaying their arms. As the democratic processes began to pervade nations, so did the habit of granting arms to plain gentlemen, and the small rancher began to record his brand. The status of brand registration has presently reached a higher degree of regulatory control than the registration of arms by the Heralds' College in London or registration by the semi-official Herolds Verein in Germany. Publication of a brand in the state brand book is comparable to publication of arms in a banner roll, although less ceremonial and perhaps marked by less dignity.

Most brands bear a striking resemblance to other marks used for different occasions and under different circumstances. Signs serve a great variety of purposes and have been used for thousands of years. The Buckle (Fig. 60), a popular brand, is found among general signs where this symbol means the male element; the symbol of the Buckle may also indicate saltpeter if used as a chemical sign (Fig. 61). The Pigpen Circle brand (Fig. 62) becomes the sign for urine if used in context with chemistry (Fig. 63). Another old brand, the Steer Skull (Fig. 66), has its counterpart in astronomy. With a little modification, the Steer Skull becomes the astronomical sign for Taurus, the bull, and for the month of April (Fig. 67). These examples clearly demonstrate the close relationship of general signs, chemical signs, astronomical and other signs to brands, no matter how original in concept they appear to be. However, all the other symbols in this category serve for identification purposes only, whereas brands normally indicate evidence of ownership, also.

32

In the similarity of marks category are grouped marks which have been specifically designed and adopted to present evidence of ownership on items of property or on items for sale. During the Middle Ages the custom of holding marks received new impetus. Personal and real items were marked to indicate ownership; the counterpart of the Rails brand (Fig. 68) was carved into fence posts, handtools, and buildings to indicate the identity of the owner (Fig. 69). Shipping marks, painted on bales of goods destined for shipment to distant locations, were the accepted mark of the merchant. The brand Four Hearts (Fig. 70) very closely resembles the shipping mark of wine merchants John and James Charlié (Fig. 71), who used it on shipments to Colonial America during the early 18th century. A remarkable similarity may be found between the sign of a Roman stone mason (Fig. 65) and an old Navaho brand, Old Woman (Fig. 64). Even though centuries and continents apart, both brand and sign display an amazing clarity and simplicity of design, necessitated by the limitations of the material upon which they were applied or chiseled. This example is also a confirmation of the statement that a good design is always good, no matter when or where or by whom it is conceived, because basic design criteria are not subject to change.

Marks of cadency are marks applied to coats of arms to indicate the relationship of the bearer to the person to whom the arms were first granted. In heraldry, a device termed a label is applied over the shield to indicate that the owner of the shield is the eldest son. There are subsequent marks to indicate cadency down to the ninth son (an octofoil). The eldest son of the eldest son applies a smaller label to his father's label, and the ninth son of the eldest son applies an octofoil to the label. By the use of this system, a great number of members of a family may be identified. In addition to heraldic cadency, a similar system was used during the Dark Ages in designing house marks. By the addition of vertical and horizontal marks, members of a family were identified. The founder of a family adopted a house mark

33

(Fig. 85); his eldest son, the eldest grandson, the son of the eldest grandson, etc., retain the original mark without modification in the line of primogeniture. The younger sons add various bars to the original mark. The second grandson adds another bar (Fig. 86). The eldest son of the second grandson retains the original mark, but his brothers add bars; the second son of the second grandson adds a bar (Fig. 87), and the third son of the second grandson adds a vertical bar (Fig. 88). In the second line a similar process of modification takes place.

This cadency system has been utilized also by the Arabs. Families of the Banu Sokhr clan of the Banu Sokhr tribe add a distinguishing mark to the basic design of their brand (Figs. 89, 90, and 91). Families of the Khur Shân clan of the Banu Sokhr tribe also add distinguishing marks, to differentiate ownership of the animals (Figs. 92, 93, and 94). Again, it may be noted that these Arabian brands are very similar to the old Navaho brands.

The brand of the Mexican Don Miguel Ascarate de la Valenzuela y Peralta was a Running P applied with a single hook running iron (Fig. 80). In lieu of cadency marks, his son Carlos added a C (Fig. 81); his son Luis, CL (Fig. 82); his son José added CLJ (Fig. 83); and his son Mario added CLJM (Fig. 84).

Among American brands indicating cadency, the H 52 Fleur-de-Lis of John French (Fig. 72) is an example similar to the cadency house marks of the Dark Ages. Mrs. John French added a single Underbar (Fig. 73). Ney French added a single Overbar (Fig. 74). Nina French added a double Underbar (Fig. 75). Homer French added a double Overbar (Fig. 76). Lonnie French added a Thrubar (Fig. 77). Burton French added a double Thrubar (Fig. 78). Among the members of the above family, each had a modified brand and was thus able to recognize any animal that was his or her personal property. The vent brand consisted of a double slash (Fig. 79).

The location of brands upon animals is important because a particular brand may only be registered in a certain location—

with possible exceptions for sheep, goats, and hogs—by one owner. Several states also restrict the location of brands to certain parts of the body. The right or left jaw is also reserved for the use of the state for disease control brands, and the right or left side of the neck for use of owners of production record brands. Both of the above brands serve for identification purposes only, and are not evidence of ownership.

The terminology relative to a portion of the body varies somewhat among the states and some locations are grouped into one description, e.g., right or left ribs and right or left flank may be indicated in the state brand book as right or left side. In addition, right or left thigh includes right or left stifle or right or left hip. The term loin is used synonymously with flank.

Almost all state brand books use abbreviations for the sake of brevity and clarity, since the number of descriptions in the brand book is very large and restricting the use of abbreviations would substantially increase its size, making it unwieldy for working use.

A prefix is used to designate the side of the animal: L for left side; R or RT for right side. A letter or letters are used to designate the location of the brand: A or W A for anywhere, for any part of the animal, or whole animal. Other commonly-used abbrevations are:

J for jaw	H for hip	S for side
SH for shoulder	ST for stifle	T for thigh
FL for flank	N for neck	RU for rump
	R for ribs	

A letter following the location of the brand designates the kind of animal: H for horses; C for cattle; and S for sheep. For example: L.R.C. designates a brand to be located on left ribs of cattle; L.SH.H. designates a brand to be located on the left shoulder of horses; and A.S. designates a brand to be located anywhere on sheep. Names of other kinds of animals are normally spelled out.

35

Below are listed the types of brands classified according to the integument of the body and to the substance of material used and the condition of the branding iron.

Hide brands, applied on the hide of an animal:
    1. Fire brands, applied with a hot iron.
        a. Fast brand (hot brand). This is an honest brand, burned through the hair and the outer layer of skin.
        b. Slow brand (cold brand, hair brand). This is a dishonest brand, burned through the hair, but not through the outer layer of skin. After the hair is shed, a rustler may then apply his own brand. The technique used in the application is burning through a wet blanket or other similar material, thus preventing the scorching of the outer layer of skin.
    2. Chemical brands—applied with a cold iron or brush and a chemical compound.
        a. Acid brands. Brands applied with a cold iron having a concave face and dipped in a solution of sodium hydroxide and barium sulfide or similar chemicals.
        b. Paint brands (dye brands). Brands applied with a paint brander or paint brush dipped in an emulsion-type liquid with lanolin base. Paint may be of different colors.
        c. Tar brands. Brands applied with a paint brander or paint brush dipped in coal tar.
Fleece brands, applied to the coat of wool of sheep only. These are chemical brands (acid, paint, and tar brands) only.
Horn brands, applied to the covering of horn which protects the ends of the digits of ungulates, and also applied to the hard process borne on the head of hoofed animals. This type of brand is always a fire brand applied with a hot iron.
Flesh brands, applied to the carcass, portions thereof, cuts of meat, meat food products, or meat by-products.
Ink brands. Hot or cold edible ink applied by means of a metal or rubber stamp or by metal rollers.
Burning (hot) brand, applied with a hot iron. Normally only to cured meat, heart, liver, and tongue.

Brand locations are listed below according to the taxonomical

36

groupings of the animals. Taxonomical groupings vary somewhat among authors of scientific works on the subject, however, the groupings listed here are generally accepted. In descending order in the animal kingdom, there are phyla, subphyla, classes, subclasses, orders, suborders, families, genera, species, and varieties. Since mammals and birds are the only classes which concern us here, the phylum and subphylum of these classes are described first:

PHYLUM: Chordata (*chorde* cord). In members of this phylum there are present at some time during their life history paired gill slits between the pharynx and the exterior, a dorsal tubular nerve cord and an axial support called a notochord.

Subphylum: Vertebrata (*vertebratus jointed*). Fish, frogs, birds, and mammals. Vertebral column at least partially replaces notochord; paired sense organs; heart with two to four chambers; usually two pairs of lateral appendages; closed circulatory system.

1. Birds (geese, ducks, chickens, and turkeys). The branding of all birds consists of tattooing numbers, letters, pictures, or any combination of these devices on the web of the left or right wing.

Class: Aves (avis bird). Birds. Feathers; bipedal; beaks; clawed toes; fetal membranes; one occipital condyle; four-chambered heart; "warm-blooded."

Subclass: Carinate birds. Capable of flight, with a keel to their breastbone.

Order: Anseriformes. Water birds; legs short, placed moderately well back; toes webbed in front; edges of beak serrated or fringed.

Family: Anatidae. With the character of the order.

Subfamily: Anserinae (geese). Lores wholly or partly feathered; beak broad and flat; tarsus with rounded scales. Tattoo applied to web of right or left wing.

Subfamily: Anatinae (dabbling ducks). Lores wholly or partly feathered; beak broad and flat; lower part of tarsus

37

with small, rounded scales; tarsus with transverse or squar-
ish scales above. Tattoo applied to web of right or left
wing.

Order: Galliformes. Gallinaceous birds. Land birds; tibia
feathered; toes usually slightly webbed; feet with short
hind toe elevated above the rest or else feet small and
weak; wings short and wide; fowl-like.

Family: Meleagridae (turkeys). Hind toe elevated; head
almost entirely bare and with comb, wattles, or other
growth. Tattoo applied to web of right or left wing.

Family: Phasianidae (pheasants, peafowl, quail, and par-
tridge).

Genus: Gallus (jungle fowl). This is the wild fowl from
which many authorities believe the domestic fowl is descended.

Specie: Gallus gallus (Gallus bankiva) (Red Junglefowl).
The principal of the four wild species from which modern
breeds have descended.

Varieties: Varieties of chickens are so numerous that a detailed discussion of all the characters they possess is not
possible in this manual. The reader is referred to the
"American Standard of Perfection," published by the
American Poultry Association. Tattoo is applied to the
web of the right or left wing.

2. Mammals (rabbits, chinchillas, foxes, dogs, minks, martens,
sheep, goats, cattle, horses, mules, asses, and burros).

Class: Mammalis (*mammalis* of the breast). Hairy animals.
Two occipital condyles; hair, nails, claws, or hooves on the
digits; coelom divided by diaphragm; fetal membranes;
young nourished by milk; usually a placenta.

Subclass: Placental mammals. The young are born alive in
an advanced state of development; the mother has no
pouch.

Order: Lagomorpha (hares and rabbits). While resem-
bling typical gnawing animals (rodents), hares and rab-

38

bits are placed in this order because of the upper incisors being four in number.

Family: Leporidae.

Genera: Lepus (rabbit) and chinchilla. Tattoos for rabbits and chinchillas are applied to right or left ear.

Order: Carnivora (*carnis* flesh). Canine teeth well developed; usually five toes with claws; placenta zonary.

Family: Canidae. Long muzzles; claws not retractile.

Genera: Vulpes (foxes) and Canis (dogs). Tattoos for foxes and dogs are applied to right or left ear or to the inside of either hind leg in the case of dogs.

Family: Mustelidae (weasel family). Elongated body and short legs, often with strong odor and valuable fur; usually ferocious.

Genera: Mustela (mink) and Martes (marten). Tattoos for minks and martens applied to right or left ear.

Order: Artiodactyla (*artios* even, *daktylos* toe). Even-toed ungulates. Weight distributed on two toes of each foot; each toe supplied with a hoof.

Suborder: Ruminants. Chewing the cud; with several stomachs; grinding teeth with crescent pattern; the feet with a single cannon-bone.

Family: Bovidae. With hollow horns, on a bony core, not shed; four-chambered stomach.

Genus: Ovis (sheep). Fleece brands (acid, paint, and tar brands) may be applied to top of neck, back, right rump, rump, left rump, right or left neck, right or left ribs, right or left flank, right or left hip, right or left stifle. Hide brands (fire brands) may be applied to forehead or nose. Horn brands (fire brands) may be applied to right or left horn. Some states restrict the placement of brands.

Genus: Capra (goats) Hide brands (fire, acid, paint or tar brands) may be applied to all locations as indicated for sheep, including horn brands (fire brands).

39

Genus: Bos (cattle). The left side of cattle is the major location for the application of brands and is preferred by approximately 85 per cent of cattle raisers. This is a holdover from the times when cowboys engaged in the custom of breaking a horse to come up on the left side of a cow. During the early years of the Texas cattle industry, the owner seared his brand on the left hip or left shoulder, while the county branded its design upon the left neck, and the counterbrand was seared on the left side. At present, the location of vent brands and counterbrands is restricted by state law in several states. Also, the right and left jaw is reserved by most states for the application of disease control brands, such as reactors to brucellosis and tuberculosis. The left and right neck is reserved by some states for the application of control brands, such as production record, tally brands, herd brands, age brands, etc. Hide brands (fire, acid, and paint brands) may be applied to the right or left shoulder, right or left ribs, right or left flank, right or left thigh, right or left stifle, right or left rump. Horn brands (fire brands) may be applied to the hooves or to the horns. Tattoos may be applied to the right or left ear.

Suborder: Pig-like ungulates. Grinding teeth with rounded tubercles; the feet with two separate bones instead of a single cannonbone.

Family: Suidae. The outer hooves do not touch the ground in walking; hooves of center toes flattened towards the middle so as to form a "cloven hoof" as in ruminanta; naked rooting snout; with tusks, those of the upper jaw curving upward.

Genus: Sus (pigs). Hide brands (acid, paint, and tar brands) may be applied to all locations as indicated for sheep. Tattoos may be applied to the right or left ear and slap marks to the left or right shoulder.

Order: Perissodactyla (*perissos* odd). Odd-toed ungulates. Odd number of toes; each toe sheathed by a hoof.

40

Family: Equidae. With a single hoof and digit (the third) on each foot.

Genus: Equus (horses, mules, asses, and burros). The left and right jaw and locations of brands on the neck are sometimes reserved by the state. Normally, a brand may be applied to right or left jaw, right or left neck, right or left shoulder, right or left ribs, right or left thigh, right or left stifle, right or left rump. Brands may be hide brands (fire or acid brands) or horn brands applied to the hooves. Usually horn brands are applied to the left front hoof. (Fig. 96).

The regions and the various parts of cattle, horses, sheep, and swine are shown in the following illustrations: Plate VII, Figure 95, for cattle; Plate VIII, Figure 96, for horses; Plate IX, Figure 97, for sheep; and Plate X, Figure 98, for swine.

TWO

Branding Implements and Methods

Various items of tools, equipment, and chemicals are required for the successful branding of animals. All items should be of the best quality; they will last longer and perform their functions more efficiently. The tools used for branding and marking are branding irons, knives for cutting marks, and tattoo markers.

Branding irons are classified according to the legal aspect of brands, the types of construction, and the design of irons. A branding iron is the means by which a brand is applied to an animal for identification. This identification may indicate the legal owner of the animal or an illegal owner; it may also indicate, by number or letter, individual identification of the animal. The venting iron is used in the legal cancellation of an existing brand upon an animal. It normally consists of a long horizontal bar which is applied over the existing brand.

There are several types of irons. The fire (heat) iron is heated over a bed of coal, wood, or other fuel, or in a special heater. The material used to make this type of iron is usually steel, if made by hand, or it may be of copper or stainless steel if commercially manufactured. Handmade irons may be electrically welded, fire welded, or riveted, or made by any combination of methods thereof.

The shank and hand hold of a branding iron should be made of half-inch round iron rod; the stamp, of spring steel. When a wooden handle is used, hardwood, such as oak, mesquite, ironwood or hickory is recommended (Fig. 118). In lieu of iron, copper or an aluminum alloy may be used.

At the intersection of parts of the stamp, a section ¼ inch by

42

¼ inch is cut out to prevent the accumulation of too much heat in one spot. The heavier the iron stock, the longer the heat will be contained and the longer the stamp will retain its shape. The center of the burning surface should be slightly higher than the edges, to allow for depressions in the surface to be branded. All edges and corners should be slightly rounded. The hand hold should have a diameter of 2 inches. The top of the handle should be painted red to indicate the top of the brand. For minimum requirements of height, width, and spacing of letters, numerals, and designs, see Plate No. XIII.

Irons for cattle are made with bars 1 inch wide by ½ inch thick, with the burning surface tapered to ¼ inch. The height of the stamp for adult stock is 5 inches, and a minimum of 3 inches for young animals. The length of the shank is about 3 feet. Irons for horses are made from bars ½ inch wide by ⅜ inch thick, the burning surface tapered to ³⁄₁₆ inch. The height of the stamp is normally 1 inch.

An iron designed to be applied to the hide of an animal is called a hide iron. Commercially manufactured irons are of solid copper, conducting heat uniformly, and are available in 2-inch, 3-inch, or 4-inch letters, numerals, or pictures, with a 30-inch wrought-iron handle with a wooden grip. A handhold is sometimes substituted for the wooden grip. Fire irons are also manufactured in stainless steel and cast bronze, with handholds, in sizes similar to solid copper ones. The hide iron is available with single letters or numerals, double letters or numerals, two letters or numerals with bar, or a universal iron shaped so that any design can be made out of it. Letter sizes are 2 inches or 3 inches.

The hoof and horn iron is applied to the horns or hooves of animals. Commercially manufactured irons are vented to lessen the scorching inside the numerals or figures. These irons are made of steel or solid copper, with wrought-iron or black-iron handles 21 inches long. They are manufactured in two sizes, ⅝ inch and ⅞ inch. The solid copper irons are obtainable with a concave face. Each letter of the horn and hoof iron is concave for easy application and is vented to prevent scorching. Height of the letters is ⅝ inch or ⅞ inch.

The meat iron is made of cast steel, for imprinting burning brands on cured meat products. It may also be used for marking heart, liver, and tongue.

The cold (chemical, acid, liquid) iron is applied only to the hide of an animal, and it is only made commercially of red bronze, with a concave face. It is manufactured in two sizes, 3 inch with ⅜-inch face, and 4 inch with ½-inch face. Sets are obtainable in numerals or letters, or may be made to order. This type of iron is used in the application of cold branding liquids.

The electric iron, a commercially manufactured iron, operates on 110-volt AC, on the same principle as the heating elements in an electric stove. It heats to a cherry red in about two minutes and maintains its rigidity while hot.

The gasoline iron burns white gasoline stored in the handle. It takes about five minutes to prepare this iron for branding. The stamp has a $\frac{3}{16}$-inch face and may be of any design or size. Consequently, it may be applied to hide or hoof or horn.

A paint iron is used for marking sheep with paint marking. Used for numbering ewes and for lambs at birth, it is made commercially of copper-coated Bessemer rod, electrically welded, with a flat face to hold paint. The 10½-inch handle is made of wood. It may consist of single or double numerals or of special designs, and it weighs four pounds.

For temporary marking of sheep, cattle, horses, and hogs, and for use in sorting or for identifying animals at sales, an iron with an aluminum stamp is used. Standard sizes are 2½ inch and 4 inch, consisting of numerals, letters, or special designs. The handle is made of wood, and the iron weighs approximately three pounds. There are also metal branders used for the application of flesh brands with cold or hot branding ink; rubber branders which are used for the application of flesh brands with cold or hot branding ink, the stamp being set in aluminum handles; and the metal roller used for the continuous application of flesh brands with cold or hot branding ink.

Branding irons are further classified relative to the method of construction, irrespective of the materials used or the type of iron. However, most irons listed below are of the fire iron type. The fixed (stamp) iron is very much like a rubber stamp with a fixed design and is applied similarly. There are two kinds of fixed irons: the boxed iron is a fixed iron with a box surrounding the design; the open iron is a fixed iron having only a design stamp with no box surrounding it.

The running iron is an iron similar to a poker and used much like writing with a pencil. That is, the design is drawn and not stamped (Fig. 117). Because rustlers used this iron prolifically, it was outlawed in several states. Subsequently, rustlers availed themselves of horseshoes, cinch rings (Fig. 119), bolts, and baling wire. A running iron was usually carried on the saddle.

The dotting iron, a primitive forerunner of the stamping iron, is made in three parts. One part consists of a bar, one part of a small semi-circle, and one part of a large semi-circle. By using various combinations of the separate parts, different designs may be made, but it takes several applications to achieve a desired brand.

A saddle iron is one of which the component parts are disassembled and inserted in a leather holster. It may be either a stamp iron or a running iron. The holster is carried on the saddle (Fig. 120).

For the marking of ears, a stockman's knife is ordinarily used. The knife contains a utility blade, a flesh blade, and a leather punch. This knife is about four inches long and has a bone stag handle.

Tattoo markers are used for numbers, letters, or figures, or any combination thereof, and are applied with special needles to the inner ears of all animals and to the web of wings of poultry. In addition, they may also be applied to the upper or lower lip of horses and to the right or left shoulder of hogs, and to either ear of fur-bearing animals. For ear, lip, and wing an inter-changeable marker is used. This has die-cast jaws and hard Monel metal points. Removable numerals or letters slide into the jaws. Sets of numerals and letters are $\frac{5}{16}$ inch and $\frac{1}{2}$ inch in height, or $\frac{1}{4}$ inch and $\frac{3}{8}$ inch. Another type of marker has an ear release which automatically frees the ear from the digit points.

The revolving head marker permits installation of letters or symbols on one side for permanent use, while the numerals, which are to be changed after each use, are installed on the opposite side. By pulling a pin at side of head, it may be revolved and locked into place automatically. Each side of the head holds up to four characters. The tongs are of malleable iron.

When large numbers of animals are to be tattooed, a rotary marker is used. The numerals are arranged in an endless chain, like a dating stamp, and any number from 1 to 999 may be made with a quick turn of the chain. Numerals may be replaced by letters or special designs.

The shoulder marker, or hog slapper, is used to slap the shoulders of hogs prior to slaughter. It is applied to each lot of hogs before the kill in order to determine which ones cut out the best. The tattoo head is attached to a wooden handle. A lever-locking hog tattoo slapper is an instrument holding four interchange-able inserts. An individual digit may be moved without moving other digits. This slapper weighs four pounds complete. The rotary head hog tattoo slapper is an instrument having two rotary number wheels of five digits each and two interchange-able inserts. This model weighs five pounds.

The ear notcher is used for notching the outer edge of ears of animals. There is an adjustable notcher, with which the size of the mark may be regulated by using the tip of the notcher so that a small, medium, or large cut can be made as desired, de-pending on the size of the animal. The steel dies are tempered steel or aluminum alloy. The shape of the dies are V, inverted

46

U, and square. The large size cuts are a maximum width of $^{13}\!/_{16}$ inch at the base and up to one inch in depth. The fixed notcher is made of malleable iron, smoothly ground and plated to resist rust. Cutting plates are ground after being hardened and tempered. The fixed notch cuts a V notch only, $^5\!/_{16}$ inch wide at the base and $^7\!/_{16}$ inch in depth. It weighs 12 ounces.

The snout cutter is used to notch the snouts of hogs, or may be used to mark the ears of hogs and other animals. The fixed cutter has an over-all length of 9 inches and makes a V cut ½ inch in depth, or any smaller size, using the tip of the cutter. It is made of tool steel and weighs approximately two pounds.

The combination cutter and marker, used for marking ears and snouts, has dies ½ inch in diameter at the base, and the dies are screwed to the jaw of the cutter. A No. 1 die is a small ear notcher for pigs. A No. 2 die is a large ear notcher and also cuts a triangle into the ear; No. 3 die cuts a square; No. 4, a ½-inch diameter hole; No. 5 die, a heart. A No. 6 die cuts the snout.

With the electric tattoo instrument any numeral, letter or design may be placed on the animal in less than one minute. This instrument is made of malleable iron and is chrome plated. It has a finger-tip control switch, and the component parts consist of the transformer, cord, and instrument. It weighs about seven pounds.

Branding heaters are used in lieu of open fires. They are portable and the asbestos-lined furnace is supported by legs. The furnace is heated by a bottle gas burner, and the temperature is regulated by the operator. For removal, it is disassembled by detaching the legs and sliding the burner out. Furnace and butane tank are carried separately. The units are made in small and large sizes. The heater, assembled, weighs 65 pounds, the butane tank twenty pounds. Using one of these heaters is quite different from the way the old-time cowman branded his cattle with a mesquite ground fire—but he got the job done just the same.

Branding chutes are used to restrain the animals during calving operations. The stanchion end of the chute has a de-horning gate built in one of several workable designs. The chute itself may be constructed of timbers and be homemade, or it may be of commercial manufacture, made of tubular steel, weighing approximately 960 pounds and measuring about 10 feet long, the stanchion being 10 feet high. One with stationary sides has two identical sides which are fixed and not movable.

A cattle squeeze is the type of chute having one of its sides movable, so that the animal can be held snugly under pressure. In closing the movable side, great pressure may be applied to the animal. Various types of tilting tables are also commercially available. All of them operate on the principle of a revolving table, or cradle, moving from a vertical position to a horizontal position with the calf securely restrained. Due to the fact that a tilting table restrains the calf in the same position, travel for branding irons is eliminated.

Chemicals are used for the cold branding of horses and cattle, and for the branding of sheep and the tattooing of livestock. Tattoo ink is an indelible black ink used in conjunction with tattooing tools and instruments. It is of a heavy, creamy consistency. A lighted flashlight held behind the ear will make reading of the tattoo mark in dark-eared animals much easier. The ink is supplied in 2-, 2½-, or 6-ounce jars; 2- or 4-ounce bottles, and 1-pint cans.

Tattoo paste in black, white, or red is also available in 4-ounce tubes. To use paste, a little is squeezed on the finger, then smeared on the skin where the tattoo is to be made. After the tattoo mark has been made, the paste is rubbed into the punctures. Black paste is also available in 2½-ounce jars and 1-pound cans.

Sheep brand paint may be used on wet as well as dry sheep, even immediately after dipping. It will hold a brand, clearly readable, for a year. The paint is supplied in red, black, green, orange, and blue colors in gallon and quart sizes; black only, in 5-gallon drums. It is applied by paint brander or brush.

48

Branding liquid contains sodium hydroxide and coal tar, and is used on cattle, horses, hogs, and sheep. The cold branding iron is dipped into the liquid and pressed lightly against the hide. If the hair is unusually long at the location of the brand, a thin coat of oil is applied before application of the branding iron. A scab will form, drop off, and leave a legible brand. This liquid is available in 1-pound cans. Another kind is supplied in half-pints, pints, and quarts. A half-pint will suffice for an average of 50 head of cattle. A pressurized 14-ounce can with black, red, green, or blue colors of liquid may be used on sheep.

Some stockmen use marking crayons. One suitable for all livestock is a soft-grease crayon manufactured in a square-base stick, 1 inch by 1 inch, 3 inches long, in red, orange, blue, green, yellow, and black in a perforated cardboard jacket which may be torn off as the crayon is used. Crayons are packed in boxes of twelve. They have a high melting point in order to withstand hot weather climates and retain easy marking qualities in freezing temperatures. A cow-marking crayon is one inch in diameter and 4 inches long. It comes in yellow, red, blue, green, white, and black colors. For best results it is applied to a clipped area on the back of cattle, either wet or dry, and remains for one month. A sheep crayon has a chalk base and is one inch in diameter at its base, four inches long, and tapered. It is for temporary marking of sheep and comes in blue, red, yellow, and green.

Chalk is sometimes used, also, and is usually one inch in diameter and four inches long. It may be soaked in oil—this makes the mark last longer. Its colors are blue and red.

The branding of animals has been documented since 2100 B.C., and has been continued to this day with very little variation in the technique. Today there are basically two ways of accomplishing the branding of livestock, namely, on the open range or in a corral. Some states have a legal requirement for corral branding, aimed at preventing hasty and illegal branding by rustlers. Most ranchers prefer to brand, mark, castrate, vaccinate, and dehorn the animals all in one operation, whether in the branding chute, corral, or on the open range. Calves are usually branded before they are weaned, because the probability of the calf's going astray is greater after it is weaned than before, and, as noted above, in the case of disputed ownership of a calf, ownership is usually conceded to the owner of the cow which the calf follows.

Physical means employed in branding may be either by throwing, or by squeezing in a chute. The throwing of cattle is particularly advantageous because it is fast and does not require a confining structure—it can be accomplished either on the range or in the corral.

Egyptian cowboys with lariats and sticks herded their spotted cattle into a yard with trees and shrubs. Then the cattle were thrown and hog-tied with piggin' strings, front legs tied to hind legs. Nearby, the iron-man was heating the very short branding irons over a container filled with hot coal. The brander applied the hot stamp to the left or right shoulder, or sometimes to the left hip, while the tally man was recording the number, kneeling on the ground and facing the owner. The stamping iron reflected the name of the owner or the herd number (Fig. 2).

What is called the Texas method is used in Texas and the Great Plains, and the roper, in a double-fire saddle and with a thirty-foot grass rope, dabs his loop on the calf he wants and starts back for the fire. There, the bulldogger goes down the rope and reaches over the calf's back, taking a double handful of loose hide, lifts the calf up on his knees, and then gets out from under it. After the calf has been thrown to the ground, the bulldogger puts his knee on the calf's neck and takes hold of the calf's uppermost front leg, bending the lower part back sharply, and holds it in that position. Meantime, the flanker has seated himself at the calf's tail, one foot hooked above the point of the hock on the leg nearest the ground, pushing it forward. At the same time, the flanker grasps the uppermost leg with both hands and pulls back hard. As soon as the calf is stretched out, the bulldogger

50

calls "Tally, bull!" and repeats it until the tally man answers, indicating that the calf has been tallied. This also gives notice to the marker and the cutter that another calf is ready, and to the brander to bring his iron. At the call of "Hot Iron!" the iron man hands the iron to the brander, who applies it to the calf with a rocking motion. The marker cuts and slits the ear, cuts wattles and dewlaps as required, and places the cut-off pieces of ear in a bag to check later with the tally man on the correct count. After completion of all operations, the calf is released and joins the rest of the herd already branded.

If the calves are big, a mounted roper brings them in with their hind legs roped and sliding on their bellies. All the bulldogger and flanker have to do is fall on the animal and apply their holds. A complete operation may involve as many as ten men: roper, iron man, brander, bulldogger, flanker, marker, tally man, cutter, vaccinator and disinfector.

What is called the California method is used in California, the Pacific Coast region, Nevada, parts of New Mexico and Arizona, and also by Mexican *vaqueros*. A team consists of two mounted ropers in center-fire saddles using rawhide *reatas* sixty-five to eighty-five feet long. The head roper eases into the herd and lassoes the calf by the neck and, taking his dallies, drags it to a spot near the fire. The other roper now rides up, snaps his *reata* around the calf's hind legs, takes up his slack and dallies, and backs away. The calf then flops to the ground. The marker, brander, and cutter attend to their chores. Upon completion of the operation, the ropers ease up on their *reatas,* shake open the loops, and let the calf scamper to its feet. On big stock, a team of mounted ropers may rope and hold both front and hind legs.

For the hog-tie method, mounted ropers lasso their calves by the hind legs and drag them near the fire. There the bulldogger hog-ties them with piggin' strings, and the calves are left there until the branding crew is ready to perform its task.

Corral branding requires fewer men. It is accomplished within a series of corrals, and stricter supervision may be exercised and

51

all ranch facilities are in close proximity. Branding can be still more easily accomplished by the use of a chute. The location of the brand on the animal can be easily reached through the sides of the chute. Care should be exercised in the application of the squeeze, because it can crush the hip of an animal. Chute branding is the preferred method for horses and for older animals. One disadvantage is the process of hazing the animal to the chute, but the chute does render it helpless very quickly. Various types of tilting tables reduce calving operations from three or four to one man, with an appreciable reduction in time and effort.

A further word on the technique of branding. The branding iron is heated to the color of ashes, a bluish white. A red-hot iron starts a hair fire and usually results in a poor brand—besides ruining the iron. The best fuel is a bed of banked coal or wood. The iron is applied to the animal by rocking it in a rotary manner, not pressing too hard, until the skin is the color of saddle leather. The brand must be deep enough to remove the hair and the outer layer of skin. If possible, the hair should be clipped before branding, because the oil in it may be ignited and cause a blotched brand. Burning a brand on long-haired animals takes patience. The burning hair clings to the iron, making it difficult to make a neat and well-burned impression, but this can be accomplished by starting to burn the hair, cleaning the iron, rubbing the burned hair off the animal, and placing the iron again on the same impression. This method will result in a good brand without the danger of burning too deep. Too much burning causes a large scab and unnecessary suffering to the animal. On a dry range stock will gather dust in their hides, making them much harder to brand. Rain will clean the hair, but it is better to wait until the hair is dry, otherwise steam develops, causing unnecessary suffering to the animal and resulting in an indistinct brand. Before branding time, all irons should be collected and inspected. They should be heated, filed or ground to proper thickness, reshaped, and all scale should be removed.

52

This iron scale slows the heating time and the time it takes to burn the brand. Holding the iron for a longer time on the animal causes a poor impression. Discard thin or burned-up irons, because they will cut too deep, leaving a thin scar which hair will cover. Horse hair is silkier and lighter than cattle hair and the skin is also more tender. The iron should, therefore, not be too hot or applied too long.

Breed registry associations are formed by breeders for the purpose of recording the lineage of their animals, protecting the purity of the breed, encouraging the improvement of the breed, and promoting the interests of the breed. A method of identification is necessary in order for animals to be registered with breed registry associations. This is accomplished by one or more, or any combination of, the methods listed below:

HOT IRON BRANDS.
   1. Hide brands, which are normally applied to the hip. Although they are the most permanent marks, they lower the market value of the hide. In the first two decades of this century, the damage to the hide was estimated anywhere from five to fifteen cents per cwt., according to size and location. In extreme cases where there was a large, sprawling brand, the discount was much higher.
   2. Horn brands, which are fairly satisfactory if applied to adult stock. However, horns may break off occasionally. Horn brands normally are not applied to young animals, because their horns continue to grow and thus require re-branding at intervals.
   3. Hoof brands, which have the disadvantage of having to be renewed at certain intervals.
EARMARKS. Earmarks are permanent, and are easily recognized. They have the disadvantage of being unsightly, and the system of marking has to be known in order for them to serve for identification.
TATTOOS. Tattoos are a permanent method of identification applied either to the ear or to the lips of animals. Tattoos are difficult to read when applied to pigmented skins. They cannot be

53

read from a distance and warts make reading them impossible.
NECK CHAINS AND NECK STRAPS. Most often used on polled cattle. They require adjustment with the change of conformation of
the animal.
EAR MARKERS (Tags, Buttons). These are easily attached, but
also easily torn off. By rubbing and scratching the skin, markers
may cause infestation with screw-worm.

The recognized domestic breeds of animals found in the
United States are classified generally according to their economic value. These breeds are listed below.

CATTLE. There are three types of cattle, classified according to
their economic value.

1. Beef breeds.
    a. Aberdeen-Angus
    b. Beefmaster (Brahman and Shorthorn and Hereford)
    c. Belted Galloway
    d. Brahman
    e. Brangus (⅜ Brahman and ⅝ Aberdeen-Angus)
    f. Charbray (¾ Charolais, ¼ Brahman to ⅞ Charolais,
        ⅛ Brahman)
    g. Charolais
    h. Galloway
    i. Hereford
    j. Highland (Scotch Highland)
    k. Indu Brazil (Zebu)
    l. Polled Shorthorn
    m. Polled Hereford
    n. Red Angus
    o. Santa Gertrudis (⅝ Shorthorn and ⅜ Brahman)
    p. Shorthorn
2. Dairy breeds.
    a. Ayrshire
    b. Brown Swiss
    c. Dexter
    d. Dutch Belted
    e. French-Canadian

54

      f. Guernsey
      g. Holstein
      h. Jersey
      i. Kerry
      j. Polled Jersey
      k. Red Danish
3. Dual-purpose breeds.
      a. Devon
      b. Milking Shorthorn
      c. Polled Durham
      d. Red Poll

HORSES. There are two types of horses, classified according to their physical conformation.

1. Light horses. This type includes horses for various purposes, such as: saddle horses, pleasure horses, parade horses, roadsters (light harness, trotters, or pacers), race horses, hunters, polo mounts, children's mounts, and carriage (heavy harness) horses.
      a. American Albino Horse
      b. American Saddle Horse
      c. Appaloosa
      d. Arabian
      e. Cleveland Bay
      f. Hackney
      g. Morgan
      h. Morocco Spotted Horse
      i. Palomino
      j. Quarter Horse
      k. Shetland Pony
      l. Standardbred
      m. Tennessee Walking Horse
      n. Thoroughbred
      o. Welsh Pony
2. Draft horses. Currently, this type is almost exclusively used for farm work.
      a. Belgian
      b. Clydesdale

c. Percheron
d. Shire
e. Suffolk

SHEEP. There are five ways in which sheep may be classified: (1) Topography of the area where the breed originated (mountain, upland, lowland); (2) Color of face (black or white); (3) Grade of wool and type of wool produced (fine, medium, long, crossbred, carpet, fur); (4) Economic value, classified according to the sheep degree of suitability for mutton or wool; (5) Bearing process, classified according to the presence or absence of horns (horned or polled). With respect to the grade of wool produced, further sub-classification is given below:

1. Fine-wool breeds.
   a. American Merino
   b. Debouillet
   c. Delaine Merino
   d. Rambouillet
2. Medium-wool breeds.
   a. Cheviot
   b. Dorset
   c. Hampshire
   d. Montadale
   e. Oxford
   f. Ryeland
   g. Shropshire
   h. Southdown
   i. Suffolk
   j. Tunis (American Tunis)
3. Long-wool breeds.
   a. Cotswold
   b. Leicester
   c. Lincoln
   d. Romney
4. Crossbred-wool breeds.
   a. Columbia (Lincoln rams and Rambouillet ewes)
   b. Corriedale (Lincoln, and Leicester rams and Merino ewes)

    c. Panama (Rambouillet rams and Lincoln ewes)
    d. Romeldale (Romney Marsh rams and Rambouillet ewes)
    e. Targhee (Rambouillet rams and Lincoln, Rambouillet
        and Lincoln-Rambouillet-Corriedale ewes)
5. Carpet-wool breeds.
    Black-faced Highlands (Scottish Blackface)
6. Fur-sheep breeds.
    Karakul

GOATS. Goats are classified according to their suitability either for hair or for milk.

1. Mohair-bearing goat breeds.
    Angora
2. Milk-goat breeds.
    a. French Alpine
    b. Nubian
    c. Rock Alpine
    d. Saanen
    e. Swiss Alpine
    f. Toggenburg

SWINE. The current classification for swine constitutes two types: lean (meat) type, and fat type. Previously, for many years, swine were classified as lard type and bacon type.

1. Lean type breeds (meat-type breeds). This type includes swine with enough finish, but no more than necessary, to produce carcasses of desired quality.
    a. Beltsville No. 1 (75 per cent Landrace and 25 per cent
        Poland China)
    b. Beltsville No. 2 (58 per cent Danish Yorkshire, 32 per
        cent Duroc, 5 per cent Landrace and 5 per cent Hamp-
        shire)
    c. Berkshire
    d. Chester White
    e. Duroc
    f. Hampshire
    g. Hereford
    h. Kentucky Red Berkshire

    i. Maryland No. 1 (62 per cent Landrace and 38 per cent Berkshire)

    j. Minnesota No. 1 (48 per cent Landrace and 52 per cent Tamworth)

    k. Minnesota No. 2 (40 per cent Yorkshire and 60 per cent Poland China)

    l. Montana No. 1 (55 per cent Landrace and 45 per cent Hampshire)

    m. Mule foot

    n. Ohio Improved Chester (OIC)

    o. Palouse (53 per cent Landrace and 47 per cent Chester White)

    p. Poland China

    q. San Pierre No. 1 (Chester White and Canadian Berkshire)

    r. Spotted Poland China

2. Bacon-type breeds. Carcasses heavier than 250 pounds produce an excessive amount of lard and cuts are less suitable to the average consumer.

    a. American Landrace

    b. Tamworth

    c. Yorkshire

Below are listed the specie and breed registry associations requiring the branding of animals for registration. Requirements for earmarks and tattoos are listed in Chapter VI. Associations requiring brands and/or tattoos are listed below; associations requiring earmarks and/or tattoos are also to be found under earmarks in Chapter VI. Tattoo requirements are enumerated in Chapter VI, also. Eartagging requirements are not listed unless as a substitute for brands, earmarks, or tattoos.

BEEF CATTLE. Branding requirements of breed registry association for registration of animals. Brands may be selected by the individual breeders.

1. Brahman.
American Brahman Breeders' Association.

Holding brand and private herd number brand.
2. Brangus.
   American Brangus Breeders' Association.
   Holding brand and private herd number brand.
3. Charolais.
   American-International Charolais Association.
   Holding brand and private herd number brand (animal number), or holding tattoo and private herd tattoo.
4. Highland (Scotch Highland).
   American Scotch Highland Breeders' Association. Founded in 1948.
   Hip or horn brand, or tattooed or eartagged.
5. Indu Brazil (Zebu).
   Pan American Zebu Association.
   Identification number brand.
6. Santa Gertrudis.
   Santa Gertrudis Breeders' International. Organized in 1951.
   Holding brand and individual number brand, or holding brand and individual number tattoo.

The latest approach to animal identification is so new that it is not yet mentioned in the brand laws, but officials are studying this unique technique, which is called cryo-branding (supercold branding). It is being developed through the co-operation of the Animal Disease and Parasite Research Division, Agricultural Research Service, United States Department of Agriculture, and the Washington State University from a study made by Dr. R. Keith Farrell, D.V.M.

This study evolved from an attempt by Dr. Farrell in 1954 to develop a method of painless branding of animals with dry ice, and his project involves both artificial pigmentation and depigmentation. This method is still in the experimental stage although it seems to be successful thus far—so successful, in fact, that there are now more than 3,000 animals thus branded in the State of Oregon, and that the fisheries biologists, with a small crew of girls, are branding fish at the rate of 4,000 an hour.

The main advantages of this method of branding over the old hot iron method are less hide damage, the absence of pain, and the later growth of white hair which is legible from a distance.

"Cattle may be branded by a variety of cryogenic techniques," writes Dr. Farrell, "but most of the preliminary work has been done on clipped animals with copper branding irons. Heavy copper branding irons were selected because they are the most efficient (as compared with steel and aluminum) for heat transfer. The experimental copper irons were ¼ to ½ inch thick, with a depth from the contact face of at least one inch. Cattle were clipped and the skin wetted with 95 per cent ethyl alcohol. They were then branded with copper irons chilled in dry ice-alcohol, with forty seconds of skin contact. These brands were effective even with a flat-faced circle iron one inch in diameter. A patchy outgrowth of white hair was observed after ten and twenty seconds of skin contact, but not when the iron was applied for only five seconds."

Only 95 per cent alcohol should be used, and it acts as a refrigerant, the dry ice chilling the alcohol and the alcohol chilling the copper branding irons. One can use either methyl alcohol, isopropyl alcohol, ethyl alcohol or acetone. The hair should be clipped as short as possible, because contact between the cold iron and the skin is one of the most critical variables. Excellent results have been gained by applying the iron from twenty to thirty seconds, but not for as short as five seconds. Applying the iron for sixty seconds leaves a legible brand with white hair growth but produces excessive loss of epithelium, although this damage is less severe than the brand with a hot iron.

"The major variables," writes Dr. Farrell, "inherent in the super-cold branding iron approach are associated with contact between the cold surface and the skin—short underfur, pressure of application, hydration of the animal, the amount of subcutaneous fat, and the anatomical site all play a part. Of major importance is the stage of hair growth. The melanocytes (pigment producing cells) are more easily destroyed when the hair is growing rapidly.

"The most frequent question asked in regard to this technique is 'will the color change be permanent?' Cryo-branded cattle have not been observed over a long period of time and we are unable to make a positive statement about the permanency of the brand. However, it is our belief that the change is permanent in hair follicle. This is based on the apparent inability of the pigment-producing cells to migrate into the hair follicle lacking this cell.

"The melanocyte occupies a unique cellular role in the skin. It has been compared with an unicellular gland. Like other glandular cells, it can be selectively destroyed by extreme cold. This selective destruction is the basis of this technique."

The branding procedure is to chill heavy copper branding irons in liquid nitrogen or dry ice and a refrigerant, and to apply them to a location where the hair has been clipped. The freezing destroys the cells that produce pigmentation in both hair and skin. The mark is visible at once, and the fur over the area falls out and is later replaced by a new growth of white hair. Cattle have two hair-growth cycles, spring and fall, so the growth of the new white hair varies with the season. Those branded in mid-winter wait until spring to replace the denuded areas.

On January 9, 1968, Dr. Farrell received Patent 3,362,381, which recounts successful branding of a black cat, two black dogs, and a black Hereford cow. Under the terms of the patent, a refrigerant instead of a chilled iron may be applied to the hair and skin.

Through the Research Corporation, New York, several manufacturers have already been licensed to produce cryo-branding equipment. The first to be licensed, Hawkeye Castings, Inc., of Manchester, Iowa, has offered single letters and figures, groups of characters, and special marks, all with the necessary handles.

THREE

Design of Brands

During the early days of the cattle industry, brands were unusually large and sometimes covered the entire side of an animal. As the price of hides went up, the size of the brand decreased. From intricate Mexican designs evolved the straightforward approach of the American design. This approach reflects the functionalism of a distinct and original American culture. For example, North American brands can normally be identified by name, whereas the large Mexican brands usually give no clue by which they can be called. The historical heritage of the American stock brand is inspiring and world-renowned. In the design of new brands, taking pains to maintain the integrity of this strictly North American custom will preserve the continuity of a particle of our otherwise limited cultural accomplishments.

In designing a brand, care must be exercised not to have lines of characters too close together, or they will blur upon application. Closed brands, such as mentioned above, should be avoided. A well-spaced design, with the components far enough apart, will not blur upon application, but will result in a clear and distinct brand. Such a brand is termed an open brand.

The component parts of a brand are termed characters. The following definition should serve as a guide in the preparation of branding literature and publications.

> *Character:* A mark made by branding on the hide, horn, or fleece of stock. Characters are divided into three classes:
> 1. Literals (letters)
> 2. Numerals (numbers)
> 3. Symbols (figures, signs, pictures)

Symbols can also be subdivided into (a) geometric, and (b) pictorial. One of the idiosyncrasies of the science of branding is the fact that geometric symbols play an important role. Many of these symbols are used to modify or to add to other conventional pictures. By their constant and overwhelming usage, they have gained in importance, and now at last have helped to make branding an interesting study, unique in the world today.

In general, the design of brands may be classified into four categories:

1. Humorous. Brand Circle Two Step (Fig. 113) is at once very descriptive in its suggestion of walking and at the same time comical in appearance.

2. Sentimental. Brand Broken Heart (Fig. 362) expresses the emotions of the brand owner in a signal manner.

3. Illustrative. The Hatchet brand (Fig. 360) is a good example of illustrating an implement used by ranchers and farmers.

4. Risqué. Brand Two Lazy Two Pee (Fig. 116) indicates a measure of ingenuity on the part of the brand owner.

In order to correctly describe a brand, several simple, fundamental rules have to be observed.

Rule One: Always read from left to right, regardless of whether the brand consists of a combination of lines, figures, numerals, or pictures. If the arrangement of the brand design is on a diagonal, read first the component of the brand projecting farthest to the left; read from upper left corner to lower right corner, or from lower left corner to upper right corner, depending upon the direction of the diagonal axis of design.

Examples:
a. A Bar X (Fig. 124)
b. R Lazy Two (Fig. 125)
c. O Bar O (Fig. 126)
d. Slash Connected E Connected Slash (Fig. 127). In order to differentiate from Figure 133, this brand may be read as *Cut Connected E Connected Cut*
e. Lapped Circles (Fig. 128)

63

f. Circle A (Fig. 130)
g. Open A Half Box Connected (Fig. 129)
h. J Slash Diamond (Fig. 131)
i. Double O (Fig. 132)
j. Diamond and A Half (Fig. 134)
k. Open A Connected Broken Bar (Fig. 135).

Rule Two: Always read from top to bottom. If the axis of design deviates from the perpendicular, read the component part of the brand farthest to the left.

Examples:
a. 4 Bar X (Fig. 136)
b. R Lazy 2 (Fig. 137)
c. O Bar O (Fig. 138)
d. Diamond T (Fig. 139)
e. Circle A (Fig. 140)
f. J Slash Diamond (Fig. 141)
g. Three O Rail (Fig. 142)
h. Diamond and A Half (Fig. 143).

Rule Three: Always read exterior to interior of design. This rule applies to boxed (framed) brands only.

Examples:
a. Circle A (Fig. 144)
b. Circle Bar (Fig. 145)
c. Double Circle or Doughnut (Fig. 146)
d. Diamond T (Fig. 147).

Rule Four: Read numeral zero as *O* (oh) when components are of numbers. In the case of numbers consisting of more than two numerals, read the number of numerals followed by the name of the numeral.

Examples:
a. One O One (Fig. 148)
b. Nine O Nine (Fig. 149)
c. Four Sixes (Fig. 150).

Rule Five: Always read letter O (oh) and numeral o (zero) as

Circle when used in conjunction with another letter or as a boxed brand. Always read letter O (oh) and numeral o (zero) as *O* (oh) when used in conjunction with characters or with numbers.

Examples:
  a. Circle A (Fig. 151)
  b. Circle A (Fig. 152)
  c. Rafter O (Fig. 153)
  d. One O One (Fig. 154).

Rule Six: Differentiate between Rafter, Half Diamond, and Vee. Rafters are obtuse angles always placed above a brand; Half Diamonds are always half of a diamond framing the brand partially. Half Diamonds and Vees may be placed anywhere around the brand. Note the exception of reading an inverted Vee in Rule Nine.

Examples:
  a. Rafter O (Fig. 153)
  b. Half Diamond O (Fig. 155)
  c. Open A O (Fig. 161).

Rule Seven: Differentiate between Quarter Circle and Swinging. Both figures are quarter circles. In a Quarter Circle O brand the component parts are distinctly separated, whereas in a Swinging O brand the parts are connected. The quarter circle of a swinging brand is always connected at the top of the character.

Examples:
  a. Quarter Circle O (Fig. 156)
  b. Swinging O (Fig. 162).

Rule Eight: Differentiate between Quarter Circle and Rocking. Both figures are quarter circles. In an O Quarter Circle brand, the component parts are distinctly separated, whereas a Rocking O brand has the component parts connected. The quarter circle of a rocking brand is always connected at the bottom of the character.

65

Examples:
  a. O Quarter Circle (Fig. 157)
  b. Rocking O (Fig. 163).

Rule Nine: Always read an inverted Vee as an *Open A*.

Examples:
  a. A (Fig. 158)
  b. Open A (Fig. 164)
  c. Open A Half Box Connected (Fig. 129)
  d. Open A Broken Bar Connected (Fig. 135).

Rule Ten: When any component parts of the brand are connected, the brand is read *Connected*.

Examples:
  a. Quarter Circle O Connected (Fig. 159)
  b. Y Four Connected (Fig. 165).

Rule Eleven: Plus signs are always read as *Cross* and multiplication signs as letter *X*. In certain cases, letter X may denote the Roman numeral 10.

Examples:
  a. Cross (Fig. 160)
  b. X or Ten (Fig. 166).

It will be noted that several brands are described alike, even though the arrangement of the design varies. This is one major disadvantage in the system used in calling brands, *e.g.*, the Diamond T brand may be arranged in three different ways, yet the description is identical in all three.

In designing a brand, a number of factors must be considered in order to achieve a design that satisfies certain requirements. A good solution to all requirements will result in a well-designed brand. In selecting a brand, attention must be given to the appearance, relative to the scale and proportion of the characters. Using good arrangement combined with good appearance will result in a well-balanced design, which will be pleasing to the eye. At the same time, it should be borne in mind that the brand definitely fulfills a function relative to identification, and should be designed in such a manner as to be easily recognized from a distance and in inclement weather.

Two sizes of brands are recommended for use on adult cattle and adult horses. Calves may be branded with a smaller brand since it will grow with the animal. Brands for sheep, goats, and hogs should generally be up to 3 inches in height. There should be 1 inch of clear space between characters. Recommended dimensions of brands and characters are listed below:

TYPES OF BRAND	DIMENSION OF CHARACTER	
	FOR CATTLE	FOR HORSES
Letters and Numerals		
Height	3 to 5 inches (Fig. 171)	1½ to 2 inches
Width	1½ inches (Fig. 171)	¾ inch
Return of projection	1 inch (Figs. 176, 177)	⅜ inch
Boxed brands		
All sides	4 to 5 inches with 2½-inch-high characters	3 to 4 inches with 1½-inch-high characters
Diameter	5 inches (Fig. 170)	4 inches
Dots		
Diameter	1 inch (Fig. 174)	1 inch
Bars		
Length of Bar:		
Above or below characters	3 to 5 inches (Fig. 167)	2 to 3 inches
Before or after characters	2 inches (Fig. 169)	1½ inches
Between characters	1½ inches (Fig. 170)	1½ inches
Stripes		
Length	6 to 8 inches (Fig. 168)	4 to 6 inches
Slashes		
Length	4 inches (Fig. 175)	3 inches
Bench		
Length	3 inches	2½ inches
Height	1 inch (Fig. 176)	1 inch
Letters and Numerals (vertical arrangement)		
Total height	4 inches	3 inches

67

There are other considerations in the selection of a brand design. First, the surface upon which the design is to be applied; second, the instrument with which the design is applied; and third, the technique of application. The surface, being hide, horn, or fleece, may be uneven, dusty, or damp. The branding iron itself has such limitations as its capacity to hold heat and the construction of the material from which it was made, the condition of the iron, and the intensity of the source of heat. Other limiting factors are the experience of the brander in applying the brand and the condition under which the brand is applied —on the ground, or in a chute.

It is well to make a preliminary inquiry from the proper authority in order to determine whether or not a selected brand is available for recordation, and if the selected brand is acceptable to the recorder. The recorder has the prerogative of refusing to accept brands which may cause confusion or which may not be acceptable under the law.

A brand should convey a definite meaning to the owner, thereby fostering a feeling of possession and pride in ownership. A brand which has no meaning or which does not tell a story in capsule form, has little significance. The brand should have as much meaning to the owner as an oil painting would have to the artist who painted it.

The following section on brand characters deals with all the possible components which may constitute a brand. It should be remembered, however, that some characters or combinations of them are not suited for application on stock. Also, it must be kept in mind that the angles appearing and forming part of the design must be as wide as possible in order to prevent blurring of the brand. Consequently, it must be emphasized again that certain characters do not lend themselves readily for inclusion in a brand design.

The Quarter Circle is a figure not to be connected to the other characters composing the brand. Ample space should be allotted in order to avoid connecting the quarter circle. If the quarter circle is connected, the brand will be read as swinging or rocking. In the latter case, the quarter circle is below the major components of the brand.

The Bench brand is one with the end projections from the exterior corners of the horizontal bar and should not be returned more than one inch. Assuming the horizontal bar to be three inches and the returns to be 1½ inches, the brand would be called a half box. For that reason, the return ends have to be less than 1½ inches (Fig. 176).

The Rafter brand has to be shown with a wide angle in order not to have it mistaken for a Vee, inverted. The rafter is only shown above a brand, because a rafter is part of the upper structure of a building, and is only located there (Fig. 53).

Letters of the complete alphabet may be used in designing brands. In the accompanying plate (Plate XVII, Fig. 182), a standard block letter is illustrated. Other, modified, block letters will be found in subsequent sections. All single letters of the complete alphabet may be used. An up and down combination consists of one certain letter in the standard position and the second letter in an inverted position. Not all letters may be so used, because some letters do not read differently if positioned in other than standard "up" position (e.g., letter H), and some letters will be confused with a different letter if positioned in crazy reverse (e.g., letter W).

Most of the letters of the alphabet may be used in twin combination with the first or the second letter in any other than the standard position (e.g., reverse E F or reverse F E). The two alphabets may be combined with each other in any combination (e.g., AA, AB, AC, AD; BA, BB, BC, BD; CA, CB, CD, etc.).

The double connected combination is similar to the double combination above, except that the two letters are connected. It will be noted that not all letters are suited for connection with each other.

The triple design consists of three separate letters in any position or with any modification (Fig. 180). The triple connected is a combination in which all letters used are connected (Fig. 181). Again, certain letters are not suitable for connection to each other. It will be noted that a very distinguished design may be achieved by positioning the letters with imagination, for example, the Triple K, shown in Fig. 112.

Since most four letter brands would take up too much space if they were in a horizontal position and unconnected, a brand of four letters is normally connected. The method of connection calls for imagination and may be solved in very ingenious ways (e.g., brand Hell, Fig. 111).

Block letters are normally used in the upper case, because the lower case letters are too intricate to produce a clear design. This alphabet is used without any embellishment and without modifications (Plate XVII, Fig. 182). Block letters may be modified by the addition of small projections from parts of the letters. This method is used for brands exclusively, and makes branding alphabets distinct from any other alphabets used for various other purposes.

The long alphabet is made by the addition of short vertical lines to either top, bottom, or center of each individual letter. This addition gives the letter a vertically elongated appearance (Plate XVIII, Fig. 188).

The bradded alphabet is made by the addition of short horizontal bars to the termini of the letter. The appearance of the letter is then similar to that of a brad, a small nail with a broad head over its shank (Plate XIX, Fig. 190). The barbed alphabet is made by the addition of a barb to the termini of the letter, either top or bottom, at an angle of 45 or 90 degrees. The barb resembles a fishhook. In considering the point of attachment of the barb to the letter, it should be borne in mind that the logical place is where an imaginary fishhook would be bent in order to make withdrawal of the hook difficult (Plate XX, Fig. 192). The forked alphabet is made by the attachment of a 90-degree fork to the termini of the letters. Normally, only one fork is attached, unless it makes the letter look unbalanced. The letter H would look out of balance with only one fork, but a second fork attached will restore the balance (Plate XX, Fig. 191). The hooked alphabet is made by the attachment of a cane or curve to the termini of the letters (Plate XIX, Fig. 189).

The walking alphabet is made by the attachment of one or two short bars to the termini of the letter. These bars are normally angling downward and to the right. This alphabet is adaptable for conveying humor by means of the short bars arranged in such fashion as to almost literally make the letters walk. For that reason, the walking alphabet is quite popular (Plate XXI, Fig. 194). The dragging alphabet differs from the walking alphabet in that the downward angling bars are turned toward the left. Because of the custom of reading from left to right, these bars appear as two feet on a body being dragged across (Plate XXI, Fig. 193).

The swinging alphabet has the letter suspended and connected to a quarter circle above. The quarter circle must be connected, or else the letter will read differently. The addition of this quarter circle makes the letter appear to be swinging from above (Plate XXII, Fig. 195). The rocking alphabet is made by the addition of a quarter circle at the bottom. The letter must be connected and must rest on the quarter circle; otherwise the letter will read differently. The attachment of the quarter circle gives the letter the appearance of resting on a rocker (Plate XXII, Fig. 196).

The flying alphabet is made by the addition of a symbolization of two wings attached to the letter. A slight curving of the outward line will emphasize the appearance of the letter as though in flight (Plate XVII, Fig. 183). Letters of the alphabet may be further modified by various positionings of the letter. Letters modified by the addition of short bars may be further modified by positioning. However, this method is not recommended, because it tends to be confusing and makes the brand extremely difficult to read. The best design is one which is easily legible and clear. The crazy (inverted) alphabet is formed by having the letters

71

simply inverted, or flopped downward (Plate XXIII, Fig. 197). The backward (reverse) alphabet has the letters turned on their left axes to the left. It will be noticed that several letters are omitted from this alphabet because, although they are turned backward, their shape does not change (*e.g.*, A, H, M, etc., Plate XXIII, Fig. 198). Crazy-backward (inverted-reverse) letters are positioned by turning them downward and then to the left. Again, several letters do not change shape (Plate XXIII, Fig. 199).

Lazy alphabets consist of letters lying on their sides. Letters are either lying on their back (left or right) sides or on their face (right or left) sides. This alphabet is descriptive of a rest position. Letters of the lazy right down alphabet are lying to the right in a prone position, that is, with their faces down (Plate XXIV, Fig. 201). Letters of the lazy left down alphabet are lying face down to the left (Plate XXIV, Fig. 200). Letters of the lazy right up alphabet are lying to the right in a supine position and facing up (Plate XXV, Fig. 203). Letters of the lazy left up alphabet are lying face up to the left (Plate XXV, Fig. 202).

The tumbling alphabets suggest action, as do all diagonal lines. Letters may either tumble to the right or to the left. Those of the tumbling right alphabet are falling on their faces and are depicted at a forty-five-degree angle (Plate XXVI, Fig. 205). Letters of the tumbling left alphabet are falling backward, or to the left, at a forty-five-degree angle (Plate XXVI, Fig. 204). Usually, letters should not be modified by both addition and position. The resultant brand probably would be confusing and difficult to identify. If a combination can be selected wherein the brand is clear, however, such modified letters may be used (*e.g.*, Flying Lazy K).

The running (script) alphabet is a stylization of script and is recommended because all angles are open, leaving no place where the brand may blur. It is also adaptable to running irons and may be applied like lettering on a sheet of paper. The brand-

72

ing iron may not leave the hide, as it is applied with a flowing motion.

The standard alphabet is the standard form for a running alphabet, and nothing more than the capital letters of script (Plate XVIII, Fig. 184). Ordinarily this alphabet is not modified in any way except that, by taking certain liberties with the standard script, certain letters are modified and read to express the similarity or resemblance to objects. The only running letters which are modified are: Open Running A (Fig. 184), Round Top A (Fig. 185), and Mustache A (Fig. 187).

In addition to the block letters of the Roman alphabet or the script alphabet, letters of the Greek, Cyrillic, and others may be used, with care.

A digit is any one of the ten Arabic numerals, 0, 1, 2, 3, 4, 5, 6, 7, 8, and 9. Any combination of these numerals is a number. Roman numerals are not satisfactory because they can be confused with letters, e.g., X equals 10, C equals 100. Numerals may be used as follows:

Although single numerals may be used, most brand recorders will not accept them because they are easily blotted by adding another number to the brand. Single numerals may be applied only for use in production records such as herd numbers, year brands, or serial numbers (Plate XXVII). Numbers consisting of two separate numerals may be used in any combination (Plate XXVII). Two numerals connected in any combination may be used. The success of any connected combination depends upon the creativeness of the designer (Plate XXVII). Any number consisting of three numerals may be used in any combination (as in Plate XXVII, Fig. 206). A number consisting of three numerals which are connected presents a challenge to the designer. A very satisfactory design is illustrated on Plate XXVII, Fig. 207.

Standard Arabic numerals are recommended because they present a clear picture. In designing a brand, attention should be directed to the proportion of the numeral, so that it will appear pleasing to the eye. Lines should be perpendicular and curves well rounded in order to obtain a well-defined numeral (Plate XVII, Fig. 182). Numerals may be modified the same as letters, but this is not recommended unless the numeral will still retain its identity and not blotch upon application. It will be noted that several numerals are omitted, either because there is no possible means of modifying them or else because modification would tend to cause confusion, *e.g.*, numerals 6 and 9.

Long numerals are formed by an additional short vertical bar either at the top, bottom, or center of the numeral (Plate XVIII, Fig. 188). Bradded numerals are formed by the addition of a short vertical or horizontal bar at the termini of the numeral (Plate XIX, Fig. 190). Barbed numerals are formed by the addition of a fishhook to the termini of the numeral (Plate XX, Fig. 192). Forked numerals, by simply adding a fork to the termini of the numeral (Plate XX, Fig. 191).

Hooked numerals are formed by the addition of a cane or hook to the termini (Plate XIX, Fig. 189). Walking numerals are formed by the addition of short bars angling downward and to the right. These bars appear to be feet in a walking position. The humorous appearance of this walking numeral makes it very popular (Plate XXI, Fig. 194). A dragging numeral is accomplished by the addition of a bar angling downward and to the left. These bars suggest dangling feet belonging to a body being dragged across a surface (Plate XXI, Fig. 193). All numerals may be made to appear swinging by the addition of a quarter circle at the top. The quarter circle must be connected to the numeral or it will read differently (Plate XXII, Fig. 195). All numerals may be made to rock by adding a quarter circle to the bottom of the numeral. The rocker and the numeral must be connected (Plate XXII, Fig. 196). By adding two stylized wings, all numerals may be made to appear as flying (Plate XVII, Fig. 183).

Like letters, numerals may be modified by placing them in a different position other than the conventional one. Crazy, or

74

inverted, numerals are those turned downward from their conventional position (Plate XXIII, Fig. 197). A backward, or reverse, numeral is made by turning it on its perpendicular axis to the left (Plate XXIII, Fig. 198). A crazy-backward, or inverted-reverse, numeral is made by turning it downward from its conventional position and then to the left (Plate XXIII, Fig. 199).

Lazy numerals lie on their sides. Numerals are either lying on their back (left or right) side or on their face (left or right) side. This stance is descriptive of a rest position. Lazy right down numerals are those lying to the right in a prone position—that is, face down (Plate XXIV, Fig. 201). Lazy left down numerals are those lying face down to the left (Plate XXIV, Fig. 200). Lazy right up numerals are those lying to the right in a supine position and facing up (Plate XXV, Fig. 203). Lazy left up numerals are those lying to the left in a supine position and facing up (Plate XXV, Fig. 202).

A tumbling numeral indicates action, and may be to the right or to the left. A tumbling right numeral is one falling to the right at forty-five degrees from the vertical (Plate XXVI, Fig. 205). A tumbling left numeral is one falling backwards to the left at forty-five degrees (Plate XXVI, Fig. 204).

Characters which are not letters or numerals can be classified as symbolic characters, and these can be subdivided into symbols which are strictly of a geometric nature and those which are of a pictorial nature. The term symbol includes figures, signs, and pictures, these terms being synonymous for all practical purposes. Geometrical characters include all characters of a plane geometric nature or portion thereof, and not necessarily representing an abstract or symbolized picture. The characters below are widely used in the design of brands and are enumerated here in a logical sequence.

LINE. Lines are the fundamental structure of any symbol. By modification and addition, they form increasingly complex symbols.

75

1. Dot. This is the very basis of a line. It should be remembered that a dot used in a brand should never be less than one inch in diameter (Plate XV, Fig. 172).

2. Bar. The bar is the horizontal elongation of a line, it may be placed in various positions around the main part of the brand, causing it to be read in various ways:

   a. Bar. Either positioned ahead of or behind the brand (Figs. 208, 209, 210).

   b. Over bar. This bar is positioned above the brand (Fig. 211).

   c. Through bar. This bar is positioned through the center of the brand (Fig. 212).

   d. Under bar. The under bar is positioned below the main body of the brand (Fig. 213).

3. Broken bar. A broken bar has one end turned up and the other end turned down, and may be read as a:

   a. Broken bar. This bar may be positioned either ahead of, or behind a brand (Figs. 238, 239, 240).

   b. Broken over bar. This bar is positioned above the brand (Fig. 241).

   c. Broken through bar. This bar is positioned through the brand (Fig. 242).

   d. Broken under bar. This bar is positioned below a brand (Fig. 243).

4. Double bar. This symbol has two bars spaced one inch apart vertically, and may be read:

   a. Double bar. This double bar may be positioned either ahead or behind the main brand (Figs. 226, 227, 228).

   b. Double over bar. This bar is positioned above the brand (Fig. 229).

   c. Double through bar. This bar is positioned through the center of the main part of the brand (Fig. 230).

   d. Double under bar. This bar is positioned below the brand (Fig. 231).

5. Rail. A bar about twice as long as a regular bar, or up to approximately 8 inches long, is termed a rail. Over, under, and through rails, double rails, and stripes are similar to bars (Figs. 220, 221, 222, 223, 224, 225), and are read similarly:

76

a. Rail. A single long bar positioned ahead of or behind a brand (Figs. 220, 221, 222).

b. Double rail. Two long bars spaced one inch apart vertically and positioned either ahead of or behind a brand (Figs. 226, 227, 228, 229, 230, 231).

c. Stripes. By common usage, three long bars, positioned either ahead of or behind the brand (Figs. 232, 233, 234).

6. Slash. A slash is a diagonal line, sometimes termed a cut, the position of which may vary:

a. Slash. The slash is positioned either ahead of or behind the brand (Figs. 244, 245, 246).

b. Reverse slash. This slash is directional from the upper right to the lower left and is also positioned either ahead of or behind a brand (Figs. 250, 251, and 252).

7. Broken slash. This slash has one end turned up and the other end turned down, and may be varied further:

a. Broken slash. This slash may be positioned either ahead of, or behind a brand (Figs. 247, 248, and 249).

b. Broken reverse slash. This slash is also used in front of and behind a brand (Figs. 253, 254, and 255).

The figures below show the progression from lines to a representation of a complete or partial plane geometric figure. When these figures are a quarter or half portion or a segment of a complete plane geometric figure, they are considered a partial box brand containing characters, and consequently should be drawn larger than the characters themselves. If so drawn, they will not be confused with characters, such as V's or C's. Complete plane geometric figures may either be used as box brands, containing characters within, or they may be placed in any position around a character.

1. Triangle. The triangle used in branding is normally a 45-degree triangle, thereby avoiding the acute angle of a 30–60 triangle. It may be read two ways:

a. Triangle. The triangle has its base at the bottom and may be positioned anywhere around a brand. Even more often, it forms the main part of the brand itself (Figs. 256, 257, 258, 259, 260, and 261).

b. Inverted triangle. This triangle has its apex at the bottom and may also be used anywhere around a brand (Figs. 262, 263, 264, 265, 266, and 267).

2. Diamond. The diamond is a plane figure with two acute and two obtuse angles, more accurately termed a lozenge. Variations are:

a. Half diamond. This character consists of half a diamond and may be placed, with the points directed outward, around the main part of the brand. (Figs. 268, 269, 270, 271, and 272).

b. Reverse half diamond. Half of a diamond, with the points directed toward the brand. (Figs. 273, 274, 275, 276, and 277).

c. Diamond. This brand may be positioned anywhere around the brand. (Figs. 278, 279, 280, 281, 282, and 283).

d. Diamond and a half. This figure may have the half diamond pointing in any direction and may also be positioned anywhere around the brand. (Fig. 284).

e. Two diamonds. This figure may point in any direction and may be positioned anywhere around the brand. Normally it forms the main part of the brand (Fig. 285).

f. Five diamonds. This figure represents a subtle combination of four diamonds contained within a larger one (Fig. 286).

3. Box (square). This is a four-sided plane figure with equal sides. Half of a box is termed an open box and is exactly one half, cut either way. The projecting ends must be exactly one half of either the horizontal or vertical side as otherwise the brand may be read a bench.

a. Box. The box may be placed all around a brand or may contain another character within. In the latter case, it is termed a box brand (Figs. 297, 298, 299, 300, 301, and 302).

b. Open box (Fig. 287). In an open box the projecting ends point downward when the box is placed above (Fig. 290); the projecting ends point upward when the box is placed below the brand (Fig. 291). The ends are pointing inward when the box is placed either before or after the brand (Figs. 288 and 289).

c. Reversed open box (Fig. 292). This figure has the projecting ends of the half box pointing away and outward from the main body of the brand, exactly the opposite from an open box (Figs. 293, 294, 295, and 296).

4. Circle. The circle is a plane figure and perfectly round. It should not be oval shaped, lest it be mistaken for an O or a zero. Because quarter circles and half circles are portions of a circle and, per se, are all box brands, they should be designed larger, in order to contain another character within. This is particularly true of a quarter circle, because it may be mis-read as a C. A segment of a circle may be placed in any position around a character.

a. Quarter circle (Fig. 303). This character consists of an arc one-quarter the circumference of a circle. It may be placed around a character with both ends pointing inward (Figs. 304, 305, 306, and 307).

b. Half circle (Fig. 313). This character consists of an arc one-half the circumference of a circle, with both ends pointing inward. (Figs. 314, 315, 316, and 317).

c. Reverse quarter circle (Fig. 308). Similar to a quarter circle, except that both ends project outward (Figs. 309, 310, 311, 312).

d. Reverse half circle (Fig. 318). Similar to a half circle, except that both ends project outward (Figs. 319, 320, 321, and 322).

e. Circle. A plane figure of 360 degrees. It normally is used only as a box brand with a character enclosed within its circumference (Figs. 323, 324, 325, 326, 327, and 328).

f. Double circle (doughnut). Two concentric circles with at least an inch of space between them. The resultant appearance is the reason for this double circle being termed doughnut (Fig. 329).

g. Broken links. Two circles separated by at least an inch of space (Fig. 332).

h. Two links. Two circles tangent to each other (Fig. 330).

i. Lapped circles. Two circles intersecting each other sufficiently not to blotch the restricted space between them (Fig. 331).

j. Goose egg (mashed O). This is an ellipse, deriving its name from the resemblance to an egg (Fig. 333).

79

The listing below includes representative pictorial symbols used throughout the animal industry. Several of these pictorial characters enjoy a special status, judged by their frequent appearance in brand books. Undoubtedly, this status has been achieved by the extensive use and popularity of these brands. Reference is made to crosses, hearts, benches, shields, etc. Inasmuch as all these preferred pictures represent an abstraction of an object in the same manner as the less popular ones, all have been included in the list here. Picture brands usually are abstractions of objects used in ranching and farming. They depict various household items, riding equipment, garden tools, camping equipment, etc. In this respect, it is worth noting that all the objects represented in picture brands are very similar to objects used in heraldic designs. The following pictures may also be modified by the addition of lines or by positioning, like the letters and numerals shown above.

SELECTED PICTURES:
1. Anchor (Fig. 334)
   a. Tumbling anchor (Fig. 335)
2. Andiron (Fig. 336)
3. Anvil (Fig. 337)
4. Arrow (Fig. 338)
   a. Broken arrow (Fig. 339)
5. Barrel (Fig. 340)
6. Bench (Fig. 341)
7. Bit (bridle) (Fig. 342)
   a. Spanish (Fig. 343)
8. Boot (Fig. 344)
9. Bottle (Fig. 345)
10. Bow and arrow (Fig. 346)
11. Buckle (Fig. 347)
    a. Cinch buckle (Fig. 348)
12. Chair (Fig. 349)
    a. Rocking chair (Fig. 350)
13. Chimney (lamp) (Fig. 351)
14. Cleaver (meat) (Fig. 352)

15. Comb (curry) (Fig. 353)
16. Crescent (Fig. 354)
17. Cross (Fig. 355)
18. Crutch (Fig. 356)
19. Dollar sign (Fig. 357)
20. Flag (Fig. 358)
21. Fleur-de-Lis (Fig. 359)
22. Hatchet (Fig. 360)
23. Heart (Fig. 361)
    a. Broken heart (Fig. 362)
    b. Crazy heart (Fig. 363)
    c. Flying heart (Fig. 364)
    d. Split heart (Fig. 365)
    e. Two hearts (Fig. 366)
24. Hook (fish) (Fig. 367)
25. Hook (hay) (Fig. 368)
26. Key (Fig. 369)
27. Keyhole (Fig. 370)
28. Knife (hash) (Fig. 371)
29. Ladder (Fig. 372)
    a. Lazy ladder (Fig. 373)
    b. Tumbling ladder (Fig. 374)
30. Leaf (clover) (Fig. 375)
31. Lightning (Fig. 376)
32. Moon (Fig. 377)
33. Pan (frying) (Fig. 378)
34. Pigpen (Fig. 379)
35. Pin (rolling) (Fig. 380)
36. Pipe (Fig. 381)
37. Pitchfork (Fig. 382)
38. Plough (Fig. 383)
39. Question mark (Fig. 384)
40. Rafter (Fig. 385)
41. Rake (Fig. 386)
42. Scissors (Fig. 387)
43. Shield (Fig. 388)
44. Shovel (Fig. 389)
45. Sled (Fig. 390)

46. Square and compass (Fig. 391)
47. Spur (Fig. 392)
48. Star (Fig. 393)
49. Stirrup (Fig. 394)
50. Sun (Fig. 395)
51. Sunrise (Fig. 396)
52. S Wrench (Fig. 397)
53. Track (horse) (Fig. 398)
54. Track (turkey) (Fig. 399)
55. Tree (Fig. 400)
56. Wind vane (Fig. 401)
57. Wineglass (Fig. 402)
58. Yoke (oxen) (Fig. 403).

FOUR

Federal Government Brands

Because the use of animals by the United States Government is quite limited and is becoming more so, certain historical facts have been included here in an effort to preserve them from oblivion. Brief descriptions of the functions of the governmental agencies have been included in order to relate the functions of these agencies to the use of branding. Branding and matters related thereto are treated in detail insofar as information is available.

Federal brands are applied to Government-owned animals to indicate ownership and, in some cases, supplementary brands are applied for identification purposes only. The agencies of the United States Government using brands are:

1. Units of the United States Army.
2. The Bureau of Indian Affairs of the United States Department of the Interior.
3. The National Park Service of the United States Department of the Interior.
4. The Forest Service of the United States Department of Agriculture.
5. The Animal Disease Eradication Division of the United States Department of Agriculture.
6. The Meat Inspection Division of the United States Department of Agriculture.
7. The Animal Husbandry Research Division, Dairy Cattle Research Branch, of the United States Department of Agriculture.
8. The Livestock Division, Meat Grading Branch, of the United States Department of Agriculture.

83

9. The United States Atomic Energy Commission.
10. The War Relocation Authority, Office for Emergency Management, Executive Office of the President.

In the Department of the Army, office of the Quartermaster General, there is the Remount Service, whose function it is to procure, train and issue animals for military use. Although the term remount is erroneous when applied to present animal activities, it has been retained. From 1775, the year the Quartermaster Corps was created, to the present, remount has been a function of the Corps.

During World War I, the Remount Service was a separate service in the Office of the Quartermaster General and consisted of forty civilians and five officers. Following World War I, the Remount Service was reduced to the status of a branch in the Supply Division. After the adoption of the Selective Service Act, the Remount Branch became a separate division, in January, 1941. In March, 1942, the Remount Division was again reduced to a branch and transferred to the Service Installation Division. Currently, Remount is a function operating within a section of a branch of a division in the Office of the Quartermaster General. It is administered by one civilian and an Animal Purchase Board which functions as required.

The horse breeding program originated in 1919 when the War Department created the Remount Board to make recommendations for regulating and supervising the breeding of public animals for the Army. The Department of Agriculture program of a similar nature was on a minor scale, and was taken over by the Army (fiscal year 1921) for expansion.

For the administration of the animal breeding and purchasing operations of the Army, the United States was geographically divided into remount areas. From 1921 to the beginning of World War II, there were seven remount areas. On September 5, 1944, that number was reduced to six, with headquarters located at: Fort Royal, Virginia; Lexington, Kentucky; Sheridan, Wyoming; San Angelo, Texas; Colorado Springs, Colorado; and

84

Pomona, California. The functions of the headquarters were to procure animals for military use, to purchase stallions for breeding purposes, and to select and inspect civilian breeding centers. These areas normally had 700 breeding stallions. At the beginning of World War II, the Army had the following permanent remount depots: Aleshire QM Depot (Remount), Fort Royal, Virginia, activated August 30, 1911; Reno QM Depot (Remount), El Reno, Oklahoma, handling capacity 15,000 horses and mules, activated May 11, 1908; Robinson QM Depot (Remount), Crawford, Nebraska, activated November 22, 1919. Later the Army added Pomona QM Depot (Remount), Pomona, California, with a holding capacity of 250 animals, activated October 28, 1943.

Under the Potsdam Agreement of Advanced Deliveries Reparations Account, horses were imported, confined to animals of known German origin. The first shipment consisted of 150 horses, including 65 thoroughbreds from the German government breeding farm established in 1934 at Altefelt, approximately a hundred miles northwest of Frankfort, and the German Army breeding farms at Monsbach and at Donauworth. A number was painted on the back of each horse and a corresponding number entered on the pedigree sheet. This first shipment left from Bremerhaven and arrived at Newport News October 19, 1945, as prizes of war. The second shipment consisting of 83 horses, arrived in 1946. At the liquidation of the United States Army horse breeding program, these horses were transferred to the United States Department of Agriculture (in July, 1948) and subsequently disposed of by public auction.

During the time of transfer of remount depots from the Army to the Department of Agriculture, 10,000 mules had been purchased and shipped to Greece from Fort Reno, Oklahoma, by December, 1949. In 1954, the Department of Agriculture loaned its processing facilities at Fort Reno to the Army. By May, 1954, 12,000 horses and mules were purchased and shipped to Turkey under the Mutual Aids Program.

85

The annual procurement level preceding the start of World War II was between 1,500 and 2,500 animals. For the fiscal year 1941, 24,000 horses and 4,000 mules were divided as follows: cavalry, 22,000 riding horses; field artillery, 1,800 riding horses; others, 250 riding horses; field artillery, 600 draft horses, and 2,400 pack mules. For the fiscal year 1941 the animals on hand at remount depots numbered 28,000. For the fiscal year 1942, 2,900 horses were procured, 6,000 animals issued, and 15,000 animals returned to depots. By June of that year 21,000 animals were on hand in depots. In the fiscal year 1943, 5,200 animals were issued and 6,000 animals returned to depots, and more than 3,000 riding horses were issued to the United States Coast Guard for beach patrol—more animals than were issued to the Army during the same period. For the fiscal year 1944, 800 horses were issued to the United States Coast Guard—more than twice as many animals as issued to the Army. From July, 1943, to December, 1945, 28,000 horses were turned over to disposal agencies.

During the period of World War II, forty-nine horses were shipped from the Zone of the Interior to overseas theaters; 39,000 foals produced; 30,523 mules were purchased, 7,800 mules were shipped overseas, 3500 mules were shipped to the United Kingdom under Lend-Lease Agreement, 15,000 pack mules were procured and 11,000 pack mules issued to forces by United States Army Quartermaster Remount Service in Italy.

The fiscal year 1941 through fiscal year 1943 brought the return of 33,000 horses by user organizations, 31,000 horses issued to units and stations, and 3,900 horses loaned to the United States Coast Guard.

During the fiscal year 1941 there were purchased in the United States 23,546 horses and 4,279 mules; in 1942 there were purchased 2,859 horses and 1,699 mules; in 1943 there were only four horses bought, but 10,217 mules were purchased. No horses were bought in 1944, but 5,129 mules were purchased; and again, no horses were bought in 1945, but 9,199 mules were acquired.

This made a total of 26,409 horses and 30,523 mules purchased during this period of five years.

It is estimated that over 650,000 horses served in the Army during the Civil War. During World War I, over 500,000 horses and mules were purchased by the Remount Service and over 68,000 horses served in the Army.

The Remount and Breeding Headquarters Offices and the Army Horse Breeding Program were transferred to the United States Department of Agriculture July 1, 1948, along with the remount depots, equipment, and breeding stock. This program was liquidated by the Department of Agriculture in 1949, and all stock was sold at public auction. The Army Horse Breeding Program was in operation twenty-eight years, from 1921 to 1948, during which time 700 stallions had been placed and 230,000 foals produced.

In 1940 the United States Army had two horse cavalry divisions, two horse-drawn artillery regiments and two mixed horse and motor transport regiments, with a total authorized strength of 20,300—16,800 horses and 3,500 mules. In 1942, seven federalized National Guard horse-mechanized regiments and the Sixth Cavalry Regiment were de-horsed, as were the First Cavalry Division in 1943 and the Second Cavalry Division and Fifty-sixth Brigade of the Texas National Guard in 1944.

In ceremonies at Fort Carson, Colorado, on February 15, 1957, the last mounted units in the United States Army were de-activated: the Fourth Field Artillery Battalion (Pack) and the Thirty-fifth Quartermaster Company (Pack). For several years following World War II, United States Constabulary units in Germany utilized mounted platoons, as did the United States Disciplinary Barracks at Fort Leavenworth, Kansas. At the U.S.D.B., horses and mules were employed for draft work and for the perimeter patrol in apprehending escaped prisoners.

The present use of animals as recorded in the Animal Register of the Army comprises seventeen horses and two mules. The horses are part of the Ceremonial Detachment at Fort Myer, Virginia; formerly the Caisson Section of the Third Infantry Regiment. This detachment consists of sixteen enlisted men, a lead horse, six horses pulling the caisson carrying the coffin of a general or a demised cavalry officer, and the caparisoned horse. The two mules are the mascots of the United States Military Academy, West Point, New York.

The last cavalry mount on the rolls of the United States Army was Chief, Preston Brand 1J84. The gelding was foaled in 1932, purchased by the Army in 1940, and received at Fort Riley, Kansas, in 1941. Chief was semi-retired in 1949 and fully retired in 1953, remaining as a symbol of the time when Fort Riley was famous as the home of the Cavalry School. Chief died May 24, 1968, at the age of thirty-six. The old cavalry horse was interred standing upright in a wooden box in front of the "Old Trooper" monument. On June 1, 1968, a brass plaque mounted on the concrete slab covering the grave was unveiled at a ceremony attended by hundreds of soldiers and civilians and presided over by Major General Roderick Weatherill, commanding general, Twenty-fourth Infantry Division, Fort Riley, Kansas.

In the fiscal year 1955 an agreement between the United States Army and the United States Department of Agriculture was reached, placing the animal processing facilities at the Beef Cattle Research Station, Fort Reno, Oklahoma, on a stand-by status for use of the Army in processing animals for future Mutual Aid Programs and for emergencies. The Army pays $1,800 annually to the Department of Agriculture for the maintenance of the facilities.

Prior to the adoption of the Preston Branding System, the US brand was used by the US Army to identify all public animals. It was first stamped by hot iron on the left hoof. Regulations for the Army of the United States, 1908, direct that the letters "US" be branded on the left foreshoulder of public animals on the day received. Horses assigned to organizations were to be branded with an additional brand designating the organization to which the horses were assigned. The US brand was specified as 2 inches in height. With the adoption of the Preston Branding System in or about 1925, reference to the US brand was omitted from Army regulations. Currently, the US is applied in conjunction with the Preston Brand to identify animals under Mutual Aid Programs (Fig. 406).

The S brand made its first appearance in Change No. 1, December 29, 1943, to Army Regulation 30–450 April 6, 1943, and "Quartermaster Corps—Public Animals." It directs that after animals have been declared surplus to the War Department and made available to the appropriate property officer of the Procurement Division, Treasury Department, for transfer to another Government agency or for sale, they must be branded with the letter "S." The brand is to be applied on the neck underneath the mane, or on the left side of the neck if the mane is roached. The dimensions of required brands were governed by Army Regulation 30–455, of November 17, 1941, and "Quartermaster Corps—Branding and Registration of Public Animals." Under this regulation, brands are specified as 2 inches in height and 1½ inches wide. The webbing of the brand is specified as between $\frac{1}{16}$ and $\frac{3}{16}$ of an inch in thickness.

Both Army regulations mentioned above are superseded by Army Regulation 880–5, September 1, 1953, "Public Animals—Horses, Mules, and Dogs." This regulation directs that after animals have been declared surplus to the needs of the military establishment and have been made available for appropriate disposition, they are to be branded with the letter "S." In the case of horses and mules, the brand is to be applied on the left side of the neck underneath the mane; in the case of dogs, on the left flank just below the regular brand. Required brands are specified to be 2 inches in height and 1½ inches wide, and the webbing of the brand to be between $\frac{1}{16}$ and $\frac{3}{16}$ of an inch in thickness (Fig. 407).

89

The IC brand signifies that public animals have been inspected and condemned. Regulations for the Army of the United States, 1908, direct that condemned animals be branded with the letters "IC" on the neck under the mane.

Army Regulation 30–450, April 6, 1943, and "Quartermaster Corps—Public Animals," directs that animals recommended for transfer to another government agency or for sale be branded with the letters "IC" on the neck under the mane, or on the left side of the neck if the mane is roached. The brand is to be applied in the presence of an inspector prior to such sale or transfer. The dimensions of this brand are governed by Army Regulations 30–455, November, 17, 1941, and "Quartermaster Corps—Branding and Resistration of Public Animals." Pursuant to this regulation, required brands are to be 2 inches in height, 1½ inches wide, with a ¾-inch open space between the nearest points of two adjacent symbols. The webbing of the brand is to be between $\frac{1}{16}$ and $\frac{3}{16}$ of an inch in thickness.

Both Army regulations above are superseded by Army Regulation 880–5 September 1, 1953, and "Public Animals—Horses, Mules, and Dogs." Except for the branding, the contents of the regulations are identical to the superseded regulations. They direct that the brand is to be applied to the left side of the neck underneath the mane in the case of horses and mules, and on the left flank just below the regular brand in the case of dogs. The dimensions of the brand also remain unchanged (Fig. 408).

Prior to the adoption of the Preston Branding System after World War I, the Organizational brand was used in conjunction with the US brand to identify public animals assigned to units of the Army. With the inception of the Preston Branding System, the Organizational hoof brand was discontinued and branding on the hoof specifically prohibited. Regulations for the Army of the United States, 1908, direct that horses assigned to organizations be branded on the hoof of one forefoot. The brand is to be applied 1½ inches below the coronet, giving the designation of the company. Letters and numerals are to be ¾ inch high,

90

to be on the same line, and the letter to precede the numeral. The brand is to be blocked so as to penetrate the hoof $\frac{1}{16}$ of an inch. Some examples of hoof brands on horses assigned to organizations in 1908 are:

Band, Ninth Cavalry	CB9
Troop A, Fifth Cavalry	A5
Band, Second Regiment, Field Artillery	AB2
Battery B, Fourth Regiment, Field Artillery	BA4
Company A, Battalion of Engineers	BEA

Army Regulation 30–455, November 17, 1941, and "Quartermaster Corps—Branding and Registration of Public Animals," directs that animals purchased and shipped to a depot before being issued to a using unit be branded with a temporary brand. The temporary brand is to be applied to public horses and mules at the time of purchase. This brand is not to exceed three digits and the purchasing officer's brand letter. It is to be applied in block letters, about 8 inches high, on the near side of the back, so that it can be read while the animal is in a chute. The brand is specified to be of nitrate of silver, or, if this is impracticable, of white paint. Animals purchased and shipped directly to a using unit without passing through a depot are branded with a permanent brand at the time of purchase.

The above Army regulation is superseded by Army Regulation 880–5, September 1, 1953, "Public Animals—Horses, Mules, and Dogs." This regulation directs that animals purchased and shipped to using units be permanently branded in accordance with the Preston System, and all animals not so branded to be temporarily branded with silver nitrate.

The Preston Branding System was adopted by the Army after World War I. It consists of serial symbols assigned by the Quartermaster General, and when branded on the animal, establish its permanent identity. With the adoption of this system, the organizational hoof brand was discontinued.

Army Regulation 30–455, April 8, 1931, "Quartermaster Corps

—Branding and Registration of Public Animals," directs that public horses and mules, on the day of purchase, be branded on the left side of the neck with a serial symbol brand in accordance with the Preston Branding System. Letters and numerals are to be 2 inches in height and 1½ inches wide. The webbing of the brand is to be between ⅛ and ¼ of an inch in thickness. Each symbol is to be so placed that there will be a ¾-inch open space between the nearest points of two adjacent symbols. The serial symbol brand is to consist of four symbols, three numerals and one letter, in the following combination:

A000 to A999	000A to 999A
0A00 to 9A99	B000 to B999
00A0 to 99A9	0B00 to 9B99

and so on, through the alphabet, omitting the letters G, I, O, and Q. Horses and mules are to be branded with the same serial symbols, each brand identifying two animals, one horse and one mule. Horse Aooo begins the horse series and mule Aooo begins the mule series.

The above Army regulation is superseded by Army Regulation 30–455, November 17, 1941, "Quartermaster Corps—Branding and Registration of Public Animals." This regulation is similar in text except that the webbing of the brand is specified as between ¹⁄₁₆ and ³⁄₁₆ of an inch in thickness. The only other revision is the option of using a four-symbol serial brand or a five-symbol serial brand. The four-symbol serial brand remains unchanged. The five-symbol serial brand is to consist of four numerals and one letter, in the following combinations:

A0000 to A9999	000A0 to 999A9
0A000 to 9A999	0000A to 9999A
00A00 to 99A99	B0000 to B9999

and so on through the alphabet, omitting the letters G, I, O, and Q. Horses and mules are to be branded with the same serial symbols, each brand identifying one horse and one mule. Horse

92

Aooo or Aoooo begins the horse series, and mule Aooo or Aoooo begins the mule series.

Army Regulation 880–5, September 1, 1953, "Public Animals—Horses, Mules and Dogs," supersedes the Army regulation above. The text of the 1953 regulation is similar, except that now only a four-symbol serial brand is authorized. In addition, it is specified that dogs are to be tattooed on the left flank. Consequently, horses, mules, and dogs are branded with the same serial symbol, each brand identifying one horse, one mule, and one dog. Horse Aooo begins the horse series; mule Aooo begins the mule series; and dog Aooo begins the dog series.

Regulations for the Army of the United States, 1908, direct that a complete descriptive list is to accompany the animal wherever it may be transferred. A file of descriptive cards of public animals is to be kept with the records of every officer accountable for public animals. When these animals are to be issued or transferred, the person in charge is to be provided with complete and accurate descriptive cards, which he is to deliver to the receiving officer.

Army Regulation 30–455, April 8, 1931, "Quartermaster Corps —Branding and Registration of Public Animals," provides for a horse and mule register to be established and maintained by the Quartermaster General. The record administrative procedure requires the purchasing officer to prepare W.D.Q.M.C. Form No. 125 (Horse [Mule] Record Card), in triplicate for each animal purchased. This form consists of three sections:

Section   I   General Description and Purchase Record
Section   II   Service Record
Section III   Final Disposition

The purchasing officer fills in the data called for in Section I of the card, plus any other pertinent remarks about the animal. The original card is sent with the animal and remains with the animal throughout its service. The duplicate is forwarded to the

Quartermaster General, and the triplicate is filed in the purchasing and breeding headquarters. The original record, with a transcript from the sick register furnished by the Medical Department, Veterinary Service (ref. AR 40–2245), completes the record of the animal.

Upon issue, the issuing officer fills in the data required in Section II of the original, which accompanies the animal. He then forwards the card with the animal to the receiving organization. The issuing officer reports to the Quartermaster General the brand of the animal and the organization to which it has been issued. This information is entered on the duplicate record card in the Office of the Quartermaster General. The remaining space in Section II of the original record card accompanying the animal is for the use of the organization to which the animal has been assigned. These entries are not reported to the Quartermaster General while the animal remains in service.

When the animal is finally separated from the service, Section III of the original record is filled in and the record card forwarded to the Quartermaster General, showing the disposition made of the animal (condemned, sold, destroyed, died, etc.), and the cause of the separation. A statement of the cause of separation is obtained by the responsible officer from the examining veterinarian, in conformity with paragraph 1, AR 40–2250, and paragraph 27, AR 40–2075. These data are entered on the duplicate record card in the office of the Quartermaster General, completing the history of the animal in that office. The original record card is then mailed to the Surgeon General, to complete the veterinary records in that office. The original horse (mule) record cards filed in the records of an organization constitute the horse (mule) register for that organization. The duplicate cards filed in the Office of the Quartermaster General constitute the horse (mule) register for the Army.

Army Regulation 30–455, November 17, 1941, "Quartermaster Corps—Branding and Registration of Public Animals," supersedes the above regulation. The 1941 regulation is similar in

94

content, save one minor variation. Instead of requiring that the triplicate be filed in purchasing and breeding headquarters, this regulation specifies that it be filed at the remount area headquarters. The regulation also prescribes the procedure to be followed when animals are shipped to a using unit by passing through a depot. The regulation directs the purchasing officer to record all data necessary to complete W.D.Q.M.C. Form No. 125 (Horse [Mule] Record Card) and R.S.Q.M.C. Form No. 9 (Assignment of Preston Brand) when animals are shipped to a depot, branded with a temporary brand. With the information contained in R.S.Q.M.Q. Form No. 9, the depot commander will then brand the animal with its permanent Preston Brand.

Army Regulation 880–5, September 1, 1953, "Public Animals —Horses, Mules, and Dogs," supersedes above regulations. The variations in the text are minor, but include dogs. The regulation directs the Quartermaster to establish and maintain an animal register. WD AGO Form 10–24 (Dog Record Card) has been added to the other record card. Triplicates of record cards are now filed in purchasing headquarters, rather than remount area headquarters. The reference for the examining veterinarian has been revised from AR 40–2250 to AR 40–905. Also, the original animal record cards filed in the records of an organization now constitute the animal register for that organization; the duplicate animal record cards filed in the Office of the Quartermaster General now constitute the animal register for the Army.

The regulation also directs that animals are to be inspected for condemnation by an appropriately designated officer. This officer prepares and signs two copies of WD IGD Form 2 (Inventory and Inspection Report of Public Animals) and a statement giving the reason the animals are submitted for inspection. This completed inventory and inspection report is a valid voucher on which to drop property from accountability.

Regulations for the Army of the United States, 1908, does not specify the person responsible for the branding of public animals.

95

The regulations only direct that public animals are to be branded on the day received.

Mimeographed "Instructions for Branding Public Animals in Accordance with the Preston System," 1925, direct that all branding will be done under the supervision of an officer. The organization of a branding detail is recommended, and this detail is to be instructed by a veterinary officer. The instructions further recommend that the first symbol of the brand be placed 6 inches from the base of the ear, and that the clear spacing should be 2 inches between symbols; the entire Preston brand is to be placed 2 inches below the root of the mane.

Army Regulation 30–455, April 8, 1931, "Quartermaster Corps —Branding and Registration of Public Animals," directs the purchasing officer to brand public horses and mules on the day of purchase. The brand is to be a serial symbol brand of the Preston Branding System and is to be placed on the left side of the neck.

Army Regulation 30–435, June 15, 1937, "Quartermaster Corps—Procurement of Horses and Mules," directs the messenger to brand animals, after completion of inspection and acceptance. The branding is to be supervised by a veterinary officer.

Army Regulation 30–455, November 17, 1941, "Quartermaster Corps—Branding and Registration of Public Animals," directs the purchasing officer to brand public horses and mules on the day of purchase. If the animals are shipped to a using unit without passing through a depot, the purchasing officer will apply a permanent brand in accordance with the Preston Branding System. If the animals are shipped to a depot for subsequent issue, the purchasing officer will brand the animals with a temporary brand of silver nitrate. Upon receipt of the shipment of animals, the depot commander will then brand each animal on the left side of the neck with the Preston brand assigned by the purchasing officer.

Superseding all above regulations, Army Regulation 880–5, September 1953, "Public Animals—Horses, Mules, and Dogs," directs all animals purchased and shipped to using units to be permanently branded, in the case of horses and mules, and tattooed, in the case of dogs, by the purchasing officer at the time of purchase, and in accordance with the Preston Branding System. All animals not so branded will be temporarily branded with silver nitrate.

Branding irons appear to have always been a Quartermaster item of supply and have been issued to posts, camps, and stations. Regulations for the Army of the United States, 1908, state that branding irons of uniform size and design will be furnished by the Quartermaster's Department. Letters of the "US" brand are to be 2 inches in height, and letters and numerals of the Organization brand are to be ¾ inch in height.

Because of limited funds, only two sets of branding irons were supplied to each Corps Area in 1925. These irons were invoiced to the Corps Area Quartermaster from the Jeffersonville Depot. One set of branding irons was considered sufficient for any particular post, and post blacksmiths were encouraged to make additional sets, using the irons furnished by the Corps Area Quartermaster as samples. In this way, the original sets could be sent on to other posts. A mimeographed sheet, 25/44/ARK, was issued for the guidance of post blacksmiths in making branding irons. These "Specifications for Branding Irons" state that letters and figures are about 1¼ inches high and about 1½ inches wide. The cross section of letters and figures should be ⁵⁄₁₆ inch thick, and should be tapered to ⅛ inch in thickness at branding edge (Fig. 412). The letters and figures should be attached to an iron rod or bar about 18 inches long. The "6" and "9" are interchangeable, and the letters and figures should be shaped so as to avoid sharp angles, which blur (Fig. 404). Air vents should be left in closed letters or figures, in order to prevent overheating the skin and flesh, thereby causing a blurred scar. See "8," "O," "D," and "B" (Fig. 404).

Army Regulation 30–435, June 15, 1937, "Quartermaster Corps —Procurement of Horses and Mules," directs that the messenger-

97

chauffeur, a member of the purchasing board, be the custodian of all equipment of the board—such as branding irons, measuring standards, and all blank books and forms. The regulation further directs the board to maintain, among other equipment, one set of branding irons (10 pieces), and all necessary equipment for temporary branding.

Superseding the regulations above, Army Regulation 880–5, September 1, 1953, "Public Animals—Horses, Mules, and Dogs," directs that a purchasing board is to consist of the following personnel:

1 Officer, QMC (Purchasing & Contracting Officer)
1 Officer, VC (Purchasing Board Veterinarian Officer)
1 Clerk, and
1 Messenger-Chauffeur.

The messenger-chauffeur is directed to be the custodian of all equipment, such as branding irons, tattoo equipment, measuring standards, and all blank forms. Each purchasing board will be provided with, among other things: silver nitrate with appropriate brush for temporary branding; and one set of branding irons (ten pieces), and necessary equipment for temporary branding. However, no tattoo equipment is mentioned in the regulation.

The Quartermaster Supply Catalog, QM 3–3, June 15, 1944, lists the stock numbers of branding irons for issue to posts, camps, and stations.

Irons, Branding. Mark IC, 2″   Stock No. 41–1–179
Irons, Branding. Mark US, 2″   Stock No. 41–1–224
Irons, Branding. Preston Branding System. Mark
    Figures 0 to 8, height 2″   Stock No. 41–1–305
    Components (Fig. 410)
Irons, Branding, Preston Branding System, Figures, Single 1.

STOCK NUMBER	MARK LETTER	HEIGHT	WIDTH
41–1–307	0	2″	1½″

41–1–308	1	2″	1½″
41–1–309	2	2″	1½″
41–1–310	3	2″	1½″
41–1–311	4	2″	1½″
41–1–312	5	2″	1½″
41–1–313	6	2″	1½″
41–1–314	7	2″	1½″
41–1–316	8	2″	1½″

Irons, Branding. Preston Branding System. Mark, Letters height 2″, width 1½″ and 2″ Stock No. 41–1–317. Components. Irons, Branding, Preston Branding System, Letter, Single 1.

STOCK NUMBER	MARK LETTER	HEIGHT	WIDTH
41–1–318	A	2″	1½″
41–1–321	B	2″	1½″
41–1–324	C	2″	1½″
41–1–327	D	2″	1½″
41–1–330	E	2″	1½″
41–1–333	F	2″	1½″
41–1–336	H	2″	1½″
41–1–339	J	2″	1½″
41–1–342	K	2″	1½″
41–1–345	L	2″	1½″
41–1–348	M	2″	1½″
41–1–351	N	2″	1½″
41–1–354	P	2″	1½″
41–1–357	R	2″	1½″
41–1–360	S	2″	1½″
41–1–363	T	2″	1½″
41–1–366	U	2″	1½″
41–1–369	V	2″	1½″
41–1–372	W	2″	1½″
41–1–375	X	2″	1½″
41–1–378	Y	2″	1½″
41–1–381	Z	2″	1½″

Note: These irons are not stocked as a complete set. Each component is procured, stored, requisitioned, and issued individually.

99

Supply Manual 9–1–5100, October 1956, and the Cataloging
Handbook, Department of the Army, November 1, 1957, list the
federal stock numbers of branding irons as shown below:

INDEX NO.	FEDERAL STOCK NO.	DESCRIPTION
1373	5120–293–1237	Branding Iron: 2 in. h, legend A
1374	5120–293–1238	Branding Iron: 2 in. h, legend B
1375	5120–193–1239	Branding Iron: 2 in. h, legend C
1376	5120–293–1240	Branding Iron: 2 in. h, legend D
1377	5120–293–1241	Branding Iron: 2 in. h, legend E
1378	5120–293–1242	Branding Iron: 2 in. h, legend F
1379	5120–293–1243	Branding Iron: 2 in. h, legend H
1380	5120–293–1244	Branding Iron: 2 in. h, legend J
1381	5120–293–1245	Branding Iron: 2 in. h, legend K
1382	5120–293–1246	Branding Iron: 2 in. h, legend L
1383	5120–293–1247	Branding Iron: 2 in. h, legend M
1384	5120–293–1248	Branding Iron: 2 in. h, legend N
1385	5120–596–0994	Branding Iron: 2 in. h, legend O
1386	5120–293–1249	Branding Iron: 2 in. h, legend P
1387	5120–293–1250	Branding Iron: 2 in. h, legend R
1388	5120–293–1251	Branding Iron: 2 in. h, legend S
1389	5120–293–1252	Branding Iron: 2 in. h, legend T
1390	5120–293–1253	Branding Iron: 2 in. h, legend U
1391	5120–293–1254	Branding Iron: 2 in. h, legend V
1392	5120–293–1255	Branding Iron: 2 in. h, legend W
1393	5120–293–1256	Branding Iron: 2 in. h, legend X
1394	5120–293–1257	Branding Iron: 2 in. h, legend Y
1395	5120–293–1258	Branding Iron: 2 in. h, legend Z
1396	5120–596–0997	Branding Iron: 2 in. h, legend IC
1397	5120–596–0995	Branding Iron: 2 in. h, legend 1
1398	5120–596–1012	Branding Iron: 2 in. h, legend 2
1399	5120–596–1013	Branding Iron: 2 in. h, legend 3
1400	5120–596–1014	Branding Iron: 2 in. h, legend 4
1401	5120–596–1015	Branding Iron: 2 in. h, legend 5
1402	5120–596–1016	Branding Iron: 2 in. h, legend 6
1403	5120–596–1010	Branding Iron: 2 in. h, legend 7
1404	5120–596–1011	Branding Iron: 2 in. h, legend 8
1405	5120–596–0996	Branding Iron: 2 in. h, legend US

One extremely unusual branding iron is on display at the Museum, United States Military Academy, West Point, New York. The card identifying the iron bears this legend: "Branding Iron for Public Animals. Transferred from the Philadelphia Quartermaster Depot, 7442." There is a second, almost identical, branding iron which is not on display. Both of these branding irons were personally secured by the Director of the West Point Museum from the Philadelphia Quartermaster Depot in 1954. At that time the depot discarded a great mass of material, and from the nature of such material secured from the depot, the branding irons have been tentatively dated as post-1900.

Figure 416 shows the front view of the West Point branding iron, the branding surface of the stamp and hook bolts securing the stamp to the face plate. Also, two screw heads are visible. These screws are fastened into the bracket behind the face plate.

Figure 414 represents a top view. The closed tops of the letters are shown, as are the upper edge of the face plate, brackets, and handle. Figure 415 is a side elevation of the branding iron; Figure 413 shows a typical fastening detail. The hook bolt can be seen passing through the face plate, through a hole in a single band of the letter, and returning to the face plate.

The construction of the West Point iron is unique and no similar type has been discovered. Essentially, the construction is identical to that of a cement finisher's wood trowel. There are three component parts: brackets and handle, face plate, and stamp letters.

The two brackets and the handle are fashioned from one piece of wood, the handle having a cross section of a dowel 1¼ inches in diameter. The ¾-inch face plate is secured to the brackets by means of two flathead wood screws. The letters, formed by two parallel bands approximately ³⁄₁₆ by ¾ of an inch are secured to the face plate by hook bolts at various locations. By turning the nut at the threaded end of the bolt, pressure is applied through the washer bearing on the face plate, which causes the hook end of the bolt to dig into the face plate and draws the

101

iron band snug against the wood. This latter action is accomplished by the inside surface of the hook bearing on the lower edge of the hole in the iron band. After the hook bolt is securely seated, the exposed portion of the thread is sawed off and the end filed smooth. Ends of the bands are closed by fire welds.

The letters are abnormally high—approximately 5 inches. The most unusual design feature is that the latters are voided, *i.e.*, there are two parallel bands forming the letter, leaving approximately a ⅜-inch void in the center. Inasmuch as the front of the face plate is only slightly scorched, it may be assumed that the branding iron was heated on a steel plate over a bed of coals. In this way, the wood did not come in direct contact with fire. The steel plate conducted the heat to the iron bands of the stamp.

The great expedition led by Captain Meriwether Lewis, 1st Regiment, United States Infantry, and Second Lieutenant William Clark, Corps of Artillerists, availed themselves of horses during part of their journey. On at least one occasion their horses were branded and left with local Indians for safekeeping until the explorers returned, making their way by canoe. The exact location where the branding occurred is now designated "Lewis & Clark Canoe Camp," and is included in the Idaho State Park System. The camp is located at the confluence of the North and South forks of the Clearwater River, a short distance west of Lewiston on US Highway 12.

The exploring party remained at Canoe Camp from September 26 until October 7, 1805. The members of the expedition were making preparations for the next phase of their voyage by water and were in the process of constructing five canoes—hence the name Canoe Camp. This mode of travel necessitated disposal of the horses and is best described in two independently kept journals, in the diarists' own words.

Journals of Lewis & Clark
(entry by Clark)

October 5th Friday Saty. 1805.
had all our horses 38 in number Collected and branded   Cut

off their fore top and delivered them to the 2 brothers and one son of one of the Chiefs who intends to accompany us down the river to each of those men I gave a Knife & Some Small articles &c.

Sergeant Ordway's Journal

Saturday 5th Oct 1805

got up all our horses 38 in number. we branded them on the near fore shoulder with a Stirrup Iron, and cropped their fore mane so as we may know them at our return. the old chief who we leave the care of our horses with has engaged to go with us past his nation and leave the horses in the care of his two sons   our officers gave them some Small presents &.C.

An original branding iron used by members of the Lewis and Clark Expedition is now on display at the museum of the Oregon Historical Society in Portland, Oregon. This iron, unusual in its design, was found in 1892 on Sepulchre Island, one of a group known as the Memaloose (Illihee or Alahee) Islands, located three and a half miles above The Dalles of the Columbia River. The iron was found in a good state of preservation, and in 1904 was in the possession of George H. Himes, assistant secretary, Oregon Historical Society.

A few years ago the iron was heated to brand hides and was consequently deformed. The present chief curator of the Oregon Historical Society Museum, Harry E. Lichter, has since restored it to its original form.

It is assumed that this iron was not used to brand animals but rather to mark bales of specimens which were sent back East wrapped in hides. The stirrup iron is basically a hollow rectangular casing with an integral square at the top containing the letters "US." The hollow interior was intended to be filled with letters, numbers, or devices as the occasion demanded, much like the movable type hand stamp of today. The two short sides of the casing have a short lug projecting outward, to which a handle can be attached. The design is much like an upright vacuum cleaner. For an imprint of the brand see Plate LXXII.

The Office of Indian Affairs of the United States Department

103

of the Interior, Bureau of Indian Affairs, was created in the War Department in 1824 and transferred to the Department of the Interior at the time of its establishment by the Act of March 3, 1849 (9 Stat. 395, U.S.C. 481).

The function of this Act was the creation of conditions under which the Indians could advance their social, economic, and political adjustment in the complex world in which they found themselves; the encouragement of Indian tribes to assume an increasing measure of self-sufficiency.

The Bureau of Indian Affairs was, and is, also to perform the function of acting as trustee with respect to Indian lands and moneys held in trust by the United States, and to assist the owners in making the most effective use of their lands and resources. About sixty Indian agencies and major field installations were set up throughout the country. The Indian brand was ID (Interior Department).

Livestock, with title thereto vested in the government and held in trusteeship for Indians on reservations, was branded with the letters "ID," as mentioned above. This practice started when the Office of Indian Affairs was still a part of the War Department. The ID brand has been recorded with livestock associations and state brand recorders (Fig. 416).

During the existence of a revolving cattle program, implemented by instructions contained in Circular No. 3156, June 26, 1936, Indians owned two classes of livestock: trust and restricted, and non-trust and unrestricted. Trust livestock was branded with the letters ID, because title to it was vested in the government. Non-trust livestock was not branded. However, non-trust livestock often became involved in legal complications and consequently in a maze of new laws and regulations. Some regulations ordered the branding of non-trust livestock while others countermanded them. Branding became an impossible procedure, resulting in difficulties in resale and title. Eventually, the conflicting laws were repealed, and Indians may now deal with trust or restricted livestock in the same manner as though the livestock were non-trust and unrestricted. All cattle loaned by the United States for use in corporate or tribal enterprises must be branded ID and also with the brand of the enterprise. Cattle loaned by the United States for relending must not be branded or marked. Relending to members of the tribe is done to promote economic development.

The authority for legislative instruments relative to the branding of livestock of Indians is contained in the following statutes:

1. Section 2138, Revised Statutes; June 30, 1919, c.4, Sec. 1, 41 Stat. 9; 25 U.S.C. 214.
2. Act of June 25, 1948, c. 645, 62 Stat. 759; 18 U.S.C. 1157.
3. Act of August 15, 1953, c. 506, Secs. 2; 67 Stat. 590; 25 U.S.C. 195.
4. Public Law 85–86; July 10, 1957; 71 Stat. 277; 18 U.S.C. 1157.
5. 25 CFR 23.14, approved June 13, 1947.
6. 25 CFR 23.13, approved December 8, 1950.
7. Sec. 467, Revised Statutes, 25 U.S.C. 266.
8. Sec. 2136, Revised Statutes, 25 U.S.C. 266.
9. Sec. 2135, Revised Statutes, 25 U.S.C. 265.
10. Act of June 18, 1934, 48 Stat. 984.
11. Act of June 26, 1936, 49 Stat. 1967.
12. Sec. 1, Act of July 4, 1884, 23 Stat. 94, 25 U.S.C. 195.
13. Public Law 281, 67 Stat. 590, approved August 15, 1953.
14. 25 CFR 92.13.

Note: 25 CFR in the above listed sources refers to Code of Federal Regulations, Title 25—Indians, followed by the respective part number.

The Executive Orders relative to the branding of livestock of Indians are contained in the following documents: Office of Indian Affairs, Circular No. 3156, June 26, 1936; Office of Indian Affairs, Circular No. 3267, September 20, 1938; Bureau of Indian Affairs, Memorandum, December 10, 1953; and Bureau of Indian Affairs, Memorandum, Indian Affairs Manual Release 47–1, July 17, 1957.

A supplementary holding brand was applied to trust or restricted livestock in addition to the ID brand. The holding brand was designated for use within the jurisdiction of the appropriate Indian Agency.

Some of the brands for cattle and horses of the different Agencies are:

AGENCY	CATTLE	HORSES	
Cheyenne River	IC rt hip, C rt neck	IC rt shoulder, C rt neck	(Fig. 425)
Crow Creek	IC rt hip, K rt neck	IC rt shoulder, K rt neck	(Fig. 429)
Lower Brule	IC rt hip, L rt neck	IC rt shoulder, L rt neck	(Fig. 426)
Pine Ridge	IC rt hip, O rt neck	IC rt shoulder, O rt neck	(Fig. 430)
Rosebud	IC rt hip, R rt neck	IC rt shoulder, R rt neck	(Fig. 427)
Yankton	IC rt hip, Y rt neck	IC rt shoulder, Y rt neck	(Fig. 431)
Sisseton	IC rt hip, T rt neck	IC rt shoulder, T rt neck	(Fig. 428)
Standing Rock	IC rt hip, S rt neck	IC rt shoulder, S rt neck	(Fig. 432)

The authority to apply reservation brands upon trust or restricted livestock is contained in the Office of Indian Affairs, Order No. 511, December 26, 1939.

The Navaho tribe is one which carries on substantial ranching operations. The Navaho Indian Reservation consists of approximately sixteen million acres of land, 95 per cent of which is used for grazing only. In the mid-thirties, this area was divided into seventeen Land Management Districts for the purpose of supervising land use.

Prior to 1939 the Navaho Indian stockman used a brand he

had acquired in any one of various ways. Some brands were symbols of objects used by medicine men; some were copied from designs used in weaving Navaho rugs. Often, an Indian would see a white rancher's brand which appealed to his fancy. Upon returning to the reservation, the Indian would brand his stock with a similar design (Figs. 444–461 inclusive). In case of duplication, the Indians earmarked their stock to identify them individually.

In 1939 the Government issued a brand to each Navaho livestock owner. This brand consists of three letters, one on top centered over two below. The top letter represents the district in which the owner has grazing rights and the two bottom letters identify the ownership of the animal. The brand is located on the left rib or hip of cattle, and on the left hip or thigh of horses (Fig. 422). The three-letter brand is recorded at the Indian Agency Office, Window Rock, Arizona. In addition to the three-letter brand, all cattle and horses grazing on the reservation have the Bar N brand applied on the left shoulder. This is the official Navaho Tribal Brand, recorded with the Arizona Livestock Sanitary Board (Fig. 423).

Figures 417, 418, 419, and 420 show brands of the Pine Ridge Agency. The illustrated brands were recorded under the title of U. S. Indian Brands, Pine Ridge Agency, Dakota, in the first volume of *Cattle Brands Owned by Members of the Wyoming Stock Growers' Association*. This book was published by the J. M. W. Jones Stationery & Printing Company, in Chicago, 1882. The brands were applied to the left ribs of animals ranging on the Pine Ridge Reserve. V. T. McGillicuddy was the agent in charge of the Pine Ridge Agency.

Brand IDS is recorded for the Unitah and Ouray Agency at Fort Duchesne, Utah, and is applied to the left ribs of cattle and horses. This brand is apparently a contraction of Indian Service (Fig. 424). Brand ID is recorded in the name of the United States Indian Service at Fort Duchesne, Utah, and applied to the left hip of cattle and horses (Fig. 418).

The letters in the ID brand are placed on the same iron, in order to maintain the letters in a uniform position. The letters are plain and without laps. In the branding of cattle, a 5-inch brand is used on adult stock and not less than a 3-inch brand on younger animals. All cattle brands have a ¼-inch face. In the branding of horses, a 2-inch minimum brand with a thin face is used.

The specifications for the design of branding irons are contained in the Office of Indian Affairs, Order No. 511, as of December 26, 1939.

Superintendents were ordered to repossess all ID branding irons on the reservation, since they were government property, and, insofar as they were able, to prevent further use of such irons. The order to repossess branding irons and to discontinue the branding of Indian-owned livestock with the ID brand is contained in the Bureau of Indian Affairs, Bulletin No. 335, Supplement No. 1 (Final), December 6, 1953.

The United States Department of the Interior National Park Service was established by the Act of August 25, 1916 (39 Stat. 535, 16 U.S.C. 1). Its object is to promote and to regulate the use of national parks, monuments, and similar reservations in order to conserve the scenery, the natural and historic objects, and the wildlife therein, and to provide for the enjoyment of the same in such manner and by such means as will leave them unimpaired for the enjoyment of future generations. Its prescribed activity is providing programs to create areas for public enjoyment and giving the fullest possible protection to natural and historic resources comprising such areas.

The continental United States is divided into five Park Service regions, each region being composed of a number of natural parks, monuments, and historic sites. The branding of government-owned livestock is contained in ten Departmental Manual, Chapter "Identification," Item 411.3.1c, "Livestock shall be branded or marked in some acceptable manner to indicate Government ownership," and National Park Service, Administrative Manual, Volume 7, Chapter 6, Section 7.

The following listed National Parks practice branding of government-owned livestock:

1. *Lassen Volcanic National Park.* Horses are branded on the left front hoof with a number brand. The number of horses maintained at the national park varies from one to seven and consequently, numbers are assigned from one to seven (Fig. 438).

2. *Rocky Mountain National Park.* Saddle and pack stock was previously branded with letters "US" on the right flank, or the existing brand was used. There are currently no government-owned animals at the park (Fig. 434).

3. *Sequoia and Kings Canyon National Park.* Horses, mules, and burros are branded with the letters "NPS" on the left shoulder (Fig. 435). Old United States Army stock on hand is branded with the letters "US" in conjunction with the existing Preston brand on the left neck (Fig. 437).

4. *Yosemite National Park.* Horses and mules are branded with the letters "NPS" on the left front hoof (Fig. 439). Old United States Army stock on hand is branded with the letters "US" and the existing Preston brand on the left neck (Fig. 437).

5. *Yellowstone National Park.* Brands are applied to saddle horses and mules. The letters "NPS" are branded on the left hip and a small numeral on the left hoof. Numbers can run from one to 111 and are reassigned when old animals are retired (Figs. 435 and 438).

6. *Grand Teton National Park.* Horses are branded with the letters "NPS" on the left hip. Presently this park owns only two horses (Fig. 435).

7. *Glacier National Park.* The letters "GNP" constitute the brand of this park. The GNP brand is recorded with the General Recorder of Marks and Brands, State of Montana, Certificate No. 24062–5, dated January 22, 1958. In addition to the recorded brand, each horse is assigned a number from one to 100. When a new horse is purchased, it is given a number previously

assigned to a horse that has been disposed of. This park also owns 25 mules purchased from the Forest Service. These mules are branded with the letters "US" on the left hip and with a number consisting of three or four digits above the brand. The mules are not assigned park numbers (Fig. 440). The GNP brand is applied on the left shoulder and the number on the left neck (Fig. 436). Each animal has also a descriptive livestock card made for it, and in addition to the neck number, each animal has a park inventory number.

The United States Department of Agriculture Forest Service was created by an act of February 1, 1905, providing for the transfer of the forest reserve from the Department of the Interior to the Department of Agriculture. It is charged with the responsibility of promoting the conservation and the best use of the nation's forest lands, and it scientifically regulates livestock grazing in order to maintain conservation concurrently with the use of the annual growth of forage. Under this program, the continental United States is divided into ten regions, each region composed of a number of national forests. The branding of government-owned livestock in national forests and other lands under its jurisdiction is provided for by the following regulations:

The National Forest Manual Regulations and Instructions issued by the Secretary of Agriculture, by W. N. Jardine and the Forester W. B. Greeley, February 1, 1926, to become effective July 1, 1926. Page 31–A.

"Branding of Animals—Government animals should be branded "US" on the left hip. This requirement may be waived by district foresters where animals secured for temporary use are to be disposed of after a short period, and also in localities where the branding is not customary or necessary.

"In the marking and identifying of animals, Government animals should be branded 'US' on the left hip. This requirement may be waived by regional foresters where animals required for temporary use are to be disposed of after a short period, and also in localities where the branding of stock is not customary or necessary."

In the Forest Service Handbook, published June, 1948, paragraph 6414.36, page 138, and the National Forest Handbook, revised May, 1958, Title 6400, Section 6414.36, the text is the same as that above.

Blank forms are used to authorize grazing of livestock upon lands owned or controlled by the United States within a specific national forest. The Forest Service application for grazing permit, Form FS–879, revised December 1954 reads:

"I will not allow livestock marked or branded otherwise as shown on the reverse side hereof to be grazed under the permit herein applied for, except with the approval of the forest supervisor."

Paragraph 1 on the reverse side provides for the indication of brands and earmarks for cattle, horses and sheep.

The Forest Service Grazing Permit, Form FS–656, revised February 1956, reads:

"The Permittee shall not allow livestock marked or branded otherwise as shown in the application upon which this permit is based to be grazed upon national forest land under this permit, except with the approval of the forest supervisor."

Branding of Government-owned livestock is practiced only in the regions enumerated below:

Region 1, Northern Region. Horses and mules used for transportation are branded with the letters "US" on the left thigh with a hot iron. Also a serial number is stamped above the US brand to maintain the identity of the individual animals only (Fig. 440).

Region 2, Rocky Mountain Region. Animals are branded in accordance with regulations contained in the latest edition of the Forest Service Handbook. There are no serial numbers used in this region (Fig. 434).

Region 3, Southwestern Region. Animals are branded under the provisions of the Forest Service Handbook published in June, 1948 (Fig. 434).

Region 4, Intermountain Region. Horses and mules are branded under the provisions of the Forest Service Handbook published in June, 1948 (Fig. 434).

111

Region 5, California Region. Animals are branded in accordance with the provisions of 3 FSM–642.7. Some forests in this region have used a neck brand of letters and numbers to identify the animals by forest. Old United States Army stock is branded with the letters "US" on the left stifle (Fig. 434).

Region 6, Pacific Northwest Region. Horses, mules and burrows are branded with letters "US" on left thigh. Some older stock is branded on the left neck. Stock obtained from other regions may carry a serial number having from one to four digits (Fig. 434).

The Bureau of Animal Industry was established by Act of May 29, 1884 (23 Stat. 31; 21 U.S.C. 119), to deal with the prevention, control, and eradication of animal diseases and parasites, conduct research on the production of livestock and their products, perform inspection duties, and otherwise seek to protect and develop the livestock, meat, poultry, and related industries. These functions were transferred to the Agricultural Research Service under the Secretary's Memorandum No. 1320, Supplement No. 4, November 2, 1953. The Agricultural Research Administration was established by Executive Order No. 9069, February 23, 1942, to consolidate most of the physical, biological, chemical, and engineering research activities in the Department of Agriculture, which was superseded by the Agricultural Research Service. The Agricultural Research Service administers livestock regulatory programs which were begun in 1884 in the former Bureau of Animal Industry. National programs of animal disease eradication, animal quarantine, and meat inspection now constitute the Service's livestock regulatory programs. The Animal Disease Eradication Branch became a Division in 1958.

This Division determines the existence and extent of infectious, contagious, and communicable diseases of livestock and poultry. It carries out inspection of stockyards, quarantine, testing, diagnosis, vaccination, condemnation and disposal, disinfection, and other measures. It administers acts and regulations governing interstate transportation of livestock and poultry.

The Division conducts testing of herds of cattle for tuberculosis and brucellosis.

All states conform to the identification of reactors adopted by the Animal Disease Eradication Division. The legend "U.S.B.A.I. Reacted" (United States Bureau of Animal Industry) has been replaced by "U.S.A.D.E. Reacted" (United States Animal Disease Eradication).

TB reactors are identified by branding the letter T on the left jaw, not less than two or more than three inches high, and attaching a metal eartag bearing "U.S.B.A.I. Reacted," or similar state reactor tag (Fig. 441).

Brucellosis reactors, the victims of an infectious and communicable disease of domestic animals known also as Bang's Disease, or contagious abortion, are identified by branding the letter "B" on the left jaw, not less than two or more than three inches high, and applying to the left ear a metal tag bearing a serial number and "U. S.B.A.I. Reacted," or similar state reactor tag (Fig. 443).

An infectious and communicable disease of domestic animals commonly known as Johne's Disease, or bacterial dysentery, is caused by an organism termed mylobacterium paratuberculosis. The disease was named after the German physician Albert Johne (December 10, 1839–December 5, 1910). The treatment consists of application of a preparation known as a johnin (after Johne). Paratuberculosis reactors are identified in the same manner as tuberculosis reactors.

Official vaccinates are identified by a national tattoo showing the letter "V" within a shield, preceded by a number showing the quarter of the year and followed by the last digit of the year. The illustration indicates a full size tattoo for the 4th Quarter, 1959 (Fig. 442). An official vaccinate is defined as:

A bovine animal vaccinated against brucellosis while from four through eight months of age, on or before June 30, 1957; or a bovine animal of the beef breed in a range or semi-range area vaccinated against brucellosis while from four to twelve

113

months of age, on or before June 30, 1957, under the supervision of a federal or state veterinary official, with a vaccine approved by the Animal Disease Eradication Division; or a bovine animal vaccinated against brucellosis while from four through eight months of age, subcutaneously, on or after July 1, 1957; or a bovine animal of the beef breed in a range or semi-range area vaccinated against brucellosis while from four to twelve months of age, subcutaneously, on or after July 1, 1957, under the supervision of a federal or state veterinary official, with 5cc. of a vaccine approved by the Animal Disease Eradication Division; permanently identified as such a vaccinate; and reported at the time of vaccination to the appropriate federal or state agency co-operating in the eradication of brucellosis.

The authority for this definition is the Meat Inspection Act, 21 U.S.G. 71 *et seq.;* and the Code of Federal Regulations, Title 9, Animal and Animal Products; Chapter I, Agricultural Research Service, U.S. Department of Agriculture; Subchapter B, Cooperative Control and Eradication of Animal Diseases; Part 51, Cattle Destroyed Because of Brucellosis (Bang's Disease), Tuberculosis, or Paratuberculosis; Subchapter C, Interstate Transportation of Animals and Poultry; Part 77, Tuberculosis in Cattle; Part 78, Brucellosis in Domestic Animals; Part 77, Tuberculosis in Cattle; Part 78, Brucellosis in Domestic Animals; and Part 80, Paratuberculosis in Domestic Animals.

At the Agricultural Research Center at Beltsville, Maryland, cattle are routinely branded on the hip with two digits of their herd number. Brands are applied when the cattle are about one year old, and serve as a permanent means of identification. Although dairy cattle are not normally branded, this method of identification is found to be helpful at Beltsville because the herd is large and the turnover of employed personnel frequent.

In the Dairy Herd Improvement Project (DHIA) a uniform numbering system for identifying cows in the production testing progress is used. Eartags, bearing a 9-digit number of a controlled series, are utilized in this program. The eartag bears a

2-digit code number of the state in which it is used, plus a 3-letter prefix, and a 4-digit number identifying the individual animal within the state.

In the United States Department of Agriculture, Agricultural Research Service, the Meat Inspection Division conducts several types of inspections to insure the wholesomeness of domestic and imported meat and meat products. Such inspection is applicable to cattle, sheep, swine, goats, and horses, and to food products derived from them.

This Division administers the Meat Inspection Act, the Horse Meat Act, the Imported Meat Act, and other acts or portions thereof. The marking and labeling program, administered directly by the Office of Labels & Standards of Identity, has been initiated for the following purposes: to require informative labeling, to prohibit the use of false or misleading labeling, to prevent adulteration of the product, and to prevent unfair trade practices.

Inspection and branding of carcasses and cuts of meat are normally conducted at establishments engaged in the slaughtering, meat canning, curing, smoking, salting, packing, rendering, and similar activities. Such establishments are designated official establishments when inspection is maintained under the regulations governing meat inspection.

In addition to the branding of carcasses and cuts of meat, the tagging and labeling of carcasses, cuts of meat, their containers, and other materials is controlled by the Meat Inspection Division. Regulations relative to tagging and labeling may be found in pertinent publications of the United States Department of Agriculture.

Another activity of the Division is the examination of food articles for various Federal agencies, for the purpose of insuring delivery of only such articles as conform to the specifications under which they are purchased. It is stated in the Manual of Meat Inspection Procedures, Meat Inspection Division of the Agricultural Research Service, that the Meat Grading Branch, of the Livestock Division of the Agricultural Marketing Service makes acceptance examinations of various processed meat food products for *non-federal* government procurement agencies. On the other hand, the Manual of Inspection and Sanitation Requirements of the Federal Meat Grading Service, Livestock Division of the Agricultural Marketing Service, states that examination of meats, prepared meats, meat food products, and meat by-products for compliance with applicable specifications, and certification thereto, is conducted by the Meat Grading Branch for *federal,* state, county or city institutions, and others. Obviously, the line of responsibility in this particular area of activity is not clearly defined between the Meat Grading Branch and the Meat Inspection Division.

The Manual of Meat Inspection Procedures, Meat Inspection Division, states that examination of meat, meat food products, and fresh sea food for specification compliance for federal government agencies will be conducted by personnel of the Meat Inspection Division. Such products as have been examined and found to conform to specifications are marked with the proper brand. There are special brands for the United States Navy, United States Marine Corps, United States Coast Guard, and the Veterans Administration. The regular United States Department of Agriculture brand is used for the United States Public Health Service purchases. Federal agencies usually purchase food articles under Federal specifications. The United States Public Health Service and the Veterans Administration have specifications of their own. The special Navy, Marine Corps, and Coast Guard brands denoting compliance with specifications are recommended to be applied to fresh meat in cloth coverings and to containers of meat food products, as follows:

1. on the heel of the bottom round on beef hindquarters;
2. on the cut known as the rib on beef forequarters;
3. on the outside of the round about halfway up on veal sides, veal saddles, and veal legs;
4. on the back, across the hips of lamb and mutton carcasses;

5. on the outside surface near the middle of the length of such cuts as beef briskits, beef chunks, beef ribs, beef loins (full, short, or ends), beef rumps, veal racks, veal forequarters, veal chucks, lamb or mutton racks, and lamb shoulders.

Food containing products derived from cattle, sheep, swine, goats, or horses and not amendable to the Meat Inspection Act, are subject to the Food, Drug, and Cosmetic Act (21 U.S.C. 301–392).

Brands are applied to carcasses, parts thereof, meat cuts, and meat food products before they are removed from the official establishment. In addition to the official inspection brand, other brands, such as grade brands, buyers' brands, and brands signifying rabbinical inspection may be applied, but so placed as not to obliterate the inspection brand. The Meat Inspection Division furnishes initial brands bearing the inspection legend at the time inspection is inaugurated at an official establishment. The establishment is required to furnish all additional brands, including replacements as they become necessary. In order to obtain a permanent and legible brand, the area where the brand is to be applied should be free of surface water. This may be accomplished by using a scraping device attached to the handle of the branding device or by permitting the carcass to hang a short time before branding.

The ink brand bearing the inspection legend "U.S. Inspected and Passed" on meat or meat food products assures the consumer that the product has been inspected and found to be free of disease, clean, wholesome, free from adulteration, and truthfully labeled. The upper portion of the brand contains the number of the official establishment as assigned by the Meat Inspection Division. This brand is not to be confused with the grade brand denoting quality which is applied by graders of the Meat Grading Branch of the Livestock Division. Tools for applying these brands vary, as listed below:

a. 1¾-inch metal brand. Used on beef and hog carcasses (Fig. 466).

117

b. 1¼-inch metal brand. Used on calf carcasses and on the larger varieties of sausage meat and meat food products in animal casings (Fig. 466).

c. ¾-inch metal brand. Used for branding sheep carcasses, loin and ribs of pork, and the smaller varieties of sausage and meat food products in animal casings (Fig. 466).

d. 2½-inch rubber brand. Used to apply inspection legend to burlap, muslin, cheesecloth, or heavy paper used to enclose carcasses or parts of carcasses. The stamp of this brand is mounted on aluminum handles (Fig. 466).

e. Hexagonal-shaped metal brand. The horizontal and vertical dimensions of this brand are 2 inches. Used for horse meat and horse meat products.

f. "U.S. Inspected and Condemned." Carcasses, meat, or meat food products so identified are unsound, unhealthy, unwholesome, or otherwise unfit for human food. The brand is not to be confused with the tag "U.S. Condemned," applied to dying animals or animals in a condition to be condemned. Animals suspected of being affected with a disease which may require later condemnation are tagged "U.S. Suspect." Carcasses held for further examination are tagged "U.S. Retained."

g. "U.S. Passed for Cooking." The meat and meat product so branded has been inspected and passed under the condition that it must be rendered into lard, rendered pork fat, or tallow.

h. "U.S. Passed for Refrigeration." The meat and meat by-product has been inspected and passed under the condition that it must be refrigerated.

i. "Tender." Branding this term or any of its derivatives on heated or smoked pork products implies that the article has been subject to sufficient heat to attain an internal temperature of at least 140° F.

j. "Ready to Eat." Finished pork products having characteristics of a ready-to-eat article and having satisfied internal temperature requirements of 140° F. are branded with this legend.

k. "Cooked" and "Fully Cooked." This brand is applied to

118

heated or smoked pork products exhibiting characteristics of a fully cooked article, such as partial separation of the meat from the bone, easy separation of tissues, and a cooked color, flavor, and texture. The normal requirement of a minimum internal temperature is 148° F.

The legibility of hot (burning) brands has been approved by drilling two holes, each $\frac{1}{16}$ inch in diameter through the face of the burning surface to permit escape of the steam that forms when the hot iron comes in contact with the surface of the wet product. The use of cast steel burning brands has been found to result in improved and more legible inspection imprints on cured products. A 2½-inch brand is used for marking cuts of cured meat (Fig. 466).

As for branding inks, official establishments furnish this for the marking of products. All inks must be made of a harmless substance. Dye designation F D & C refers to Food, Drug and Cosmetic Act (21 U.S.C. 301–392), administered by the Food and Drug Administration of the United States Department of Health, Education, and Welfare.

Cold purple branding ink is composed of "F D & C Violet No. 1 dye," water, alcohol, and sugar. Acetone may be added to shorten the drying time. Hot inks may be prepared without sugar, using an acceptable dye, and specially denatured alcohol 23A (alcohol plus 10 per cent acetone) is desirable. A brand equipped with thermostatic control to regulate the temperature of the electrically-heated element has been found to greatly improve legibility on meat, meat by-products, and meat food products. Purple ink may be used to brand all fresh meats except horse meat.

Green ink is exclusively used for the branding of horse meat. Cold or hot ink may be used. Hot green ink has proved to leave more permanent marks on boneless horse meat, such as horse tenderloins. The formula giving the most satisfactory results is furnished below:

Component	Per cent
F D & C Green No. 3 (fast green FCF)	3½
Dextrose (corn sugar)	3
Water	16
Edible shellac	2
95% ethyl alcohol	75

Cooked, cured, or smoked meats or meat food products may be marked with ink of any color, except green, that will insure permanence of marking and legibility. The color of the selected ink should provide a distinct contrast to the color of the product to which it is applied.

For the reader wishing to examine the laws regulating this type of branding, the following information will be helpful. The Meat Inspection Act is an act making appropriations for the Department of Agriculture, for the fiscal year ending June 30, 1907, approved June 30, 1906, (34 Stat. 674–679), as re-enacted by an act making an appropriation for the Department of Agriculture, for the fiscal year ending June 30, 1908, approved March 4, 1907 (34 Stat. 1260–1265), as amended and extended (21 U.S.C. 71–91, 96), Section 5.

The Code of Federal Regulations, Title 9, Animal and Animal Products, is found in Chapter I, Agriculture Research Service, United States Department of Agriculture, and Meat Inspection Regulations in Subchapter A. Marking, branding, and identifying products is in Part 16; imported products in Part 27, and inspection and handling of horse meat and products thereof in Part 29. Identification and certification service for meat and other products is in Part 40, while subchapter A of Title 9, Code of Federal Regulations, is contained in the following publications: Regulations Governing the Meat Inspection of U.S. Department of Agriculture, as contained in Title 9, Chapter I, Subchapters A and K, Code of Federal Regulations, 1959 Edition, and amendments issued through June 1, 1959. U.S. Government Printing Office, Washington, 1960; Manual of Meat Inspection Procedures of the U.S. Department of Agriculture, Edition of

January 1956, reprinted December 1957 without change in text, U.S. Government Printing Office, Washington, 1957, 0–447599.

The Federal grading and stamping of beef was started by the United States Department of Agriculture May 1, 1927. The original request for establishing a grading service originated with the Better Beef Association, a producers' organization. At the beginning, the Department set up a beef grading program on an experimental basis in ten major market centers. In 1929, the service was established on a self-supporting basis by charging fees for the service to packers requesting grading. Grading was expanded to include veal, calf, lamb, and mutton, and the demand for graded meats has continued to increase.

The Meat Grading Service performs the following functions: the grading of carcasses and wholesale cuts of beef, veal, calf, lamb, yearling mutton, and mutton; the examination of meats, prepared meats, meat food products, and meat by-products for compliance with applicable specifications, and certification thereto, when requested by an interested applicant, such as federal, state, county, or municipal institution, steamship line, railroad commissary, etc. Slaughtering, processing and/or fabricating plants are only eligible to receive federal meat grading service if operating under the federal meat inspection system or an approved system.

In addition to U.S. grades for carcasses, there are U.S. grades for slaughter and/or market. Classes and grade factors vary slightly. Beef carcasses are graded on composite evaluation of the three general factors, conformation, finish, and quality. Classes and grades are as follows:

Class				Grade				
Steer	Prime	Choice	Good	Stand.[1]	Comm.[2]	Utility	Cutter	Canner
Heifer	Prime	Choice	Good	Stand.[1]	Comm.[2]	Utility	Cutter	Canner
Cow	————	Choice	Good	Stand.[1]	Comm.[2]	Utility	Cutter	Canner
Bull	————	Choice	Good	————	Comm.[2]	Utility	Cutter	Canner
Stag	————	Choice	Good	————	Comm.[2]	Utility	Cutter	Canner

[1] Standard.
[2] Commercial.

121

Veal carcasses are graded on composite evaluation of the three general grade factors, conformation, finish, and quality. Vealers are usually three months of age or less and have primarily subsisted on milk. Definitions for steer, heifer, and bull are identical to beef (see glossary).

Class	Grade					
Steer	Prime	Choice	Good	Standard	Utility	Cull
Heifer	Prime	Choice	Good	Standard	Utility	Cull
Bull	Prime	Choice	Good	Standard	Utility	Cull

Calf carcasses are graded on composite evaluation of the three general grade factors, conformation, finish, and quality. Calves are usually between three and eight months of age and have primarily subsisted on food other than milk.

Class	Grade					
Steer	Prime	Choice	Good	Standard	Utility	Cull
Heifer	Prime	Choice	Good	Standard	Utility	Cull
Bull	Prime	Choice	Good	Standard	Utility	Cull

Sheep, or Ovine, carcasses are graded on a composite evaluation of two general grade factors, conformation and quality. The classes of carcass meat are predominantly determined by age of the animal.

Class	Grade				
Lamb	Prime	Choice	Good	Utility	Cull
Yearling mutton	Prime	Choice	Good	Utility	Cull
Mutton	Prime	Choice	Good	Utility	Cull

Pork carcass grades are based on three factors, relationship between carcass measurements, lean cut yields, and quality of cuts.

Class	Grades				
Barrow	U.S. No. 1	U.S. No. 2	U.S. No. 3	Medium	Cull
Gilt	U.S. No. 1	U.S. No. 2	U.S. No. 3	Medium	Cull
Sow	U.S. No. 1	U.S. No. 2	U.S. No. 3	Medium	Cull
Stag	U.S. No. 1	U.S. No. 2	U.S. No. 3	Medium	Cull
Boar	U.S. No. 1	U.S. No. 2	U.S. No. 3	Medium	Cull

The basic device for all grade brands of the United States Department of Agriculture is the United States Shield. The chief of the shield bears the legend USDA. The appropriate grade designation is indicated below, in the lower half of the shield. Underneath the shield are shown the class designations: Stag, Bull, Veal, Calf, Yearling Mutton, or Mutton. In roller-applied brands, the code identification of the grader appears after six consecutive imprints of the grade shield with or without class designation as prescribed. The grade brands are applied with purple ink (Figs. 467, 468, 469, 470, 471, 472, 473, 474, and 475).

Institutional brands constitute official identification showing compliance of products. Upon acceptance, each product is branded. Code identification of the grader may appear below the acceptance legend, or the date and place of service may appear on special brands (Figs. 462, 463, 464, and 465).

Official grading terms Prime, Choice, Good, and Commercial formerly had the following letters associated with them: AA, A, B, and C respectively. Pertinent regulations did not apply to

Class	Grade							
Beef and Lamb	U.S. Prime	U.S. Choice	U.S. Good	U.S. Comm.	U.S. Utility	U.S. Cutter	U.S. Canner	U.S. Cull
Calves	U.S. Prime Calf	U.S. Choice Calf	U.S. Good Calf	U.S. Comm. Calf	U.S. Utility Calf	____	____	U.S. Cull Calf
Veal	U.S. Prime Veal	U.S. Choice Veal	U.S. Good Veal	U.S. Comm. Veal	U.S. Utility Veal	____	____	U.S. Cull Veal
Yearling Mutton	U.S. Prime Yrl'g	U.S. Choice Yrl'g	U.S. Good Yrl'g	U.S. Comm. Yrl'g	U.S. Utility Yrl'g	____	____	U.S. Cull Yrl'g
Mutton	____	U.S. Choice Mutton	U.S. Good Mutton	____	U.S. Utility Mutton	____	____	____
Stag	____	U.S. Choice Stag	U.S. Good Stag	U.S. Comm. Stag	U.S. Utility Stag	U.S. Cutter Stag	U.S. Canner Stag	____
Bull	____	U.S. Choice Bull	U.S. Good Bull	U.S. Comm. Bull	U.S. Utility Bull	U.S. Cutter Bull	U.S. Canner Bull	

terms "Army-AA," "Army-A," "Army-B," or similar terms applied to meats in conjunction with standard Army veterinary inspection by inspectors of the U.S. Army.

The authority for grading terms is the Agricultural Marketing Act of 1046 (Title II of the Act of Congress approved August 14, 1946, 60 Stat. 1087, as amended by Public Law 272, 84th Congress, 69 Stat. 553, 7 U.S.C. 1621–12627).

The Code of Federal Regulations is found in Title 7, Agriculture, Subtitle B, Regulations of the U.S. Department of Agriculture. Chapter I, Agricultural Marketing Service (Standards, Inspections, Marketing Practices), U.S. Department of Agriculture, (Part 53–209); Subchapter C, Regulations and Standards under the Farm Products Inspection Act.

Also in Part 53, Livestock, Meats, Prepared Meats, and Meat Products (Grading, Certification, and Standards). Subpart A, Regulations; Subpart B, Standards. A portion of the above regulations are contained in: Service and Regulatory Announcement No. 98 (Revised): (S.R.A.-A.M.S. 98 Revised); Agricultural Marketing Service, U.S. Department of Agriculture, U.S. Government Printing Office, Washington, 1959, (C–522752), as well as the Manual of Inspection and Sanitary Requirements of the Federal Grading Service AMS 332, U.S. Department of Agriculture, Agricultural Marketing Service, Livestock Division, Washington, September 1959.

The United States Atomic Energy Commission was established by the Atomic Energy Act of 1946 (60 Stat. 755), as amended by the Atomic Energy Act of 1954 (68 Stat. 919; U.S.C. 1801 *et seq.*). Pursuant to Section 9 of the Act, certain interests, property, and facilities of the Manhattan Engineer District were transferred to the Commission as of midnight December 31, 1946, by Executive Order 9816 of the same date.

It is the purpose of the Atomic Energy Act to put into effect the declared policy of the United States that, subject at all times to the paramount objective of making the maximum contribu-

124

tion to the common defense and security, the development, use, and control of atomic energy shall be directed to promote world peace, improve the general welfare, increase the standard of living, and strengthen free competition to private enterprise.

The Commission is composed of five members, who appoint the general manager. The general manager has assistant general managers who co-ordinate the activities of various divisions under a director. Certain directors of divisions are responsible for operations offices under a manager.

In this department, the branding of government-owned cattle is performed by authority of the Office of Test Operations, Albuquerque Operations Office, Albuquerque, New Mexico. The brand "AEC" was registered in November, 1957, in the name of the Chief, Las Vegas Branch Office, United States Atomic Energy Commission, with the Nevada State Department of Agriculture; the brand to be applied to the left ribs of cattle and the left shoulder of horses (Fig. 433).

At the Nevada Test Site, the United States Atomic Energy Commission maintains an offsite Animal Investigation Project Herd consisting of fifty cattle. Research on fallout and atomic bomb material is conducted on the herd, and detailed records are maintained. This herd was established in November, 1957, and is to continue for an indefinite period. Supervision is conducted by an officer of the United States Army Veterinary Corps.

The authority of this department was created within the Office for Emergency Management by Executive Order 9102, March 18, 1942. It was transferred to the Department of the Interior by Executive Order 9423, February 16, 1944.

During World War II it became imperative to provide for the relocation, maintenance, supervision, and placement in public and private employment of persons whose removal from areas designated by military commands was necessary in the interest of national security. Such areas were designated under authority of Executive Order 9066, February 19, 1942.

The brand "US" was recorded in the name of the War Relocation Authority at Topaz, Utah. It was applied to the left hoof and to the left hip of cattle and horses (Fig. 434). These animals were furnished to people of Japanese ancestry who were relocated at this camp for reasons of national security. The livestock was used in the pursuit of agricultural endeavors by the camp inmates.

The War Relocation Authority was terminated by Executive Order 9742, June 15, 1946, effective June 30, 1946.

FIVE

State Government Brands

State brands are applied upon state-owned animals to indicate ownership. For purposes of identification the state also requires the application of brands upon reactors to disease and animals in other special categories. Several typical examples of state brands have been selected to show type and purpose.

The state Department of Agriculture is normally charged with the responsibility for administration and implementation of the laws and other pertinent regulations concerning branding and brands. This department also issues the state Brand Book. All state brands are recorded in the state Brand Book and are reserved exclusively for the use of the state. This applies to both brands on state-owned animals and state-required brands. Within the department, the office of the state brand recorder conducts the actual administration of the branding laws, with the exception of the veterinary provisions thereof, which are administered and implemented by the state veterinarian.

Ownership brands are applied upon state-owned animals or animals possessed by the state. This brand may also be of a ceremonial nature, and may be used for display purposes only.

In estray brands the Circle E is applied on the left neck of an animal found running at large (Fig. 480). If prescribed processes of law designed to locate the owner of the animal produce negative results, it is then claimed by the state and branded, state of Idaho. There are special brands, such as the Dog Iron brand used by the late Will Rogers of Oologah and Claremore, Oklahoma, which is reserved by the state of Oklahoma for historical purposes. However, any blood relative of said Will Rogers has the privilege of recording the brand in order to perpetuate it (Fig. 486).

There are various brands required by law to be applied to privately owned animals in order to control the spread of disease or for other causes relative to sanitation and marketing. For example, the brand "S" is applied to the left side of the jaw by the person spaying a heifer in the state of Alaska (Fig. 478). Another example may be found in the case of quarantined registered feed lots. Brand "F," followed by a number assigned to the feed lot by the state Department of Agriculture, is applied on any point ahead of the left shoulder blade to the left jaw of cattle in the State of Washington (Fig. 483).

Usually, the Veterinary Division of the state Department of Agriculture is the agency implementing the state laws and regulations pertaining to livestock diseases and the use of disease control brands. The division headed by the state veterinarian also has the authority to issue and enforce rules governing the handling, sale, and use of vaccines, antigen and other biological products used in connection with livestock. A program for control and eradication of disease is promulgated and maintained by the state Department of Agriculture. Such a program is based upon recommendations by the United States Livestock Sanitary Association, and is approved by the state Department of Agriculture and the United States Agricultural Research Service.

Brucellosis (*brucella abortus* or Bang's disease) is one of the diseases for which a number of regulations have been set up. The test for brucellosis is an agglutination blood test made at a joint state-federal laboratory. The person drawing the blood sample affixes a metal tag with a distinctive number thereon to the right ear of the animal, and submits the sample and a written report to the state Department of Agriculture. If the animal has given a positive reaction to such test, the state Department of Agriculture declares it to be infected with brucellosis and notifies the person who drew the blood sample for the test to place the letter "B" on the left jaw of the affected animal. The letter "B"

128

is normally not less than two and not more than three inches in height (Fig. 477). In addition to the brand, a state reactor tag is affixed to the left ear of the affected animal. All livestock declared to be infected with brucellosis is immediately quarantined on the premises, and may only be disposed of by slaughter.

The *brucella abortus* ring (brucellosis ring) test, made by a person approved by the state and federal agricultural agencies, using whole milk or cream and an antigen, may be used to indicate the possibility of the presence of reactors in the herd from which the milk or cream samples were taken. If the test indicates that reactors may be present in a herd, the state Department of Agriculture conducts an official agglutination test of the herd in order to identify the reactors. Indemnity payments to owners of slaughtered cattle are made with funds available from the state and federal agencies, after an appraisal by the owner and agencies. Positive reactors to the test for brucellosis are not considered to be diseased provided that official calfhood vaccinates have a positive blood agglutination in dilutions of 1 to 100 or higher.

Official calfhood vaccination means vaccination under federal or state supervision with *brucella abortus* vaccine between the ages of four and eight months. (Some states define the period as between six and twelve months.) Animals so vaccinated are either branded with the letter "V" on the right jaw or left jaw (Fig. 479), or identified with a tattoo as prescribed by the state Department of Agriculture. Adult animals officially vaccinated against brucellosis, in lieu of eartags ordinarily used for such identification of vaccinated animals, may use the letter brand "AV," applied to the left jaw (Fig. 481).

All cattle found to be affected with bovine tuberculosis, either by a tuberculin test or a physical examination by a veterinarian, is branded immediately with the letter "T" on the left jaw. The "T" must be not less than two inches and not more than three inches in height (Fig. 476). A state reactor tag is also affixed to the left ear. The state veterinarian or any other accredited veterinarian, upon reliable information that tuberculosis exists in a herd may order the tuberculin test to be applied to such cattle. Any herd in which tuberculosis reactors are present is quarantined and is disposed of by immediate slaughter. Indemnity payments are made to the owner in the same manner as for brucellosis reactors.

Animals affected with mastitis are branded with the letter "M" on the left jaw (Fig. 482). When cattle are yarded at the premises of a livestock market for sale as dairy, breeding, or feeding stock, and comingle with cattle not known to be affected with brucellosis but are designated for removal to a slaughtering establishment, all cattle yarded there for whatever purpose are deemed slaughter cattle. They must immediately be removed to a slaughtering establishment for immediate slaughter. Prior to removal from the premises, however, they are branded with the letter "S," state of Wisconsin (Fig. 478).

Many brands have been reserved for the use of various departments in the different states. For example, in the state of Colorado brands are applied to the Game and Fish Department's livestock which ranges in Rio Blanco county (Fig. 489), and the Board of Stock Inspection Commissioners in that state has the same brand recorded for livestock ranging in Denver county. The Bar One Bar brand is used by the Livestock Commission in Montana (Fig. 484).

In the state of Idaho brand IFG is applied to the left shoulder of horses belonging to the Fish and Game Department (Fig. 487). The Fish and Game Commission of Nevada applies brand NFG to the right shoulder of its horses (Fig. 488).

The state of Hawaii has recorded the K brand for its Department of Institutions.

Other such state-owned brands are listed below, grouped according to the type of institution using them.
Penal Institutions.

a. The State Reformatory at Buena Vista, Chaffee county, state of Colorado, uses the brand illustrated in Figure 504.

b. The State Penitentiary of the state of Idaho applies brand ISP to the left hip of cattle and the left hip of horses (Fig. 503).

c. By legislative act, the Five Point Star brand is used by the Texas prison system. It is worn by several thousand cattle on the system's ranches (Fig. 509).

Hospitals.

a. Brand TH and brand 234 are recorded in the name of the Territorial Hospital, Oahu, state of Hawaii (Figs. 508 and 507).

b. The brand illustrated in Figure 493 is recorded in the name of State Hospital South at Blackfoot, Idaho, and is applied to the left hip of cattle, the left shoulder of horses, and anywhere on sheep.

c. Colorado State Hospital at Pueblo uses the brand illustrated in Figure 494.

d. The Northern State Hospital at Sedro Woolley, state of Washington, uses the NS brand on the right hip of cattle (Fig. 495).

Schools.

a. Colorado State College at Fort Collins uses brand A Bar C (Fig. 492).

b. Brand U is recorded in the name of Division of Training Schools, Oahu, state of Hawaii (Fig. 506).

c. The University of the state of Idaho applies brand UI to the left hip of cattle (Fig. 490).

d. Brand I is applied to the left hip of cattle and the left hip of horses of the State School for the Deaf and Blind, state of Idaho (Fig. 496).

e. The State School and Colony, state of Idaho, applies brand CHR to the left hip of cattle (Fig. 497).

f. Brand NX is used by the Agricultural Experiment Station of the University of Nevada, and is applied to both the right and the left side of cattle and to the right and the left side of horses (Fig. 491).

g. The Utah State Training School at American Fork has brand STS recorded. This brand is applied to the right hip of cattle and horses (Fig. 498).

Homes.

a. The State Home for Dependent Children at Denver, Colorado, uses the brand illustrated in Figure 499.

b. Brand NH is used by the State Children's Home of the state of Nevada and is applied to the left hip of cattle and the left thigh of horses (Fig. 502).

c. Colorado State Soldiers' and Sailors' Home at Homelake uses brand/H7 (Fig. 500).

d. The State Welfare Farm at North Idaho Falls, Idaho, uses the illustrated brand on the left ribs of cattle, the left thigh of horses, and anywhere on sheep (Fig. 501).

SIX

Marks

A mark is a sign of ownership or identification made upon an animal. It may be applied in the form of cuts into the flesh or skin or by the sawing of horns. A mark may also be tattooed into certain portions of the skin. Logically, therefore, marks may be grouped by type into earmarks, fleshmarks, hornmarks and tattoos.

Earmarks are made with a knife or other instrument, such as a punch or a notcher, into the ears of cattle, sheep, hogs, or goats. The mark is made either by removing a portion of ear, or by cuts made into the ear, or by a combination of both. Earmarks were recorded as early as 1678 in Staten Island, and an entry in the Record of Registry in New England, December 25, 1734, in the name of James Frie describes the earmark as follows: "A half-cross cut of the underside of the left ear split or cut out about the middle of the top of the ear called by some a figure of seven."

In the United States, it appears that in the early days earmarks were made predominantly on the underside of the ear. Below are given several examples of the terminology used:

Modern Term	Early-day Term
crop	crope
halfpenny	hapene
left ear	near ear
right ear	off ear
swallow-tail	swallow-fork
a square cut in the underside	nicke

Others were: foor gad, hind gad, latch, crabb, half-still, and slitt.

The American Guernsey Cattle Club, founded in 1877, has a rule that solid-colored or nearly solid-colored animals must be identified for registration by either tattoo or earmark. A vaccination tattoo or eartag is not acceptable. Only three earmarks are recognized: upper bit, lower bit, and end bit; a notch at the upper edge, lower edge, or the tip of the ear respectively. The tattoo may be selected by the owner.

Earmarks are not recordable as a legal means of identification, but may be indicated on brand applications. They are range marks, and serve as supplementary means of identification. An animal that has not been earmarked is known as a slick ear or full ear (Fig. 512).

Earmarks are of different designs and may be cut into either ear. In calling them, the roper dragging a calf up to the bonfire during the branding and marking calls the right ear first and the left ear second; e.g., over-slope-crop and under-slope-hack the right, and under-slope-swallow-fork the left. When the mark is the same on both ears, it may be called flickerbob the right, flickerbob the left; or flickerbob the right and left. In making marks, the marker usually cuts from the center of the ear outward in order to eliminate the danger of cutting his hand or making the cut too large. The nomenclature of an earmark is based on the following criteria:

    1. A certain portion of the ear removed.

    2. A particular type of cut made into the ear.

    3. The shape of the cutting line. The descriptions of these lines are similar to those applicable to brands. The modification of straight cutting lines is not to be mistaken for the description of a certain portion of the earmark.

    a. Rimmed. A long curved line.

    b. Curved. A gradual bending of a straight line.

    c. Curl. A sharp, abrupt bending of a straight line.

    d. Tipped. A small upward line at the termination of the bottom bar of the letter L.

    e. Drag. Obtuse angle at the termination of the cutting line and cut toward the base of the ear.

f. Sloped. Obtuse angle at the termination of the cutting line and cut toward the tip of the ear.

g. Barb. Acute angle at the termination of the cutting line.

(1) Raised barb. Cut made toward the upper edge of the ear.

(2) Dropped barb. Cut made toward the lower edge of the ear.

4. Location of cut.

a. Over. Cut made along the upper edge of the ear.

b. Under. Cut made along the lower edge of the ear.

c. Others. Cuts made at the tip, base, or center of the ear normally have distinct and different names, whereas cuts along upper or lower edge of the ear may have the same name with the additional prefix of over or under.

5. Extent of cut.

a. Fanned. Three cuts diverging from the centerpoint of the ear.

b. Double. Two identical cuts in adjoining positions.

c. Full. A cut through the entire surface of the ear.

d. Three quarter. A cut through three quarters of the surface of the ear.

e. Half. One half of a particular cut.

f. Quarter. One quarter of a particular cut.

g. Reverse. A particular cut made in reverse at any location on the ear. When the cut is described, the normal position is assumed unless reverse is specified.

6. Indeterminate cut. When an earmark is of such design that it cannot be classified, a special term is adopted. Usually, earmarks that are of Mexican origin and indeterminate are given Spanish names.

The various types of earmarks for cattle are listed below:

MARKS INVOLVING REMOVAL OF A PORTION OF THE EAR

1. Tips. Marks made by cutting off the tip of the ear or portions thereof; half as much as is removed by a crop.

a. Over half tip (Fig. 513).

b. Under half tip (Fig. 514).

135

c. Tip (Fig. 515).

d. Button tip (pennant) (Fig. 510).

e. Point tip (Fig. 511).

2. Crops. Marks made by removal of one half the ear or portions thereof. This mark is accomplished by folding the ear lengthwise and cutting at right angles the folded edge.

a. Over quarter crop (Fig. 517).

b. Under quarter crop (Fig. 518).

c. Over half crop (Fig. 516).

    (1) V over half crop (Fig. 524).

    (2) Key over half crop (Fig. 533).

    (3) Round top over half crop (Fig. 529).

    (4) Dutch over half crop (Fig. 528).

    (5) Over slope half crop (Fig. 520).

    (6) Flicker over half crop (Fig. 532).

d. Under half crop (Fig. 519).

    (1) V under half crop (Fig. 527).

    (2) Key under half crop (Fig. 534).

    (3) Round top under half crop (Fig. 530).

    (4) Dutch under half crop (Fig. 531).

    (5) Under slope half crop (Fig. 523).

    (6) Flicker under half crop (Fig. 535).

e. Crop (Fig. 536).

    (1) Button crop (Fig. 537).

    (2) Point crop (Fig. 538).

    (3) Round crop (Fig. 539).

    (4) S crop (Fig. 543).

    (5) Lightning crop (Fig. 551).

    (6) Reversed lightning crop (Fig. 555).

    (7) Over slope crop (Fig. 540).

    (8) Under slope crop (Fig. 544).

    (9) Button over slope crop (Fig. 541).

    (10) Button under slope crop (Fig. 545).

    (11) Point over slope crop (Fig. 542).

    (12) Point under slope crop (Fig. 546).

    (13) Pelow crop (Fig. 619).

    (14) Tip hook crop (Fig. 549).

136

(15) Chihuahua crop (Fig. 550).

(16) Ching-whala crop (Fig. 547).

(17) Half over slope crop (Fig. 548).

(18) Half under slope crop (Fig. 552).

f. Three quarter crops.

(1) Three quarter over one quarter crop (over step) (Fig. 521).

(2) Three quarter under one quarter crop (under step) (Fig. 522).

(3) Three quarter over crop (Fig. 556).

(4) Three quarter under crop (Fig. 559).

3. Grub. A grubbed ear is cut off close to its base. This type of mark is prohibited by law in many states, because it may be used to eliminate other earmarks and also for humanitarian reasons. Grubbing has been effectively used by rustlers to discard legitimate earmarks (Fig. 558).

4. Bits. This type of earmark may have the shape of V bits, U bits, Square bits or Quarter circle bits. It is made by the removal of small portions of the ear from either its upper or lower edge.

a. Over bits.

(1) Half V over bit (Fig. 560).

(2) V over bit (peak). Made by doubling the ear in and cutting a portion out of the upper part, 1 inch measured on the diagonal and ⅜ of an inch in depth (Fig. 561).

(3) Double V over bit (Fig. 565).

(4) Bench over bit (Fig. 564).

(5) Key over bit (Fig. 568).

(6) U over bit (Fig. 569).

(7) Dutch over bit (Fig. 572).

(8) Square over bit (Fig. 573).

(9) Quien sabe over bit (Fig. 576).

(10) 7 over bit. Made by cutting the ear from the upper edge near the tip down 1 inch; then making a sloping cut from near the upper base of the ear to meet the first cut (Fig. 577).

(11) Reverse 7 over bit (Fig. 581).

b. Under bits.

(1) Half V under bit (Fig. 563).

(2) V under bit. Made by doubling the ear in and cutting a portion out of the lower part, 1 inch measured on the diagonal and ⅜ of an inch in depth (Fig. 562).

(3) Double V under bit (M punch) (Fig. 566).

(4) Bench under bit (Fig. 567).

(5) U under bit (Fig. 570). When this mark is cut in both ears, the mark is termed earrings.

(6) Square under bit (Fig. 574).

(7) Key under bit (keyhole) (Fig. 571).

(8) Dutch under bit (Fig. 575).

(9) 7 under bit. Made by cutting the ear from the lower edge near the tip up 1 inch; then making a sloping cut from the lower base of the ear to meet the first cut (Fig. 578).

(10) Quien sabe under bit (Fig. 579).

(11) Reverse 7 under bit (Fig. 582).

(12) Chihuahua under bit (Fig. 583).

5. Rounds. Made by removal of a large semi-circular section of ear, either from the upper or lower edge.

a. Over round (Fig. 554).

b. Under round (Fig. 553).

6. Slopes. Made by a primary cut which may be modified by a secondary cut of a particular design.

a. Over slope. Formed by making a cut two-thirds of the distance from the base to the tip of the lower edge, to the center line of the ear on the upper edge (Fig. 584).

(1) Point over slope (Fig. 593).

(2) Key over slope (Fig. 585).

(3) S over slope (Fig. 592).

(4) Rimmed over slope (Fig. 588).

(5) Drop over slope (Fig. 589).

b. Under slope. Formed by making a cut on the under edge two-thirds of the distance from the base of the ear to the tip, to the centerline of the ear on the lower edge (Fig. 587).

(1) Point under slope (Fig. 594).

(2) Key under slope (Fig. 586).

(3) S under slope (Fig. 595).

(4) Rimmed under slope (Fig. 591).

(5) Drop under slope (Fig. 590).

7. Straights. Made by a diagonal cut from near the base of the ear to the tip.

a. Over straight (lop) (Fig. 525).

b. Under straight (Fig. 526).

8. Sharps (points). Made by shaping the ear to terminate in a point.

a. Sharp (Fig. 614).

b. Dutch point (Fig. 615).

c. Over sharp (Fig. 612).

d. Under sharp (Fig. 613).

9. Swallow Forks. Made by removal of a section of ear from the tip similar in appearance to the tail of a swallow. This is accomplished by hollowing the ear lengthwise and cutting from a point 1 inch from the tip toward it at a 45-degree angle (Fig. 600).

a. Over half swallow fork (Fig. 608).

(1) Full over half swallow fork (Fig. 601).

b. Under half swallow fork (Fig. 611).

(1) Full under half swallow fork (Fig. 605).

c. Round swallow fork (Fig. 596).

d. Square swallow fork (Fig. 599).

e. Key swallow fork (Fig. 597).

f. Over slope swallow fork (Fig. 602).

g. Under slope swallow fork (Fig. 606).

h. Quien sabe swallow fork (Fig. 598).

i. Pelow swallow fork (Fig. 603).

j. Reversed pelow swallow fork (Fig. 607).

k. Double swallow fork (Sawtooth, saw) (Fig. 604).

l. X split swallow fork (Fig. 616).

10. Punch. Made by removal of a circular portion of the ear from its center (Fig. 557).

11. Miscellaneous.

a. Steeple fork. Made by cutting two parallel splits, 1 inch apart, to the vertical centerline of the ear, and then cutting out the central portion (Fig. 618).

b. Quedow (Fig. 609).

c. Reverse quedow (Fig. 610).

d. Kitchen split (Fig. 580).

e. Dutch split (Fig. 617).

MARKS REQUIRING SELECTED COMBINATIONS OF PORTIONS
OF THE EAR TO BE REMOVED.

1. Tips.

   a. Over half crop and tip (step, stair) (Fig. 620).

   b. Over straight and tip (Fig. 622).

   c. Reversed 7 over bit and tip (Fig. 624).

   d. Three-quarter over crop and tip (Fig. 626).

   e. Three-quarter under crop and tip (Fig. 627).

2. Crops.

   a. Over slope and under half crop (Fig. 629).

   b. Over slope and crop (Fig. 628).

   c. Reverse 7 over and under slope crop (Fig. 623).

   d. Over and under quarter crop (fingermark, fingerprint, thumbprint) (Fig. 621).

3. Bits.

   a. Half V over and under bit (Fig. 631).

   b. Reverse 7 over and reverse 7 under bit (paddle, double figure seven) (Fig. 632).

   c. Under slope and V under bit (Fig. 634).

4. Rounds. Over round and under round (Fig. 625).

5. Slopes.

   a. Tip and under slope (Fig. 630).

   b. Over half crop and under slope (Fig. 633).

6. Straights. Over and under straight (Fig. 635).

CUTS MADE INTO THE EAR. A gotch ear is one with a deep undercut near the base, causing the ear to hang below its normal level, *e.g.*, (Fig. 654). Other variations are:

1. Slits. Made by cutting into the ear without cutting out at the ends.

   a. Slit (Fig. 636).

(1) Over half key slit (Fig. 639).
(2) Under half key slit (Fig. 640).
(3) Key slit (Fig. 637).
   b. Double slit (Fig. 638).

2. Hacks. Made by splitting the ear from either the lower or upper edge, down or up 1 inch; or 1 inch from the tip inward.
   a. Over hack. Made by splitting the ear from midpoint on the upper edge down 1 inch (Fig. 642).
(1) L over hack (Fig. 645).
(2) Slash over hack (Fig. 644).
   b. Under hack. Made by making a 1 inch cut upward from the midpoint on the lower edge (Fig. 643).
(1) L under hack (Fig. 646).
(2) Slash under hack (Fig. 647).
   c. Hack (Fig. 641).

3. Splits. Made by splitting the ear from centerpoint to the tip; or to the upper or lower edge.
   a. Over split (Fig. 648).
(1) Slope over split (Fig. 658).
(2) Drag over split (stovepipe) (Fig. 654).
(3) Barb over split (Fig. 655).
(4) Hooked over split (Fig. 675).
(5) Curl over split (Fig. 671).
(6) Fanned over split (Fig. 678).
(7) Curved (bent) over split (Fig. 667).
(8) Half key over split (Fig. 679).
(9) Cross over split (Fig. 679).
(10) L over split (Fig. 651).
(11) Tipped L over split (Fig. 650).
(12) Key over split (Fig. 662).
(13) Comet over split (Fig. 666).
(14) Pelow over split (Fig. 663).
(15) Y over split (Fig. 659).
   b. Under split (Fig. 649).
(1) Sloped under split (Fig. 661).
(2) Drag under split (Fig. 657).
(3) Barbed under split (Fig. 656).

141

(4) Hooked under split (Fig. 676).
(5) Curl under split (Fig. 672).
(6) Fanned under split (Fig. 681).
(7) Curved (bent) under split (Fig. 672).
(8) Half key under split (Fig. 674).
(9) Cross under split (Fig. 680).
(10) L under split (Fig. 652).
(11) Tipped L under split (Fig. 653).
(12) Key under split (Fig. 665).
(13) Comet under split (Fig. 669).
(14) Pelow under split (Fig. 664).
(15) Y under split (Fig. 660).
c. Split (Fig. 686).
(1) Hack split (Fig. 690).
(2) Double hack split (Fig. 691).
(3) Full split (Fig. 687).
(4) Slash split (Fig. 707).
(5) Raised barb split (Fig. 694).
(6) Dropped barb split (Fig. 695).
(7) Over slope split (Fig. 708).
(8) Under slope split (Fig. 711).
(9) Double over slope split (Fig. 709).
(10) Double under slope split (Fig. 710).
(11) Over slope key split (Fig. 670).
(12) Under slope key split (Fig. 673).
(13) Key split (Fig. 706).
(14) Over half key split (Fig. 704).
(15) Under half key split (Fig. 705).
(16) V split (Fig. 702).
(17) Rocker split (shoestring) (Fig. 697).
(18) Dropped L split (Fig. 699).
(19) L split (Fig. 698).
(20) S split (Fig. 700).
(21) T split (split and downfall) (Fig. 703).
(22) Y split (Fig. 696).
(23) Finger split (Fig. 689).
(24) Fantail split (cloverleaf) (Fig. 693).

(25) Flickertail split (Fig. 692).

(26) Ching-gow split (Fig. 701).

(27) Double split (Fig. 688).

(28) Over split-split (Fig. 682).

(29) Under split-split (Fig. 685).

(30) X over bit split (Fig. 683).

(31) X under bit split (Fig. 684).

4. Jiggers. Made by splitting the ear on either the upper or lower edge in the shape of a chevron.

a. Over jigger (Fig. 712).

b. Under jigger (Fig. 713).

5. Slash. An oblique split made on either the upper or lower edge of the ear.

a. Over slash (Fig. 714). Curved over slash (Fig. 715).

b. Under slash (Fig. 717). Curved under slash (reef, hatchet) (Fig. 716).

6. Flicker. A two inch split made running parallel to the edge of the ear.

a. Over flicker (Fig. 719).

b. Under flicker (Fig. 720).

c. Tip flicker (Fig. 718).

7. Jinglebobs. Pendant sections of the ear. Made by different types of splits, cut in the direction of the base of the ear.

a. Half jinglebob (Fig. 721).

b. Jinglebob (Fig. 722).

c. Ching-gow jinglebob (Fig. 724).

d. Rocker split jinglebob (Fig. 726).

e. Full curved jinglebob (Fig. 723).

f. Sonora jinglebob (holy split) (Fig. 730).

g. Chihuahua jinglebob (Fig. 729).

h. Over slash jinglebob (Fig. 725).

8. Flickerbob. Pendant section of the ear. Made by slits from the base toward the tip of the ear.

a. Flickerbob (Fig. 727).

b. Under slope flickerbob (Fig. 728).

143

SELECTED COMBINATIONS OF MARKS
MADE BY CUTTING INTO THE EAR.

1. Hacks. Slash over and slash under hacks applied to ears as a secondary cut are termed overslope and underslope hacks, respectively; e.g., a slash over hack applied to a rimmed overslope is called an overslope hack (Fig. 747). A slash under hack applied with an overslope crop is called an underslope hack (Fig. 752).

    a. Over and under slash hack (Fig. 762).

    b. Over and under L hack (Fig. 763).

2. Splits.

    a. Over and under hack and split (Fig. 765).

    b. L over hack and split (Fig. 767).

3. Flickers. L over split and under flicker (Fig. 764).

SELECTED COMBINATIONS OF MARKS MADE BY THE REMOVAL OF A PORTION OF THE EAR AND OF CUTS MADE INTO THE EAR.

1. Tip and split (Fig. 731).
2. Tip and double split (Fig. 732).
3. Tip and V split (Fig. 733).
4. Tip and over and under slash hack (Fig. 739).
5. Tip and over slash (Fig. 735).
6. Tip and double under slope split (Fig. 743).
7. Over half tip and split (Fig. 751).
8. Tip and over and under L hack (Fig. 746).
9. Crop and split (Fig. 760).
10. Under slope and split (Fig. 737).
11. Over slope and split (Fig. 736).
12. Over slope and under slash hack (Fig. 740).
13. Over slope and rocker split (Fig. 753).
14. Under slope and over slash hack (Fig. 741).
15. Swallowfork and slash over and under hack (Fig. 738).
16. Over slope and over slash (Fig. 744).
17. Over round and hack (Fig. 759).
18. Under round and hack (Fig. 761).
19. Under slope and under slash (Fig. 745).
20. Rimmed under slope and under slope hack (Fig. 748).

21. V over bit and slash (Fig. 755).
22. Curved under slope split and under bit (Fig. 754).
23. Half under slope crop and hack (Fig. 757).
24. Round swallow fork and split (Fig. 742).
25. Swallow fork and split (Fig. 734).
26. Reverse under slash and under bit (Fig. 749).
27. Under rim and under slope hack (Fig. 750). Note that an under rim is slightly smaller than a rimmed under slope (Fig. 591).
28. Over three-quarter crop and hack (Fig. 756).
29. Chingadero jinglebob (Fig. 758).
30. Over flicker and half jinglebob (Fig. 766).

A system has been devised for earmarking sheep in order to identify by number the individual sheep of a flock. Ears are notched with a V at either upper or lower edge, or the tip, or punched in the center of the ear. By the number, location, and type of cut, a serial number may be properly and permanently marked. This system is based on combinations of numbers 1, 3, 10, 30, 100, 200, 400, and 800; e.g., serial number 4 is a combination of cuts 1 and 3. Single-digit numbers are cut into the left ear, two-digit numbers into the right ear, and three-digit numbers into either right, left, or both ears. This system has been in use for over a hundred years in Germany and in the United Kingdom, especially in areas where flocks are not as extensive as they are on large sheep ranches in the United States. With a little practice, this system is easily learned and applied (Fig. 768–96).

For sheep, most breed registry associations require eartagging in combination with tattoos. The associations listed below require notching the ear for various purposes.

The Columbia Sheep Breeders' Association of America requires that sheep rejected for registration be identified by cutting the left ear or tattooing oooo (four zeros) in the left ear. Accepted sheep are tattooed and tagged in the left ear.

The American Panama Registry Association specifies that sheep accepted for registration are to be identified by cutting a small V-notch in the extreme tip of the right ear. Such sheep also receive the breed insignia tattoo, followed by the flock number, in the right ear.

The National Suffolk Sheep Association requires the breeder's individual identification to consist of an ear notch, tattoo, or eartag.

Goats may also be identified by earmarks. By notching or by punching the ear, or both, serial numbers for individual goats may be obtained. The illustrated system utilized only numbers 1, 10, 100, and 1,000 in the left ear, and 3, 30, 300, and 3,000 in the right ear (Fig. 797).

With the American Angora Goat Breeders' Association the breeder has a choice of required methods of identification for the purpose of registration: the earmarking method as illustrated in Figure 797; the owner's private number in one ear, either branded or tattooed; an eartag with the owner's initial and private number.

There are several systems used for the individual identification of swine. Normally, the individual pigs of a specific litter are earmarked. Several of the systems for marking swine are described in detail below.

The Beltsville system has been utilized at the Agricultural Research Center, United States Department of Agriculture, Beltsville, Maryland, for a period of years. The pig's ear is notched its first day of life with a small "v" cutting plier. As the pig's ear grows, the cut becomes larger and easier to read. One disadvantage of this marking system is that it places marks on very thick portions of the ear. The upper and lower edge of the right ear and the upper edge of the left ear are for indicating the number of the litter, while the lower edge of the left ear is reserved for the indication of the individual pig's number in the litter. The system uses the following basic numbers: 1, 3, 9, 10, 30, 90, 100, 300, 900, 1,000, 3,000, and 9,000. These numbers are indicated on the ear by one "v" notch in a prescribed location on the ear. Because certain numbers cannot be attained by a combination of the above basic numbers, another "v" notch is cut alongside the notch indicating the basic number; e.g., number 2 is attained by cutting another "v" notch adjoining the notch indicating number 1; number 6 is similarly attained; number 8 consists of four notches, two near the base (number 1 plus number 1) and two near the tip of the ear (number 3 plus number 3).

All litters are numbered consecutively, omitting litter numbers 1 to 9, inclusive. Pigs in litters are numbered in series, starting with number 1. In the event that there are more than ten pigs in the litter, pigs are sorted by sex, first the boars and then the sows. In this manner, since the individual pig number within the litter is limited to 10, the identical number can be notched on two pigs of the same litter but of a different sex. In addition, pigs with numbers larger than 10 also may receive a small punch in the center of the left ear.

Pigs of the same litter with numbers of more than 10 are designated by an S; e.g., Litter 33, consisting of 13 pigs, has pig numbers 11, 12, and 13 designated as 331S, 332S, and 333S, respectively. Pigs having the same number are recorded as B or as S; e.g., Litter 33, consisting of 13 pigs, has pig numbers 1, 2, 3, etc., recorded as 331S, 332S, 333S etc., and pig numbers 11, 12, and 13 as 331S, 332S and 333S respectively. The number assigned to a pig at birth identifies that animal throughout its life; e.g., pig No. 332S is put into the herd and remains pig No. 332S at all times, and may farrow litters numbered in consequence each season in accordance with the time she farrows.

SAMPLE NUMBERING:

Litter No. (Omit 1 through 9)	Number of pigs in litter	Pig No.
10	4	101, 102, 103, 104
11	5	111, 112, 113, 114, 115
33	13	331, 332, 333, 334, 335, 336, 337, 338, 339, 340, 331S, 332S, 333S

34	3	341, 342, 343
507	2	5071, 5072
1976	7	19,761, 19,762, 19,763, 19,764, 19,765, 19,766, 19,767

This system should not cause confusion to any great extent, because the number of litters on a farm at any one time is in small series (Fig. 800).

Under the Hampshire system all pigs in the same litter are marked with identical earmarks in the right ear, making this the litter number. Earmarks to identify the individual pigs within the litter are cut into the left ear. This system uses a geometric progression of numbers with the constant factor of 3: Number 1, 3, (3 x 3), 9, (3 x 9), 27, (3 x 27) 81 (Fig. 798).

The Tamworth system uses only numbers 1 and 10, and 3 and 30, in the right ear and the left ear respectively. Only notches are used (Fig. 799).

The system illustrated in Plate LIV has been used for many years in Germany. By notching or by pinching and notching the ear in various locations, a serial number is permanently marked on the pig. This system utilizes a combination of numbers: 1, 2, 5, 10, 20, 50, 100, 200, and 400. By combining notches for numbers 2 and 5, serial number 7 is obtained. Single-digit numbers are notched in the left ear and two-digit numbers are notched in the right ear. Three-digit numbers are punched in either left or right or both ears (Figs. 801–24).

The marking methods required by breed registry associations vary, but most of them specify the identification of pigs by a system of earmarks.

1. With the American Landrace Association, Inc., animals must have either an earmark or a tattoo. The Beltsville System is recommended (Fig. 800).

2. For the American Berkshire Association all pigs must be

earmarked prior to registration. Any individual system may be used.

3. With the Chester White Swine Record Association, all pigs may be earmarked prior to registration; all pigs in the same litter must be given identical earmarks. The association recommends, but does not require, a specific earmarking system.

4. The United Duroc Record Association requires that all pigs in the same litter shall be earmarked identically. An exception to this requirement is the identification with different earmarks for each individual pig of a litter during Sow Testing Programs.

5. With the Hampshire Swine Registry, the association recommends the Hampshire System for the application of earmarks prior to registration (Fig. 798).

6. The National Hereford Hog Record Association requires earmarks or tattoos prior to registration.

7. With the Ohio Improved Chester Swine Breeders' Association, Inc. and the Ohio Improved Chester Swine Association, all pigs in the same litter must bear identical earmarks. An exception is made to this rule in the case of participation in experimental programs.

8. The Poland China Record Association requires that all pigs be earmarked prior to registration. The association recommends, but does not require, a specific earmarking system.

9. The American Spotted Poland China Association and the National Spotted Poland China Record specify that all pigs in the same litter must be earmarked identically, and each litter must be marked differently.

10. The Tamworth Swine Association requires the Tamworth System of earmarks (Fig. 799).

Fleshmarks, made by cutting, splitting, or slitting the skin with a knife, may serve as a supplemental device of ownership and identification, since they are recognizable during any season of the year. An additional advantage is the difficulty of obliterating this type of mark, because it leaves a scar on the flesh. Flesh-

149

marks are not extensively used, especially not where the climate is conducive to the activities of the screwworm, which attacks the exposed portions of flesh. Such climate is prevalent throughout the Southwest. Variations of two types of fleshmarks are described below:

1. Dewlaps. Dewlaps are cuts, slits, or splits made in the folds of skin hanging from the chin, under the jaw, from the throat under the neck down to and including the brisket of cattle. The name is derived from the action of the loose skin lapping or licking the dew when the animal is grazing.

a. Single Dewlap Up. Made by slashing upward in the brisket (Fig. 825).

b. Double Dewlap Down. Made by slashing downward in the brisket (Fig. 826).

c. Single Dewlap Down. Made by slashing downward in the brisket (Fig. 827).

d. Double Dewlap Down. Made by two downward slashes in the brisket (Fig. 828).

e. Dewlap Throat. Made by cutting the loose skin at the throat (Fig. 829).

f. Dewlap between front legs. Made by splitting the brisket between the front legs (Fig. 830).

g. Necktie Dewlap. Made by one upward and by one downward slash at the edge of the brisket. The resulting hanging skin resembles a four-in-hand necktie (Fig. 831).

h. Bell Dewlap throat. Made by cutting the hanging skin at the throat in the shape of a vertical half-bell. With the movement of the animal, the hanging skin resembles a ringing bell (Fig. 832).

i. K Dewlap brisket. Made by making one upward and one downward slash in the brisket. The resulting shape of the hanging skin resembles the letter K. Note that the cuts are made further from the edge of the brisket than the necktie dewlap (Fig. 833).

j. Jughandle Dewlap. Made by slitting the skin of the brisket with a long slash and not cutting out at either end. The resulting shape resembles that of a jughandle (Fig. 834).

150

k. Broken Jughandle Dewlap. Made like the jughandle dewlap except an additional cut at the center of the slash causes the skin of the handle to separate (Fig. 835).

l. Wire Through Brisket. A slit cut into the brisket with a length of rope inserted therein. After the incision has sufficiently healed, the rope is withdrawn and a loop of wire is tied through the orifice (Fig. 836).

m. Notch in Brisket. Notch cut out of the brisket (Fig. 837).

n. Chin Dewlap (chin whisker). Made by cutting the loose skin under the chin to form a flap (Fig. 844).

o. Bell Dewlap chin. Made similar to bell dewlap throat (Fig. 846).

p. Dewlap Jaw. Made by splitting the skin under the jaw (Fig. 845).

2. Wattles (Tadpoles). Wattles are made by pinching up a quantity of skin and cutting it downward, but not entirely off. The cut is about three inches long and will heal very quickly. The result is a hanging flap of skin. Wattles may be made all over the hides of cattle.

a. Nose Wattle (bud, snub) (Fig. 838).

b. Wattle between eyes (Fig. 839).

c. Wattle forehead (Fig. 840).

d. Wattle over right (left) eye (Fig. 841).

e. Wattle under right (left) eye (Fig. 842).

f. Wattle right (left) jaw (Fig. 845).

g. Wattle top neck (Fig. 848).

h. Wattle right (left) side neck (Fig. 847).

i. Wattle right (left) shoulder (Fig. 849).

j. Wattle right (left) shank (Fig. 850).

k. Wattle right (left) ribs (Fig. 851).

l. Wattle right (left) hip (Fig. 852).

m. Wattle tail (Fig. 853).

n. Wattle right (left) stifle (Fig. 854).

Snoutmarks are made by removing part of the snout of a hog by using a cutter. This cutter consists of pliers with various kinds of shaped dies set into its jaws. This kind of mark is not recordable, and serves only for supplementary identification purposes.

151

Cattlemen occasionally use hornmarks. The Broken Bow brand is made by sawing notches at the base of the horns of two- or three-month-old calves. This operation causes the horns to grow downward in a distinctive direction. This brand, which is not recordable, has the advantage of not being susceptible to the infections caused by screwworms or other bacteriological actions. Because this type of brand is almost impossible to alter, it is an excellent method of identification.

Tattoos are a mark of ownership not recordable as legal identification except for poultry and fur-bearing animals in some states. They are considered to be marks, and serve as supplementary identification and may be so indicated on brand applications. The tattoo is applied by using a type of pliers with perforation points set into the jaws. These points, arranged in numerals, letters, or symbols, or in any combination of these, puncture the skin when the jaws of the pliers are closed. After releasing the points, ink or paste is rubbed into the punctures, leaving an indelible mark. The rows of perforation points may be arranged in single or double lines. In order to read ear tattoos, a lighted flashlight is held behind the ear causing the tattoo to appear distinctly on the back-lighted inner surface of the ear.

A calf should be tattooed when only a few days old, preferably before it is taken from the dam. This practice is followed in order to eliminate the possibility of having calves of approximately the same age mixed up. In order to obtain a permanent and easily read tattoo, the following procedure is recommended:

1. Select tattooing pliers with fine and straight perforation points of uniform length. Small punctures cause a minimum amount of bleeding.

2. Insert the perforation points, consisting of the adopted tattoo (letters, or letters and numbers), into the jaws of the pliers.

3. Test the performance of the marker by clamping it on a piece of cardboard.

4. Clean the inside of the animal's ear, removing all dirt, wax,

and oil with a rag soaked in gasoline or alcohol, or with soap and water.

5. Dry the ear with a clean cloth.

6. Select the location for the tattoo, avoiding hair and large veins. Crossing large veins results in excessive bleeding, which will wash out the ink.

7. Apply the marker to the selected spot, and clamp with firm and uniform perforation.

8. Release the jaws of the marker immediately, to avoid tearing the ear if the animal should move its head suddenly.

9. Place ink or paste on the perforations and rub thoroughly with the thumb, so that each puncture is filled with ink or paste.

10. Do not permit the cow to suck on the calf's ear for several days after tattooing, because she may suck the ink out of the perforations before it has set.

Tattoos are normally applied to the species listed below:

1. Cattle. The tattoo is preferred for breeding and show stock because it does not disfigure the skin and spoil the appearance of valuable animals. It is also used for the identification of reactors to brucellosis and tuberculosis, and to vaccinates. The tattoo is normally applied to the ears. Tattooing requirements of breed registry associations for the registration of animals are as follows:

a. Beef cattle:

With the Aberdeen-Angus, the American Angus Association, founded in 1883, tattoos must be applied to both ears prior to registration. The breeder may devise his own system, but each animal must be tattooed differently.

The American Hereford Association, founded in 1881 as the American Hereford Cattle Breeders' Association and renamed in 1934, rules that each animal must be tattooed in one ear. Tattoos in both ears are recommended, as is using the tattoo number as the horn brand number also.

With the American Polled Hereford Association, each animal must be tattooed in one ear. The association recommends tattoo-

153

ing both ears. Each animal to be registered must have a different tattoo.

The American Shorthorn Breeders' Association (first consolidated herd book issued in 1883), rules that each animal must be tattooed in either the right or the left ear. Duplication of numbers in the same sex and herd is not permissible.

b. Dairy cattle:

With the Ayrshire Breeders' Association, organized in 1875 and incorporated in 1886, tattoos or eartags are not required, but recommended. Any system may be used.

The Brown Swiss Cattle Breeders' Association rules that all animals must be tattooed. Brands, eartags, and neck chains are not acceptable substitutes. The breeder may select his own system of tattooing.

The Holstein Herd Book Association, founded in 1873, and the Dutch Frisian Association, founded in 1878, were combined and incorporated in 1885 to form the present organization, the Holstein Frisian Association of America. No tattoo or eartags are required. When an animal bearing such marks is registered, no official recording of them is made.

With the American Jersey Cattle Club, incorporated in 1880, all animals offered for registration must be tattooed in the ear with at least one letter and one number, as the owner may select. No two animals in the same herd and of the same sex may have identical tattoos. Both ears may be used. The Club has a voluntary herd tattoo program. Under this system, the identity of each individual animal is provided by recording the herd of birth, the year of birth, and the sequence of birth within that herd during the designated year. A letter and number in the left ear indicates the year in which the animal was born and its numerical sequence of birth in the herd. Letters have been assigned as follows: 1959 A, 1960 B, *et. seq.* through 1984 Z. For example, the third calf born in the herd during 1962 bears in its left ear D 3. The right ear bears the herd identification tattoo

154

as assigned by the Club, and a Bange's vaccination tattoo if applicable. The herd identification tattoo may consist of two or three letters.

c. Dual-purpose cattle:

With the American Devon Cattle Club, Inc., formerly known as the American Devon Cattle Breeding Association, founded in 1905, each breeder is assigned a herd tattoo code of three letters to be tattooed in the right ear. The individual herd number and the letter code for the year must be tattooed in the left ear.

The American Milking Shorthorn Society, founded in 1920, requires that animals be tattooed in the ear with an individual identification number. This number must be different from any number used for another animal of the same sex and in the same herd. However, there are certain exceptions to this requirement.

Rules of the Red Poll Cattle Club of America, founded in 1883, state that animals must bear a tattoo in both ears, either identical or of a different design. Each animal must be tattooed differently. The breeder may select his own system of tattooing.

2. Horses. Tattoos are normally applied to the upper or lower lip of horses. They may be applied with either tattoo markers or tattoo stamps. In case of the latter, a three-pronged bar is used, through which the lip is threaded, over, under and over, exposing the inside of the lip for the application of the tattoo by a stamp having perforation points (Fig. 48).

The Jockey Club requires the lip tattoo and a photograph of the chestnuts (night eyes) of each animal. The Thoroughbred Racing Protective Bureau established this system of identification in 1946 (Fig. 48).

3. Sheep. For the American Cheviot Sheep Society, Inc., all sheep to be registered must have a tattoo with the breeder's name or initials, or a metal tag.

The Continental Dorset Club, accepts tattoos only in conjunction with the association tag.

With the National Lincoln Sheep Breeders' Association, a tattoo or metal tag may be used for private or flock number.

The American Rambouillet Sheep Breeders' Association recommends supplementary means of identification, such as tattoos, in addition to metal eartags.

For the American Romney Breeders' Association, the left ear must bear the assigned record number and tattoo, and the right ear may be used for the breeder's tattoo.

With the American Shropshire Registry Association, all sheep must bear a tattoo in the ear, with the breeder's initials and number.

For flock registration with the U. S. Targhee Sheep Association, the right ear must bear the association's tattooed individual number and the association numbered eartag.

4. Goats. For milk goats, such as Saanen, Nubian, Toggenburg, French Alpines, Swiss Alpines, and Rock Alpines, with the American Goat Society, Inc., and the American Milk Goat Record Association, herd number tattoos are assigned to be applied to the right ear. The left ear bears a herd letter and an individual number.

5. Swine. For swine, tattooes are normally applied to the ears of hogs; however, all breed registry associations require ear marks. A slap mark may also be applied to the shoulder for permanent identification of the carcass after slaughter. The slap mark is applied with a hog slapper.

6. Poultry (Turkeys, Chickens, Geese). Poultry tattoos are recordable in several states as a legal means of identification and listed as such in the brand book. The tattoo is applied to the web of the right or left wing.

7. Fur-bearing Animals. Furbearers such as chinchillas, foxes, rabbits, and even dogs can be tattooed and such a mark considered legal identification in some states and so listed in the brand book. It is applied to either ear or to the inside of the legs.

156

SEVEN

California Mission Brands

Twenty-one mission churches were built in California by Franciscans of the Roman Catholic Church in the period from 1769 to 1832. Some of them have been restored or rebuilt, and some of them are in ruins. They are located on or near El Camino Real, the Royal Highway, now U.S. 101. After Spain expelled the Jesuits in 1768, Father Junípero Serra led a missionary expedition from Mexico City and founded six churches before he died at Carmel in 1784. The friars from the missions converted many of the Indians, and raised livestock and grain. Mexico secularized and sold the missions in the 1830's, but after the Mexican War the United States returned the missions to the church. In 1915, all Franciscan monasteries, convents, and Indian missions in California, Oregon, Washington, and Southern Arizona were united into a Province under the patronage of Santa Barbara. The buildings had suffered from fire, earthquake, military and secular use, and some have been entirely replaced.

The twenty-one California mission churches made a positive imprint upon the history of livestock because of the large numbers of cattle raised. At some missions as many as fifty beeves were slaughtered each week to feed the Indians. In 1821 there was a total of 21,196 Indians living in the missions. Under each mission listed below is indicated the number of livestock for the peak year. These figures are based on the annual reports in the Franciscan archives at Mission Santa Barbara, California, and in Mexico. The missions are listed in the order of their founding. Some of them used more than one cattle brand, especially if it covered a large territory.

157

1. *San Diego de Alcalá, San Diego.* Founded July 16, 1769, by Father Junípero Serra, Vizcaíno, and Parron. Brands shown in Figures 855 and 856.

	Cattle	Sheep	Goats	Hogs	Horses	Mules
Year:	1822	1825	1789	1791	1830	1822
Number:	9,245	19,654	805	763	1,250	395

2. *San Carlos Borromeo (Carmelo), Monterey.* Founded June 3, 1770, by Fathers Junípero Serra and Juan Crespi. See Figure 857 for brand.

	Cattle	Sheep	Goats	Hogs	Horses	Mules
Year:	1819	1805	1793	1800	1831	1807
Number:	3,000	7,000	400	60	1,300	40

3. *San Antonio de Padua, near Jolon.* Founded July 14, 1771, by Fathers Junípero Serra, Miguel Pieras, and Buenaventura Sitjar. Brand shown in Figure 858.

	Cattle	Sheep	Goats	Hogs	Horses	Mules
Year:	1825	1814	1790	1817	1806	1830
Number:	8,000	11,500	293	150	3,304	107

4. *San Gabriel, Arcángel, San Gabriel.* Founded September 8, 1771, by Fathers Angel Somera and Pedro Cambón. See Figures 859 and 860.

	Cattle	Sheep	Goats	Hogs	Horses	Mules
Year:	1828	1829	1785	1802	1828	1832
Number:	26,300	15,000	1,380	300	2,065	364

5. *San Luis Obispo de Tolosa, San Luis Obispo.* Founded September 1, 1772, by Fathers Junípero Serra and Cavaller. Brand shown in Figure 861.

	Cattle	Sheep	Goats	Hogs	Horses	Mules
Year:	1818	1813	1785	1788	1813	1823
Number:	8,900	11,000	602	270	1,350	340

6. *San Francisco de Asis (Dolores), San Francisco.* Founded June 29, 1776, by Fathers Francisco Palóu and Pedro Cambón. See brand in Figure 862.

	Cattle	Sheep	Goats	Hogs	Horses	Mules
Year:	1809	1814	1784	1818	1816	1819
Number:	11,340	11,324	104	12	800	130

7. *San Juan Capistrano, near Santa Ana.* Founded November 1, 1776, by Fathers Junípero Serra, Mugártegui, and Gregorio Amúrrio. Figure 863 shows the brand.

	Cattle	Sheep	Goats	Hogs	Horses	Mules
Year:	1819	1800	1784	1818	1824	1832
Number:	14,000	17,030	1,353	206	1,070	82

8. *Santa Clara de Asis, San José.* Founded January 12, 1777, by Father Tómas de la Peña. See brand in Figure 864.

	Cattle	Sheep	Goats	Hogs	Horses	Mules
Year:	1828	1822	1786	1820	1822	1812
Number:	14,500	19,000	500	60	1,320	340

9. *San Buenaventura, Ventura.* Founded March 31, 1782, by Fathers Junípero Serra and Pedro Cambón. See Figure 865.

	Cattle	Sheep	Goats	Hogs	Horses	Mules
Year:	1816	1816	1790	1803	1831	1813
Number:	23,400	13,144	488	200	1,239	42

10. *Santa Barbara, Santa Barbara.* Founded December 4, 1786, by Father Fermin Francisco Lasuén and Antonio Paterna. Brand shown in Figure 866.

	Cattle	Sheep	Goats	Hogs	Horses	Mules
Year:	1809	1803	1822	1812	1806	1813
Number:	5,200	11,221	290	250	1,408	183

11. *La Purísima Conception, Lompoc.* Founded December 8, 1787, by Father Fermin Francisco Lasuén. See brand in Figure 867.

	Cattle	Sheep	Goats	Hogs	Horses	Mules
Year:	1821	1820	1791	1816	1814	1813
Number:	11,000	12,600	292	160	4,652	442

12. *Santa Cruz, Vera Cruz.* Founded August 28, 1781, by Father Fermin Francisco Lasuén. Brand shown in Figure 868.

	Cattle	Sheep	Goats	Hogs	Horses	Mules
Year:	1828	1826	1818	1818	1827	1832
Number:	3,700	8,300	50	150	1,630	186

13. La Soledad, Soledad. Founded October 9, 1791, by Fathers Fermin Francisco Lasuén, García Diego, and Buenaventura Sitjar. See Figure 869.

	Cattle	Sheep	Goats	Hogs	Horses	Mules
Year:	1831	1808	1826	1814	1825	1824
Number:	6,599	9,500	60	90	1,910	72

14. San José, San José. Founded June 11, 1797, by Father Fermin Francisco Lasuén. For brand, see Figure 870.

	Cattle	Sheep	Goats	Hogs	Horses	Mules
Year:	1826	1826	no	1807	1830	1825
Number:	15,000	20,000	report	50	2,690	345

15. San Juan Bautista, San Juan Bautista. Founded June 24, 1797, by Fathers Fermin Francisco Lasuén, Magin Catalá and Joseph Manuel de Martiarena. See Figure 871.

	Cattle	Sheep	Goats	Hogs	Horses	Mules
Year:	1819	1816	no	1812	1806	1826
Number:	11,000	13,000	report	91	1,600	53

16. San Miguel, Arcángel, Paso Robles. Founded July 25, 1797, by Fathers Fermin Francisco Lasuén and Buenaventura Sitjar. Brand shown in Figure 872.

	Cattle	Sheep	Goats	Hogs	Horses	Mules
Year:	1822	1819	1832	1813	1823	1824
Number:	10,558	14,079	42	245	1,389	300

17. San Fernando Rey, Los Angeles. Founded September 8, 1797, by Fathers Fermin Francisco Lasuén and Francisco Dumétz. For brand, see Figure 873.

	Cattle	Sheep	Goats	Hogs	Horses	Mules
Year:	1819	1819	1816	1812	1816	1832
Number:	12,800	7,800	600	270	2,258	364

18. San Luis Rey, near San Diego. Founded June 13, 1798, by

Fathers Fermin Francisco Lasuén, Antonio Peyri, and Juan de Santiago.

Year:	Cattle 1832	Sheep 1828	Goats 1832	Hogs 1819	Horses 1805	Mules 1797
Number:	27,500	28,913	1,300	372	984	47

19. *Santa Inés, Buellton.* Founded September 17, 1804, by Fathers Estévan Tápis, Marcelino Cipres, José Antonio Calzada, and José Romualdo Gutiérrez. Brand shown in Figure 875.

Year:	Cattle 1831	Sheep 1811	Goats 1817	Hogs 1813	Horses 1811	Mules 1827
Number:	7,300	6,000	120	300	2,750	40

20. *San Rafael, Arcángel, San Rafael.* Founded December 14, 1817, by Fathers Sarría, Ramón Abella, Narciso Durán, and Luis Gíl y Taboada. See Figure 876.

Year:	Cattle 1816	Sheep 1826	Goats no report	Hogs 1831	Horses 1831	Mules 1832
Number:	15,000	20,000		46	1,300	50

21. *San Francisco Solano (Sonoma), Sonoma.* Founded July 4, 1823 by Father José Altimira. Figure 877 shows the brand.

Year:	Cattle 1832	Sheep 1829	Goats no report	Hogs 1826	Horses 1832	Mules 1824
Number:	3,500	5,000		80	900	16

161

EIGHT

Brand Registration

First registration of brands and marks was begun during the Colonial era. It is generally assumed that the custom of branding and marking was brought to this country by the early settlers of Staten Island. One of the first, if not the very first, brand registers is a small book in the office of the County Clerk, Richmond County, St. George, Staten Island 1, New York, entitled "Court and Road Record." This is a "town" book wherein for nearly 150 years miscellaneous court cases, road surveys, grievances and other official matters were recorded. The earliest recordings of brands and marks are not dated, but could have been made as far back as 1678. The last recording date is 1806. While the majority of more than two hundred entries are for earmarks, there are many for brands, using either the initials of the owner or a made-up brand. According to the entries, branding was often done on one of the cattle's horns. Since cattle or horses would sometimes stray from the place where they were kept—on the commons, for example—some means of marking became necessary for owner identification.

Probably early records of all colonies show entries for branding similar to those in the "town" book of Richmond County (Figs. 9, 11 and 13, Pl. II). Along the Gulf Coast, the first Louisiana brand of record was registered in 1738. In the Southwest, the first recorded brand was that of Richard H. Chisholm, registered with the County of Gonzales, Texas, in 1832 (Fig. 16, Pl. II). Legislation during the period from 1830 to about 1885 usually specified the county clerk to be the recorder of brands. With the creation of the state cattle growers' associations, state registration in a limited form was achieved because the associations registered brands of their members on a state-wide basis. This system prevailed until legislatures of the various states provided for the establishment of state brand recording offices. Conversion from county registration to state registration is still being accomplished up to the present time. Progress is made as it becomes necessary to establish order from the profusion of brands and resulting confusion in identification.

The purpose of brand registration is twofold. First, to make a permanent and legal record of past and present ownership of brands; and second, to prevent duplication or conflicting brands on animals that may range together or be shipped to the same market. Brand registration by counties has proved to be almost useless because of duplications and conflicts with adjoining counties, or even within the county itself. Under these conditions, inspection is almost impossible and brands are useless as positive identification of ownership.

Units of the executive branch of the federal government, namely the Department of the Army, Department of the Interior, Department of Agriculture, and the Atomic Energy Commission are the only ones providing for a system of recordation for public animals. The Animal Register of the Army has dwindled to a mere seventeen horses and two mules; the National Park Service and the Forest Service care for several hundred horses and mules; the animals of the Bureau of Indian Affairs are gradually being turned over to the Indians; and the Atomic Energy Commission maintains its Test Herd of fifty head of cattle.

There are twenty-five states providing for state-wide registration of brands under a system normally administered by a state brand recorder in the state department of agriculture. There are nine states whose statutes provide for the registration of stock brands by the county clerk in which the applicant resides, and there are nineteen states without brand registration requirements. Most of these states, however, have legislation providing for the branding of livestock under disease control laws and regulations.

163

Subjects relative to the process of such action have been grouped under the category of brand registration. Branding and marking within a state is specified by law. In addition, and authorized by state law, certain states have branding regulations promulgated by the state department of agriculture or the equivalent thereof, such as livestock commissions. Several states have agricultural codes incorporating all laws pertaining to livestock and agriculture into one comprehensive act. In general, laws are similar, dealing with specific aspects of branding and marking and other related matters. It will be noted that some states place a great amount of emphasis upon certain aspects of branding, while leaving other important matters vague or couched in dubious terms. Missouri law dwells almost exclusively on the subjects of minors and servants owning livestock, while Kansas law leaves nothing to chance as far as estrays are concerned. The particular branding acts of the respective states normally have the following sections enumerated: general provisions, definitions, administration and enforcement, brands and brand records, brand fees and penalties, cattle record and vent brands, inspection of cattle, estrays, transfers, unlawful branding and marking, enforcement, remedies, and penalties.

Brand laws were first enacted during the revolutionary period. Several sections of the Georgia brand law were enacted in 1792 and are unchanged to this day. The oldest brand law in effect is that of Wisconsin, enacted in 1849 and still in use to this day. Territorial legislatures began enactment of branding laws as early as 1854, when the Legislative Assembly of the Territory of Oregon passed an act regulating the use of brands. The second oldest brand law in effect in its entirety is the brand law of Illinois, enacted in 1872. Nevada's brand law was first enacted in 1873; Washington's in 1881. Sections of the Michigan brand law of 1897 are still in effect, as is the entire brand law of Wisconsin, passed in 1905. The brand law of Missouri dates back to the early 1920's, but it never has been revised to make it effective for today's requirements.

Most branding laws have been revised innumerable times and have become so cumbersome and ambiguous that many states have seen fit to repeal the original law with all its amendments and enact a new law, clear and precise, to meet the requirements of this century. It can be stated that starting during the late 1930's a steady number of brand laws have been repealed and new ones enacted in a vigorous manner.

Brand books were first compiled by cattle growers' associations during the 1880's. At that time, the prevailing condition was that complete lists of brands were kept by the county clerks in territories where county lines meant nothing and the distances were great, as was the case in the Territory of Montana and the Territory of Wyoming. When small local associations were consolidated, it was felt that a brand book should be published with the brands and marks of all the members. Annual revisions to the brand book became necessary when livestock purchases comprised entire herds, thereby adding more brands. A local brand book, such as the La Junta Tribune Brand Book of 1886, listed brands in Las Animas and parts of Pueblo, Huerfano, and Bent counties in Colorado, and Colfax County in New Mexico. These local books were published with descriptive cuts, usually two to a page, and accompanied by a large fold-out map of the region, upon which were superimposed the brands and the range area of the owner's cattle.

The Wyoming Stock Growers' Association Brand Book of 1884 was arranged in alphabetical order of the members' names, with a descriptive cut of a bull bearing one brand and additional brands and marks indicated by facsimile cuts. In addition to the name of the owner, the range location was indicated.

Present-day brand books are published by the state brand recorder, printed on thin Bible paper and bound in heavy cardboard or similar material. The format is usually narrow, designed for working use by cattlemen and officials. The price of current brand books ranges from a gratuitous issue to $10.00 a copy.

Brand books are usually issued after completion of the brand

165

renewal date, with supplements quarterly, semi-quarterly, annually, or biennially. The issue is regulated by law, stating the date of the first issue with subsequent issues at an interval, or it may be issued at the discretion of the state brand recorder.

The problem of brand arrangement has been solved in a very satisfactory manner. In the front portion of the book is usually found a copy of the state brand law and other regulations pertinent to branding. Listed next are abbreviations used, laws and regulations, and instructions relative to locating a brand in the book. A typical arrangement consists of brands in alphabetical order. Each modification of the letter is listed immediately after the letter. For example, letter A is succeeded in all its forms (lazy, tumbling, etc.) by modifications (bar, quarter circle, etc.). After the last modification, letter A is followed by an additional letter, and so on through the alphabet—e.g., AA, AA Bar, AA Quarter Circle. This process is continued for the entire alphabet. Next are the letter-number combinations with their modifications as stated above. Following the complete alphabet is the number section. Starting with single numbers, it gradually is extended in the same manner as the prior section on letters—e.g., following 1 is 1 with modifications; number 1 through numbers, number 1 through numbers with modifications, and number 1 through the alphabet. The last section consists of picture brands in alphabetical order—e.g., anvil, arrow, barrel, turkey tracks, etc.

A typical page has from twenty to fifty-six brands listed, either in single or double columns. The individual brands are numbered by line or square number. On the line or in the square is a facsimile of the brand with an adjoining smaller square reserved for the indication of earmarks on an outline drawing of ears. To the right is stated the name and address of the owner, the location of the brand on the specie, and the name of the county or range where the animals are located. Wattles and dewlaps also are indicated below the location of the brand. Normally, cattle and horse brands are listed together in one section, sheep, hog, and goat brands in another, and tattoos for poultry and fur-bearing animals in a third section. The last section of the brand book contains an alphabetical listing of owners, with the page and line numbers of their brands.

In brand recording, the office of the state brand recorder in most states is a division within the state Department of Agriculture. One exception is the supervisor of brands of the state of Mississippi. This particular bureau is subordinate to the Department of Public Safety. Another exception is found in Nebraska, where the secretary of state is ex officio the chairman of the brand committee. The title of the state brand recorder varies considerably in the different states; however, his duties are similar no matter what the title may be. The state brand recorder may also be a commissioner, recorder, secretary, director, president, executive officer, or chief of the recording office, bureau, division, or board. His duties include, among others, recommending or promulgating departmental regulations or orders relative to branding. Such orders are supplementary to existing legislation and are concerned with the application of brands and limitations of design. Also, certain brands, such as disease control brands, are reserved for the use of the state, by law and by administrative order.

In states where registration is by county, the appropriate county official, normally the county clerk, administers the provisions of the law relative to registration. Duties of the state brand recorder, acting in the name of the director of the state Department of Agriculture, including publication of the state brand book and supplements, and issuing applications, certificates, transfers, and renewals. He also collects all fees for transaction of documents and aids the applicant in the design of his brand. It is noted that several of the state brand recorders are women who have administered the recording office with efficiency over an extremely long period of time.

In 1943 a meeting of the stockmen of Nebraska, South Dakota,

167

and Wyoming was held at Belle Fourche, South Dakota. Brand officials of these states met to discuss mutual problems relative to brand inspection. There are no minutes of this meeting available. A second meeting was held the next year at the same place, the states of Montana and North Dakota joining the group. There are no minutes of this meeting, either.

In 1945 a similar meeting was held in Dickenson, North Dakota, the same five states being represented. At this meeting the Five State Brand Conference was founded. The next year (1946) the meeting was held at Miles City, Montana, and the same five states were represented. The following year the meeting was again held in Belle Fourche, and this convention constituted the first official meeting of the Five State Brand Conference. In 1948 Dickenson, North Dakota, again acted as host, and three new states, Colorado, Idaho, and Washington were represented. At this meeting the name of the Five State Brand Conference was changed to Western States Brand Conference.

On June 27, 1949, the meeting was held in Sheridan, Wyoming, at which time Louisiana was represented, and the following year the meeting was held at Salt Lake City, Utah, at which time Alabama, Kansas, Nevada, New Mexico, Oklahoma, Oregon, and Utah were represented. To the meeting held at Billings, Montana, in 1951, Alberta, British Columbia, California, and Texas sent representatives. At this meeting the name of the Western States Brand Conference was changed to National Livestock Brand Conference, and a constitution and by-laws were approved.

The twenty member states of the National Livestock Brand Conference plus Georgia met at Denver, Colorado, in 1952. Since accurate records of this organization are in existence, only miscellaneous dates of subsequent meetings are noted here, as follows: At the meeting in New Orleans, Louisiana, January 8, 1956, by-laws were proposed; in July of 1958, at the meeting at Salt Lake City, Utah, a constitution and by-laws were adopted. In July of 1960 the annual meeting was held in Seattle, Washington; during the next year a mid-year meeting was held in January at Salt Lake City, the annual meeting of that year being held in July at Flagstaff, Arizona. In 1962 the annual meeting was held at Las Vegas, Nevada, and in 1963 the annual meeting was held at McCall, Idaho, at which time the State of Alabama terminated its membership and the Oklahoma Cattlemen's Association joined the National Livestock Brand Conference. In 1963 the annual meeting was held at Glacier National Park, Montana. Later annual meetings were held at Craig, Colorado, in 1965; at Dodge City, Kansas, in 1966; at Calgary, Canada, in 1967; and at New Orleans, Louisiana in July of 1968.

The National Livestock Brand Conference is an association of official livestock brand inspection and theft investigation agencies. The object and purposes of the Conference, unchanged since its creation, are: First, the study of problems relating to the administration and enforcement of brand inspection laws in the several member states and provinces. Second, to promote and develop uniform laws, administration, and enforcement procedures relating to brand inspection insofar as such ends are consistent with the needs of the several member states and provinces. Third, to secure close and effective co-operation between the several member states, provinces, and agencies in the matter of detection of livestock wrongfully or illegally removed from one jurisdiction to another. Fourth, to work toward the removal of conflicts between the several states and agencies conducting brand inspection in public markets under the jurisdiction of the Packers' and Stockyards Act of 1921, as amended.

There are two classes of membership, associate member and official member. An associate member is any person who is interested in the objects and purposes of the Conference, and the annual dues for this type of membership are $2.00. An official member is one representative of the recognized brand inspection agency of each state or province. In case there are two inspection agencies, the membership is divided, but both together have only one vote, and the annual dues are $25.00.

169

Member states, provinces, and organizations through 1964 were Alberta, Arizona, British Columbia, California, Colorado, Idaho, Kansas, Louisiana, Montana, Nebraska, Nevada, New Mexico, North Dakota, Oklahoma, Oklahoma Cattlemen's Association, Oregon, South Dakota, Texas, Utah, Washington, and Wyoming.

More recent memberships are listed below.

1965 Memberships

Texas and Southwestern Cattle Raisers Association
North Dakota Stockmen's Association
Wyoming Stockgrowers Association
South Dakota Stockgrowers Association
State of Kansas
State of Montana
New Mexico Cattle Sanitary Board
State of Nebraska
Victoria, British Columbia
State of Oregon
State of Arizona
State of Washington
Edmonton, Alberta, Canada
Idaho Brand Board
Colorado Board of Stock Inspection
Utah Department of Agriculture
California Department of Agriculture
Nevada Department of Agriculture
Louisiana Department of Agriculture

1966 Memberships

North Dakota Stockmen's Association
Texas and Southwestern Cattle Raisers Association
South Dakota Stockgrowers Association
Montana Livestock Commission
Wyoming Livestock Growers Association
Manfred Wolfenstine (Individual Membership)
Cattle Sanitary Board of New Mexico
Idaho Board, State Brand Inspector

Kansas Livestock Brand Commission
Utah Livestock Brand Inspector
Oklahoma Cattlemen's Association
Livestock Sanitary Board of Arizona
State of Washington
British Columbia recorder of Brands
State of Oregon Department of Agriculture
State of Nevada Bureau of Livestock Identification
State of California Brand Inspector
Nebraska Brand Commission
Province of Alberta, Canada
Colorado Board of Stock Inspection
State of Louisiana, Department of Agriculture

1967 Memberships

Arizona Livestock Sanitary Board
Colorado State Board of Stock Inspections
Idaho State Brand Board
Louisiana Livestock Brand Commission
Montana Livestock Commission
North Dakota Stockmen's Association
Oregon Division of Animal Services
South Dakota Stockgrowers Association
New Mexico Livestock Board
Kansas Livestock Brand Commission
Alberta Animal Division (Edmonton, Alberta, Canada)
Utah State Department of Agriculture
Texas and Southwestern Cattle Raisers Association
Nebraska Brand Commission
Victoria, British Columbia, Canada
Nevada Department of Agriculture
Oklahoma State Bureau of Investigation
California Department of Agriculture
Wyoming Stockgrowers Association
Washington Regulatory Division

1968 Memberships

Texas and Southwestern Cattle Raisers Association
State of Oklahoma

171

New Mexico Livestock Board
Wyoming Stockgrowers Association
South Dakota Stockgrowers Association
North Dakota Stockmen's Association
State of Louisiana, Department of Agriculture
State of Kansas
State of Colorado
State of Oregon
State of Nebraska
State of Arizona
Province of British Columbia, Canada
State of California
State of Utah
State Brand Board, Idaho
Nevada Bureau of Livestock Investigation
State of Montana
Oklahoma Cattlemen's Association
Province of Edmonton, Alberta, Canada
Province of Saskatchewan, Canada
State of Washington
State of Alabama
Manfred Wolfenstine (Individual Dues Membership)

Certain items appear on the application blank forms of all states. In addition to name and address of the applicant, there are outline drawings of cattle, right and left side, and an outline drawing of ears for the indication of the desired earmarks. The location of the brand on the animal is indicated on the outline drawing of the specie. Unless there are separate application forms for horses and for sheep, an outline drawing of a horse is normally included, showing right and left sides. Several states have identical outline drawings of cattle and horses on their respective application blanks. The format varies anywhere from 6 by 8 inches to 8½ by 14 inches. Normally, the applicant is permitted three choices of brands, to be drawn and described in the appropriate spaces provided. Fleshmarks may also be indicated. The name of the county and the range of the animals on which the desired brand is to be applied must be indicated on most application blanks. Explanatory notes refer to branding laws and specific requirements of the recorder; e.g., that branding irons must be examined by the recorder prior to issue of the brand certificate, and that the recorder reserves the right to alter the desired brand. Some applications have to be notarized, and others have printed excerpts from the state brand law printed on the reverse side thereof.

No brand law states the amount of the recording fee precisely, and this condition is open to interpretation. The fee has to be considered from three aspects, the number of brands (designs), the location of the brand, and the specie on which the brand is to be applied. Consequently, there are the following possible combinations.

1. One brand design, one location, one specie; e.g., Bar X, right hip, cattle. This fee system is used in California.

2. One brand design, one location, two species; e.g., Bar X, right hip, cattle, right hip, horses. Kansas is using this system.

3. One brand design, two locations, two species; e.g., Bar X, right hip, cattle, left hip, horses. This system is used by most of the states.

4. One brand design, one location, one color, one specie; e.g., Bar X, right ribs, red, sheep. This system is used by Montana, in addition to system 3., above.

In general, one fee is charged for each separate brand design, with choices for different locations on cattle and on horses. A separate fee is charged for sheep, goats, and hogs, even though the brand design is identical for all the owner's livestock. Reference to horses always includes mules, asses, and burros. The amount of the fee ranges from $1.00 (Florida, Hawaii, North Carolina), $2.00 (Alabama, Alaska, California, Mississippi, Nebraska, Nevada), $3.00 (New Mexico, Oklahoma, Washington), $5.00 (Arkansas, North Dakota, Oregon, South Dakota, Utah, Wyoming), $8.00 (Montana), to $10.00 (Arizona, Kansas). It should be borne in mind that the amount of the fee is dependent upon the length of the renewal period and the budget system under which the recorder operates. The term "recording fee" is synonymous with the term "application fee." Recording fee is preferable, since the fee is paid for recording the application and not for the application blank form.

Transfer blank forms, variously labeled Assignment of Brand, Brand Transfer, etc., are for the purpose of transferring or assigning a brand from the brand owner and seller to the assignee and buyer. The blank form normally has space for the description and location of the brand to be transferred and the names of the parties concerned. The transfer form is countersigned by two witnesses. In addition to the transfer, a notarized bill of sale may be required from the seller before the transfer of his recorded brand is granted.

State law in several states specifically designates a recorded brand as personal property, subject to sale, assignment, transfer, mortgage or lien, devise, and descent. Some of the states having specific sections in their respective state laws designating brands as personal property are Alaska, Arkansas, California, Oklahoma, Oregon, South Dakota, Utah, and Washington. The law in several states (Alabama, Florida, Georgia, and North Carolina) does not mention brands as personal property, and it can be assumed that in those states brands are not subject to transfer. In Montana, whose state law does not specifically designate brands as personal property, court cases have established that brands are personal property. Upon the death of a brand owner the recorded brand becomes a part of the estate and is subject to transfer in the same manner as other personal property. Transfer fees vary with the different states. They range from $1.00 (Alabama, Mississippi, Oklahoma, Oregon, South Dakota, Utah, Washington), $1.50 (Alaska, Nebraska), $2.00 (California, Kansas), $5.00 (Wyoming), to $6.00 (Montana).

The format of the brand certificate is essentially the same as that of the application form. It is a legal document stating that a certain brand has been recorded in the name of the applicant.

The certificate states the recording number and the effective date of the brand. The expiration date is also indicated, and the certificate is signed by the state brand recorder. A bill of sale blank form may be printed on the reverse side. There is no fee for the certificate, since the recording fee includes all charges for the processing of brand registration. The brand certificate is considered to be a certified copy of the brand record.

Additional certified copies of the brand record may be obtained from the state brand recorder. The charge for a duplicate brand certificate is, in most states, $1.00, and is specifically provided for in most brand laws. In California, the recording fee includes the issuance of one duplicate certificate, and each additional duplicate is issued for a fee of $1.00.

A brand is valid only for a legally specified period of time. The length of the period varies with the different states. No renewal is required in Florida, Georgia, or North Carolina. Annual renewal is required in California; four years is the renewal period in Nebraska; five years in Alabama, Alaska, Hawaii, Kansas, Mississippi, Nevada, Oklahoma, Oregon, South Dakota, and Washington; and ten year periods are legal in Montana, New Mexico, North Dakota, Utah, and Wyoming. At the termination of the renewal period, all recorded brands have to be renewed in order for them to remain valid and to appear in the brand book.

The state recorder is required by law to apprise brand owners of the expiration date of their brands prior to the termination of the renewal period. The state legislatures in the different states pass on the provision to determine the first renewal date and the period of renewal subsequent to the first date. Fees for applications are paid to the next renewal date in order for all renewals to fall due in the year provided under the law. Brands on which the renewal fee has not been paid within a reasonable time from the date of renewal are subject to cancellation and forfeiture. This period of grace varies from 30 days to one year in the different states. After the period of grace has expired, the brand is considered in the same way as a new application.

The term "renewal" means the interrupted continuance of the brand in the brand records. Re-recording means that a recorded brand has been permitted to lapse after the termination of the renewal date and the end of the grace period, and a desire has been expressed by the original brand owner to re-record the same. For re-recording purposes, the original owner has priority on his previously recorded brand unless another person had already selected this particular brand for his own and applied to record it before the original owner's application. This situation would have undesirable consequences in regard to proper identification of stock and would most certainly add expenses and cause for concern. Brands can not be renewed for less time than the specified period.

As in all other aspects of brands and marks, renewal fees vary in the different states. Fees are generally the same for recording and for renewing of a brand. Renewal fees range from $1.00, as in the states of Alaska and Nebraska—$2.00 in Alabama, California, and Mississippi, $2.50 in South Dakota, $3.00 in Oklahoma, Utah, and Washington, $5.00 in Oregon—to $10.00 in Kansas.

Physical inspection of brands is controlled by the individual states after certain requirements by the Federal Government have been satisfied. Brand inspection usually is conducted in order to verify identification of livestock upon change in ownership. Therefore, it is desirable to have well-designed and legible brands, not only for a successful livestock operation, but also for the protection of market operators, sellers, and buyers. Inspection takes place in intrastate and interstate movement of stock and is conducted at: (1) point of origin, a preferred location for interstate shipments; (2) intermediate points, where livestock may not be shipped beyond a specified distance from the point of origin without inspection; (3) point of destination; and (4) stockyards, sales rings, sales markets, auction markets, etc., either public or private, and bonded, licensed, or posted. Prior to sale, slaughter, or release for other reasons from such stockyards, livestock is inspected for brands and marks. Co-ordination of brand inspectors and market operators is imperative for the efficient and rapid movement of stock and for the general operation of the market.

Inspections are conducted by brand inspectors or fieldmen employed by the state department of agriculture, livestock commission, or other state agency, or by arrangement with the state cattlemen's association. State-employed inspectors are either civil service employees (having successfully passed an examination) or persons directly hired by the director of agriculture or commission chairman. A hired inspector may be hired full time, part-time, or may work on a fee basis. An inspector in the last category is paid according to the number of head inspected. At the completion of a required brand inspection, a certificate of inspection is issued after the payment of a fee based on the number of head of livestock inspected. The inspection fee varies between ten and twenty-five cents a head.

Inasmuch as each state has its individual inspection and brand problems, the procedure of inspection naturally varies. The Livestock Sanitary Board of Arizona concluded an agreement with the 8,000 to 10,000 livestock owners on the Navaho Reservation to inspect all cattle leaving the reservation.

In Colorado, the state licenses and requires a bond for auction markets. Brand inspection is conducted after the cattle are sorted for sale and number. This procedure eliminates inspection outside the sales rings. Brand clearance is issued by the selling agency from records furnished by the brand inspectors. Furthermore, any change of ownership necessitates conducting a brand inspection, as does any movement of cattle over a distance exceeding seventy-five miles in Colorado. All out-of-state shipments also require an inspection.

Among the activities of the Division of Animal Husbandry of the Oregon State Department of Agriculture is collection of ten cents per head inspected for the purpose of beef promotion and the back tagging of cattle under the Brucellosis program. A re-

177

cently enacted law provides for the inspection of brands upon any change of ownership. However, this statute is presently not enforced. All markets in Oregon are bonded under the Packers and Stockyards Act, even though the state law does not provide for bonding.

Kansas has a livestock community sale law and regulations under which 140 markets are licensed in the state. All but five of these are posted under the provisions of the Packers and Stockyards Act. Upon demand, an owner identification is made by one of eight fieldmen employed by the Livestock Sanitary Commissioner. By contrast, the Livestock Brand Commissioner is charged with the transaction of business relative to brands and marks only. A 1957 Kansas statute provides for the inspection of livestock on a county option basis.

A new law enacted by the Wyoming legislature provides authority for the Live Stock and Sanitary Board to contract all inspection, both intrastate and interstate, to another agency. The Wyoming Stock Growers' Association has contracted to perform the required inspections.

A fast and efficient brand inspection service is maintained for the livestock industry by the Montana Livestock Commission, in order to provide for a rapid and free movement of cattle. Montana is primarily an exporting state and therefore does not have all the problems encountered by other states. Despite experienced and qualified inspectors, large losses of cattle by theft are still reported in Montana.

In South Dakota, the state stockgrowers' association conducted inspections prior to the creation of the State Brand Board. Current brand inspection is still carried on by the South Dakota Stockgrowers' Association under authority granted by the State Brand Board, which is appointed by the governor. The association operates the inspection service from fees collected. The present rate is fifteen cents per head inspected. In 1960 the association held 3,000 head of cattle during inspections made, and only four head of these were not finally cleared.

178

Some western states also issue annual permits for rodeo or other show stock moving interstate.

Under Federal control, the secretary of agriculture may authorize the charging and collection of fees for the inspection of brands and marks as a means of establishing ownership. This inspection may be authorized to be performed by any state agency or department, or by a state livestock association, operating in a posted stockyard subject to the provisions of Federal laws. The stockyard must be located in a state where branding and marking of livestock prevails by custom or by statute.

No charges can be assessed until an agency or association has been registered with the Department of Agriculture as a market agency. There may only be one agency in a state. If more than one department or agency applies for the authorization to collect inspection fees, a hearing by the Department of Agriculture is held to determine the best-qualified applicant. The applicant is evaluated according to experience, financial responsibility, extent and efficiency of service, possession of necessary records, and any other factor relating to the ability of the applicant to perform the proposed service. After registration as a market agency, the state department, state agency, or livestock association may collect the inspection fee. Market agencies selling livestock deduct the fee, as set forth in the registered tariff, from the proceeds of the sale of livestock which has been inspected, and pay over to the authorized agency or association the amount of such fees due them.

An amendment to the Packers and Stockyards Act, 1921, Section 317, approved by Congress June 19, 1942, provides for brand inspection by various states or agencies in a state where either branding or marking, or both, prevails by custom or statute. The primary purpose of this amendment was to designate a specific agency in each eligible state to perform inspections and to collect fees. The act further permitted one state inspection agency to act as agent for another state, under a reciprocal agreement.

There have been a number of dockets relative to authorizations under the Act to inspect livestock for brands, marks, and other identifying characteristics, and relative to enforcement of brand inspection by state agencies and livestock associations which perform brand inspection. Dockets related to brand inspection are reported in the "Agricultural Decisions," available in law libraries. Specific cases may be located by referring to the subject index of the "Agricultural Decisions." Two cases of interest are: *Peterson* vs. *Valley Packing Company,* 1954, 276 Pa. 2d. 403; and *State of Colorado* vs. *U.S., C. A.* Colorado, 1954, 219 F. 2d. 474.

In some cases the decisions rendered by the judicial officer, United States Department of Agriculture, were not based on the question of inspection by custom or statute, but rather on the question of public interest. Two cases where the decision rendered against the respondent was based on the fact that performance of inspection by him was not in the public interest are: Packers and Stockyards Docket No. 2410 *in re Texas and Southwestern Cattle Raisers' Association;* and *in re Northwest Oklahoma Cattlemen's Association,* 13, A. D. 225, 231 (1954).

Most states with large numbers of recorded brands have limitations on the design of brands. Authority to limit design of certain brands is derived either from state law directly, or by departmental orders issued under the provisions of the state law. Limitations usually are concerned with single numerals, letters, and certain figures which are no longer acceptable to the state brand recorder. For example, Brand A, Brand 1, or Brand quarter-circle are not accepted. The reason for this limitation is that many older brands consisting of single letters, numerals, and figures exist, although in different locations, and any further recording of such brands would add to the confusion. Certain other brands are reserved for the use of the state or federal government and cannot be accepted. This category consists mostly of disease control brands.

A production record brand is usually a number brand, applied for production identification only, and may be recorded only in conjunction with the owner's recorded brand. Several states authorize specific locations for the application of such brands. These brands are applicable to beef and dairy breeds and cannot be registered. Production record brands comprise age brands (age, tally mark, year brand), identifying individual animals by age; serial number brands (numerical mark, tally brand), identifying individual animals by serial numbers; and a herd brand, identifying individual animals belonging to a specific herd. States having production record brands as provided directly by law are Alabama, California, New Mexico, Oregon, and Kansas. Washington's production record brands are established by law and by regulation, and in the state of Montana, by an amended regulation.

California and Montana have articles of the brand law pertaining to the use of vent brands. In Montana a seller of livestock must vent his brand by counter-branding at the time of sale, whereas in California, venting is optional. In both cases the vent brand must be a counter-brand—that is, a facsimile of the owner's recorded brand. Both states specify the exact location for such a brand.

Under the provisions of Kansas law, horn and hoof brands are not considered brands by definition, and consequently cannot be recorded.

State laws either specify, prohibit, or make no mention of the type of brand which may be applied. Most states do, however, specify that brands may be applied by hot iron, acid, or chemical (Alabama, Alaska, Utah, California, Kansas, Mississippi, Oregon, among others). Oklahoma prohibits the use of acid brands and Arkansas specifies application by hot iron only.

The requirements of states relative to the branding of livestock may be classified into three categories.

1. Compulsory branding and recording of brands prior to branding. There are very few states having this requirement. The requirement is usually qualified by compelling branding upon the open range only, applicable to animals of specified age

only. In Missouri, hogs and sheep must be branded at six months of age and cattle at twelve months of age, without any other qualifications. In Montana all livestock running at large or on the open range must be branded; Utah qualifies this requirement by specifying livestock over six months of age.

2. Branding is not required and neither is the recording of brands where these are optional in a state. States permitting recorded and unrecorded brands are Arkansas, Illinois, Michigan, Minnesota, North Carolina, and Wisconsin; but none of these states can be regarded as cattle states.

3. In some states branding is optional but brand recording is compulsory. Brands may be used after proper recordation only, and unrecorded brands are illegal. The majority of states have this requirement, e.g., Alabama, Alaska, California, Florida, Georgia, Hawaii, Kansas, Mississippi, Illinois, Michigan, Nebraska, Nevada, North Carolina, Oklahoma, Oregon, South Dakota, Washington, Wisconsin, and Wyoming.

Earmarks are recordable in conjunction with the owner's recorded brand. They do not serve as a legal identification of ownership, however, and are recorded only as an additional aid to identification. Earmarks are range marks, recorded as a courtesy, and are subject to assignment and transfer. In Oregon, earmarks have a conditional legal status. Several states have provisions in the brand law making it illegal to shape brands— to cut off more than one half of the ear, or to shape the ears to a point, starting at the base of the ear and making two cuts, on the upper and lower edge respectively, converging at the tip of the ear. Among the states having legislation prohibiting the marking of ears as described above are California, Nevada, Oregon, and Utah. Several state brand recorders do not accept such marks for recordation, e.g., Arizona, New Mexico. Missouri law prohibits cutting off the complete ear.

Wattles and dewlaps are also considered range marks and are recorded only as additional aids to identification in conjunction with the owner's recorded brand. They are also subject to assignment and transfer, but have no legal standing. States providing specific space for wattles and dewlaps on their application blank forms are Mississippi, Oregon, and Washington.

Tattoos are regarded as legal brands only when applied to poultry or fur-bearing animals. When applied to such specie, they may be referred to as tattoo brands. They are unrecordable in Oregon, Colorado, and several other states, and until 1959 were not recordable in Washington.

Most state brand recorders issue various kinds of literature to applicants for brands. Such literature consists of instruction sheets for filling out forms, specifications for branding irons, excerpts of pertinent sections of the brand law, and applicable departmental policies. Other publications include historical abstracts of the history of branding, and a suggestion sheet for brand designs. There are also information sheets enumerating the limitations of brand design and the brands which are not acceptable to the state brand recorder.

Branding information from all states having state-wide registration and a state brand recorder are included in the summary below. The only exceptions are Georgia and North Carolina, which have a system of dual registration (namely, by the state brand recorder and also by the local county official in whose county the brand applicant resides), and Nevada, where the state brand recorder records all livestock brands except those for sheep, which are recorded by the local county official.

In the following paragraphs, wherein the registration of brands in each state is discussed, only positive information has been included, e.g., in cases where the brand book is not mentioned, the state does not issue one. In order to make the survey as complete as possible, several state branding laws have been included in their entirety, provided that brevity and historical value warranted such treatment. Branding information varies somewhat in quantity from state to state, according to the availability of research material. Nevertheless, this condition does not detract from the unity of the over-all pattern relative to branding practices and procedures. For the purpose of retaining a measure of compactness for each state, branding literature issued by a state has been included at the end of the subsection devoted to that state, rather than listed in the bibliography.

Alabama. In the state of Alabama the law is Act No. 861, Regular Session, 1951, which repeals Sections 393 and 394 of Title 2, of the Code of Alabama, 1940. The Alabama State Brand Book is published every five years, with annual supplements between years of publication. The brand book published in 1956 is priced at $2.00. The application blank has three choices of brands and line drawings of a bull, left and right side. The recording fee is $2.00 for one brand, for one location, for cattle. The transfer of a brand is recorded for a fee of $1.00, and the renewal period is five years, starting with October 1, 1951, at a fee of $2.00.

The law does not compel branding, but all brands must be recorded. Hot iron, chemical, and acid brands are recognized, and single letters and numerals are permissible. Brands may be applied in any location upon any live animal. Production record or age brands cannot be recorded. Earmarks may be indicated on the application, but cannot be recorded. Tattoo marks in the ear are not recognized as brands and cannot be recorded.

Alabama brand publications: (1) Alabama Law, Act No. 861, (Regular Session, 1951), S. 14. Brown Printing Co., Montgomery, 1951. (2) Application (undated). Department of Agriculture and Industries, Division of Stockyards and Brands. (3) "Cattle brands: Questions and Answers on the Alabama Brand Law in Which You May Be Interested and Which All Persons Who Brand Livestock Should Know," by Ralph Eagle (undated). Department of Agriculture and Industries, Division of Stockyards and Brands.

Alaska. The Alaska brand law was enacted in 1933 and required filing of a brand with the Territorial Auditor. The recording fee was $2.50 and it was required that brands should not be similar.

184

Renewal period was every five years, at a fee of $1.00. A list of recorded brands was furnished the United States Commissioner for each of the various parts of the Territory. A new law, State of Alaska, Chapter 161, an act pertaining to the branding of livestock, was enacted by the first state legislature and approved May 1, 1959. It repeals Sec. 33–3–61 through and including Sec. 33–3–67, ACLA, 1949.

Under provisions of the law, a brand book is to be issued from time to time, with issues of supplements in between publications. The price of books and supplements is not to exceed $2.00. For brand applications the recording fee is $2.00. A recorded brand may be sold, transferred, or assigned by an instrument of writing, for a fee of $1.50. The renewal period is five years, commencing with January 1, 1960, and the renewal fee is $1.00.

The director of the Division of Agriculture, or any agent duly authorized by him, may make inspection of branded livestock. A recorded brand or mark is the property of the person causing such record to be made and is subject to sale, assignment, transfer, devise, and descent. Branding of livestock is optional, but a brand must be recorded before it is burned into the hide of cattle, horses, mules, asses, or sheep. The brand may be applied to either side of the animal. The state reserves Brand S, on the left jaw of cattle, for the use of spayed heifers (Fig. 478). This brand must be applied by the person spaying heifers. A duly recorded mark is evidence of ownership. The publication for the state of Alaska is State of Alaska, Chapter 161 (S.B. 58).

Arizona. A commission created in 1885 was charged with the responsibility for the administration of brands and brand tax for the state of Arizona. It did not include inspection service. In 1895 a brand commission was appointed and authorized to make inspections and to publish a brand book. The first Territorial Brand Book was published in 1897. Statutes of 1913 governing branding administration were brought up to date by Chapter 48, Revised Statutes of Arizona, 1928, as amended by Session Laws of 1931. The brand book is priced at $5.00.

185

The brand application form for cattle, horses, mules, and asses has line drawings of a bull, left and right side, and of a stallion, right and left side. Location of range is required, choice of one location. The application fee is $10.00 for one brand, one location, for cattle, horses, mules, or asses. The application blank for sheep and goats has line drawings of a face for fire brands on sheep and goats, a line drawing of a back for tar brands, and a line drawing of ears for earmarks, for ewes and wethers respectively. Location of range is required. There is one choice for each location of tar brand and fire brand. The application fee is $5.00.

A brand certificate for cattle, horses, mules, and asses shows line drawings of a bull, right and left side, and of a stallion, right and left side. For sheep and goats the form has the identical drawings as shown on the application.

A recorded brand may be sold, transferred, or assigned by an instrument of writing for a fee of $1.00. There are 79 state brand inspectors employed, working in districts and sales auction yards.

A recorded brand or mark is the property of the person causing such record to be made, and is subject to sale, assignment, transfer, devise, and descent. Brands may be applied to right or left jaw, neck, shoulder, ribs, loins, hip, or thigh upon cattle, horses, mules, and asses. Sheep and goats may be fire branded on the face and fire or tar branded on back of neck, back, and rump. Earmarks are recorded with brands in order to facilitate identification of animals on the range. Earmarks made by cutting off the ends of both ears are unacceptable.

Arizona brand publications: (1) Brand Application (cattle, horses, mules, and asses) (undated). (2) Brand Application (sheep and goats) (undated). (3) Brand Certificate (cattle, horses, mules, and asses) (undated). (4) Brand Certificate (sheep and goats) (undated). (5) Bill of sale (undated).

Arkansas. For the state of Arkansas, the Arkansas Brand Registration Law, Act No. 179, was enacted in 1959. This law cancels the old system of county registration, and records of the county clerks' offices have been turned over to the State Division of Brand Registry. A State Brand Registration Book will be priced at $10.00 when published.

On brand applications the forms have line drawings of cattle, right and left side, breeching, and face; and of horses and mules, right and left side, face and breeching. There are three choices of brands and three locations as required by law. Description of the range area is required, as is a statement that only a hot iron brand is to be used. The recording fee is $5.00 for one brand, one location, for all specie. Under provisions of the law, brands have assumed personal property status for the first time and are subject to sale, assignment, transfer, device, and bequest. The brand certificate has the identical cuts on the obverse side as the application blank, and a transfer and assignment form on the reverse side.

A brand is defined as a permanent mark not less than three inches in length or diameter and applied with a hot iron. Registration is not required by law. Single unit brands consisting of one letter or numeral, or simple lines and figures such as bar, slash, or quarter-circle, are not acceptable. Brands may be recorded for head, left or right jaw, shoulder, leg, rib, hip, thigh, or breeching for cattle, horses, and mules, except the left jaw of cattle, which is reserved for the use of B and T brands, identifying reactors to brucellosis and tuberculosis respectively.

Publications are: (1) Summary of Arkansas Brand Registration Law, Act No. 179, Arkansas Livestock Sanitary Board, Division of Brand Registry (undated). (5) Application for Registration, 5M–5–59–147261–C.–McB. Arkansas Livestock Sanitary Board, Division of Brand Registry. (6) Livestock Brand Certificate, 5M–6–59–147744–C.–McB. Arkansas Livestock Sanitary Board. (7) Brand File, 15M–6–59–147745–C.–McB. (green). (8) Name File, 15M–6–59–147745–C.–McB. (buff). (9) County File, 15M–6–59–147745–C.–McB. (white).

California. The California state law governing the registration

187

of brands, the inspection of hides and animals for ownership, the handling of stray animals, and the prosecution of cattle thieves was first enacted May 28, 1917. The Hide and Brand Law of 1921 provided for a recording fee of $2.00, and a renewal fee for the right to use a brand was $1.50 a year. Branding districts were established consisting of a county and all counties adjoining the same. Under the provisions of Chapter 25, Statutes of 1933, an act to establish an Agricultural Code was passed, and became effective August 21, 1933. The Agricultural Code consolidated and revised the law relating to plant and animal industry and the products thereof, and repealed some acts and parts of acts, as specified in the Agricultural Code of California, Pertaining to Marks and Brands, Slaughterers' and Public Sales Yard Licenses, Poultry Theft, Estrays, Packers and Stockyards, Revised to September 7, 1955. Under the provisions of the law, Statutes of 1947, 1949, and 1953, the entire state became a branding district on January 1, 1959, with state-wide recordation of brands.

The brand book published in 1954 has had at least two subsequent supplements. The price of the brand book is $7.73 and the price of each supplement, $1.50.

The California brand application form lists three choices for the design of brands, a line drawing of the right and left side of a bull, and a line drawing of ears. The recording fee is $2.00. For horses, mules, and burros this form lists three choices for the design of brands, line drawings of the right and left side of a horse, and a line drawing of ears. The recording fee is $2.00, also. For sheep this form lists three choices for the design of brands, line drawings of the right and left side of a sheep, and a line drawing of ears. Again, the recording fee is $2.00.

The use of a recorded brand is a property right and may be sold or otherwise transferred. This fee is also $2.00. The renewal period of brands is annual and terminates with the end of the calendar year, and the renewal fee is $2.00. When the renewal fee is not paid within a specified time, the brand is suspended, but it may be reinstated within the calendar year in which the

188

suspension occurs for a fee of $4.00. When the brand is suspended for more than a year, it becomes forfeited, but it may be re-recorded for a fee of $2.00. Brand inspectors are employed from a list of eligibles certified by the State Personnel Board after a competitive civil service examination.

Branding is optional. The brand may be applied by hot iron, acid, or chemical compound. Brands on either jaw, the face, the nose, either loin, or the breeching of an animal are not accepted. Only right or left neck, shoulder, ribs, and hips are acceptable locations for brands. A duly recorded brand is a property right until such brand is forfeited.

Vent brands must be the owner's recorded brand and can only be applied on either loin of an animal. No recording of a V brand on the left shoulder is granted. A cattle record brand may be placed upon either loin in front of the hips and behind the ribs or on the right jaw. Record brands for dairy cattle of the Holstein, Jersey, Guernsey, Ayrshire, Brown Swiss, Dutch Belted, and Milking Shorthorn breeds may be placed upon the right hip in lieu of on the loin. When placed upon the loin or right jaw, the brand must consist of consecutive numerals, letters, or combination of numerals and letters; when placed upon the right hip, the brand must consist of at least three consecutive numerals constituting a number greater than 200. Cattle record brands in any location may not be registered.

A mark is a design cut into or from the ear, dewlap, or other part of the animal. It may be recorded only in conjunction with a brand. No marks made by cutting off more than half of an ear or cutting an ear to a point are accepted.

Some publications of California are: (1) Extracts from the Agricultural Code of California, Revised to September 7, 1955, State of California, Department of Agriculture, California State Printing Office, Sacramento. (2) Application for Cattle Brand for State-wide Use (white, undated). Bureau of Livestock Identification, Department of Agriculture, Sacramento. (3) Application for Horse, Mule or Burro brand (green, undated, 60346–

8–57 250 SPO). Bureau of Livestock Identification, Department of Agriculture, Sacramento. (4) Application for Sheep Brand for State-wide Use (Pink, undated, 60347–8–57 250 SPO). Bureau of Livestock Identification, Department of Agriculture, Sacramento.

Colorado. The first law for the administration of brands for the state of Colorado was enacted in 1869, and the first brand book was published in 1885. The state brand law is Chapter 160 of the 1935 Colorado Statutes Annotated. The brand book published in 1957 is priced at $4.00. The 1948 Colorado Brand Book contains, in addition to a section on cattle and horse brands, a section of sheep and goat brands, a section of hog brands, a section of fur brands (foxes and rabbits), a section of turkey brands, and a separate section devoted to earmarks of sheep and goats only. The Colorado State Board of Stock Inspection Commissioners employs forty-five full time brand inspectors.

Florida. In Florida the marks and brand law was enacted in 1945 and amended in 1951. The law is contained in Chapter 534, Florida Marks and Brands Law, filed in the office of the secretary of state June 11, 1951. Prior to 1951, recordation of brands was administered by counties.

The application form has a line drawing of cattle, right and left side, and a line drawing of a face with ears. There is one choice for the design of brand; locations are limited to right and left hips, ribs, shoulder, neck, and jaw. Earmarks may be indicated, and the name of the county in which the cattle are located is required. The recording fee is $1.00. All persons having cattle in this state must record their marks and brands.

The commissioner of agriculture is authorized to appoint as many inspectors as he deems advisable, in addition to being authorized to determine their salary. At time no inspectors are employed, because of a lack of sufficient funds.

The publications of this state are: (1) Application for Brand Record (undated). Marks and Brands Division, Department of

190

Agriculture, Gainesville. (2) Chapter 534, Florida Marks and Brands Law, Department of Agriculture, State of Florida.

Georgia. In the state of Georgia the brand law is Code of Georgia, Chapter 62–1, known as the Marks and Brands Law of Georgia, enacted in 1933 and amended by Georgia Laws, 1953. Prior to 1953, recordation of brands was administered by the ordinary of the county. Sections of Chapter 62–1 (62–102, 62–103, and 62–9901) date back to Acts of 1915. Sections 62–104 and 62–105 date back to Acts of 1792.

The marks and brands laws of Georgia under Code 1933 and Chapter 62 are as follows:

62–101 (2016). *Marks and brands must be recorded.* All persons having marks and brands on cattle shall have them recorded by the Ordinary of the county where the owner resides, or if a non-resident, where the cattle frequent, in a book kept by him for that purpose.

62–102. *Only one mark and brand allowed.* No person or corporation owning live stock running at large on open range shall be allowed to have more than one mark and brand. (Acts 1915, P. 50)

62–103. *Mark and Brand of increase.* Should any person buy live stock for breeding purposes, he shall mark and brand the increase thereof in the mark and brand he already has. In the event he has no mark and brand, he may adopt the mark and brand so purchased. Any person who already has two or more stocks of live stock marked in different marks and brands shall mark and brand the increase thereof in one mark and brand. (Acts 1915, pp. 50, 51)

62–104. (2017) *Preference in favor of marks and brands recorded.* If live stock are in dispute between one whose marks and brands are recorded, and one whose are not, both having the same mark and brand, and such live stock shall be found in possession of him whose marks and brands are recorded, the other party claiming may not get possession of same, but must sue and prove his right to the property and damages. (Act 1792, Cobb 17)

62–105. (2018) *Oldest record has preference.* When two or

more persons have the same marks and brands and both are recorded, the prima facie right is with the older record. (Acts 1792, Cobb 17)

62–106. (2019) *Marking, etc. by whom done.* There shall be no marking or branding of live stock except by or under the supervision of some competent person, on pain of forfeiting $50.00 for each violation, to be recovered at the suit of the informer, who shall have one-half of the recovery. The other half shall go to the educational fund.

62–107. (2020) *Change of recorded marks and brands.* No recorded mark or brand shall be changed so as to be of any avail to the owner, unless permission is first granted by the Ordinary, and a minute made thereof.

62–9901. *Single brand and mark: Branding and marking increase.* Any person or corporation who shall violate the provisions of section 62–102 or 62–103 allowing owners of live stock to have but one mark or brand, and providing for the marketing and branding of the increase of live stock, shall be guilty of a misdemeanor. (Act 1915, pp. 50, 51)

26–2613. (162 P. C.) *Altering brands or marks of animals–punishment.* Any person who shall mark and brand (or mark, or brand) any animal before mentioned, or alter or change the mark or brand of any such animal being the property of another with an intention to claim or appropriate the same to his own use, or to prevent identification by the true owner thereof, shall suffer the same punishment as is inflicted for the theft of said animal. (Cobb, 792)

Code of Georgia (Chapter 62–1) known as the Marks and Brands Law of Georgia are amended by adding new sections as follows:

All persons having marks, brands, or tattoos shall have them recorded in the office of the Commissioner of Agriculture, and by the Ordinary of the County where the owner resides, or if nonresident, where the cattle frequent. In a book kept for that purpose.

It shall be the duty of the Commissioner of Agriculture to carry out and enforce the provisions of this chapter. (Georgia Laws, 1953)

Publications for the State of Georgia: (1) Application for Brand Record (undated). (2) Marks and Brands, Laws of Georgia, Code 1933, Chapter 62–1.

Hawaii. In the state of Hawaii the first brand law was enacted in 1888. Act 235, Session Laws of Hawaii 1953 amended the law, transferring livestock brand registration duties from the sheriff of the city and county, or the chiefs of police of other counties, to the Territorial Board of Agriculture and Forestry. Act 73, Session Laws of Hawaii 1955, required the Board of Agriculture and Forestry to record brands in a Hawaii Brand Book. This act also changed the right to register from a county basis to a territory-wide basis. The first Hawaii Brand Book was compiled and printed in December 1955. Supplements were issued September 30, 1955, October 1 to December 31, 1955, January 1 to March 31, 1956, April 1 to June 30, 1956, July 1 to September 31, 1956, January 1 to March 31, 1957, April 1 to June 30, 1957, July 1 to September 30, 1957, October 1 to December 31, 1957, January 1 to March 31, 1958, April 1 to June 30, 1958, July 1 to December 31, 1958, and January 1 to March 31, 1959. The Hawaii Brand Book and Supplements are gratuitous.

Hawaii's brand application form has one space for indicating a brand and another space for indicating earmarks. The application fee is $1.00. A certificate form is similar to the application and has two identical spaces, for brand and earmarks respectively. Brand renewal period is five years, commencing with January 1, 1961.

Every owner of livestock must have his brand recorded. Unmarked or unbranded livestock running wild and at large for six months or over, belongs to the owner of the land upon which the animals are found. Numerals from 1 to 9 and 0, not used in combination or with symbols, are the common property of all persons. No record is made of earmarks, except as supplementary identification with a brand.

Publications of Hawaii are (1) Application for Livestock

Brand Registration (undated). Board of Agriculture and Forestry, Territory of Hawaii. (2) Brand Registry Receipt (undated). Board of Agriculture and Forestry, Territory of Hawaii.

Idaho. For the state of Idaho there is no information available concerning brand laws, brand books, brand recordation, and inspection. In that state, no neck brands may be recorded on any animal, nor may jaw brands be recorded on cattle. Dots must be at least one inch in diameter and dashes must be at least two inches long. A brand must be recorded before application upon animals. In order to be eligible to record a brand, a person, association, or corporation must be able to produce evidence of actually paying taxes on cattle, horses, or mules. No person may cut ears to a point, or cut off or remove more than half of one ear of any head of livestock.

Kansas. In Kansas a state-wide brand registry was adopted in 1939. Prior to that time, brands were registered county-wide. Current livestock brand regulations are contained in Chapter 47, Law of 1939, with subsequent revisions. The first official brand book, state of Kansas, was published in 1940. The edition published in 1955 was priced at $5.00. A supplement, the Kansas Brand Book Supplement 1956, was published, priced at $2.00.

The application form for brands has a line drawing of cattle, right and left side, and of horses, right and left side. Three choices of brands may be indicated on neck, shoulder, ribs and hip. Single letters or figures are not acceptable as cattle brands. When cattle and horse brands are the same, only one fee is charged; but when different, two separate fees are charged. The application fee is $10.00. County in which animals are to range must be indicated.

The brand certificate has line drawings of cattle and horses similar to the application. On the reverse side is a bill of sale. Brands are personal property, subject to sale, assignment, transfer, devise, and descent. The transfer fee is $2.00. Record brands may be registered separately for a fee of $1.00, unless recorded with an ownership brand, in which case no fee is charged. Record brands of single numeral digits spaced six inches from the ownership brand may be recorded. Record brands comprise age brands, serial number brands, and herd number brands. The renewal period is five years, with all livestock brands expiring March 29, 1959. The renewal fee is $10.00.

The livestock sanitary commissioner appoints state brand inspectors in accordance with the provisions of the civil service law. Brands may be applied to cattle, sheep, horses, mules, or asses by any acid, chemical, or hot iron. Paint and tar brands are accepted for sheep. Horn and hoof brands are excluded from registration. Earmarks may be recorded in conjunction with the recordation of a brand, but have only limited recognition.

Kansas brand publications are: (1) Application for Brand Record. 27–3900–2–S–2–17–18–5–58–15M. (2) Certificate of Brand Title. 27–7095–2–S–31–78–79–12–58–10M. (3) Bill of Sale (undated). (4) Approval for Registration (undated). (5) Brand Renewal Notice. 27–4522–4.S–4A13–6–58–14M. (6) Livestock Brand Regulations, State of Kansas, July 1958. The State Printing Plant, 1959. 27–7542.

Louisiana. For the state of Louisiana, the first brand law was enacted in 1884 and remained unchanged until 1944. The brand law comprises Part I of Chapter 7 of Title 3 of the Louisiana Revised Statutes of 1950, as amended by Acts of 1950, No. 105; on Acts of 1946, No. 352; and on Acts of 1948, No. 103 and No. 57. The Acts of 1944 became effective August 1, 1944. The law pertains to organization and recording of brands by the Livestock Brand Commission of Louisiana. The Commission is composed of four livestock producers, one from each of the four agricultural extension districts, who are appointed by the governor. The commissioner of agriculture and immigration is chairman ex officio. Brand books are published from time to time with a price fixed not to exceed $3.00 a copy.

The first brand was recorded in Louisiana in 1735. The appli-

195

cation form has a line drawing of a cow, showing right and left sides, with elongated ears upon which to indicate earmarks. The application is for one brand for either cattle, horses, or sheep. The application fee is $2.00. The certificate of brand is similar to the brand application. It bears the notation that the certificate becomes void after July 1, 1969, the date of the next renewal period. The fee for a duplicate certificate is $1.00.

Recorded brands are the property of the person or association causing the record to be made. Brands may be sold, assigned, or donated as personal property. No transfer forms are used, but upon presentation of the old certificate and a notarized bill of sale, a new brand certificate is issued with a notation that the brand has been transferred. The fee required for recording a transfer is $1.50.

The brand renewal period is five years, beginning with July 1, 1949. The renewal fee is $1.00. Livestock brand inspectors are hired by the commissioner of agriculture and immigration and are deputized by the Department of Public Safety. The branding and marking of livestock, cattle, sheep, horses, or mules is optional, but use of unrecorded brands is prohibited. Animals may be branded on either side, except the jaw of cattle, which location is reserved for federal disease control brands. Sheep and goats, however, may be branded on the jaw. Means of branding include hot irons, chemicals, or acids. Single letters are legal, but their use is discouraged. Earmarks are not considered brands, nor are they evidence of ownership, but they may be indicated on the brand application.

Publications of the state of Louisiana are: (1) Brand Laws, Louisiana Livestock Brand Commission (undated). (2) Brand Application. Livestock Brand Commission (undated). (3) Certificate of Brand. Livestock Brand Commission of Louisiana, Form Al 2000 (undated). (4) "Questions and Answers on the Louisiana Brand Laws in Which You May Be Interested and Which All Persons Who Brand Should Know." Department of Agriculture and Immigration, Livestock Brand Commission of

Louisiana, Baton Rouge (undated). (5) Regulation 1, for the Prevention of Livestock Theft by Regulation or Livestock Movement on the Highways of the State, Louisiana Department of Agriculture and Immigration, Livestock Brand Commission, May 16, 1951. (6) For the Prevention of Livestock Theft by Requiring Butchers and Slaughter Establishments to Keep Certain Records and Providing for the Inspection of Premises, Records, etc., Louisiana Department of Agriculture and Immigration, Livestock Brand Commission, January 16, 1952.

Mississippi. In the state of Mississippi the brand law, Senate Bill No. 149, Laws of the Regular Session 1952, Mississippi Legislature, went into effect and has been in force since July 1, 1952. This act is entitled Livestock Brand Registration and Records of Sale. The first brand book was published in 1954 and the second edition was published in 1959, at a price of $3.00.

The brand application form has a box in which the desired brand may be placed, a line on which the location for horse or mule brands may be described, a line for cattle brands, and a line drawing of ears for showing earmarks. There is also space for additional fleshmarks. The county in which the branded livestock is to be ranged must be indicated, and the registration fee is $2.00. The certificate of brand registration is identical to the application. The renewal period is five years, commencing with July 1, 1952, and the renewal fee is $2.00. Brands may be applied to any location on the hide of a live animal by means of acid, chemical, or hot iron.

The Mississippi Livestock Theft Bureau, Department of Public Safety, is composed of a commissioner, director, assistant director, supervisor of brands, and four special investigators whose duties are to investigate thefts of all types of livestock, and also thefts of agricultural products of the state.

Publications of the Mississippi Brand Division are: (1) Application for Recording of Brands (undated). (2) Certificate of Brand Registration (undated). (3) Senate Bill No. 149, laws of

Regular Session 1952 Mississippi Legislature, Livestock Brand Registration and Records of Sale (undated). (4) Instruction sheet (undated). Department of Public Safety, Mississippi Livestock Theft Bureau, Jackson.

Montana. The first law regarding brands of Montana was introduced in the territorial legislature in 1864 and became law January 31, 1865. The Board of Livestock Commissioners, Territory of Montana, was created in 1884. A new statute was enacted in 1921, with subsequent amendments; Chapter 285, Revised Codes of Montana 1935, and amended 1949; Chapter 46, Revised Codes of Montana 1947, with subsequent amendments; Chapter 184 (1953 Session Laws) and amendments by the 1957 legislature.

There was no brand book published, because of the many changes in ownership and the number of new brands issued. Some of the local county associations have compiled brand books with brands recorded in their respective counties. On the brand application for cattle and horses, there are open boxes wherein three choices of brands may be indicated. The name of the county in which the branded animals are to be ranged also has to be stated, and the application fee is $8.00. For sheep, three choices of brands may be indicated for right or left hips or ribs only. Brands on rump or back may not be recorded. The choice of color of paint is either red, black, blue, or green. The name of the county where sheep are to be ranged has to be indicated. The application fee is $8.00 for one location for one color of paint. The charge for each additional color of paint is another $8.00.

Brand certificates have line drawings of the left and right sides of a bull and the left and right sides of a stallion, on which the brand may be indicated. The reverse side is printed with an assignment of brand form. Under the provisions of Opinion 219, Volume 16, Opinions of the Attorney General, State of Montana, it has been held that a livestock brand is property. The transfer of title to property owned by a party at the time of his death can be adjudicated only by an order or decree of a court of competent jurisdiction, and the transfer fee is $6.00.

The renewal period is ten years, commencing with 1921. The next renewal is during the year 1971, and the fee is $4.00. The state employs stock inspectors with salaries ranging from $300 to $450 a month. There are approximately three hundred deputy state stock inspectors employed on a fee basis.

Upon the sale of horses, mules, or cattle, a vent brand must be applied to the same side of the animal as the original brand. The vent brand must be of the same design as the original brand, except that it may be reduced to half the original size. Single letters, numerals, monograms, or character brands may not be recorded, except record brands. Record brands comprise age tally marks and numerical marks. Age tally marks consisting of single digits may be applied high on the shoulder, and numerical marks limited to three digits may be applied to the shoulder or hip. Both record brands must be applied to the same side as the recorded brand used for ownership identification. Earmarks may be recorded in conjunction with the recording of a brand.

Publications for the state of Montana are: (1) Application for Recording Brand, B#12, 2/6/59. (2) Application for a Sheep Brand, B#17, 1/2/58. (3) Certificate, 6 M 56D. (4) Assignment of Brand B#13, (undated). (5) "Complete Brand Inspection Law," reprinted from *Montana Stockgrower,* June, 1957. (6) Chapter 285, *Revised Codes of Montana,* 1935. (7) Amended Regulation No. 29, 4 (undated). (8) Instruction Letter, B#1, 7/17/58. (9) Instruction Letter, Circ. #2B, 7/24/58. (10) Instruction Letter, Circ. #3B, 5/7/58. (11) Instruction Letter, Circ. #4B, 6/25/56. (12) Instruction Letter, Circ. #5B, 8/27/58. (13) "A Word About Brands," B1 #3, 9/20/57. (14) "Your Brand Protects Your Livestock," (undated). (15) Branding and Brand Inspection, B1 #8, 9/20/57. (16) Livestock Brands, Recording Transfer of Title Thereof Upon Death of Owner. Opinion No. 50, Volume 24, December 20, 1951. Opinions of the Attorney General.

Nebraska. Legislation providing for official registration of brands on a state-wide level in Nebraska was enacted in 1898. Prior to that date, brands were registered with the Cattlemen's Association. Brands have been registered since Nebraska became a territory. In 1941, legislation was enacted creating the present Nebraska Brand Committee, consisting of the secretary of state, chairman ex officio, and four practicing cattlemen. The first brand book was published in 1898. Price of the Nebraska brand book is $10.00.

The application form allows four choices of brands, which may only be applied to the right or left shoulder, ribs, or hips. There are boxes for indicating the brand. The application fee is $2.00 for each location or $6.00 per side (three locations). Brands may be transferred by securing a notarized bill of sale from the owner. A brand is personal property and, upon the death of the brand owner, becomes a part of the estate and is subject to transfer in the same manner as other personal property. The transfer form is identical to the application form. Both have spaces to indicate the county in which the branded stock will be ranged. The transfer fee is $1.50. The renewal period is four years; the renewal fee is $1.50. No single letters or numerals may be used, or block brands, or brands having dots or periods.

The state of Nebraska publications are: (1) Application for Livestock Brand (undated). (2) Application for Livestock Brand Transfer (undated), and (3) Bill of Sale (undated).

Nevada. In the state of Nevada the first act to regulate marks and brands of stock was approved February 27, 1873. Acts providing for the registration of brands were approved March 20, 1909, March 25, 1915, and, Section 6745 and Section 7172, Revised Laws of Nevada, 1912. In 1923 a new law was passed, Chapter 26, Nevada Brand Law, enacted February 19, 1923, and amended by statutes in 1925, March 17, 1937, and Section 564.010 through Section 564.150, Nevada Revised Statutes 1957 and 1959. Prior to 1923, recording was accomplished by the various county recorders. Sheep brands are still registered by recorders of the county.

The first official brand book was published in 1924. Subsequent editions were issued in 1932, 1936, 1941, 1946, 1951, and 1956. Supplements were printed in 1924, 1926, 1938, 1943, and 1949. A mimeographed supplement was issued in 1954. Mimeographed supplements to the 1956 brand book were issued as follows: July 1 to December 31, 1956; January 1 to March 31, 1957; April 1 to July 31, 1957; August 1 to December 31, 1957; January 1 to June 30, 1958; and July 1 to December 31, 1958.

The 1924 brand book was published by the Nevada Brand Book Company and was sold for $3.00. A group of interested parties founded this company for the purpose of publishing a brand book. In order to reduce the price, advertising matter was included. The Board of Stock Commissioners assumed responsibility for editing the book and certified, insofar as possible, to the accuracy of the brands. The Board also censored the advertising matter. The first supplement to the original brand book also was published by the Nevada Brand Book Company, in 1924. The second official brand book was issued by the State Board of Stock Commissioners and was printed by the State Printing Office in Carson City in 1936. All subsequent publications have been printed by the State Printing Office. The cost of the 1956 brand book is $2.50.

The application form provides for two choices of brand to be indicated in boxes, and the location thereof on line drawings of the right and left side of cattle and horses. Earmarks may be indicated on separate line drawings of ears. The approximate boundaries of that part of the state in which the brand is intended to be used must be indicated. The application fee is $2.00.

Here, again, brands are the property of the person to whom they stand of record and are subject to sale, assignment, transfer, mortgage or lien, devise, and descent. The renewal period is five years, commencing with January 1, 1926. The first two brand inspectors were employed by the State Board of Stock Commissioners in 1920. In 1959, four full time supervising brand inspectors were employed, with about 175 fee brand inspectors being paid ten cents per head inspected. Brands may be recorded only for horses, mules, asses, cattle, and hogs. Earmarks are recorded as accessory marks. It is unlawful to remove more than half the ear or to cut the edge of the ear to a point. Dewlaps and wattles may be recorded in conjunction with a brand.

Publications for the state of Nevada are: (1) Application for the Recording of Stock Brand, 134 (undated); (2) Nevada Brand Law, State Printing Office, Carson City, 1955; and (3) Amendment to Nevada Brand Law, (undated).

New Mexico. The Cattle Sanitary Board of New Mexico, with offices at East Las Vegas, was established November 28, 1887. The first brand book was published under the title of Brand Book of the Territory of New Mexico, July 1, 1900, with 7,786 recorded brands. It was published by the New Mexican Printing Company, Santa Fe, New Mexico, and contained 321 pages, each page listing about 25 brands. The 1958 edition of the brand book is $10.00 a copy.

The state's application form has space for one choice, to be placed on a right and left outline drawing of cattle and horses, including enlarged ears for both species for indication of earmarks. Locations are limited to ten for cattle, right or left jaw, neck, shoulder, ribs, and hips; and to eight for horses, right or left jaw, neck, shoulder and hips. There is also a place to indicate the name of the county where the animals are to be ranged. The application fee is $3.00. The law on brand renewal specifies not less than five or more than ten years. The latest renewal period started April 1, 1958; the prior period ended in 1948.

Brand inspectors are employed after approval by members of the Cattle Sanitary Board, following submission of a letter of application, giving experience, references, etc. Registered cattle are exempt from branding and receive a gratuitous certificate. Tally or year brands are illegal, since they may be identical to another person's recorded brand. Brands must consist of two letters, two numerals, or a combination of a letter and a numeral, with the addition of a bar, slash, or quarter-circle. Earmarks are optional and may be recorded at the time the brand application is submitted or at a later date. In the case of the latter, a charge of fifty cents is made. Ears cut to a point or completely cut off can not be recorded.

The state's publication is Application for Brand Record, Form No. 16 5M 2–59, Baser Printing Co., Albuquerque.

North Carolina. North Carolina's brand law is put forth in An Act Relating to the Records Required to be Kept by Persons or Firms Conducting Stock Yards, Chapter 232, P. L. 1935. There is no brand book issued, but the state recorder maintains a file. Neither is there an official blank published by the state recorder. Application fees are fifty cents, but there is no official application fee published by the registers of deeds.

Brands are applied for and recorded by the state recorder. After proper state recordation, the brand may be recorded by register of deeds of the county in which the stock grower resides. The only publication is the act mentioned above.

North Dakota. The first North Dakota brand law was enacted on March 9, 1891; however, ranchers were using livestock brands prior to that time. The law to authorize printing of the state brand book was enacted in 1943 and became effective January 1, 1944. The first brand book was published by the Little Missouri Cattlemen's Association in 1892. The Little Missouri Cattlemen's Association, founded in 1884, largely through the efforts of Theodore Roosevelt, was the forerunner of the North Dakota Stockmen's Association, founded in 1929. Subsequent issues of the brand book were in 1899, 1902, and 1937. The first state brand book was printed in 1944. The 1956 edition was followed by Supplement No. 1 for 1957 and Supplement No. 2 for 1958. The first association brand book contained 1,300 brands.

In applications for brand recording, there are five choices of brands which may be indicated in boxes and also located on line drawings. There are line drawings of the left and right side of a horse or cow. The recording fee is $5.00 for one brand location on all animals. The brand renewal period is every ten years, regardless of when the brand was recorded. The next date of renewal is January 1, 1976.

Brand inspectors are employed by the North Dakota Stockmen's Association. All cattle sold or transferred in ownership must be inspected for brands. This is done in the county by local brand inspectors, or at auctions, or at terminal markets. Cattle being sent outside the state to markets where inspection is maintained by the Association are inspected at destination. Only brands with at least two letters, two numerals, or one letter and one numeral are accepted.

Publications of the state are: (1) Application for Brand (undated); (2) Branding Suggestions (undated).

Oklahoma. The brand law of the state of Oklahoma is contained in the Senate Bill 202, S.L. 1949, which provides for registration on a state-wide basis. Prior to that time, brands were registered with the various county clerks of seventy-seven counties. The current law is contained in Article 4 of the Oklahoma Agricultural Code, enacted by the 1955 Legislature.

The first state brand book was published in 1950, with subsequent issues in 1955 and 1960. The price of the brand book is $3.00. Supplements are issued quarterly and are priced at fifty cents each. However, the state brand book and all supplements thereto within a specified five-year period cannot be sold for more than $5.00. The 1950 Oklahoma Brand Book was compiled and published by the State Board of Agriculture in pursuance of the provisions of 4 O.S. 1951, para. 276.

On brand applications there are three choices of brands. Line drawings of cattle (right and left side, breeching, and head) and of horses or mules (right and left side, head, and breeching) are provided for indicating the position of the brand. The location on which livestock with the described brand will range must be indicated according to sections and townships. The recording fee is $3.00 for one brand in one location.

Brands have recently assumed personal property status in Oklahoma, and are subject to sale, assignment, transfer, devise, and bequest. The transfer fee is $1.00. The brand renewal period is five years, with the first registration period closed March 31, 1950. The renewal fee is $3.00. Under Oklahoma law, no provisions have been made for brand inspection service, although Senate Bill 202 authorizes the Board of Agriculture and its brand division to co-operate with livestock associations and law enforcement agencies in this phase of the work. The Oklahoma Cattlemen's Association co-operates to the fullest extent with the state brand division.

The state reserves Brands B (*brucellosis abortus*, Fig. 443), T (Bovine Tuberculosis, Fig. 441), V (calves officially vaccinated, Fig. 479), AV (adult animals officially vaccinated against brucellosis, Fig. 481), and the Dog Iron brand (the brand used by the late Will Rogers and reserved by the state for historical purposes, Fig. 486). The location of the disease control brands is the left jaw, also reserved by the state. Brands may be applied to horses, mules, and cattle at the following locations: head, right and left jaw, right and left shoulder, legs, right and left ribs, right and left hips, right and left thigh, right and left breeching, except the left jaw of cattle. Brands must be at least three inches in height or diameter and must be applied with a hot iron only; acid brands are illegal. Single-unit brands, such as one initial, numeral, or single character, such as a bar, slash, or quarter-circle are not acceptable for registration. Earmarks may be recorded as a means of permanent identification. They are considered marks, cut from the ear or ears of a live animal.

Publications of this state are: (1) Application for Registration (undated); (2) Summary of Oklahoma Brand Registration Law Senate Bill 202 (undated); (3) The Oklahoma Agricultural Code of 1955, State Board of Agriculture; and (4) Oklahoma

205

Agriculture, 1958 *Annual Report*, State Board of Agriculture and the Agricultural Marketing Service, United States Department of Agriculture.

Oregon. The first Oregon brand law, enacted January 12, 1854, by the Legislative Assembly of the Territory of Oregon reads:

Sec. 1. Be it enacted by the Legislative Assembly of the Territory of Oregon, that it shall be the duty of the register of deeds of each county, on the application of any person residing in such county, to record a description of the marks and brands with which said person may be desirous of marking his horses, cattle, sheep or hogs; but the same description shall not be recorded for more than one resident of the same county.

Sec. 2. No two persons residing within fifteen miles of each other shall use the same mark or brand in this Territory, but in such cases, the person having the oldest recorded mark shall have the preference, but nothing contained (herein) shall prevent the parties from agreeing which one of them shall change his mark or brand; and any person offending against the provisions of this section shall, on conviction before a justice of the peace of the proper county, be fined for each offence, in any sum not exceeding $5.00.

Provision that this shall be effective May 1st, 1854.

More recent branding regulations are contained in Chapter 604, Oregon Revised Statutes, as amended in 1953, 1957 and 1959.

The first brand book was compiled and published for Samuel Van Dersal by a Portland book firm in 1917. The book shows "the recorded marks and brands of each (stock raiser) as they appear in the state records in the office of the State Veterinarian, Salem, Oregon." The brands were listed by counties. The brand book published in 1955, with supplements, is priced at $5.75.

Brand application forms have space for one choice of brand to be drawn in a box, a line to indicate the location of the brand, and an outline drawing of ears for the indication of earmarks. Fleshmarks may also be indicated. The name of the county in which the animals are to be ranged has to be described. The recording fee is $5.00 for each brand on each specie of livestock or poultry. Any recorded brand is the property of the person causing such record to be made, and it is subject to sale, assignment, transfer, devise, and descent, and the transfer fee is $1.00. The renewal period is five years, beginning with January 1, 1955. There are thirty full time brand inspectors and sixty-five brand inspectors working on a fee, hourly, or part-time basis.

Brands may be applied to the hide, hoof, horn, skin, or wool of sheep, horses, asses, mules, cattle, goats, hogs, poultry, or foxes by a heated iron, tattoo, caustic chemical substance, or paint. No brand consisting of three numerals or letters may be recorded for the shoulders of cattle, and no brand may be recorded for the jaw of any cattle. These locations are reserved for the purpose of indicating age, breeding, or such other information as the owner may desire.

Earmarks are taken in evidence in conjunction with recorded brands for all animals other than sheep, goats, or hogs. In the case of sheep, goats, or hogs, earmarks are taken in evidence regardless of whether or not paint, wool, or tattoo brand is duly recorded under the provisions of the law. It is illegal to cut off more than half of the ear or to shape it to a point by cutting the upper or lower side. Fleshmarks such as dewlaps and wattles are considered a brand and may be used. Tattoos, both ear and lip, are considered brands and may be used. Tattoos for all foxes raised or bred in captivity or enclosures are proof of ownership and may be recorded in the same manner as brands.

The state's publications are: (1) Application for Record and Brands (undated); and (2) Chapter 604, Oregon Revised Statutes (undated).

South Dakota. In South Dakota, legislation enacted in 1861 made possible the registration of brands by the registers of deeds of various counties. Legislation enacted in 1897 provided for state-wide registration of brands. The 1949 session of the legislature amended the law covering brand registrations and renewals.

The first brand book was published in the 1890's. The cost of the present brand book is $5.00. Four choices of brands can be indicated in appropriate boxes on the application form. Line drawings of the left and right side of cattle and horses are provided for showing the location of the brand. A bill of sale is printed on the reverse side. The recording fee for one brand for one location for either cattle or horses or both is $5.00. Separate fees are required for both different brands and for different locations for cattle and horses. Brands are considered personal property, and the transfer fee is $1.00. The renewal period is five years. The last renewal date was January 1, 1965; the next date is January 1, 1970, and the renewal fee is $2.50.

Brand inspection is under the general supervision of the State Brand Board. However, the Board has contracted with the South Dakota Stock Growers' Association to do inspection work. Employment of inspectors is administered by the Association, with the approval of the Board. Brands must consist of two, and not more than three, letters or numerals. Single designs or characters are acceptable. The location of brands may be the right or left side of the jaw, neck, shoulder, ribs, and hips. The thigh is considered as hip.

Publications of this state are: (1) Application for Record Brand (undated); (2) Letter of Requirements (undated).

Utah. In the state of Utah, the basic law is contained in Chapter 7, Session Laws of Utah 1939, repealing sections of Revised Statutes of Utah 1933. The law contained in Title 3, Chapter 5, Sections 113 to 181, Utah Code Annotated 1943, as amended by Chapter 1, Laws of Utah 1949, and Chapter 5, Laws of Utah 1951, and Chapter 8, Laws of Utah 1943, was in effect until it was changed by the Utah Livestock Brand and Anti-Theft Act, Title 3, Chapter 5, Sections 113 to 181, Utah Code Annotated 1953, as amended by Chapter 7, Laws of Utah 1959. Pursuant to

Chapter 7, Laws of Utah 1939, the State Board of Agriculture on October 16, 1941, designated Brand Inspection Districts, locations of brands on cattle and horses and location of brands on sheep and goats. It further designated earmark districts for cattle, earmark districts for sheep and goats, and designated as official brands the tattoos on fur-bearing animals.

The first brand book was published in Utah about 1850. Subsequent issues include the Official Brand Book, State of Utah, 1940–41, with Brand Book Supplement 1942–43, 1944, 1945, and 1947. The brand book differs in one respect from the brand books of other states. Following the section on cattle and horse brands and earmarks, a special section is devoted exclusively to cattle earmarks, arranged by the type of earmark, e.g., Crop Right Ear, Crop Left Ear, Crop Both Ears. Within each subsection of types, earmarks are arranged in order of the four earmark districts for cattle.

The next section of the brand book contains brands and earmarks for sheep, followed by a section of earmarks by type for sheep. The earmark districts are omitted in this section because the entire state of Utah is designated as one district for earmarks for sheep. Consequently, earmarks are found in conjunction with brands in one section, and by type and district (the latter applicable only to cattle) in another section of the brand book. Earmark districts for cattle are also noted in the first section of the book, which lists brands and earmarks together.

Brand application forms provide for two choices of brands and two choices of location on cattle, horses, and sheep. There are outline drawings of the left and right sides of cattle and horses; an outline drawing of a face for cattle, and one of a back of a sheep. Counties in which the stock is to be ranged must be indicated. The recording fee is $5.00 for each brand for each location.

The earmark application form has outline drawings of ears upon which three choices of earmarks for cattle and horses may be indicated, and another set of drawings providing for four choices of earmarks for sheep. The schedule of fees for recording of earmarks is $5.00 for each earmark for cattle and horses in each district, and the same for sheep.

Any brand or mark duly recorded is the property of the person causing such record to be made, and is subject to sale, assignment, transfer, devise, and descent. The transfer fee for a brand is $1.00, and the same for a mark. The renewal period is ten years, starting with 1940, so the next renewal period is in 1970. The renewal application is similar to the original application except for the addition of outline drawings of ears for cattle earmarks and sheep earmarks. The renewal fee for each brand for each location is $3.00, which includes the renewal for earmarks.

There are eleven brand inspection districts in Utah. All livestock moving across district boundaries must be brand inspected. Also, all livestock slaughtered and sold through regular sales are brand inspected. There are seven full time brand inspectors and forty-seven part-time brand inspectors employed. A brand may be applied to cattle, horses, mules, asses, sheep, goats, and hogs. The brand may be applied by means of heat, acid, or chemicals. Livestock over six months of age must be branded with a recorded brand when ranging on the open range or without an enclosure. The following brands are reserved by Federal or state authorities: ID, for use by the Bureau of Indian Affairs, United States Department of Interior; Brand B, applied to the left jaw, Brand T, applied to the left jaw, and Brand V, applied to the right jaw, reserved for reactors to brucellosis, T. B. tested, and vaccinated calves, respectively. Designated locations of brands on cattle and horses are:

face (including forehead and nose)—F.

right jaw—R.J.	left jaw—L.J.
right neck—R.N.	left neck—L.N.
right shoulder—R.S.	left shoulder—L.S.
right ribs—R.R.	left ribs—L.R.
right hip-thigh—R.H.T.	left hip-thigh—L.H.T.

Designated locations of brands on sheep and goats (face and back only):

face—F.	center back—C. of B.
withers—W.	rump—R.

Cutting off more than half of the ear or pointing the ear is prohibited. The state is divided into four districts for the recording of cattle earmarks, and the entire state is designated as one district for the recording of earmarks of sheep and goats. A tattoo is designated as an official brand and is evidence of ownership of animals so branded. Formerly recorded for fur-bearing animals, tattoos are no longer recorded at all.

Publications of the state of Utah are: (1) Utah Livestock Brand and Anti-Theft Act, 1951, State Board of Agriculture; (2) Utah Livestock Brand and Anti-Theft Act, 1959, State Board of Agriculture; (3) Application for Recording of Livestock Brand (undated); (4) Application for Recording of Livestock Earmarks (undated); (5) Renewal Application for Recording of Livestock Brand and/or Earmark (undated); (6) Assignment of Estate Livestock Marks and Brands (undated); and (7) Assignment of Livestock Marks and Brands (undated).

Washington. In the state of Washington, the first territorial law relating to the identification of livestock was enacted under the Code of 1881. State-wide registration of brands was first accomplished under the provisions of Chapter 156, Laws of 1935. Prior to that date, registration was accomplished by the auditors of the thirty-nine counties. Subsequent legislation amending Laws of 1935 are found in Chapter 75, Laws of 1937; Chapter 198, Laws of 1939; Chapter 161, Laws of 1945; Chapter 30, Laws of 1947; Chapter 98, Laws of 1949; and Chapter 160, Laws of 1951. The above acts or parts of acts were repealed by House Bill No. 246, 36th Regular Session, 1959. The livestock laws of the state have been codified in the Revised Code of Washington under Chapter 16. In addition to the statutes passed, the Director of the Department of Agriculture has issued various Executive Orders affecting livestock branding.

There is in existence a brand book of Thurston County containing brands and marks dating back to 1852, and also a brand book published by Whitman County in 1886, which includes Adams County and Lincoln County, among others. The brand book published in 1957 is priced at $5.00.

Brand applications have space for three choices of brands, and line drawings of the left and right side of cattle and horses. Earmarks may be indicated on an outline of ears. There is also a space to indicate dewlaps. The recording fee for one brand for cattle and horses, in a different location if desired, is $3.00. Here again, a brand is the personal property of the owner of record, and the transfer fee is $1.00. The brand renewal period is five years, commencing with September 1, 1960.

Production record brands for dairy cattle may be applied to any point between the hock and stifle of the right hind leg; any digit or combination of digits may be used. Production record brands for beef cattle may be applied high on either the right or left shoulder; any digit or combination of digits may be used (with the exception of digits 6, 7, 33, 60, 401, and 717) on the right shoulder, and 14, 25, and 77 on the left shoulder. Only the above numbers are recorded for evidence of ownership. The following brands are reserved by the state for federal and state departments: US (United States), ID (Interior Department), IC (inspected and condemned), B on left jaw (brucellosis), F on right jaw (feeder), M on left jaw (mastitis, Fig. 482), T on left jaw (tuberculosis), V on right jaw (vaccinated). Earmarks, dewlaps and wattles are considered range marks and are published only as a courtesy. Prior to the Laws of 1959, tattoos were recorded for poultry and fur-bearing animals, including all foxes, minks, and martens bred and reared in captivity or enclosures.

Publications for the State of Washington are: (1) Application for Recording of Livestock Brand, S. F. No. 4836-2-58-3M 52219; (2) House Bill No. 246, 1957; (3) Laws and Regulations

Relating to Livestock, State Printing Plant, Olympia, 1954; (4) Order No. 483, December 20, 1946; (5) Order No. 676, January 13, 1955; (6) Order No. 753, September 9, 1957; (7) General Instructions Relating to Livestock Branding Irons, February 18, 1954; and (8) General Instructions Relating to Livestock Branding Irons, July 9, 1958.

Wyoming. While the state of Wyoming was still a territory, the first law requiring the branding of livestock was enacted in 1879, Chapter 69, Sections One and Two, pertaining to the branding of trail herds only. The law pertaining to all livestock on Wyoming ranges was enacted in 1890, Chapter 39. This chapter is the basic foundation for a later brand recording law, Chapter 56, Wyoming Compiled Statutes, 1945.

The first brand book, entitled "Cattle Brands," and containing brands owned by the Wyoming Stock Growers' Association, was printed in 1882 by The J. M. W. Jones Stationery & Printing Co., Chicago. The second edition was published in 1884. Copies of the Wyoming Stock Growers' Association Brand Book for the years 1882–86 may be found in the office of the Wyoming State Historian. The Wyoming Brand Book published in 1956 was priced at $4.00. The First Supplement, containing new brands and transfers from July 1, 1956, to July 1, 1958, is priced at $2.00. Subsequent supplements were issued in 1960, 1962, and 1964. A new brand book was issued in 1966.

The Wyoming brand application form has one box for the drawing of the desired brand, another box with an outline drawing of outsized ears to indicate earmarks, and left and right outline drawings of cattle and horses. Also, a space is allotted for describing the locality where the stock is to range. The fee is $5.00 for one brand for one specie of livestock, or $10.00 for two or more species of livestock. Here again, brands are personal property and may only be transferred by a notarized bill of sale, at a transfer fee of $5.00. The brand renewal period is ten years, on years ending in the number five. The last renewal date was

1965. There are eleven state brand inspectors who work at licensed sales rings. In addition, there are approximately 140 county inspectors who inspect livestock in their respective counties. Brands are recorded to be used only in a specified county or counties and for specified location or locations on the animal. Cattle, horses, and sheep may be branded. For sheep, hot iron, paint, and tattoo brands are acceptable. Earmarks are used, in conjunction with brands, for personal herd identification.

The state of Wyoming publications are: (1) Application for Stock Brand, The Herald-Lusk, 2M–6–57; (2) Bill of Sale of Brand, Buffalo Bulletin, 5M–2–56; (3) Instructions to Brand Applicants (undated); (4) Branding Instructions (undated).

In the following table, states are listed in the order of the highest number of brands recorded by each state, using the number of brands on record as of March 1, 1959.

1.	Texas	230,000*	15.	Utah	12,130
2.	Montana	60,000	16.	Washington	12,000
3.	Nebraska	36,000	17.	Florida	9,913
4.	Colorado	33,771	18.	Oklahoma	8,866
5.	California	30,000	19.	Mississippi	5,073
6.	Louisiana	25,050	20.	Nevada	4,091
7.	Wyoming	25,000	21.	Alabama	3,236
8.	New Mexico	23,065	22.	Hawaii	1,639
9.	Kansas	23,000	23.	Georgia	181
10.	Idaho	21,095	24.	Arkansas	176
11.	South Dakota	20,500	25.	Alaska	40
12.	North Dakota	16,040	26.	North Carolina	14
13.	Oregon	13,000			
14.	Arizona	12,263		Total	626,143

* Record file maintained by the Texas and Southwestern Cattle Raisers' Association.

The states having county-wide registration of stock brands are listed below. By law, the county clerk, or the equivalent thereof, is charged with the registration of brands in his respective county. Among the states listed are three exceptions:

Georgia and North Carolina, which also have state-wide recording of brands, and Nevada, where the state recorder of brands registers all livestock except sheep, which are registered on a county-wide basis by the respective recorders of the counties.

In the state of Georgia the brand recorders are the ordinary of the county and the commissioner of agriculture. In the state of Illinois the recorder is the clerk of the county, and the recording fee is fifteen cents. The Illinois brand law states:

An Act in regard to marks and brands, approved March 29, 1872. How cattle etc., may be marked—Record 1. Be it enacted by the People of the State of Illinois, represented in the General Assembly: That every person in this state, who hath cattle, horses, hogs, sheep or goats, may have an ear mark and brand, and but one of each, which shall be different from the ear mark and brand of his neighbors; which ear mark and brand may be recorded by the county clerk of the county where such cattle, horses, hogs, sheep and goats shall be.

2. Book—Record—Fee—Examination of book. It shall be the duty of the county clerks, in the respective counties of this state, to keep a well bound book in which they shall record the brands of each individual who may apply to them for that purpose, for which they shall be entitled to demand and receive the sum of fifteen cents; and the book in which the same are recorded shall be open to the examination of every citizen of the county, at all reasonable office hours, free of charge.

3. If any dispute shall arise about any ear mark or brand, it shall be decided by reference to the book of marks and brands kept by the county clerk, but such book shall be prima facie evidence only.

4. Any person purchasing or acquiring horses, cattle, hogs, sheep or goats, when he brands or marks the same in his brand or mark, after the acquisition of the same, may do it in the presence of one or more of his neighbors, who are authorized to certify to the fact of the marking or branding being done, when done, and in what brand or mark the same were, previously, and in what brand or mark they were re-branded or re-marked. Such certificate shall not be deemed evidence or property in the animal branded, but only prima facie evidence of the facts therein certified to.

215

The only other brands used for official identification among Illinois cattle brands are the B and T brands, applied with a hot iron to the left jaw of brucellosis and tuberculosis infected animals.

In the state of Michigan the brand recorder is the clerk of the county, and the recording fee is twenty-five cents. Its brand law is:

Act 122, 1883, p. 114; imd. Eff. May 25. The people of the State of Michigan enact; 287.221. Ear mark or brand; recording dissimilarity.

Sec. 1: That every person who has cattle, horses, hogs, sheep, goats, or any other domestic animals, may adopt an ear mark or brand, which ear mark or brand may be recorded in the office of the county clerk of the county where such cattle, horses, hogs, sheep, goats or other domestic animals shall be; Provided, That the mark or brand so adopted and recorded shall be different from all other marks or brands, adopted and recorded in such county.

History: How. 2074a; —CL 1897, 5660; —CL 1915, 7350; —CL 1929, 5290. 287.222 Record Book of County Clerk: recording fee.

Sec. 2: It shall be the duty of the county clerks of the several counties of this state, to keep a book in which they shall record the mark and brand adopted by each person who may apply to them for that purpose, for which they shall be entitled to demand and receive twenty-five cents.

History: How. 2074b; —CL 1897, 5661; —CL 1915, 7351; —CL 1929, 5291.

Sec. 3: History: How. 2074c; —CL 1897, 5662; —CL 1915, 7352; —CL 1929, 5292; —Rep. 1931, p. 742, Act 328, Eff. Sept. 18. [This section has a penalty section. See Compilers 750.68.]

Act 309 of the Public Acts of 1939 provides a procedure for the registration and identification of dogs. The Michigan Department of Agriculture administers this law and permits an owner to designate a veterinarian who is provided with instructions for tattooing the dog, and the tattoo number is assigned to the applicant and is placed on record in the Department of Agriculture.

Pertinent publications of the state of Michigan are: (1) Application for Dog Registration, LDC–49; (2) Instructions to Owners Desiring to Have Dogs Tattooed in Accordance with Act 309, Public Acts of 1939, as Amended, LDC–213; (3) Assignment of Tattoo No. LDC–214; (4) Dog Identification Certificate Cover Letter, LDC–215; (5) Acknowledgment of Request (undated); (6) Instructions to Veterinarians (undated).

For the state of Minnesota the brand recorder is the register of deeds, and the brand law is:

> Minnesota Statutes 1949. Sec. 386–35. On the application of any person residing in his county, the register shall record a description of the marks or brands with which such person may be desirous of marking his horses, cattle, sheep, or hogs, but the same description shall not be recorded for more than one resident of the same county [R.L. s. 541] (898).*
>
> Sec. 620.43. Willful False Branding of Animals. Every person who shall willfully mark any of his horses, cattle, sheep, or hogs with the same mark or brand previously recorded by any other resident of the same county, and while such a mark is still used by such other resident, or shall willfully mark or brand horses, cattle, sheep, or hogs of any other person with his own brand or mark, or shall willfully destroy or alter any mark or brand upon any horses, cattle, sheep, or hogs of another, shall be guilty of a misdemeanor. [R.L. s. 5065] (10339).

*The source notes enclosed in brackets are references to Revised Laws 1905, followed by Mason's number in parentheses.

The publications of the State of Minnesota are: (1) Laws of the State of Minnesota, Relating to Duties and Powers of the Live Stock Sanitary Board and Local Boards of Health, Pertaining to Diseases of Animals and Poultry, October 1st, 1952.

In the state of Missouri the brand recorder is the clerk of the county court, and Chapter 268, Missouri Revised Statutes of 1949, is the brand law, but it actually predates 1929 and is inadequate to meet present needs. Every person must brand or mark his cattle over twelve months old and his sheep and hogs over six months old, with a brand or mark different from those used by his neighbor. No person can use more than one brand or mark for his stock. No minor living with his parents or guardian and no apprentice or servant can use any mark or brand other than that of his parents or guardian, or his master, respectively. A minor, apprentice, or servant may record a separate brand for stock received as a gift or devise from any person other than his guardian or master. If any person kills any hog, sheep, or head of cattle running at large, he must show within three days the head and ears of such hog, or the hide and ears of such sheep or cattle, to a magistrate or two respectable householders of the township, under the penalty of ten dollars. It is also illegal to adopt as an earmark for cattle, sheep, or hogs a mark for which the entire ear is either removed or so mutilated as to destroy it. The penalty for this offense is forfeiture of a hundred dollars. The sheriff of each county is ex officio the brand inspector, and may appoint assistant brand inspectors for his county.

For the state of Nevada the brand recorder is the recorder of the county, and under the provisions of the law, sheep brands are recorded by the recorder of the county in which the applicant resides. All cattle, horse, and hog brands are recorded by the State Board of Stock Commissioners. For details see state registration, state of Nevada, p. 200, above.

For the state of North Carolina brand recorders are the register of deeds, and the state recorder of marks and brands, and the recording fee is fifty cents. For details of the brand law see state registration, state of North Carolina, page 203, above.

In Texas the brand recorder is the clerk of the county. In the late 1830's the Republic of Texas began registering brands. The present practice of registration in counties began in the spring of 1848. Brand laws have been passed in rather piecemeal fashion, therefore it is extremely difficult to establish dates for each legislative act passed. In 1943 the Texas Legislature passed an act nullifying all brands which were on record as of that date in all Texas counties. The owners of such brands were given preferential rights to re-record their brands, but any brand not re-recorded within the two-year period specified became available for anyone's use. The purpose was to eliminate from the books any inactive brands, thus making them available for use by persons currently in the cattle business. Beginning in 1945, the Texas and Southwestern Cattle Raisers' Association accumulated a record of all brands which had been recorded in all Texas counties, and this file is kept up to date. It is the only complete file of recorded brands in existence. The record is maintained in card index files, and all brands are indexed two ways: according to brand, and according to the name of the brand owner. No attempt has been made to publish this record because of the very large number of brands and also because of the difficulty of keeping it current.

There has been in effect for many years a law requiring that reactors to the tuberculin test be identified with the letter T on the left jaw. This has to be a hot iron brand, not less than three inches high. H.B. No. 525, passed May 23, 1947, amends Article 1525d and Article 1525e, Title 17 of Vernon's Annotated Penal Code, being Acts 1937 and 1939, Forty-fifth and Forty-sixth Legislature, respectively. This act provides for the identification of animals reacting to the brucellosis agglutination test by branding of the letter B on the left jaw. Regulations of the Sanitary Livestock Commission require that the identification brand is to be three inches high and shall be firebranded in such a manner as to produce a permanent mark.

Cattle of beef breeds, between the ages of four and twelve months, must be individually identified with an ear tattoo showing the number of the month, the letter V and the last number of the year. A hot iron V brand not less than three inches high may be substituted for the tattoo on the right jaw. The brand is applied in the correct position, designating the year vaccinated or such other identification as may be authorized by the Live-

219

stock Sanitary Commission. For April 1959, the position of this brand is three clockwise. The V is placed in four different positions, representing the year in which the animal is vaccinated.

In the state of Wisconsin the brand recorder is the town clerk. The state brand law is contained in Chapter 95, Wisconsin Statutes 1957, Animal Health. Section 95.11 of Wisconsin Statutes 1957 was originally enacted in 1849, during the first legislative session of the state of Wisconsin. There has been no change in the law since that time. Some of the requirements are:

> Every Town Clerk shall, on the application of any person residing in his town, record a description of the marks or brands with which such person may be desirous of marking his horses, cattle, sheep, or hogs; but the same description shall not be recorded or used by more than one resident of the same town. If any person shall mark any of his horses, cattle, sheep, or hogs with the same mark or brand previously recorded by any resident of the same town and while the same mark or brand shall be used by such resident, he shall forfeit for every such offence $5.00; if any person shall willfully mark or brand any of the horses, cattle, sheep, or hogs of any other person with his own mark or brand he shall forfeit for every such offense $10.00; and if any person shall willfully destroy or alter any mark or brand upon any of the horses, cattle, sheep, or hogs of another he shall forfeit $10.00 and pay to the party injured double damages.

All animals between the age of four months and eight months, having been vaccinated by an approved veterinarian, are identified by a tattoo on the inner surface of the right ear, using symbols as prescribed by the department of agriculture. The veterinarian may also, with the herd owner's permission, cut a half-inch notch into the lower edge of the calf's left ear as a more readily visible mark indicating calfhood vaccination. When properly vaccinated, tattooed, and reported to the department, the calf becomes an official "Vaccinate."

All cattle, yarded for whatever purpose at the premises of a livestock market, while there are cattle located at such premises which have been moved there pursuant to certain exceptions from brucellosis tests, are considered to be slaughter cattle. Such cattle have to be removed directly to a slaughtering establishment for immediate slaughter. Prior to removal, such cattle, except calves under four months of age, must be branded with the letter "S," in a manner prescribed by the department of agriculture (Fig. 478).

The publication of Wisconsin is Chapter 95, Wisconsin Statutes 1957, Animal Health. Wisconsin State Department of Agriculture, State Capitol, Madison, Wisconsin.

Most Eastern states have no legislation in regard to brands for the identification of ownership of livestock. They do, however, have disease control legislation. The state of Connecticut has no branding laws except for brands applied to tuberculosis and brucellosis reactors. Animals are identified by ear tags, tattoos, or registrations. The majority of animals are milk producers, kept on separate farms, and are cared for by individual owners. There are no laws or regulations in the state of Delaware relative to the use of brands other than the official B and T brands used on reactors. Brands as a means of identification are not used in this state. Neither are they used in the states of Indiana, Iowa, Kentucky, Maine, Maryland, Massachusetts, New Hampshire, New Jersey, or New York.

Checking the statutes of the state of Ohio even as far back as 1898 uncovered no reference indicating that branding laws as such were utilized at any time, up to and including the present. Since there are no branding laws in this state, the only means of identifying livestock is that provided in accordance with the disease control laws which have regulations indicating where tags, tattoos, and, in the case of purebreds, registration numbers are acceptable.

Pennsylvania does not have a branding law, but regulations governing branding reactor animals in the disease program are as follows: When reactors are disclosed as the result of a tuberculin test, it shall be the duty of the veterinarian applying the test to quarantine, tag, and brand with a hot iron the letter "T" on the left jaw of the reactor animals. When reactors are disclosed as a result of a Johnin test, it shall be the duty of the veterinarian applying the test to quarantine, tag, and brand with a hot iron the letter "T" on the left jaw of the reactor animals. When reactors are disclosed as a result of a brucellosis test, it shall be the duty of the appraiser to quarantine, tag, and brand with a hot iron the letter "B" on the left jaw of the reactor animals.

Other states having no branding laws are Rhode Island, South Carolina, Tennessee, Vermont, Virginia, and West Virginia, although most of these states do have the usual disease regulations.

NINE

Foreign Brands

Branding practices in the western provinces of Canada are very similar to such practices in the western states of the United States. Canadian systems of registration are, for all practical purposes, the same as those used in the United States. In marked contrast, however, is the precision and unity of the branding laws of the various provinces. These laws and the administration of them by a recorder of brands are uniform for all provinces. Geographical differences are responsible for minor deviations from a standard system of registration, but the fact that the provinces previously were united as a territory before they were established as provinces of the Dominion encouraged uniform regulations.

Brand acts and stock inspection acts similar to United States laws were first enacted in the 1860's. Canadian brand laws are quite clear and comprehensive and pertain strictly to the subject matter. They are infrequently revised or amended, but apparently fill all requirements very satisfactorily. Terminology differs somewhat from American usage. Generally, the structure of the law is built on a logical progression and all matters are well defined and clearly stated.

Brand books were issued in territorial days, as were supplements. Current brand books are published either annually or at irregular intervals of from four to five years. Supplements are issued between years of publication. The prices of current brand books range from $1.00 to $5.00.

In brand recording the procedure employed in Canada is almost identical to procedures used in the United States, including the progressive steps from application to renewal and transfer. It can be said that Canadian procedures are more clearly defined, more effective, and less confusing than their American counterparts. The legislation providing such procedure obviously was more concerned with improvement of the entire system than with specific local aspects, as was the case with many American legislative acts.

In Canada, the provincial brand recorder is normally the livestock commissioner, who is in charge of the livestock branch of the Department of Agriculture. All departments of agriculture are headed by a minister who exercises general supervision over the recorder of brands. The recorder of brands carries out the duties as specified by law, namely, the administration of the branding registration system.

Canadian brand application forms are small in size and have no outline drawings of cattle and horses for the indication of brands in different locations on the animal. They also lack outline drawings of ears, and the application forms for cattle and horses are separate documents. The fee for allotment of a brand is from $1.00 to $3.00. Canadian terminology prefers allotment to recordation.

Upon recordation of the application, a certificate of allotment is issued. This certificate is always considered to be prima facie evidence of ownership of the brand. Brands are renewed on the thirty-first day of December in the third or fourth year subsequent to the year in which the brand was first recorded (allotted). Upon failure to pay the renewal fee, the brand is cancelled, but it may be re-recorded (re-allotted) upon payment of the renewal fee within a three-month period, the thirty-first day of March being the last day of the grace period. If the brand owner still fails to pay the required fee, he forfeits his right to the brand. The forfeited brand can not be re-recorded (re-allotted) to any person for four or five years from the day of cancellation or the day of forfeiture. The length of the renewal period and the

224

effective date for the non-recording period vary slightly in different provinces. The fee for renewal is $1.00 or $2.00, depending upon the province.

Full time inspectors and part-time deputy inspectors are employed by the Department of Agriculture. Under provisions of the law, the Royal Canadian Mounted Police carry out a large share of brand inspection at public stockyards, abattoirs, and places where stock is held prior to shipment out of the province.

Brands consisting of a single letter or numeral are not acceptable in any province having a brand law. All recorders insist on clear brands and place many restrictions on brand design. The locations for brands are usually limited to six: for cattle, right or left shoulder, right or left ribs, and right or left hips; for horses, right or left jaw, right or left shoulder, and right or left hip. No brand is allotted to an Indian living on a reservation in Alberta or Saskatchewan. Cattle and horse brands are recorded separately on applications and published in separate sections of the brand book.

Disease control brands of the Canadian Department of Agriculture are recognized by the provinces whether or not they are recorded. They are reserved by the province. Production record brands may be applied to specified locations on livestock, but must consist of an Arabic numeral from 0 to 9, inclusive, and may be used only in conjunction with a recorded brand. Production record brands cannot be recorded. A vent may be a vent brand recorded prior to March 1, 1889, or a second brand below the recorded brand. The second brand may be identical to the recorded brand, or may consist of a portion of the design of the recorded brand, or of a letter or numeral; but in all cases it must be applied immediately below the recorded brand in a horizontal, or lazy, position. Upon transfer of livestock, the vent brand must be applied unless the brand has also been transferred.

The branding of livestock is optional, but when branding is used, the brand must first be recorded. Also, it is illegal to use a brand that has not been renewed. Earmarks are not recordable except in Alberta, where earmarks are considered brands when applied to sheep. Dewlaps and wattles are not recordable, but tattoos are considered brands when applied to the web of either wing of poultry or to the ears of fur-bearing animals. It is illegal to destroy, mutilate, or remove the web of either wing of poultry in Alberta.

Like their United States counterparts, Canadian recorders of brands issue instructions for designs, extracts from the brand law, and other literature pertaining to brands and branding.

Several federal departments of Canada use brands. The departments are headed by ministers, and are divided into branches or services, each under a director. Branches and services are further sub-divided into divisions, each headed by a chief.

The Department of Justice, established in 1868 by "An Act respecting the Department of Justice" (S.C., 1867–68, Chapter 39 [31 Vic. Chap. 39] now the Department of Justice Act, R.S.C., 1952, Chapter 71), was constituted to superintend the administration of justice whenever it was not within the jurisdiction of the provinces, and to supervise the prison system of the Dominion. Duties imposed on the Minister of Justice and the attorney general of Canada are by numerous statutes, including the Royal Canadian Mounted Police Act (R.S.C., 1952, Chapter 241, as amended). The minister of justice is the minister responsible for the Royal Canadian Mounted Police.

This body was originally established in 1873 as the North West Mounted Police by "An Act respecting the Administration of Justice," and for the establishment of a police force in the Northwest Territories (S.C. 1873, Chapter 35 [36 Vic. Chap. 35], now the Royal Canadian Mounted Police Act, R.S.C., 1952, Chapter 241, as amended) to provide police protection in the unsettled portions of the northwest. In 1904 the title "Royal" was given to the Force. In 1920 the Dominion Police was amalgamated with this force and the name was changed to "Royal Canadian Mounted Police." The headquarters was moved from Regina to Ottawa, and the Force may now be called upon to perform duties in any portion of the Dominion. In 1928 the Royal Canadian Mounted Police absorbed the Saskatchewan Provincial Police, and in 1932 the Provincial Police Forces of Alberta, Manitoba, New Brunswick, Nova Scotia, and Prince Edward Island were absorbed in like manner.

During 1932 the Force also assumed administration of the Preventive Service Branch of the Department of National Revenue. On August 1, 1950, the duties of the Newfoundland Rangers and certain members of the Newfoundland Constabulary were taken over by the Royal Canadian Mounted Police, and on August 15, 1950, the British Columbia Provincial Police were similarly absorbed. These arrangements were made by agreement between the respective provincial governments and the federal government. Royal Canadian Mounted Police now enforce some fifty-five federal statutes throughout Canada. The Force has about 25 police service dogs, 268 sleigh dogs, 1,344 cars and trucks, 58 motorcycles, 13 aircraft, and 76 ships and boats. The strength, including civilian clerks and reserves, is about 7,233, and the term of engagement is five years. The Force operates through seventeen divisions, twelve land police divisions, and five special divisions. Divisions are divided into sub-divisions and detachments.

Although horses are no longer used in actual police work, every Royal Canadian Mounted Police recruit learns how to ride in order to develop courage, stamina, poise, confidence, and co-ordination. There are mounted sections stationed at Regina and Ottawa, in addition to the troop performing the noted Musical Ride. The Musical Ride, usually performed by a full troop of thirty-two men and horses, is made up of a variety of intricate maneuvers executed at the trot and canter to music of an appropriate tempo. It originated in Canada in the 1880's. The Musical Ride participated as part of the Canadian Tattoo during the Seattle World's Fair, September 10 to 16, 1962, with Inspector J. C. Downie as officer-in-charge. The ride was presented throughout Canada that year, with other performances presented in Portland, Oregon, and San Francisco, Fresno, and Pomona, California.

The participating police officers for the Musical Ride are hand-picked from the Force. There is an annual turnover, however, since police work is still the prime function of the Mounties. The horses of the Musical Ride are also handpicked. Mounts of the Force have ranged through all the solid colors, but some years ago black was prescribed as official. The public selects the names of the horses, submitting them to Royal Canadian Mounted Police headquarters. Each year, all colts born during that year are given names starting with the same letter.

The brand "MP Connected" was allotted to the Northwest Mounted Police in 1887 and is applied on the left shoulder. Horses of the Musical Ride also receive a temporary brush brand prior to performances. It consists of a solid maple leaf, about 9 inches along the stem, and is placed on the left and right rump. The leaf points upward, its axis on a diagonal to the back-bone. This brand is achieved by placing a stencil in the described location and brushing the hair against the growth with a damp brush. The effect is that of a glowing, luminous maple leaf, dis-tinctively offset from the black coat of the mount. During night performances the brush brand becomes even more distinct un-der the spotlights.

The Royal Canadian Mounted Police now have about two hundred horses, which are trained at the "Depot" Division, Re-gina, Saskatchewan, under the command of a superintendent. Rules and regulations of the Force require that a register num-ber be assigned each horse, and the registration number must be branded on the near forefoot. The regulations also require horses to be branded on the near shoulder with the brand MP (Fig. 878). This brand is recorded in Alberta and Saskatchewan to be applied to the left shoulder, and in British Columbia to the right shoulder. The vent brand in Alberta is an inverted MP (Fig. 879), and in British Columbia it is Brand C (Fig. 880), both applied below the original brand.

228

The Department of Citizenship and Immigration was established in December of 1949 by the "Department of Citizenship and Immigration Act (S.C., 1949, Second Session, Chapter 16 [13 George VI, Chapter 16]—now R.S.C. 1952, Chapter 67). The act came into force January 18, 1950, affecting certain branches of the former Department of Mines and Resources and the Department of the Secretary of State of Canada. The functions of this department include all matters over which the Parliament of Canada has jurisdiction, relating to naturalization, citizenship, Indian affairs, immigration, and colonization which are not assigned by law to any other department. There are four operational branches, Canadian Citizenship, Canadian Citizenship Registration, Immigration, and Indian Affairs; and five staff divisions, Editorial and Information, Inspection, Legal, Personal, and Technical Services.

The Indian Affairs Branch administers the Indian Act (R.S.C., 1952, Chapter 149, as amended by 1952–1953, Chapter 41, and 1956, Chapter 40). It consists of six divisions: Administration, Education, Engineering and Construction, Indian Agencies, Reserves and Trusts, and Welfare.

With an Indian population of over 180,000 in 1960, the Canadian government has introduced programs to speed the establishment of Canadian Indians within the social and economic life of the country. Indians engaged in agriculture are assisted and encouraged by supervision and practical training, and are provided, where necessary, with breeding stock, seed grain, and farm machinery. Emphasis is now placed on the introduction of cattle-raising and other mixed farm operations. ID is the registered brand used to designate livestock placed on Indian reserves by the federal government. The ID brand (Fig. 896) is recorded for cattle and horses, in any location on the animal, in Alberta and Saskatchewan. The recorded vent brand in Alberta is a bar through the ID (Fig. 897). Brand IND, applied to the left hip of cattle, is recorded for the Indian Affairs Branch in British Columbia (Fig. 898). For many years, on the Canadian prairies, Indians with their own herds used the brand ID followed by a number. These numbers were not registered under the Provincial Acts but were for purposes of local identification only. It has been the practice in recent years to encourage the Indians to register their own herds with their own individual brands, and a number of them have done so.

The education of Canadian Indians is the responsibility of the federal government, which has established four types of schools: day schools established on reserves for children who can attend from their homes; residential (boarding) schools operated under the auspices of various religious denominations for children from broken homes, orphans, or those unable to attend day schools; seasonal schools at places where migratory families gather during the year; and hospital schools for children confined to hospitals. Currently there are 470 schools of all types in operation.

The following Indian Residential schools have recorded brands: (1) St. Cyprian Indian Residential School, Brocket, Alberta. The Arrow Seven Bar brand is applied to the right hip of cattle (Fig. 901). (2) St. Paul's Residential School, Blood Reserve, Cardston, Alberta. The illustrated brand is applied to the left ribs of cattle (Fig. 902). (3) St. Anthony's Indian Residential School, Onion Lake, Saskatchewan. Brand IS Bar is applied to right hip of cattle (Fig. 910). (4) St. Michael's Indian Residential School, Duck Lake, Saskatchewan. Brand SM Bar is applied to the right hip of cattle (Fig. 911). (5) St. Philips' Indian Residential School, St. Philips, Saskatchewan. Brand Reverse SP is applied to the left hip of cattle (Fig. 912). (6) Kamloops Indian Residential School, Kamloops, British Columbia. Brand I Bar D is applied to the right hip of cattle and right hip of horses (Fig. 903). (7) Kootenay Indian Residential School, Cranbrook, British Columbia. Brand OM is applied to the right hip of cattle and left shoulder of horses (Fig. 904); and (8) Lejac Indian Residential School, Lejac, British Columbia. Brand OMI is applied to the left hip of cattle (Fig. 905).

Canadian federal publications are: Report of Indian Affairs

Branch for the Fiscal Year Ended March 31, 1959. 79193–9–1, The Queen's Printer and Controller of Stationery, Ottawa, 1960; The Canadian Indian, a Reference Paper, Department of Citizenship and Immigration, Indian Affairs Branch, Ottawa, Canada, 1959; and Regulations with Respect to Teaching, Education, Inspection, and Discipline for Indian Residential Schools, Made and Established by the Superintendent General of Indian Affairs Pursuant to Paragraph (a) of Section 114 of the Indian Act (undated), stencil 519.

The Department of Resources and Development was constituted in January 1950 (13 George VI, Chapter 18), and was reconstituted under the present name, Department of Northern Affairs and Natural Resources, in December of 1953 by the Department of Northern Affairs and Natural Resources Act (S.C., 1953–54, Chapter 4 [2 Elizabeth, Chapter 4]), in order to give greater emphasis to its function of developing the north and administering Eskimo affairs. It consists of certain branches of the former Department of Mines and Resources. The functions assigned to the minister extend, among other matters, to affairs relative to national parks.

The department is divided into five branches: Administration, National Parks, Water Resources, Northern Administration and Lands, and Canadian Government Travel Bureau.

The National Parks branch administers the national parks of Canada, the national historic parks and sites, federal interests in the conservation, protection, and management of wildlife, and the natural museum of Canada. It also administers the National Parks Act (R.S.C., 1952, Chapter 189, as amended) and the Migratory Birds Convention Act (R.S.C., 1952, Chapter 179). Horses belonging to the National Parks branch at the Banff National Park, Banff, Alberta, are branded with a Sheep's Head on the left shoulder (Fig. 900).

The Department of Mines and Technical Surveys was created by the Department of Mines and Technical Surveys Act (S.C., 1949, Second Session, Chapter 17, now R.S.C., 1952, Chapter

73), and consists of certain branches of the former department of Mines and Resources. Its primary functions are to provide technological assistance in the development of Canada's mineral resources through studies, investigations, and research in the fields of geology, mineral dressing, and metallurgy, and to carry out geodetic, topographical, and other surveys of use in development of Canada's natural resources. The department consists of five branches, Dominion Observatories, Geographical Branch, Geological Survey of Canada, Mines Branch, and the Surveys and Mapping Branch. It administers, among others, the Canada Lands Surveys Act (R.S.C., 1952, Chapter 26). Horses owned by this department are branded on the left shoulder with a Bar Broad Arrow (Fig. 899). This brand is recorded in Alberta and British Columbia.

The Department of Agriculture (originally the Bureau of Agriculture established by an Act of the Legislature of the Province of Canada in 1852) was created by "An Act for the Organization of the Department of Agriculture" (S.C., 1867–68, Chapter 53 [31 Vic. Chapter 53], now the Department of Agriculture Act, R.S.C., 1952, Chapter 66). The present organization of the department is designed to implement the principle of bringing activities of a similar character and purpose together under one administrative head. There are eight components: Agricultural Prices Support Board, Departmental Administration, Experimental Farms Service, Information Service, Marketing Service, Production Service, Rehabilitation Service, and Science Service.

The Experimental Farms Service has branch farms, laboratories, and illustration stations in important agricultural regions throughout Canada, and provides a broad program of experimental and research work in agricultural problems. Branch farms may specialize in the type of agriculture practiced in their districts and may undertake experimental projects in areas where the results will have direct application. In addition to the field installations, there are eight divisions in the service: Animal

Husbandry, Forage Crops, Horticulture, Agriculture, Soils and Agricultural Engineering, Illustration Stations, Poultry Husbandry, and Tobacco. These divisions, in addition to conducting research at Ottawa, co-ordinate the work in their respective fields which is conducted on various branch farms throughout the country.

Various brands are used at the experimental stations. At the Dominion Range Experimental Station at Manyberries, Alberta, the cattle are branded with the Pigpen brand on the left hip (Fig. 884). The brand used at the Experimental Station at Kamloops, British Columbia, is the Bar Lazy E F, applied to the left hip of cattle and the left hip of horses (Fig. 885). And the Experimental Farm at Lethbridge, Alberta, uses the brand D Bar on the right shoulder of horses (Fig. 886).

The Production Service administers legislation and policies relative to agricultural production. It is composed of four divisions, Health of Animals and Animal Pathology, Livestock and Poultry Production, Plant Products, and Plant Protection.

Bulls owned by the Department of Agriculture and leased to districts in the Province of Alberta, British Columbia, and Manitoba, are branded C A Bar on the right hip. (Fig. 887). This brand is recorded in British Columbia. Brand D is recorded in the name of the Production Service in Saskatchewan and is applied to the left neck of cattle (Fig. 883).

The Health of Animals Division administers legislation designed to prevent the introduction and spread of contagious animal diseases and for the health and inspection of meat products entering into inter-provincial or export trade. This division also administers the Animals Contagious Disease Act.

By provincial statute in Alberta, brand B on the right jaw of cattle (Fig. 881), and brand T on the left jaw of cattle are reserved for the use of the federal government (Fig. 882). The Health of Animals Division uses a tamperproof clinch tag to identify reactor animals ordered slaughtered as a disease control measure. This tag is used in connection with the depart-

233

ment's tuberculosis, brucellosis, and Johne's disease eradication programs. The tag is dyed red, its high visibility assisting in the identification of reactors.

The Livestock and Poultry Division administers performance testing programs and breeding policies in various classes of livestock, and also administers legislation dealing with the pedigree registration of purebred animals, such as the Live Stock Pedigree Act (S.C., 1949, Second Session, Chapter 28, as amended by R.S.C., 1952, Chapter 168). Supervision of race track betting is also the responsibility of this division. Bulls bought by this division are branded CDA (Fig. 888), in British Columbia; however, the brand is not recorded. Brand D (Fig. 883), used with consecutive numbers, is recorded in Alberta and applied to the left neck of cattle.

The Canadian National Live Stock Records is an affiliation of livestock associations in a national system of registration of purebreds. The affiliation is under the general supervision of the minister of the Department of Agriculture and is headed by a director. The governing body is known as the Canadian National Live Stock Record Board and the administrative committee, under a chairman, is known as the Canadian National Live Stock Record Committee. Incorporation of purebred livestock record associations is governed by the Live Stock Pedigree Act. The organization is primarily concerned with the registration of purebred livestock and the usual method of identifying utility breeds of livestock by tattooing in either or both ears is followed. A breeder is assigned a combination of code letters to be used in tattooing each animal of a particular breed owned by him at birth. In addition to the code letters, a breeder is also required to tattoo a specific letter in the ear designating the year of birth, as well as a number to identify the different animals born as his property in any particular year.

The Rehabilitation Service administers rehabilitation acts through the Maritime Marshlands Rehabilitation Administration, the Prairie Farm Assistance Administration, and the Prairie Farm Rehabilitation Administration.

The Prairie Farm Rehabilitation Administration administers the Prairie Farm Rehabilitation Act (R.S.C., 1952, Chapter 214), which provides for reclamation of drought and soil-drifting areas in the provinces of Manitoba, Saskatchewan, and Alberta. The policies vary widely in their nature and scope, but each has as its objective the better utilization of land in order to minimize problems of drought or the conservation of water for farm use. Community pastures are established in municipalities and operated by a community pasture manager appointed by P.F.R.A. and assisted by an advisory committee of the Community Pasture Grazing Association.

Any livestock not bearing the recorded brand of the pasture patron when it is placed in a community pasture is branded and eartagged for identification purposes by the government of Canada at the community pasture branding chute. The pasture manager performs branding, with the assistance of the pasture patron.

The P.F.R.A. brands cattle in the community pastures with four individual brands, C, D, CD, and 5. The CD is used on the shoulder and the 5 on the flank, as a rule. Only one brand is generally used, unless there is danger of conflict when two community pastures are located close together; then the combination adding the 5 brand is used. Eartags are used, as a rule, on swine and sheep. The illustrated brands are recorded in Saskatchewan and all may be applied to any location on cattle (Figs. 889, 890, 891, 892, 893, 894, and 895).

Publications are: (1) Procedure for the Establishment of Community Pastures and Rules and Regulations for the Operation Thereof, Cat. No. A22-1658, Edmond Cloutier, C.M.G., O.A., D.S.P., Queen's Printer and Controller of Stationery, Ottawa, 1958. (2) Canada Agricultural Products Standards Act. (R.S.C. 1955, Chapter 27; 3-4 Elizabeth II), Edmond Cloutier,

C.M.G., O.A., D.S.P., Queen's Printer and Controller of Stationery, Ottawa, 1955. (3) Live Stock Pedigree Act, R.S., 1952, Chapter 168. Edmond Cloutier, C.M.G., O.A., D.S.P., Queen's Printer and Controller of Stationery, Ottawa, 1952. (4) Statutory Orders and Regulations SOR/58–295, Beef and Veal Carcass Grading Regulations, Edmond Cloutier, C.M.G., O.A., D.S.P., Queen's Printer and Controller of Stationery, Ottawa, 1958. (5) Statutory Orders and Regulations SOR/58–305, Lamb and Mutton Carcass Grading Regulations, Edmond Cloutier, C.M.G., O.A., D.S.P., Queen's Printer and Controller of Stationery, Ottawa, 1958. (6) Statutory Orders and Regulations SOR/58–358, Hog Carcass Grading Regulations, Edmond Cloutier, C.M.G., O.A., D.S.P., Queen's Printer and Controller of Stationery, Ottawa, 1958. (7) Statutory Orders and Regulations SOR/59–323, Hog Carcass Grading Regulations, amended, The Queen's Printer and Controller of Stationery, Ottawa, 1959.

Provincial brands are applied to animals belonging to different agencies of the various provincial governments. The province of Alberta, in addition to the provincial brands listed below, has approximately fifty-three brands recorded for municipal districts in the province. The Roundtop A brand is recorded in the name of the Department of the Attorney General, and is applied to the right hip of cattle (Fig. 906). This brand is also recorded in the Department of Agriculture for the Domestic Animals Act, Part 2, and is applied to the left shoulder of cattle and of horses. Vent brand D is applied immediately below the original brand (Fig. 907). In addition, the Roundtop A brand is recorded for the Domestic Animals Act, Part 3, but is applied to the left hip of cattle and of horses. Again, the vent brand D is applied immediately below the original brand.

For the University of Alberta, the illustrated brand is recorded for the Department of Animal Husbandry. It is applied to the left hip of cattle, with consecutive numbers below (Fig. 908). For the Provincial Auxiliary Mental Hospital, the illustrated brand is applied to the right ribs of cattle (Fig. 909). The Department of Agriculture of British Columbia uses the Arrow brand, applied to the left hip of cattle (Fig. 916). Cattle belonging to the University of British Columbia at Vancouver are branded on the left hip with the illustrated brand (Fig. 915). In the province of Manitoba no provincial brand is used, but in the province of Saskatchewan, cattle of the Local Improvement Branch of the Department of Municipal Affairs are branded with the LID brand on the rump (Fig. 913), and cattle of the Department of Social Welfare and Rehabilitation at the Willow Bunch Ranch are branded with the brand illustrated in Fig. 914.

Below are listed the provinces having provincial branding laws and provincial recorders of brands. There are five provinces having such systems of livestock registration. They are: Alberta, British Columbia, Manitoba, Ontario, and Saskatchewan. In addition, Quebec has been included for information purposes.

Province of Alberta (North West Territories). The North West Territories roughly approximate Alberta and Saskatchewan today. The first brand ordinance passed by the North West Territories government was termed "An Ordinance Respecting the Marking of Stock," in the year 1878. Prior to that time, some registration was carried out under the general direction of the North West Mounted Police at Fort McLeod, which is now Alberta. Three different brand commissioners were appointed in different parts of the territory; however, the recording was not satisfactory because of the number of duplicate brands issued. The first brand recorded under the new ordinance was filed March 16, 1880, in the name of Samuel B. Steele and Percy R. Neale of Fort McLeod. The brand recorder was H. Hinder. This brand was a 71, and was described as required to be applied to the near ribs of each of the owners' cattle. Some time later the registration of brands was transferred from Fort McLeod to Regina. The record was maintained at

Regina until 1906, when it was moved to Medicine Hat, which is now in Alberta. This move was occasioned by the establishment of the province of Alberta and the province of Saskatchewan in 1909. Brand recording was maintained at Medicine Hat until 1922, at which time it was transferred to Edmonton, capital of Alberta. The current law is The Brand Act (Chapter 89, R.S.A. 1951 and Chapter 321, R.S.A. 1955, the latter being amended by Chapter 82, R.S.A. 1959, assented to April 7, 1959. Chapter 30, R.S.A. 1955 was also amended by Chapter 6, R.S.A. 1959, assented to April 7, 1959). Stock inspection is regulated under the provisions of the Stock Inspection Act, Chapter 86, R.S.A. 1951 and Chapter 321, R.S.A. 1955, the latter being amended by Chapter 82, R.S.A. 1959, assented to April 7, 1959.

The first brand book on record to have been published as revised and corrected to January 1, 1903, is the sixth edition of the North West Brand Book. There are copies of two earlier editions in private hands. Supplements to the North West Brand Book were published in 1904, 1905, and 1906. The next edition was a joint Alberta and Saskatchewan Brand Book published in 1907. Following this joint edition, brand books were published as Alberta Brand Books at irregular intervals. The issue published in 1958 is priced at $5.00.

The brand application form blank is small. In addition to the applicant's name and address, and the range or farm where the brand is to be used, there is a space for indicating the location of the brand and also space for six choices of brands. Applications for horse and cattle brands are separate, but identical in text. The brand certificate is prima facie evidence of ownership of the brand.

A brand may be transferred by a notarized memorandum of transfer to the recorder, who makes the necessary changes in the record. The renewal period is four years, ending on the thirty-first day of December of the fourth year after the recordation of the brand. If non-payment of the renewal fee is not effected by the thirty-first day of March of the following year, the owner forfeits his right to ownership of the brand. Such a forfeited brand cannot be re-recorded for a period of four years from the day of forfeiture. This entire period, then, is a total of four years and three months from the date of cancellation (thirty-first day of December).

Inspectors are employed by the Department of Agriculture. Every member of the Royal Canadian Mounted Police is also, ex officio, an inspector. Branding is optional, but the recordation of brands is compulsory. Brands are restricted to six locations for cattle, right and left shoulder, right and left ribs, and right and left hips; for horses, right and left jaw, right and left shoulder, and right and left thigh. There are twelve other restrictions enumerated and compounded by the recorder, limiting the design of brands. No brand is allotted to an Indian living on a reservation without the approval of the regional supervisor of the Indian Agency for the province of Alberta.

A vent may be a vent brand recorded prior to March 1, 1898, or a second brand in the form of a letter or numeral in a horizontal or lazy position immediately below the location of the recorded brand. At the time of transfer of livestock branded with a recorded brand, the vent brand must be applied unless the recorded brand is also transferred. An owner of a recorded brand may apply an age brand consisting of one Arabic numeral, from 0 to 9, inclusive, on the shoulder or thigh and on the same side of a horse or cattle as the recorded brand is applied.

The cattle brand B on the right jaw and cattle brand T on the left jaw are reserved exclusively for the identification of reactors to brucellosis and tuberculosis respectively. These brands are applied under the provisions of the Animal Contagious Disease Act. Earmarks are considered brands when applied to the ears of sheep, and tattoos applied to the web of either wing of poultry or to either ear of fur-bearing animals constitute a brand. It is illegal to remove, mutilate, or destroy the web of a wing of any poultry.

The schedule of fees for poultry brands is:

On application for allotment of a brand	$1.00
On application for renewal of a brand	.50
On application for re-allotment of a brand	1.00
On application for change in the record of a brand	1.00
On every transfer of a recorded brand	1.00
For every search of a brand record	.25
For every certified extract from the brand record	1.00

For all other brands:

On application for allotment of a brand	$2.00
On application for renewal of a brand	1.00
On application for re-allotment of a brand	2.00
On application for change in the record of a brand	2.00
On every transfer of a recorded brand	2.00
For every search of a brand record	.25
For every certified extract from the brand record	1.00

Publications are as follows: (1) Application for Horse Brand, A.R. 8–2; (2) Application for Cattle Brand, A.R. 8–4; (3) Memorandum of Transfer of Brands (undated); (4) Information Regarding Brand Registration in the Province of Alberta (undated); (5) The Brand Act, Chapter 30, A. Shnitka, Edmonton, Queen's Printer for Alberta, 1957; (6) Chapter 9, 1956, A. Shnitka, Edmonton, Queen's Printer for Alberta, 1956; (7) Chapter 6, 1959, L.S. Wall, Edmonton, Queen's Printer for Alberta, 1959; (8) The Stock Inspection Act, Chapter 321 (undated), and (9) Chapter 82, 1959, L.S. Wall, Edmonton, Queen's Printer for Alberta, 1959.

Province of British Columbia. Concerning the brand law for the province of British Columbia, the first record available is an application for the draft of an act to regulate branding and marking. This application is dated April 8, 1868. The first registration of brands apparently was kept in 1860 by the local magistrate who acted ex officio as general superintendent of brands; or by some other authority in one of the various sub-divisions of each district which included government agents.

In 1931 the Stock-brands Act was revised, a central registry was established in Victoria, and all previous records were turned in to the office of the recorder of brands. Previously, brands had been registered only on the local level instead of on a province-wide basis. The act was amended in 1950.

The brand book published in 1956 had supplements issued in 1957, 1958, and 1959. The price of the brand book, including supplements, is $2.00. The next British Columbia Horse and Cattle Brand Book was published in 1960. It is noteworthy that in the brand book Indians are identified by the letter I in parentheses after their names, e.g., LOUIE, Chief James (I). The brand book also incorporates a system whereby the expiration date of the brand is indicated after the location of the brand by a series of dashes, e.g., L.H.C.,–. One dash in the 1956 brand book indicates that the brand expires in 1957; two dashes, 1958; three dashes, 1959; and four dashes, 1960. In the 1957 Supplement No. 1, one dash indicates that the brand expires in 1961; two dashes, 1958; three dashes, 1959; four dashes, 1960. The same system is used for Supplement No. 2, issued in 1958, and Supplement No. 3, issued in 1959. In the last supplement, three dashes indicate that the brand expires in 1963, and four dashes, in 1964.

It is noteworthy that in British Columbia the renewal falls due four years after the first recordation of the brand, and does not fall due upon a fixed date, regardless of the year of recordation, as it does in the United States.

Brand application form blanks have spaces for five choices for the location of the brand. Location of range has to be indicated. Horse and cattle brand applications are separate, but identical in text. When a brand is sold, the owner must deliver to the transferee a declaration and his brand certificate; the transferee then applies to the recorder with the declaration and brand certificate and fee. Transfer of single-character brands is now limited to a direct descendant only. The renewal period is four years from the thirty-first day of December of the year the brand was recorded.

Three full time brand inspectors and twenty-three deputy brand inspectors are employed by the Department of Agriculture. Detachments of the Royal Canadian Mounted Police carry out brand inspection at seventy shipping points and otherwise enforce the provisions of the Stock-brands Act. Branding is optional, but brands must be recorded. Present policy does not permit issuance of single-character brands, arbitrary signs, or letters J, L, and P, or numerals 1, 7, and 8. In an amendment to the Stock-brands Act in 1950, the provision requiring the use of a single stamp iron for branding of stock was removed, now permitting the use of several irons to apply the brand. Earmarks, dewlaps, and wattles are not recorded, and the fee for the application for allotment of a brand is $3.00; upon application for renewal of a brand, $1.00; and upon transfer of a recorded brand, $3.00.

Publications for the province of British Columbia are: (1) Application for Cattle-brand, 2M–458–4563; (2) Application for Horse-brand, 1M–456–3147; (3) Stock-brands Act (extract), 13.12.57; (4) Instruction Letter, re: Applications for Cattle and Horse Brands (undated); (5) Making and Using Your Branding-Iron, (undated); (6) How to Make a Good Branding Iron and Apply It, 29.11.55; and (7) Branding, Branding "Don'ts" (undated).

Province of Manitoba. For the province of Manitoba, the first brand act was passed on March 18, 1903. This act, an individual brand act in itself, was entitled "The Cattle Brand Act of Manitoba." It was later incorporated into the Animal Husbandry Act and the branding of horses was also included. The present brand law is contained in Part III of the Animal Husbandry Act, being Chapter 6 of the Revised Statutes of Manitoba, 1954. The act was amended by Chapter 3, assented to March 15, 1956. The province of Manitoba does not publish a brand book, and the

application fee for the allotment of a brand is $2.00. The owner-
ship of a brand and the right to use it may be assigned to another party for a fee of $2.00.

All allotted brands are cancelled on the thirty-first day of December in the second year next following the year during which
the brand was allotted. During the year in which the brand is
subject to cancellation, it may be renewed for a period of three
years from the end of that year. If a brand has been cancelled, it
may be re-allotted to the original owner or allotted to a new
applicant not less than five years from the date of cancellation.

Brands of any description and in any location may be placed
on livestock belonging to the federal government, on stock
grazed in a federally operated pasture, and specifically on stock
grazed in any pasture operated under the provisions of the
Prairie Farm Rehabilitation Act (Canada). Brands may be
applied to cattle, horses, mules, and asses.

Vent brands are recordable for a fee of $1.00. Upon the trans-
fer of cattle, horses, mules, and asses, the vent brand must be
applied on the animals so transferred. The vent brand may be
omitted if the transferor's brand has also been transferred to
the transferee, and the vent may also be omitted in the event
the transferor executes a statement establishing the omission
of the vent.

The publications relative to Manitoba are: (1) An Animal
Husbandry Act, Chapter 6, Revised Statutes of Manitoba, 1954;
and (2) Chapter 3, An Act to Amend the Animal Husbandry
Act. R. S. Evans, Printer to Her Most Excellent Majesty, Winnipeg, 1956.

Province of Ontario. Relative to the province of Ontario, the first
brand law enacted and in effect witihout amendments is entitled The Live Stock Branding Act, R.S.O. 1937, c. 341. No
brand book has been published, and the application blank form
provides spaces for the name and address of the applicant and
three choices of brands to be described by name and by loca-

tion on the animal. There are no outline drawings. The reverse side has a complete copy of the brand law printed thereon. Upon recordation of the applicant's brand, a certificate of allotment is issued.

The brand owner is entitled to transfer the ownership of his brand to anyone. A certificate of transfer is issued upon such transfer. A recorded brand is valid for a period of three years. In case the owner does not renew his brand, he forfeits his right to ownership. A forfeited brand is not recorded to any person for a period of three years.

There are brands recorded only for cattle and sheep in the province. Federal brands have not been recorded, but it is felt that the federal government may use its prerogative in the application of its various brands. Branding is optional, but the recordation of brands is mandatory. Horses, cattle, sheep, and fowl may be branded. Ontario has no legislation dealing with the earmarking of livestock. Its schedule of tariff or fees: (1) On an application for allotment of a brand for a period of three years, $1.00; (2) on application for renewal of a brand allotment for a further period of three years, $1.00; (3) on application for a change in the record of a brand, $0.50; (4) on transfer of a recorded brand, $0.50; (5) for every search of a brand record, $0.50; (6) for every certified extract from the brand recorded, $0.50.

Ontario's only publication seems to be the Application for Allotment of Brand, 3M–52–4183.

Province of Saskatchewan. In 1905 the province of Saskatchewan and the province of Alberta were created from the North West Territory. The Brand Act and the Stock Inspection Act of the North West Territory were taken over by the new province of Saskatchewan. For a description of the early laws see *Province of Alberta* section, above.

In 1909 the legislature of Saskatchewan amended the Stock Inspection Act so that any area in the province could be taken out of stock inspection by an order-in-council, the cabinet of the day. In 1937 an order-in-council was passed taking all of the province out of stock inspection, and there was no stock inspection from the summer of 1937 until the summer of 1943. At the session of the legislature in 1943, the old Brand Act and Stock Inspection were repealed and a new act passed. At that time only a small area in the southwest part of the province was included in stock inspection. Since then this area has increased, and it now composes a third of the province. More recent legislation is The Brand and Brand Inspection Act, R.S.S., 1953, Chapter 191. This act was amended and assented to, March 29, 1957, by Chapter 59.

For the first issues of the brand book, see the paragraph on the province of Alberta, in the *Province of Alberta* section, above. The brand book was published every three years after establishment of the province, with annual supplements. Later the Saskatchewan Cattle and Horse Brands Book was published annually at a price of $1.00.

The application form is of small format. In addition to the applicant's name and address and the range or farm where the brand is to be used, there is a space for indicating the location of the brand, and also space for six choices of brands desired. Application for horse brands and cattle brands are separate, but identical in text. The brand certificate is prima facie evidence of ownership of the brand. A brand may be transferred by a notorized memorandum of transfer sent to the recorder, who makes the necessary changes in the records. The renewal period is four years. It ends on the thirty-first day of December of the fourth year after the recordation of the brand. If the brand is not renewed, it is cancelled and is not subject to re-recording or to reallotting for a five-year period starting from the date of such cancellation.

The Department of Agriculture presently employs eleven brand inspectors. In addition to that, the Royal Canadian Mounted Police do considerable inspection in the country. Any stock moving westward to inspection points in Alberta are inspected by the Alberta brand inspectors, and any cattle moving from Alberta eastward to points in Saskatchewan and to St. Boniface, Manitoba, are inspected by Saskatchewan brand inspectors under a co-operative program.

Branding is optional, but the recordation of a brand is specifically required by law. Brands may be located on any part of the body of any stock, except the ribs. No brand is allotted to an Indian living on a reservation. Cattle brands must consist of two characters, or three characters if two are not available. Brands of any description may be allotted to the minister of agriculture of Canada, for the identification of stock grazed in any pasture operated under the provisions of the Prairie Farm Rehabilitation Act (Canada), and to the Department of Agriculture of Saskatchewan, for the identification of stock owned by the department or grazed in any pasture operated by the department.

A vent brand is defined as one recorded prior to March 1, 1898; also, a second brand in a horizontal or lazy position immediately below the recorded brand, either identical to the recorded brand or forming part of the design only. At the time of transfer of livestock branded with a recorded brand, the vent brand must be applied, unless the recorded brand is also transferred.

Brands consisting of Arabic numerals, o to 9 inclusive, may be applied in conjunction with a recorded brand. They must be applied on the neck and on the same side of the animal as that upon which the stock is branded with the recorded brand. This type of brand need not be recorded.

The schedule of fees is: (1) on application for allotment, renewal, or reallotment of a brand, $2.00; (2) on application for a change in the record of a brand, $1.00; (3) on every transfer of a recorded brand, $1.00; (4) for every search of the brand record, $0.50; and (5) for every certified extract from the brand record, $0.50.

Publications for Saskatchewan are (1) Application for Horse

Brand, Form No. 72a–5C–12–56; (2) Application for Cattle Brand, Form No. 72–5M–12–56; (3) Memorandum of transfer of Brand (undated); (4) R.S.S. 1953, Chapter 191; Thos. H. McConica, Regina, Queen's Printer for Saskatchewan, 1954; and (5) 1957, Chapter 59; Lawrence Amon, Regina, Queen's Printer for Saskatchewan, 1957.

A tabulation of recorded brands would show:

Brands recorded by the Provincial Brand Recorder of	Number of brands recorded as of March 1, 1959
ALBERTA	
horses	3,500
cattle	28,500
sheep	16
poultry and fur-bearing animals	29
Total	32,045
BRITISH COLUMBIA	
horses	1,741
cattle	3,777
Total	5,518
MANITOBA (not available)	
ONTARIO	
cattle	1,311
poultry	3,185
Total	4,496
SASKATCHEWAN	
horses	498
cattle	13,178
Total	13,676
Grand Aggregate	55,735

Province of Quebec. The province of Quebec has no brand or stock inspection act. Earmarks are sometimes used on a private basis, pending proper identification for the registration of pure-bred animals, but not under provincial supervision. Animals

tested for TB or brucellosis under federal supervision are identified by eartag numbers in the left ear. Under a brucellosis
control system operated by the provincial government, animals
found positive are tattooed with a B in the right ear, by agreement with the owner. There is no law forcing such identification.

The United Kingdom of Great Britain and Northern Ireland
have no statutory requirement that a person's livestock should
be marked in a distinctive way to indicate ownership, and branding on the hide by any method is very seldom practiced.

The Fatstock (Guarantee Payments) Order of 1957 provides
for the making of guarantee payments to producers of livestock
in accordance with Part I of the Agricultural Act, 1957. In order
to qualify for any guarantee payment, fatstock of the prescribed
guarantee classes must be certified by authorized officers at livestock markets, slaughterhouses, bacon factories, or other places
approved for that purpose. Guarantee payments may be made
upon fat steers, fat heifers, fat lambs, fat hoggets, fat sheep, and
home-bred, clean fat pigs, provided they meet prescribed standards and qualifications. All fatstock presented at a liveweight
certification center and accepted for guarantee purposes, which
are sold by auction or by private treaty, or which are intended
for sale in the producer's own butchery business, will be permanently marked before removal from the center. Statutory
provision for such marking is made in the Fatstock Order of
1955. Temporary paint marks are applied to animals to show
their eligibility as follows: (1) fat cattle, "C" on the left plate;
(2) lambs, hoggets, and sheep, a small paint mark on the head;
and (3) pigs, a small paint mark between the shoulders.

Animals which are rejected as ineligible are temporarily marked
thusly: (1) cattle, an "X" on both plates; (2) sheep and pigs,
with a line across the back. Permanent marks for fatstock accepted for guarantee purposes are: (1) cattle, a circular hole
approximately half an inch in diameter in the right ear of an imported animal, and in the left ear of a home-bred animal. The

248

right ear of a home-bred animal is also marked if it does not bear a similar mark; (2) sheep, a green tattoo mark, or both a hole approximately a fourth of an inch in diameter and a green tattoo mark in the right ear of a home-bred, and in the left ear of an imported animal; and (3) pigs, a slap mark on the right shoulder, or a hole approximately a fourth of an inch in diameter and a green tattoo mark in the right ear.

The authorities for these statements are the following United Kingdom offices and publications: Ministry of Agriculture, Fisheries and Food, Department of Agriculture for Scotland. Ministry of Agriculture, Northern Ireland. Fatstock Guarantee Scheme 1958–59. London: Her Majesty's Stationery Office, 1958; the Ministry of Agriculture, Fatstock (Guarantee Payments) (Marking) Order, 1957. Statutory Instrument No. 852/1955. London: Her Majesty's Stationery Office, 1955; the Ministry of Agriculture, the Imported Livestock (Marking) Order, 1954. Statutory Instrument 760/1954. London: Her Majesty's Stationery Office, 1954; and the Ministry of Agriculture, Amending Statutory Instrument No. 1223/1955. London: Her Majesty's Stationery Office, 1955.

Identification of cattle is accomplished by three methods, tattooing in the ear, metal or plastic eartags, and numbering on the horn. When breeders mark pedigreed cattle they usually employ a registered code of letters representing the birth year, the breeder, and an individual number for the calf. Herd index letters are approved by breeding societies. The Great Glen Cattle Ranch uses the following ear tattoo: $\frac{G.G.C.R.}{K.450}$ The letter "K" signifies the year, followed by the number of the animal. All cattle are required to be either tattooed or eartagged with an identification number for the use of the Ministry of Agriculture in connection with the movement of cattle after being tested for bovine tuberculosis.

Sheep have been branded on the Isle of Skye by making a mark on the animal's nose. Sheep branding irons are in common use today in Lewis and Harris counties, Hebrides Islands, since

almost all the crofters own sheep, and all of them have their identifying mark branded on the sheep's horns. These marks are
usually an abbreviation of the number and site of the croft (Figs.
917 to 961). There are located at Stornoway, Lewis Island, two
blacksmiths engaged in the practice of shaping branding irons.

Sheep are identified by four methods: tattooing in the ear, by
earmarking, horn-branding, and paint-branding the fleece. The
latter is applied with a buisting iron dipped in a mixture of
boiling tar and pitch.

The buisting irons usually consist of two or three letters, the
owner's initials, and possibly a number indicating the age of
the animal. These irons are usually made by a local blacksmith
and examples of them are found in local museums of country
crafts. The irons are about four or five inches in diameter, with
the letter or number enclosed in a toothed ring. Flocks of sheep
have a distinctive mark, either a notch or notches in a particular
part of the ear. There is no register maintained by the Department of Agriculture for such marks, and duplication of them is
inevitable. Individual marking of sheep is carried out for pedigreed stock which is registered with a society, but the number
of those so marked is small. The flocks which are registered with
a society are usually of a breed of sheep suitable for the lower
and better land, as distinct from the hill breeds.

Tattooing is used for identification of individual sheep in registered flocks. All sheep markings are registered with the county
and they are keyed for identification purposes, such as: blue on
the kidney for one kind of identification, blue on the head for
another, red on the left shoulder for another, etc. In addition,
breeding ewes are branded on the horn with an identification
letter denoting the year born, together with a number, viz: K.964.

Pigs are usually marked by the breeder to suit his own requirements. This may be either collectively as a litter shortly after
birth, with individual marking for stock later selected for breeding, or with individual marking shortly after birth, which is
necessary in any case if the stock is registered with a breeding

society. Notching is used for marking black or colored pigs in preference to tattooing. However, tattooing is the most common method.

In the Federal Republic of Germany and German Democratic Republic, hide brands have been used for a long time by German horse breeders. The design and the location, i. e., the part of the body used for the application of the brand, give possible clues to the breeding places. These brands are called stud farm brands. The design and the location also may give clues to the origin or type of bloodlines of the animal.

Brands in this category are termed foal brands. In addition, in conjunction with registration of mares and stallions in the stud book, breeders' associations use stud book brands, sometimes termed registration brands. Stud farm brands are still being used by several state stud farms for all the horses bred at the main stud farm (Prussia and her successor states, also Württemberg-Baden) or pedigree stud farm (Bavaria). This brand is applied to the right side of the body. Stud farm brands are descent brands, as are the foal brands used by horse breeders' associations for the descendants of stud book registered mares and registered, recognized, and service qualified stallions at stud. Stud farm brands and foal brands are applied to several-months-old foals while they are still with the mare. Thus the design of the brand indicates the breeding place, the stud farm brand, or the breeding region and the horse breeders' association maintaining the stud book, foal brand, and registration brand.

Foal brands are used, in accordance with regulations for the respective breeding region, for all descendants of stud book registered horses, including geldings. Foal brands are also used for all foals bred by main pedigree book and pedigree book registered mares, in addition to descendants of registered or recognized, service qualified stallions at stud. In some breeding regions, foal brands of various designs are applied to descendants of mares registered in the main pedigree book, pedigree book, and pre-register. In that case, foal brands are identification for the section of the stud book in which the dam has been registered.

Stud book brands or registration brands are used for breed stallions and brood mares registered in the stud book. These brands are listed after the entries in the stud book. Registration in the stud book includes entries in the following sections: main pedigree book, pedigree book, and the pre-register. For each section a different brand is used. In case of similar design, a different location, a different size, or an additional mark is used. Frequently, a main pedigree book brand may be different from a pedigree book brand only by the addition of three points forming a triangle under the former. In some breeding regions, breed stallions selected for the first time are registered in the stallion book of the stud book of the horse breeders' association, and are branded with the main pedigree book brand.

Mares meeting the requirements of horse breeders' associations in respect to pure breeding, form and body, and certified descent from selected or registered sires and dams and grand-sires and grand-dams, are registered in the main pedigree book. Brood mares not meeting these evaluation criteria and not having evidence of descent, but having satisfactory form or appearance, are registered in the pedigree book. Mares not meeting evaluation criteria for registration in the pedigree book, but which in conjunction with pureblood stallions may start a new breeding circle, are registered in the pre-register.

In German horse breeding, two different types of purebreds (Vollblut) are recognized: (1) saddle, pack, and light draft horses (Warmblut), such as Hanoveraner, Oldenburger, Mecklenburger, and Holsteiner; (2) heavy draft horses (Kaltblut), such as the Rhenish-Belgian horse. Both the saddle horses and the heavy draft horses are further sub-divided into light and heavy classes, e.g., a Hanoveraner is a light saddle horse, and an Oldenburger a heavy saddle horse; a Schleswiger is a light draft horse, and a Rhinelander a heavy draft horse. Breeding of saddle horses is conducted by the government at state stud farms (Staats-gestüt), to satisfy its own requirements. State stud farms are comprised of main stud farms (Hauptgestüt) and pedigree stud farms (Stammgestüt). Stallions at stud at government-operated farms are called main service stallions (Hauptbeschäler). The government also maintains regional stud farms (Landgestüt) in order to satisfy the requirements of private breeders. Actually, this type of farm can only be considered a service facility (Hengst-depot), with regional service stallions (Landesbeschäler). At times, stallions for breeding purposes may be selected and pur-chased from outside sources. Such stallions must pass an evalu-ation examination by a selection committee (Körkommission), and if such stallions are accepted they are called selected (Ge-körte) stallions.

Stallions of the heavy draft horse type are not bred and fur-nished by the government, but are maintained by private breed-ers and associations. The names of all the varieties of the two types of breeds are derived from the region where they were originally bred. The breeding region (Zuchtgebiet) is usually a German state or province which offers particular advantages for raising either saddle or heavy draft horses. Such advantages may be of climatic, topographic, or other nature, including certain partic-ular types of feed. However, most saddle horses are raised in the eastern part, and heavy draft horses in the western part of Ger-many. During the past several decades there has been a steady ascent in popularity of small horses (Kleinpferde). Even though they differ in many respects from the characteristic saddle and heavy draft horses, they are classified "cold blooded," the same as the draft horse. The German criterion for classification is that all saddle, pack, and light draft horses are "warm blooded" and heavy draft horses are "cold blooded," the latter not showing as much temperament.

The following are translations of terms used in connection with horse breeding in Germany:

1. BRANDS:

Gestütsbrand	stud farm brand
Fohlenbrand	foal brand
Stutbuchbrand (Eintragungsbrand)	studbook brand (registration brand)
Hauptstammbuchbrand	main pedigree book brand
Stammbuchbrand	pedigree book brand
Nachzuchtbrand	descent brand
Körbrand	selection brand
Kontrollbrand	control brand
Prämienbrand	blue ribbon

2. STUD FARMS:

Staatsgestüt	state stud farm
Hauptgestüt	main stud farm
Landgestüt	regional stud farm
Stammgestüt	pedigree stud farm
Zuchtgebiet	breeding island
Deckstelle	service facility

3. REGISTRATION:

Stutbuch	stud book
Hauptstammbuch	main pedigree book
Stammbuch	pedigree book
Vorbuch (Vorregister)	pre-register
Hauptstutbuch	main brood mare book
Hilfsstutbuch	auxiliary brood mare book
Übergangsregister	transition register
Anhang	annex

4. SOLIPEDES:

Vollblut	purebred
Edles Warmblut	thoroughbred
Warmblut	riding horse; light draft
leicht	light
schwer	heavy
Kaltblut	draft horse
leicht	light
schwer	heavy
Kleinpferd	small horse
Zwergpferd	dwarf horse

254

Pony	pony
Hengst	stallion
Wallach	gelding
Deckberechtigster Hengst	service qualified stallion
Gekörter Hengst	selected stallion
Hauptbeschäler	main stallion at stud
Landbeschalër	regional stallion at stud
Deckhengst	stallion at stud
Stute	mare
Fohlen	foal

The Reich Food Agency (Reichsnährstand) was created under the provisions of the law of September 13, 1933, to unify the diverse interests of various agricultural organizations. The Reich chief of farmers (Reichsbauernfüher), who also was the secretary of agriculture (Reichsminister für Ernährung und Landwirtschaft), administered the programs, with the aid of staff sections and divisions on three different levels of organization. The highest division was on a provincial, or equivalent, level. These divisions, land farmers' associations (Landesbauernschaften), were responsible for the application of brands.

Some brands of the regional farmers' units are:

Baden
 light horses, left hip (Fig. 1033)
 draft horses, left hip (Fig. 1031)
Upper Bavaria
 light horses, for registered mares and stallions, left hip (Fig. 1116)
Lower Bavaria
 light horses, for registered mares and stallions, left hip (Fig. 1097)
Brunswick
 light horses and draft horses, left hip (Fig. 1039)
Hanover
 light horses, stud book brand for descendants of stud book mares, left hip (Fig. 982)
 light horses, for stud book mares, left neck (Fig. 1045)

255

East Frisia
  light horses, stud book brand, left neck (Fig. 1067)
Electoral Marche (Brandenburg)
  light horses, left hip (Fig. 973. The brand depicts a stylized version of the coat of arms of the former province of Brandenburg, the Red Eagle.)
  draft horses, left hip (Fig. 1034)
Mecklenburg
  light horses, left hip (Fig. 1085)
Oldenburg
  light horses, stud book brand, left hip (Fig. 1088)
East Prussia
  light horses, stud book brand, left neck (Fig. 963)
  light horses, mares in pre-register I, left neck (Fig. 964)
  light horses, for descendants of mares in pre-register II, left hip (Fig. 965)
  draft horses, for main pedigree book mares, left hip (Fig. 1011)
  draft horses for pedigree book mares, left hip (Fig. 1091)
Danzig
  light horses, for mares and stallions of the East Prussian stud book, left hip (Fig. 963)
Pomerania
  light horses, left neck (Fig. 974)
Rhineland
  draft horses, left hip (Fig. 1100)
  foal brand, right neck (Fig. 1100)
Saar-Palatinate
  light horses or Zweibrücken descent, right hip (Fig. 1113)
  draft horses, left hip (Fig. 1042)
Saxony-Anhalt
  light horses, left hip (Fig. 1096)
  draft horses, left neck (Fig. 1066)
Saxony
  light horses and draft horses, left hip (Fig. 1058)
Silesia
  light horses and draft horses, left hip (Fig. 1016)
Schleswig-Holstein
  light horses, left hip (Fig. 1114)

draft horses, left hip (Fig. 1068)
light horses, control brand for foals, left neck (Fig. 992)
Westphalia
light horses, right hip (Fig. 1013)
draft horses, left hip (Fig. 1013)
Württemberg
light horses, right hip (Fig. 1084)
light horses and draft horses for stallions in private possession, left hip (Fig. 976)

During the 1930's the following state stud farms were in existence:

1. Prussian main stud farms, where the state bred horses for use by the regional stud farms. Stallions at the state stud farm were termed main stallions at stud. At the Trakehnen (East Prussia) the Moose Palm brand, right hip (Fig. 962), was used, and at Graditz (Saxony) the Crossed Arrow and Snake brand, right hip (Fig. 983). At Neustadt a.d. Dosse (Brandenburg) the Arrow and Snake brand was used, right hip (Fig. 984).

2. Prussian regional stud farms. Below are listed several important regional stud farms, actually only service facilities at which the state service stallions, regional service stallions and, at times, main service stallions were at stud for privately owned mares: Braunsberg (East Prussia) (Fig. 1049), Marienwerder (West Prussia), Labes (Pomerania), Leubus (Lower Silesia), Kreuz (Saxony), Celle (Hanover) (Fig. 980), and Wickrath (Rhineland).

3. Other stud farms were those in which the respective states engaged in their own breeding and furnished regional stallions at stud for private breeding purposes. The Bavarian Pedigree Stud Farm Achselschwang branded on the right hip (Fig. 1072); Pedigree Stud Farm Zweibrücken, Saar Palatinate branded on the right hip (Fig. 1026); Pedigree Stud Farm Schwaiganger branded on the left hip (Fig. 1102); Württemberg Main Stud Farm Marbach a.d. Lauter branded on the right hip (Fig. 1084). Regional Stable Office Moritzburg (Saxony) is similar to the

Prussian regional stud farm. The brand for the stud farm at Alte-feld is shown in Fig. 988, for Stud Farm Beberbeck, the Arrow and Snake Brand, right hip, see Fig. 986, and for Stud Book West Prussia see Fig. 1023.

State stud farms consist of main stud farms and pedigree stud farms. Stud farm brands are used for all horses bred at these establishments. Main Stud Farm Trakehnen (East Prussia) brands on right hip (Fig. 962) are no longer in use; Main Stud Farm Graditz (Saxony-Anhalt) brands on right hip (Fig. 981) are no longer in use; Main Stud Farm Neustadt a.d. Dosse (Brandenburg) brands on right hip (Fig. 984) are no longer in use; Württemberg Main Stud Farm Marbach a.d. Lauter brands on right hip, bred and selected stallions and mares at the main stud farm over three years old (Fig. 1084). Also right hip, foals; left neck, selected brand for regionally purchased and selected stallions (Fig. 966). Bavarian Pedigree Stud Farm Achselschwang brands on the right hip, since 1864 (Fig. 1072); Pedigree Stud Farm Zweibrücken (Rhineland-Palatinate) brands on the right neck, since 1850 (Fig. 1026), and Pedigree Stud Farm Schwaiganger brands on the left hip (Fig. 1102).

Horse breeders' associations of the Federal Republic of Germany use a system of listing the brands comforming generally to the following sequence: first, the breed, second, the name of the association, and third, the method of registration by the divisions of the stud book, that is, (1) main pedigree book mares, foals by main pedigree book mares; (2) pedigree book mares, foals by pedigree book mares; (3) preregister mares, foals by preregister mares; (4) mares listed in annex; and (5) stallions and other pertinent information, listed in the appropriate place. The following paragraphs will identify a great many of the brands used by German associations.

Horse breeders' associations for light horses within the Federal Republic of Germany:

The East Prussian Association of Breeders of the Light Horse Trakehnen Ancestry, Inc., Hamburg, uses for the main pedi-

258

gree book a brand (small) on the left neck (Fig. 963), and for foals, left neck (large) (Fig. 963). The Hanover Association of Hanoverian Light Horse Breeders, Inc., for the main pedigree book, since 1946, on left neck (Fig. 982), and foals, left hip (Fig. 982). Until 1945, this brand was used for foals by stud book mares and for foals by mares listed in the annex. In the case of the latter, the granddam of the mare also had to be registered in the stud book. The brand was applied on the left hip. For the pedigree book, since 1946, the brand was on the left neck (Fig. 878); for foals, the left hip (Fig. 978); for pre-register, the left neck (Fig. 985), for foals, left hip (Fig. 985). This was the control brand for all foals. These foals or their dams had to be sired by half or full-blooded regional stallions at stud. The sire for all main pedigree book, pedigree book, and pre-register foals has to be certified as being recognized by the Hanoverian stud book. Mares after acceptance in the Hanoverian stud book, until 1945, were branded on the left neck (Fig. 1045). Mares after acceptance in the annex of the Hanoverian stud book, until 1945, were branded on the left neck (Fig. 1070).

For Westphalian Horse Pedigree Book, Inc., Riding Horse Division, Münster, Westphalia, brands in the main pedigree book, pedigree book, and pre-register book were on the left neck (Figs. 1013, 1014, 1104), and for foals, left hip (Fig. 1112). The Association of Breeders of the Holstein Horse, Inc., Elmshorst, Holstein, had no stud book in use, but its stud farm book, since 1944, branded on the left hip (Fig. 1038), and for foals, until 1943, the left hip (Fig. 1024).

In the Association of Breeders of the Oldenburger Horse, Oldenburg, branded brood fillies, marked in the Oldenburger stud book, since 1897, were branded on the left hip (Fig. 1088), and mares registered in the annex and their descendants in Regierungsbezirk Osnabrück, since 1948, were branded on the left neck (small) (Fig. 1093). The Blue Ribbon brand, since 1861, is on the right hip (Fig. 1092).

For East Frisian Stud Book, Inc., Norden, East Frisia, in the main pedigree book, mares, since 1869, and stallions, for more than 150 years, were branded on the left neck (Fig. 1089). In the pedigree book, mares, since 1921, were branded on the left neck (Fig. 1076) and foals, since 1919, on the left hip (Fig. 1094). In East Frisian also, the Association of Horse Breeders Hesse-Nassau, Light Horse Division, in the main pedigree book, mares and selected stallions are branded on the left hip (Fig. 1079) as they are in the pedigree book and the pre-register book (Figs. 1081 and 1111), as well as the foals (Fig. 1081). Again in East Frisian, for the Electoral-Hessian Horse Pedigree Book, Inc., Light Horse Division, the main pedigree book, since 1947, the brand is on the left hip (Fig. 1001), while the pedigree book, since 1947, and the pre-register book both call for a brand on the left neck (Figs. 1002 and 1111); but for the pre-register for thoroughbreds, since 1947, brand on the left hip (Fig. 1111), and foals, since 1946, are branded on the right neck (Fig. 1083).

For the Association of Württemberger Light Horse Breeders, Inc., the main pedigree book lists, since 1907, a brand on the left neck (Fig. 966), and for foals, since 1940, on the left hip (Fig. 966). In the pedigree book, since 1907, the brand is on the left neck (Fig. 1104), and for foals, by pre-register mares, since 1940, on the left hip (Fig. 968).

For Rottalers, in the records of the Regional Association of Bavarian Horse Breeders, Inc., in the main pedigree book and pedigree book, the brand is on the left hip (Fig. 1101), while for foals it is on the left neck (Fig. 1101). For the Rottaler, also, the Badian Horse Pedigree Book, Inc., Light Horse Division, seat Heidelberg, in the main pedigree book (Fig. 1032), the pedigree book (Fig. 1033), and the pre-register book (Fig. 1108), all brands are on the right hip, while foals are branded on the left neck (small) (Fig. 1033). For the Badian Horse Pedigree Book, Inc., Light Horse Division, seat Neustadt (Black Forest) the brands are identical to those above.

For the Regional Association of Horse Breeders, Palatinate Light Horse Division, in the main pedigree book, since 1936,

(Fig. 1028), and the pedigree book and pre-register, since 1936, the brands are on the left hip (Fig. 1027) and for the foals, on the left neck (Fig. 1027). Breed stallions, since 1850, carry brands on the right hip (Fig. 1029).

For the Haflinger, according to the Regional Association of Bavarian Horse Breeders, Inc., in the main pedigree book, pedigree book and foals, since 1950, and the pre-register until 1949, brands were on the left neck (Figs. 1007 and 1104).

Defunct horse breeders' associations for light horses, and existing associations outside the boundaries of the Federal Republic of Germany:

For the Regional Association of Horse Breeders in the Saarland, Inc., Light Horse Division, Saarbrücken, in the pedigree book and stallions, and the pre-register, brands are on the left hip (large) and the left neck (large), respectively (Fig. 1051). Foals are branded on the right neck (small) (Fig. 1051), and all the above brands have been used since 1946.

For the Association of Branderburger Horse Breeders, Inc., Light Horse Division, Potsdam, in the main pedigree book the brand is on the left neck (Fig. 1075), and for foals, since 1945, on the left hip (Fig. 1075); in the pedigree book, on the left neck (Fig. 1073), and foals, since 1945, on the left hip (Fig. 1073); pre-register, on the left neck (Fig. 1074), and foals, since 1945, on left hip (Fig. 1074).

For the Regional Association of Mecklenburger Horse Breeders, Light Horse Division, Schwerin, former Mecklenburger breeding region, in the main pedigree book the brand is on the left neck (Fig. 1071), in the pedigree book, on the left neck (Fig. 1109), in the pre-register, on the left neck (Fig. 1093) and for foals by main pedigree and pedigree book mares, on the left hip (Fig. 1085). Foals by pre-register mares, on the left hip (Fig. 1086); foals by main pedigree book and pedigree book mares of East Prussian descent and East Prussian stallions, on the left hip (Fig. 1085). In addition, since 1949, the Double East Prussian foal brand is on the right hip (Fig. 963). Foals since 1949, right hip (Fig. 963). This is the Double East Prussian foal brand applied to foals by requirements of the main pedigree book, pedigree book, and pre-register mares of East Prussian descent and by East Prussian stallions in addition to the above- and below-mentioned brands, as indicated.

In the former Fore-Pomeranian counties in the main pedigree book the brand is on the left neck (Fig. 972), the pedigree book, left neck (Fig. 974), the pre-register, on the left neck (Fig. 1018), and foals by main pedigree book and pedigree book mares of East Prussian descent and East Prussian stallions are branded on the left hip (Fig. 972). In addition, since 1959, the Double East Prussian brand is on the right hip (Fig. 963). For foals by pre-register mares and branded on the left hip (Fig. 1018), and in addition, since 1949, for foals by pre-register mares of East Prussian descent and East Prussian stallions, the Double East Prussian foal brand is on the right hip (Fig. 963).

On the breeding island Hanover, service facilities are at Haar, Bitter, and Stiepelsee (County of Hagenow). In the main pedigree book, the brand is on the left neck for horses and the left hip for foals (Fig. 982). Foals by main pedigree book and pedigree book mares of East Prussian descent and East Prussian stallions are also branded on left hip. In addition, since 1949, the Double East Prussian foal brand is on the right hip (Fig. 963); pedigree book, on the left neck (Fig. 978); foals, left hip (Fig. 978), and foals by pre-register mares of East Prussian descent and East Prussian stallions, also on the left hip. In addition, since 1949, the Double East Prussian foal brand is on the right hip (Fig. 963); pre-register, on left neck (Fig. 979), and foals, on left hip (Fig. 979).

For the Saxonian Horse Pedigree Book, Light Horse Division, Dresden, main pedigree book mares and stallions, since 1946, are branded on the left hip (Fig. 1057); pedigree book mares and stallions, since 1920, branded on left hip (Fig. 1058), and Blue Ribbon brand, since 1937, applied on the left neck (Fig. 1058).

For the Regional Horse Breeding Association Saxony-Anhalt, Light Horse Division, Halle/Saale, in the Heavy Light Horse Section (Oldenburger, East Frisian, and their cross breeds), in the main pedigree book and selected stallions, the brand is on the left hip (Fig. 1059); foals, since 1950, on left neck (small) (Fig. 1059); pedigree book, left hip (Fig. 1060); foals, since 1950, small on left neck (Fig. 1060); pre-register on left hip (Fig. 1104), and foals, since 1950, on left neck (small) (Fig. 1104).

For the Thoroughbred Section (Hanoverian, Holsteiner etc.), and their cross breeds, in the main pedigree book and selected stallions, the brand is on the left hip (Fig. 1040), and foals, since 1950, left neck (small) (Fig. 1040); pedigree book, left hip (Fig. 1041), and foals, since 1950, left neck (small) (Fig. 1041); pre-register, left hip (Fig. 1104), and foals since 1950, left neck (small) (Fig. 1104).

For the Regional Association of Thuringian Horse Breeders, Light Horse Division, Weimar, in the main pedigree book, since 1929, the brand is on the left hip (Fig. 1061); the main pedigree book for thoroughbreds, since 1948, the left hip (Fig. 1063); for pedigree book, since 1929, left hip (Fig. 1062); pedigree book for thoroughbreds, since 1948, left hip (Fig. 1064); the pre-register, left hip (Fig. 1106); pre-register thoroughbreds, since 1941, left hip (Fig. 1106); foals, left neck (Fig. 1050), and foals by thoroughbreds, since 1929, left neck (Fig. 1050).

For East Prussian Stud Book Corporation for Light Horses of Trakehnen Ancestry, Inc., Königsberg i.Pr., in the main pedigree book and stallions the brand is on the left neck (Fig. 963), and foals, on the left hip (Fig. 963). For pre-register I, left neck (small) (Fig. 964); foals on left hip (Fig. 963). For pre-register II, brand on right neck (small) (Fig. 963), and foals, left hip (Fig. 965).

For the West Prussian Stud Book Corporation for Light Horses of Trakehnen Ancestry, Inc., Danzig, brands are identical to those above.

For the Association of Pomeranian Light Horse Breeders, Inc.,

Stettin, in the stud book, since 1927, the brand is listed as on the left neck (Fig. 974); for the Auxiliary stud book, since 1927, the left neck (Fig. 1018), and foals by service qualified stallions, since 1927, left hip, (Fig. 972).

For the Silesian Horse Pedigree Book, Inc., Light Horse Division, Breslau, in the main pedigree book, since 1941, the brand is on the left neck (Fig. 1015), and foals, since 1941, left hip (Fig. 1025); for pedigree book, since 1941, the left neck (Fig. 1016), and for pre-register, since 1941, the left neck (Fig. 1104).

For the Regional Association of Horse Breeders Wartheland, Posen, Light Horse Division, in the main pedigree book, the brand is on the left neck (small) (Fig. 987), and foals, left hip (small) (Fig. 987); in the pedigree book on the left neck (small) (Fig. 989), and foals, left hip (small) (Fig. 989).

Records on Rhenish-German draft horses kept by breeders' associations for draft horses within the Federal Republic of Germany contain the following brand specifications:

Included in records on Rhenish-German draft horses, the Rhenish Horse Pedigree Book, Inc., Draft Horse Division, Bonn, in its main pedigree book has the brand on the left hip (Fig. 1099), and for foals on the left neck (Fig. 1100); pedigree book, left hip (Fig. 1100).

For the Westphalian Horse Pedigree Book, Inc., Draft Horse Division, in the main pedigree book, the brand is on the left hip (Fig. 1013); for the pedigree book, left hip (Fig. 1014); for pre-register, left neck (Fig. 1104), and for foals, left neck (Fig. 1112).

For Pedigree Book for Draft Horses, Lower Saxony, Inc., in the main pedigree book and selected stallions, the brand is on the left hip (Fig. 1046); in the pedigree book, left hip (Fig. 1047); in the pre-register, left hip (Fig. 1105), and for foals by pedigree book and main pedigree book mares and service qualified stallions, left neck (Fig. 1069).

For Association of Horse Breeders Hesse-Nassau, Draft Horse

Division, in the main pedigree book and selected stallions, the brand is on the left hip (Fig. 1079); the pedigree book, left hip (Fig. 1080); the pre-register, left hip (Fig. 1082), and for foals, left neck (Fig. 1082).

For the Electoral-Hessian Horse Pedigree Book, Inc., Draft Horse Division, in the main pedigree book, since 1947, the brand is on the left hip (Fig. 1048); the pedigree book, since 1947, left hip (Fig. 1048); pedigree book, since 1947, left hip (Fig. 977), and foals, until 1945, right neck (Fig. 977). Pre-register, since 1947, left neck (Fig. 1104), and foals, since 1946, right neck (Fig. 1083).

For the Pedigree Book for Rhenish-German Draft Horses in Holstein, Inc., in the main pedigree book, since 1938, the brand is on the left hip (Fig. 1020), and for foals, since 1938, left neck (small) (Fig. 1021); pedigree book A and B, left hip (Fig. 1021), and foals, since 1938, left neck (Fig. 1021); pre-register, since 1938, left hip (Fig. 1022).

For Schleswiger draft horses registered with the Association of Schleswiger Horse Breeders' Clubs, Inc., in the main pedigree book, since 1939, the brand is on the left hip (Fig. 1065); pedigree book, the brand is on the left hip (large) (Fig. 1006); pedi-1939, left hip (Fig. 1104), and foals, since 1951, right hip (Fig. 1068). This brand was applied to foals, left neck (small) from 1891 to 1951.

In the case of South German draft horses, for the Regional Association of Bavarian Horse Breeders, Inc., in the main pedigree book, the brand is on the left hip (large) (Fig. 1006); pedigree book, left hip (small) (Fig. 1006); pre-register, since 1950, left hip (Fig. 1104). Until 1949 a small brand was applied to the left hip (Fig. 1006), and for foals, since 1950, left neck (small) (Fig. 1006).

For the Association of Württemberg Draft Horse Breeders, Inc., in the main pedigree book, since 1938, the brand is on the left neck (Fig. 971), and for foals, since 1940, the left neck (Fig.

971); pedigree book, since 1938, left neck (Fig. 970), and foals, since 1940, left hip (Fig. 970); pre-register, since 1938, left neck (Fig. 1104), and foals, since 1940, left hip (Fig. 969).

For Badian Horse Pedigree Book, Inc., Draft Horse Division, seat Neustadt (Black Forest), the main pedigree book has the brand on the left hip (Fig. 1030); the pedigree book, left hip (Fig. 1031); pre-register, left hip (Fig. 1103), and foals, left neck (small) (Fig. 1031).

Rhenish-German draft horses registered with the Badian Horse Pedigree Book, Inc., Draft Horse Division, seat Heidelberg, in the main pedigree book and all others, brands are the same as those in the paragraph above.

For the Rhenish Horse Pedigree Book for Rhineland-Nassau, Coblence (Rhenish-German draft horses), in the main pedigree book the brand is on the left hip (Fig. 1099), and foals, left hip (Fig. 1100); pedigree book, left hip (Fig. 1100), and foals, left neck (Fig. 1100).

Ardenner draft horses registered with the Regional Association of Horse Breeders Palatinate, Draft Horse Division, in the main pedigree book, from 1936 to 1949, the brand is on the left hip (Fig. 1042), and foals, from 1936 to 1949, left neck (Fig. 1042); main pedigree book, pedigree book and pre-register, since 1950, left hip (Fig. 1095), and foals, left neck (Fig. 1095); pedigree book and pre-register, from 1936 to 1949, left hip (Fig. 1043), and foals, from 1936 to 1949, left neck (Fig. 1043).

Defunct horse breeders' associations for draft horses, and existing associations outside the boundaries of the Federal Republic of Germany (breeds not indicated):

For the Regional Association of Horse Breeders in the Saarland, Inc., Draft Horse Division, Saarbrücken, in the pedigree book and stallions, brands are on the left hip (large) (Fig. 1052); pre-register, left neck (large) (Fig. 1052), and foals, right neck (small) (Fig. 1052). All brands since 1946.

For the Association of Brandenburger Horse Breeders, Draft Horse Division, Potsdam, in the main pedigree book, since 1923, brands are on the left hip (Fig. 1034), foals, since 1945, left neck (Fig. 1034); pedigree book, left hip (Fig. 1035), and foals, since 1945, left neck (Fig. 1035); pre-registers, left neck (Fig. 1017), and foals, since 1945, left neck (Fig. 1017).

For the Regional Association of Mecklenburger Horse Breeders, Draft Horse Division, Schwerin, former Mecklenburger breeding region, in the main pedigree book, brands are on the left hip (Fig. 1044), and foals on left neck (Fig. 1087); pedigree book, left hip (Fig. 1090), and foals, left neck (Fig. 1087); pre-register, left hip (Fig. 1098), and foals, left neck (Fig. 1087).

For former Fore-Pomeranian counties, in main pedigree book the brand is on the left hip (Fig. 1037), and for foals, on left neck (Fig. 1019); pedigree book, left hip (Fig. 1036), and foals, left neck (Fig. 1019); pre-register, left hip (Fig. 1098), and foals, left neck (Fig. 1019).

For the Saxonian Horse Pedigree Book, Draft Horse Division, Dresden, for the main pedigree book mares and stallions, since 1946, the brand is on the left hip (Fig. 1057); the pedigree book mares and stallions, since 1920, left hip (Fig. 1058), and Blue Ribbon brand, since 1927, left neck (Fig. 1058).

For the Regional Horse Breeding Association Saxony-Anhalt, Draft Horse Division, Halle/Saale, the main pedigree book and selected stallion, since 1942, the brand is on the left hip (Fig. 1053), and foals, since 1942, left neck (Fig. 1055); pedigree book, since 1942, left hip (Fig. 1054), and foals, since 1942, left neck (Fig. 1056); pre-register, since 1942, left neck (Fig. 1104).

For the Regional Association of Thuringian Horse Breeders, Draft Horse Division, Weimar, the main pedigree book, since 1929, has the brand on the left hip (Fig. 990); pedigree book, since 1929, left hip (Fig. 994); pre-register, since 1941, left hip (Fig. 1106), and foals, since 1929, left neck (Fig. 1050).

For the Danzig Stud Book for Heavy Work Horses, Inc., Danzig, in the main pedigree book and registered stallions, since 1940, the brand is on the left hip (Fig. 1077), and foals, since 1940, left neck (small) (Fig. 1077); pedigree book, since 1940, left hip (Fig. 1078), and foals, since 1940, left neck (small) (Fig. 1078); pre-register, since 1940, left hip (Fig. 1107), and foals, since 1940, left neck (small) (Fig. 1107).

For East Prussian Stud Book for Heavy Work Horses, Inc., Königsberg i.Pr., the main pedigree book, since 1940, has the brand on the left hip (Fig. 1010); pedigree book, until 1940, left hip (Fig. 1091), and since 1940, left hip (Fig. 1011); pre-register, left hip (Fig. 1110), and foals, left neck (Fig. 1091).

For the Association of Pomeranian Draft Horse Breeders, Inc., Stettin, in the main pedigree book both mares and stallions, since 1924, were branded on the left hip (Fig. 1037), and foals, since 1924, left neck (Fig. 1019); pedigree book mares and stallions, since 1924, left hip (Fig. 1036), and foals, since 1924, left neck (Fig. 1019).

For Silesian Horse Pedigree Book, Inc., Draft Horse Division, Breslau, in the main pedigree book, since 1941, the brand is on the left hip (Fig. 1015), and foals, since 1941, left neck (Fig. 1025); pedigree book, since 1941, left hip (Fig. 1016); and pre-register, since 1941, left hip (Fig. 1104).

For the Regional Association of Horse Breeders Wartheland, Inc., Draft Horse Division, Posen, the main pedigree book has the brand on the left hip (Fig. 1115), and foals, left neck (Fig. 1115); pedigree book, left hip (Fig. 1117), and foals left neck (small) (Fig. 1117).

Small horse breeders' associations within the boundaries of the Federal Republic of Germany:

Small horses registered with the Regional Association of Pony and Small Horse Breeders, Schleswig-Holstein—Hamburg in Elmshorn, the main pedigree book and selected stallions, the brand is on the left hip (Fig. 1012); pre-register, left hip (Fig. 1009), and foals, left hip (small) (Fig. 1012).

For the Association of Pony and Small Horse Breeders Hanover, the main pedigree book, pedigree book, and selected stallions, since 1948, have the brand on the left hip (Fig. 1012);

pre-register, since 1948, left hip (Fig. 1009), and foals, since that date, left hip (small) (Fig. 1012).

For the Association of Small Horse and Pony Breeders Weser-Ems, in the main pedigree book, the brand design has not been finally selected; for the pedigree book, left hip (Fig. 1012); pre-register, left hip (Fig. 1009), and foals, left neck (small) (Fig. 1012).

For the Association of Pony and Small Horse Breeders of the North Rhine Province, mares and stallions, since 1947, have been branded on the left hip (Fig. 1012), and foals, since that same year, left neck (small) (Fig. 1012).

For the Westphalian Horse Pedigree Book, Inc., Small Horse Division, in the main pedigree book and pedigree book, brands are on the left hip (Fig. 1012); pre-register, left neck (Fig. 1104), and foals, left neck (small) (Fig. 1012).

For the Association of Pony and Small Horse Breeders Hesse, Inc., in the pedigree book and selected stallions, the brand is on the left hip (Fig. 991); pre-register, left hip (Fig. 993), and foals, left neck (Fig. 991).

For the South German Small Horse Pedigree Book, Inc., in the main pedigree book and stallions, the brand is on the left neck (Fig. 995), and foals, left hip (Fig. 997); pre-register, left neck (Fig. 996), and foals, left hip (Fig. 996); transition register, left neck (Fig. 1000), and foals, left hip (Fig. 1000).

For the Association of Small Horse Breeders of Bavaria, draft horses up to 120 centimeters high, and small horses from 120 to 140 centimeters high, brands are valid for both draft and small horses. In the main pedigree book the brand is on the right neck (Fig. 999), and foals, left hip (Fig. 998); pedigree book, left neck (Fig. 999), and foals, left hip (Fig. 998), and pre-register, right hip (Fig. 999).

In the German Democratic Republic, small horses are registered in the German Small Horse Pedigree Book, in the main pedigree book and stallions, the brand is on the left neck (Fig. 1003), and foals, since 1942, left hip (Fig. 1003); pedigree book, left neck (Fig. 1005), and foals, since 1942, left hip (Fig. 1005); pre-register, left neck (Fig. 1004), and foals, since 1942, left hip (Fig. 1004); transition register, left neck (Fig. 1008), and foals, since 1942, left hip (Fig. 1008).

In the Republic of Mexico, fighting bulls are raised on large tracts of rolling grasslands with wooded areas and a good water supply. These tracts are the ranches *(ganaderías)* where one-year-old calves are rounded up for the branding *(herradero)* and subsequently trained for fighting. The ranch brand is placed on the left hip, and a number consisting of two digits is applied with a running iron on the right ribs, the latter method having been in practice since about 1950. This number is entered in a record book and identifies the calf as to its mother's fighting characteristics. Earmarks and dewlaps are cut, also. At present there are fourteen Grade A bull ranches. In addition to the brand, another emblem of identification is used for fighting bulls. This is a small bunch of ribbons attached to a staff with a very sharp harpoon point. This staff of ribbons *(divisa)* is planted into the bull's *morrillo* as he enters the arena. The *divisa* may be compared to the racing colors of racing stables, each bull ranch having its distinctive color. Of seventeen original bull ranches, only fourteen remain:

Grade A Bull Ranch		*Divisa*
Atenco	(Fig. 1118)	sky-blue and white
Ayala	(Fig. 1119)	pink and white
Coaxamalucan	(Fig. 1120)	red and dark violet
Pasteje	(Fig. 1121)	black and gold
La Punta	(Fig. 1122)	grey, red and gold
La Laguna	(Fig. 1123)	tobacco and gold
Peñuelas	(Fig. 1124)	sky-blue and gold
Piedras Negras	(Fig. 1125)	red and black
Rancho Seco	(Fig. 1127)	yellow and red
(San Diego de) los Padres	(Fig. 1128)	red and white
San Mateo	(Fig. 1129)	pink and white

Xajay	(Fig. 1126)	red and green
Zacatepec	(Fig. 1130)	lead and red
Zotoluca	(Fig. 1131)	sky-blue and red

Hungary has produced some of the finest purebred horses. Similar to practices in Germany, horses are bred at state stud farms. Some of the important farms in existence prior to World War II are listed below. It will be noted that all brands have a similar crown above the letter designation. This crown is from the former national coat-of-arms, discontinued in 1949. The cross atop the crown of St. Stephen I, 997–1083, first king of Hungary, is bent. Legend has it that thieves once stole the crown and placed it in an iron casket which was not of sufficient depth to accommodate it. The thieves, however, forced the lid down, thus bending the cross. It also will be noted that the brands contain various types of letters, such as running, block, bradded, and reverse.

Hungarian State Stud Farms:

Radautz	(Fig. 1132)
Piber	(Fig. 1133)
Kísber	(Fig. 1134)
Babolna	(Fig. 1135)
Mezö-Hegyes	(Fig. 1136)
Fogaras	(Fig. 1137)

In the Kingdom of Thailand, there is no compulsory branding of livestock for purposes of ownership identification. The government has enacted the "Identity Card Act" providing for the registration of cattle, buffaloes, elephants, horses, asses, and mules over three years of age, except animals used for driving or drafting. After proper registration, an identity card is issued. Elephants are normally paint-branded on the rump.

There are regulations providing for the branding of livestock to control infectious diseases, including rinderpest, foot and mouth disease, haemorrhagic septicaemia, and swine fever. Animals vaccinated or inspected, or those from an infected area, are branded with a disease control brand. There are also regulations providing for the branding of livestock in inter-provincial travel, as evidence of clean health as certified by veterinary inspectors. Hot iron brands are used for cattle and buffaloes, and earmarks for hogs.

Miscellany

The entrance to Pioneer Hall, Teachers' College, Canyon, Texas, has branding irons displayed. . . . McMurray College, Abilene, Texas, has a large collection of branding irons. . . . The wall of the dining room, First National Bank of Dallas, Texas, has 100 brands displayed. . . . The elevator doors, Potter County Courthouse, Amarillo, Texas, have 70 brands displayed. . . . Mess Hall, The Chuckwagon, University of Texas, Austin, has brands displayed . . . . Rock Bunkhouse, Texas Cowboys' Reunion Association, Stamford, Texas, has dozens of brands carved in stone. . . . In Bison, South Dakota, the local museum's front wall is covered with 200 cattle brands. . . . In Garrison Hall, University of Texas, Austin, 32 brands are displayed.

Wyoming's oldest existing brand, used by John Walker Myers in 1857, is now used by Charles Myers in the Evanston region. . . . Washington's oldest brand is the Bar Balloon of Fred C. Schnebly, Ellensburg, used since 1839. Second oldest is the brand of H. B. James, Dayton, used since 1863; third oldest brand, used since 1869, is that of Frank Graham, Wilson Creek. . . . In 1916 Wyoming had 14,400 brands recorded. . . . In 1907 New Mexico had 24,380 brands recorded in the Brand Book of the Territory. . . . Brand number 5,000 was issued to Joe Zeb, near Ellensburg, Washington, in 1939; registration started in 1935. . . . Montana had 65,000 brands recorded in 1952; Washington, 10,500. . . . Colorado had 12,000 brands recorded in 1885; 23,250 in 1906; and 15,087 in 1940. . . . Brand number 10,000 was issued to H. E. Erskine and L. M. Sieght of Diamond Bell Ranch, Wauconda, Washington, the brand being the milestone insignia. . . . The Bexar County Clerk, Texas, had 1,200 brands recorded between 1943 and 1951. . . . In 1951 Washington had 12,655 recorded brands; and in 1957, 11,310.

Annual county registration is not feasible, because if a rancher was late for registration and someone else obtained his brand, he would have to rebrand his entire stock. . . . Queena Stewart, Buffalo Gap, South Dakota, Secretary, South Dakota Brand Commission, Secretary, Association of Secretaries of State Cattle Raisers' Associations, Vice-President of Western South Dakota Livestock Growers' Association, is considered the foremost student of brand nomenclature. . . . Miss Dora Criddle was Recorder of Brands, State of Washington, from 1935 to 1955. . . . Arizona had 7,360 brands recorded in 1933. . . . "Cattle Trails in the Live Stock Market Development," *Monthly Newsletter to Animal Husbandmen*, Vol. VIII, No. 1 (April 1926), published by Armour's Livestock Bureau, Chicago, has an accompanying map describing all of the Texas cattle trails. . . . The longest name of any recorded brand owner is that of Mosteenbihnahatinihbitsih in Utah.

In the Cashmere, Washington, Willis Carey Historical Museum, are original Chelan County cattle brands on pieces of wood, shoe leather, and scraps. These sample brands were rescued from the basement of the county auditor's office. . . . At the eighty-third annual Texas and Southwestern Cattle Raisers' Convention at Austin, March, 1960, Field Inspector Leonard Stiles (2210 POB 532, Sweeney, Texas) exhibited his collection of 540 branding irons. His collection was started in 1953 when he persuaded a country storekeeper to give him the branding iron he was using to poke his pot-bellied stove. Some branding irons were given to him by cattlemen in the Coastal Plains he covers as a TSCRA inspector, others he found hanging in trees, barns, and in out-of-the-way places. Recently, a rancher who knew that a branding iron was placed in his concrete porch for reinforcing some fifty years ago, demolished the porch in order to donate the iron to Stiles' collection. About 75 per cent of the brands in Inspector Stiles' collection are still in use on South Texas ranches. . . . During 1959–60, the Texas and Southwestern Cattle Raisers' Association registered more than 5,000 new brands, an indication that the custom of branding cattle in Texas is growing. . . . During fiscal year 1959–60, a total of 183 cattle thefts were reported in Texas. . . . Membership in the Texas and Southwest Cattle Raisers' Association amounted to 10,599 and the number of cattle rendered by members to 1,418,976 in 1960.

The Arabic term for brand is *ousm or wasm;* brands *ousoum* or *wusum.* . . . The United States Border Patrol (Immigration and Naturalization Service, United States Department of Justice) on occasion finds it desirable to use horses in patrol work. With the advent of quarter-ton trucks with front-wheel drive (jeep), the need for horses has become limited. When horses are needed, they are obtained on a rental basis from local sources. . . . The French term for brand is *le tatouage.* . . . The cattle drive of another era was revived when rancher Don Hight and seven cowboys drove his herd of 1,800 Herefords (1,100 cows and 700 steers) from his ranch to a sales ring in Winner, South Dakota, a distance of sixty-five miles. The drive took place, through blinding snowstorms and high winds, across private lands in the rolling hills of South Central South Dakota, during the early part of January, 1962. . . . Three cattle-rustling incidents in the Enumclaw-Auburn area of the state of Washington were solved February 27, 1962, with the arrest of four men by the sheriff of King County. The men admitted to killing beef animals in farm fields and taking about 1,200 pounds of dressed meat. The incidents took place in April, October, and February. . . . Lapp herdsmen work on foot during fall roundup and use their backs for hitching posts when cutting out a deer. Owners brand ears with registered notches. Unmarked strays are sold to help the aged. The tribe also outlaws rustlers.

ENCO, Humble Oil & Refining Company, issued a brochure titled "Montana Adventures, Territorial Centennial 1864–1964," which contains, on pages 8 and 9, respectively, articles called

"The Story of Cattle Brands," and "The Language of Cattle Brands," the latter explaining the method of reading a brand and also giving examples of forty-six brands. . . . *Mainliner,* a magazine for United Air Lines guests, contains in its January 1963 issue (Vol. 7, No. 1, p. 9) an article by Eugene Dunlop on "Brands and Irons." . . . The front cover of the March–April 1965 (Vol. 21, No. 2) issue of *Steelways,* a magazine published bi-monthly by the American Iron and Steel Institute bears a color photograph by I. G. Holmes featuring branding irons. These irons are from the museum of the Texas Technological College at Lubbock. Among this collection of famous brands, the Matador V and the XIT are easily recognized. The editorial describing the front cover is appropriately entitled "Frontier Symbolism." . . . Harter's, manufacturers of hunting and fishing equipment in Waseca, Minnesota, advertised in its Catalog No. 76, 1966, Item 29–1100 "Western Used Branding Irons." They were described as about four feet long and were used at top western ranches. Shipping weight, 3½ pounds. . . . In the Knoedler Galleries of the Library of Congress hangs an oil painting by artist Albertus Browere depicting a prospector on mule back, carrying new equipment in search of gold. The mule bears the Circle Four Arrow brand ⊕ .

Turistas shopping in Mexico in the summer of 1967 found it worth their while to drop in at the "Weston Reforma," Paseo de la Reforma 157, México 5, D.F. In an antique store jammed with genuine treasures, the genial resident Englishman sold *"fierros antiguos para marcar ganado"* for as low as forty pesos, a true bargain for ornate Mexican branding irons . . . The bull country of France lies in a triangle at the mouth of the Rhône, bounded by Avignon in the north, by Montpellier in the west, and by Marseille in the east. The base of the triangle is formed by the marshes of the Camargue. Bullfighting takes place in a dozen cities within this triangle. In the summer of 1969 spectators at the bullfight in Arles were presented with a chart, depicting fifty-one brands, various earmarks, and breeders' colors. The chart is entitled: *"Marques–Escoussures–Devises des Manades de Taureaux"* (Brands–Earmarks–Bull Ranch Colors). This chart is published under the auspices of Club Taurin, siège social, 4, rue Berthelot; Marseille, 14e, and is dated Janvier 1963 . . . .

In the *Rügianisches Landbuch* (Landgebrauch), a volume on the subject of land use dating back to the sixteenth century, livestock, goose, and duck marks are discussed. The book pertains to the Isle of Rügen, off the coast of Pomerania. . . . The Ripuarian Franks had a code book entitled *Edictum Rotharis*, which has been edited by Bluhme in Monum. Leg. IV. The original code dates back to 550 A.D. and deals with identification of animals. There is a separate section on horse marks. . . . In France we find a book by Coutume v. Berry, dated 1539, on the subject of mandatory animal marking. . . . A Belgian law of July 15, 1896, prescribes marking of cattle. . . . Icelandic law relating to livestock marking and abuse has a long history. In 930 A.D. the Ulfejöts law with its Stadarholsbook came into being. This edict became the law of the land in 1118. Subsequently there appeared the Konungsbok, Codex regius of 1250–60, and the later amalgamation of the ancient republican Icelandic laws to Grágás. The first Book of Laws was compiled by King Magnus Hakonsohn in 1280–81, the second Book of Laws by Magnus Lagabätir (The Law Improver). In these books are laws on blotting of sheep brands, laws concerning marks on livestock, regulations for the marking of cattle and *einkumit* (sheep), and also regulations for unmarked livestock.

Glossary

1. *Brands and Branding Terms*

AGE BRAND—a number of digits indicating the date of birth of the animal. Usually it is applied to the neck and is not recordable as evidence of ownership.

BRAND—a design consisting of numerals, letters, or pictures, or any combination thereof, permanently impressed in a specified location upon the skin, hide, fleece, horn, or hoof of livestock, including cattle, horses, mules, asses, burros, sheep, goats, hogs, foxes, mink, marten, dogs, chickens, geese, ducks, and turkeys, by a hot iron, or by a chemical compound such as acid, paint, tar, and ink. The term brand includes all marks, such as earmarks, dewlaps, and wattles; and all tattoos, including slapmarks, snout marks, and horn marks. A registered brand is evidence that the animal bearing such brand is the personal property of the owner in whose name the brand is registered.

BARBED BRAND—one with a short projection from some part of the design.

BENCH BRAND—one resting upon a bench.

BLOTCHING—defacing a recorded brand with a hot iron, causing a large scar which obliterates the original brand and renders it useless for evidence of ownership.

BLOTTING—defacing a recorded brand willfully in order to achieve a new design. This is one of the techniques used by rustlers to alter brands.

BOSAL BRAND—this brand consists of a stripe burned around the

278

animal's nose. The term is derived from the brand's similarity in appearance to a bosal. The bosal is the front piece of the noseband of a bosalea, a riding headstall for breaking broncs; from the Spanish *bozal* (muzzle).

BOTCH—an unsuccessfully defaced brand.

BOXED BRAND—one whose design bears framing lines, either curvilinear or rectilinear.

BRADDED BRAND—one with a short projection from some part of the design.

BRAND ARTIST—an expert at defacing brands.

BRAND BLOTTER (BRAND BLOTCHER, BRAND BURNER)—a cattle thief who defaces a recorded brand in order to destroy the evidence of ownership; a brand artist.

BRAND BOOK—official publication of recorded brands; issued by state recorders of brands and, formerly, by cattle raisers' associations.

BRANDER—a man who applies the branding iron to the hide, fleece, skin, horn and hoof of livestock.

BRANDING CHUTE—a narrow, boarded passage into which cattle are driven and held so that they may be branded without having to be thrown.

BRAND INSPECTOR—a man hired to inspect brands at shipping points, sales auctions, and markets for compliance with legal requirements. Inspectors are employed by the state or by cattle raisers' associations.

BRAND YOU CAN READ IN THE MOONLIGHT—a large brand, covering a large area of hide.

CHARACTER RECORD BRAND—a brand used to classify an animal for the purpose of keeping records relating to it. It is usually applied to the flank and is not recordable as evidence of ownership.

CHARACTER BRAND—a brand testing the character of a person suspected of engaging in the practice of brand artistry. It is of a design which can easily be worked into the design of a brand used by the person suspected of brand artistry. The brand is also of a design not usually found in that particular locality.

CLOSE BRAND—one whose characters are set too close, blurring the brand on application.

CONNECTED BRAND—one which has two or more characters connected.

COLD BRAND—a hair brand.

CORRAL BRANDING—branding accomplished in a corral, as opposed to range branding.

COUNTERBRAND—a brand legally cancelling the original one by application either above or below it. The counterbrand supersedes the original one either by purchase or by brand error. In addition to being placed either below or above the original brand, the counterbrand is also applied at the proper location, differently situated and so registered. During the 1880's in the Texas cattle industry, counterbranding was accomplished by repeating the undesired brand and then applying the new brand in its proper location, thus discontinuing the use of the long bar burned through the existing brand. See vent brand.

COUNTY BRAND—a brand used in Texas. It consisted of a letter or a group of letters for each Texas county and was always placed on the neck of the animal. This brand was intended to make rustling more difficult, since the rustler would have to record the blotted brand at the county clerk's office or else blot the county brand, too.

CRYO-BRAND—see Freeze Brand.

DECOY BRAND—a small and unobtrusive brand burned on the ventral side of an animal in order to trap rustlers. Usually choicest steers and calves are used and are left unbranded otherwise. This ruse, however, seldom works.

DRAG BRAND—one with a downward projection angling to the left.

FLUIDY MUSTARD—an odd-looking brand brought in from outside the district and having no recognizable character by which it might be called, e.g., Quien Sabe brand (Fig. 114).

FLYING BRAND—one with characters having symbolized wings.

FOOL BRAND—one too complicated to describe with a brief name.

FORKED BRAND—one with a V-shaped fork attached to a part of the character.

FREEZE BRAND (Cryo-Brand)—a brand applied with a super-cold copper branding iron. The brand is distinguished by white hair on the brand site, in contrast to the animals' natural hair-color.

GREASER MADHOUSE—an occasional name for the intricate Mexican brands.

HAIR BRAND—a brand made by holding the branding iron against the animal just long enough to burn the hair and not the hide.

HAIR OVER—said of a brand when the hair grows back over it.

HAIRY-DICK—an unbranded animal, especially a calf.

HERD BRAND—a brand consisting of the number designation or other identification of a specific herd. It is usually applied to the neck, is not recordable, and may be used only for purposes of identification.

HOLDING BRAND—a brand of any design denoting ownership, as opposed to a production record brand. It is the primary brand of the owner and all other marks and brands on the animal are of a supplementary nature.

HOOKED BRAND—one with a cane-shaped projection attached to a part of the characters.

HOT IRON!—the call of the brander when he wants a freshly heated iron.

HOT STUFF—a slang name for heated branding irons.

IRON—a short name for branding iron.

IRON MAN—the man handling the branding irons at branding time.

IRON TENDER—the man who heats and tends to the branding irons.

KETCH HAND—the man who ropes the calves for branding.

LAZY BRAND—one with its characters lying on their sides, either to the right or to the left.

LONG BRAND—one with vertically extended letters and numerals.

MAP OF MEXICO—the American cowboy's name for the intricate Mexican cattle brands, which are usually large and give no clue to any name by which they may be called.

MAVERICK—an unbranded calf or adult cow. In 1855, Colonel Samuel A. Maverick of San Antonio sold his branded and unbranded cattle to Toutant de Beauregard who systematically rounded up all cattle, branded or unbranded. Whenever his riders found an unbranded animal, they called it a maverick and applied Beauregard's brand. An early brand used by Colonel Maverick was the MK. After 1886 this brand was used by the Magnolia Land and Cattle Company on 625 sections in and around Borden County.

MAVERICK BRAND—an unrecorded brand. This brand is used by thieves to hold an animal on the range until such time as they are able to drive it off.

MAVERICKER—a man who rode the ranges in order to brand mavericks in the early days when it was considered that calves not following cows were anybody's cattle. Subsequently, laws were enacted to prohibit such practice. Thereafter, the meaning of the word mavericker became a cow thief.

MAVERICKING—the act of hunting down and branding unbranded calves. In later years the meaning of the word changed to stealing.

MAVERICK FACTORY—the procedure of creating mavericks by killing the cow with her tell-tale brand.

MORE STRAW—the call of the brander for more calves to be brought to the branding fire.

OPEN BRAND—one not boxed with framing lines. Also, a brand whose characters have been separated sufficiently so that upon application it produces a clearly defined brand.

PICKED BRAND—a brand made by picking the hair by means of knife and thumb in order to form the design of the brand. It is not a permanent brand and serves only the rustler, since it appears to be an honest brand when seen from a distance.

282

PICKING A SLEEPER—the process of attempting to identify a brand which is not readily discernible by plucking the hair around the obscured brand.

PRODUCTION RECORD BRAND—a brand used for the identification of dairy or beef cattle. It is usually applied to a point between the hock and stifle or to the shoulder. It consists of a digit or a combination of digits and may not be recorded as evidence of ownership.

RAFTER BRAND—one having semi-cone-shaped lines above the letter or figure, similar to the roof of a house.

RANGE BRANDED—branded on the range, away from the corral.

RENEGADE RIDER (OUTSIDE MAN, STRAY MAN, REPRESENTATIVE, REP)—a hand who represents his boss at other ranches and round-ups, and who is charged to return any cattle carrying the brand of his own ranch.

ROAD BRAND—a brand used on trail herds. Cattle were driven through a chute and the road brand applied lightly. It was a common brand for a particular drive, because the animals in the trail herd might belong to different owners using various types of brands. This brand originated in Texas, where a law was enacted that all cattle driven beyond the northern limits of the state were to be branded with a large and plain mark of any design, to be applied to the left side of the stock behind the shoulder. With the passing of the trail herds, this brand is no longer needed.

ROCKING BRAND—one resting upon and connected to a quarter circle.

ROUNDUP—the gathering in of cattle. The spring roundup is for the branding of calves and the fall roundup for the gathering of beeves for shipment and the branding of late calves or those overlooked in the spring. The roundup originated in Kentucky, North Carolina, Tennessee, South Carolina, Virginia, and West Virginia.

RUNNING A BRAND—to use a brand; to give a brand; to sear a brand with a running iron.

RUNNING BRAND—one with flowing curves at its ends.

RUSTLERS' BRAND—a resolution, passed November 8, 1883, by the Wyoming Stock Growers' Association, declared cattle so branded to be treated as mavericks, because the owner was suspected of being a rustler. Innocent small cattle owners and grangers had to prove their innocence before they were able to recover their property. This arbitrary exercise of power of the Association in violation of fundamental constitutional rights soon caused it to be entangled in litigation.

SCORCHER—a branding iron.

SET BRAND—one made with a stamp branding iron.

SKILLET OF SNAKES—cowboy's name for the intricate Mexican brands.

SLEEPER BRAND—a brand unrecorded and unknown on a particular range.

SLEEPER—an unbranded calf earmarked by rustlers with the marks of its rightful owner. As a result, the rustlers hoped the calf would be overlooked at the round-up and would be assumed to be branded. Next season the rustlers would return, apply their own brand, and cut new earmarks of such nature as to obliterate the old ones.

SLEEPERING—the act of such action.

SLICKS—unbranded animals, particularly horses.

SLICK EAR—an unbranded calf.

SLOW BRAND—an unrecorded brand, employed in one form of cattle stealing. It is unlawful for anyone to mutilate a brand, and the law also requires that every brand must be recorded in the county of its origin. A rustler who blots out one brand and puts another in its place hesitates to record this new brand. He simply uses it, trusting that he can get the cattle out of the county before discovery.

STAMP BRAND—one made with a stamp branding iron.

STRAY BRAND—branded cattle unintentionally shipped in a large consignment. Proper reimbursement to the rightful owner was made at the shipping terminus through cattlemen's associations and inspectors.

SWING BRAND—one suspended from and connected with a quarter circle.

TALLY BRAND—a brand consisting of a numerical designation for an animal. This brand is used for identification purposes only and may not be recorded.

TALLY BRANDING—taking an inventory of cattle.

TUMBLING BRAND—one leaning in an oblique position, either to the right or to the left.

VENT BRAND—(venta-sale) legal voiding (venting) of a brand after sale to a new owner. There are two types of vent brands. First, it may consist of a long bar applied through the original brand with a vent iron at the time of sale. Or second, it may consist of the owner's registered brand, applied in a legally specified location, but not necessarily of the same size as the original brand. This type of venting is termed counterbranding. Consequently, only if an iron is smaller than the original branding iron can it properly be called a vent iron.

WALKING BRAND—one with an upward projection angling to the right.

WHANGDOODLE—a brand with interlocking wings and with no central flying figure.

WORKING BRANDS—changing brands from one type to another through the use of a running iron.

WORK OVER—to change a brand.

2. Terms Used by Breeders and Associations

APPLICATION FOR REGISTRY—the owner of an animal at the time the application for registry is made.

BREED—race or variety of animals related by descent and similar in most characteristics. They are additionally classified according to their economic value: cattle bred for beef production; cattle bred for milk production; or cattle bred for the dual purpose of both milk and beef production.

285

BREEDER—the breeder of an animal is the owner of the dam at the time she was served.

BREED ASSOCIATIONS—maintain herd books and registration records. Associations may also maintain additional registration for meritorious performance of animals and administer programs to determine the performance of breeders' animals. Animals showing a high order of merit may be registered in the Advanced Registry.

CROSS-BREEDING—the crossing of distinct breeds, thereby interfering with the transmission of distinct factors accounting for the typical characteristics of the two breeds. The result is not a blending of the characters of the two breeds, but a combination of the factors. The first cross between distinct breeds usually has good results, while many of the second generation prove unsatisfactory in their characteristics.

FIRST OWNER—the first owner of a calf is the owner of the dam at the time the calf is born.

FREEMARTIN—the imperfectly-sexed and infertile female of mixed twins in cattle. Not all heifers born twin with bulls are freemartins.

GRADE—used in conjunction with a certain breed name, such as Grade Jersey. The animal has half or more of the characteristics of the grade mentioned. High Grade implies a high proportion of purebred characteristics. Grade cattle are ineligible for registration.

HERD BOOK—a record of ancestry in systematic order maintained by a breeders' association.

IN-BREEDING—mating of closely related individuals, such as brother to sister, sire to daughter, or son to dam. An individual is in-bred when its parents show 50 per cent or more common ancestry in their pedigree. The primary effect of in-breeding is the intensification and fixation of hereditary qualities, such as the white faces of Hereford cattle.

LINE-BREEDING—is the mating of related animals to a lesser degree than that of in-breeding. The common ancestry of parents range from 25 per cent to 50 per cent. This system is said to possess all the excellencies of in-breeding, with a greatly lessened tendency toward the production of defectives.

OUT-CROSSING—mating of entirely unrelated individuals, or those of less than 25 per cent common ancestry. In breeds where families or strains have become well established, such practice is usually avoided.

OWNER OF SIRE—is the owner at the time of service.

PEDIGREE—a list or table indicating the ancestors of an individual. It is usually presented in graphic form.

POLL—is a naturally polled animal that will never grow horns. A dehorned animal is not a natural poll.

PUREBRED—an animal descended in all lines of its ancestry from animals imported from the locality in which the breed to which the animal belongs originated. The ancestry is documented. Purebred is not synonymous with thoroughbred, since this term is only applied to a distinctive English horse breed.

REGISTERED PUREBRED—a purebred animal which has been registered by its owner with a brand registry association.

SCORE CARD—a concise description of the conformation of the body desired, with a numerical expression of the relative importance of each point considered. Perfection is normally 100 per cent. Score cards are adopted by breed registry associations for their respective breeds.

SCRUB—an animal of mixed or unknown breeding, without type or markings of any recognized breed.

TYPE OF CATTLE—refers to the conformation of an animal which indicates or suggests the purpose it serves; e.g., the extraordinary development of the udder and milk veins in cattle of the dairy type.

3. *Terms Applicable to Meat Grading*

ANIMAL—cattle, sheep, swine, or goats.

CARCASS—the commercially prepared or dressed body of any animal intended for human food.

CLASS—a subdivision of a product based on essential physical characteristics that differentiate between major groups of the same species. These physical characteristics are associated with age and sex.

CONDITION—the physical characteristics of a product which affect its marketability, with special reference to its state of preservation, cleanliness, soundness, wholesomeness or fitness for human food.

CONFORMATION—the general build, shape, form, contour, or outline of a carcass, side, or cut. Superior conformation consists of a plump, thick, or meaty carcass with short neck and shanks. Lower degrees of excellence are evidenced by ranginess and angularity.

FABRICATING—cutting into wholesale or retail cuts, or dicing or grinding.

FINISH—the amount, quality, and distribution of fat. Superior finish is a smooth, even covering of fat over most of the exterior surface of the carcass, a much thinner covering over the interior surface of the ribs, and a liberal mixture of fat with lean (marbling).

GRADE—a commercial subdivision of a product based on certain definite preference-determining factors: conformation, finish, and quality.

KIND—refers to different species of animals, such as cattle, swine, sheep, goats, and horses.

MEAT—the edible part of the muscle of a skeletal animal, or that which is found in the tongue, in the diaphragm, in the heart, or in the esophagus, and which is intended for human food, with or without the accompanying and overlying fat and the portions of bone, skin, sinew, nerve, and blood vessels which normally accompany the muscle tissue and which are not separated from it in the process of dressing. This term does not include the muscle found in the lips, snout, or ears.

MEAT-BY-PRODUCT—all edible (other than meat and prepared

meats) intended for human food, derived from one or more animals, and including but not limited to such organs and parts as livers, kidneys, sweetbreads, brains, lungs, spleens, stomachs, tripe, lips, snouts, and ears.

QUALITY—a combination of the inherent properties of a product which determine its relative degree of excellence.

PREPARED MEATS—the products intended for human food which are obtained by subjecting meat to drying, curing, smoking, cooking, grinding, seasoning, or flavoring, or to any combination of such procedures, and to which no considerable quantity of any substance other than meat or meat by-products has been added.

PROCESSING—drying, curing, smoking, cooking, seasoning, or flavoring, or any combination of such processes, with or without fabrication.

PRODUCTS—meats, prepared meats, meat by-products, or meat food products.

SPECIFICATION—description of official and tentative standards for products with respect to the class, grade, quantity, other quality, or condition of product.

STANDARDS—the official and tentative standards of the U.S. Department of Agriculture for the class, grade, other quality designation, or condition of the product.

Animal Definitions as to Class

BULL—uncastrated male bovine.

Cow—female bovine that has developed through reproduction or with age the typical characteristics of a mature female.

HEIFER—immature female bovine that has not yet developed the physical characteristics typical of cows.

STAG—male bovine castrated after it has developed or begun to develop the secondary physical characteristics of a bull.

STEER—male bovine castrated when young and prior to development of the secondary physical characteristics of a bull.

EWE—female ovine.

LAMB—immature ovine, usually under fourteen months of age, that has not cut its first pair of permanent incisor teeth.

RAM—uncastrated male ovine.

SHEEP—an ovine, usually over twenty-four months old, that has cut its second pair of incisor teeth.

WETHER—male ovine castrated when young and prior to developing the secondary physical characteristics of a ram.

YEARLING—an ovine usually between one and two years old, that has cut its first pair of permanent incisor teeth but has not cut its second pair.

BARROW—male swine castrated when young and prior to the development of the secondary physical characteristics of a boar.

BOAR—uncastrated male swine.

GILT—young female swine that has not yet produced young and has not reached an advanced stage of pregnancy.

Sow—mature female swine that shows evidence of having produced young or has reached an advanced stage of pregnancy.

STAG—male swine castrated after development or beginning of development of the secondary physical characteristics of a boar.

5. *Definitions Used in Cattle Marketing*

DEALER—any person, not a market agency, engaged in the business of buying or selling livestock in commerce, either in his own account or as the employee or agent of the vendor or purchaser.

MARKET AGENCY—any person or organization engaged in the business of (1) buying or selling commercial livestock on a commission basis or (2) furnishing stockyard services.

PACKER—any person engaged in the business of buying livestock in commerce for purposes of slaughter; or of manufacturing or preparing meats or meat food products for sale or shipment in commerce; or of manufacturing or preparing livestock products for sale or shipment in commerce; or of marketing meats, meat food products, livestock products, dairy products, poultry, poultry products, or eggs in commerce. In addition, there may be various other qualifications.

STOCKYARD—any place, establishment, or facility known as stockyards, conducted or operated for compensation or profit as a public market, consisting of pens or other enclosures, and their appurtenances, in which live cattle, sheep, swine, horses, mules, or goats are received, held, or kept for sale or shipment in commerce.

List of Abbreviations

AMS—Agricultural Marketing Service, U.S. Department of Agriculture.

AR—Army Regulation, Department of the Army.

ARS—Agricultural Research Service, U.S. Department of Agriculture.

CFR—Code of Federal Regulations.

CL—Collections of Laws, State of Michigan.

CMG—Companion of the Most Distinguished Order of St. Michael and St. George (7th ranking Order of British Knighthood; 3rd Class of this particular order).

DA—Department of the Army.

DHIA—Dairy Herd Improvement, Animal Husbandry Research Division, Agricultural Research Service, U.S. Department of Agriculture. (The chief of this agency did not specify what the final A in the abbreviation stood for; probably agency or administration).

DSP—this abbreviation has defied definition, but is probably a distinguished service award (Canada).

FS—Forest Service, U.S. Department of Agriculture.

FSM—Forest Service Manual.

ID—Interior Department (U.S. Department of Interior).

IGD—Inspector General's Department.*

IGO—Office of Inspector General.*

NPS—National Park Service, U.S. Department of Interior.

PFRA—Prairie Farm Rehabilitation Administration (Canada).

RSA—Revised Statutes of Alberta (Canada).

RSC—Revised Statutes of Canada.

RSO—Revised Statutes of Ontario (Canada).

RS QMC—Remount Service, Quartermaster Corps, U.S. Army.

RSS—Revised Statutes of Saskatchewan (Canada).

SC—Statutes of Canada.

SPO—State Printing Office (California).

SRA-AMS—Service and Regulators Announcement, Agricultural Marketing Service, U.S. Department of Agriculture.

USADE—U.S. Animal Disease Eradication Division, Agricultural Research Service, U.S. Department of Agriculture. Successor to the U.S. Animal Disease Eradication Branch which in turn succeeded the U.S. Bureau of Animal Industry (USBAI).

USBAI—U.S. Bureau of Animal Industry, U.S. Department of Agriculture. Succeeded by U.S. Animal Disease Eradication Branch of the Agricultural Research Service.

USDA—U.S. Department of Agriculture.

USDI—U.S. Department of Interior.

WD—War Department.*

WD AGO—The Adjutant General's Office, War Department. Used for blank form identification, discontinued in 1947.

WD QMC—Quartermaster Corps, War Department. Used for identification of blank forms for quartermaster items of equipment, discontinued in 1947.

* The Inspector General's Department and the Quartermaster Corps, services, as opposed to branches, of the U.S. Army, are headed by the inspector general and the quartermaster general. These two officers have always worn two hats, i.e., they are the senior technical advisers to the chief of staff, U.S. Army, in their respective areas, and also are chiefs of services. Before World War II they were elements of the Chiefs of Service Section under the chief of staff, U.S. Army, and as such were members of the General Council.

From the offices of the Chiefs of Service Section various blank forms and other publications emanated, designated "IGO" or "IGD" and "IWD QMC" or "RS QMC," terms which obviously lacked military uniformity.

During World War II, the inspector general became a member of the Special Staff, but subordinate directly to the chief of staff, U.S. Army, while the quartermaster general was subordinate to the Commanding General, Service of Supply.

Under the provisions of the National Security Act of 1947, 61 Statutes 499, 5 USC 171, a national military establishment was created in which the War Department was renamed Department of the Army (DA). Additional acts prescribed and amended the organization of the Department of the Army.

After the reorganization, the inspector general remained as a member of the Special Staff and retained his position as a chief of a special branch (formerly known as a service). The quartermaster general, as chief of a basic branch (formerly known as a service) was subordinated to the deputy chief of staff for Logistics, the latter being a member of the Department of the Army General Staff.

Because of the almost total disappearance of Public Animals (horses, mules, dogs, pigeons) used by the U.S. Army, no blank forms bearing DA designation have been printed, stocks of old WD forms being exhausted to administer the few remaining Public Animals.

Bibliography

Books

Adams, Ramon F. *Come An' Get It*. Norman, University of Oklahoma Press, 1952.

———. *Cowboy Lingo*. Boston, Houghton Mifflin, 1936.

———. *Old-Time Cowhand*. New York, Macmillan Co., 1961.

———. *Western Words*. Norman, University of Oklahoma Press, 1944.

———. ed. *The Best of the American Cowboy*. Norman, University of Oklahoma Press, 1957.

Allaugh, R., and B. Anderson. *How to Identify Livestock*. Santa Cruz, California, Davis Publishing Co., 1951.

Allen, Jules Verne. *Cowboy Lore*. San Antonio, Naylor Printing Co., 1933.

Arndt, Ernst Moritz. *Bomärce in Island, auf den Orkneys-Shetland-Inseln fur wilde und zahme Tiere*. Nebenstunden, 1826.

———. *Kennzeichen der Schafe in England, auf den Shetlands und Orkneys*. Nebenstunden, 1826. (Cited from Hibbert, *Description of the Shetland Islands*. Edinburgh, 1822.) (Sheep marks in England and in the Shetland and Orkney islands).

Arnold, Oren, and John P. Hale. *Hot Irons, Heraldry of the Range*. New York, Macmillan Co., 1940.

Brown, Dee, and Martin F. Schmitt. *Trail Driving Days*. New York, Charles Scribner's Sons, 1952.

Brown, Mark H., and W. R. Felton. *Before Barbed Wire*. New York, Henry Holt and Co., 1956.

Bye, John O. *Backtrailing In the Heart of the Shortgrass Country*. Everett, Washington, 1956.

Cailliaud, Frédéric. *Recherches sur les arts et métiers*. Paris, Debure frères, 1831.

Calver, William Louis, and Reginald Pelham Bolton. *History Written With Pick and Shovel*. New York, New York Historical Society, 1950.

Carter, Amon C., Molyneau, Peter, and Reeves, Frank Sr., *A Century of Texas Cattle Brands*. Fort Worth, '36 Fair Publication Company, 1936.

Casteel, Homer. *The Running of the Bulls*. New York, Dodd, Mead and Company, 1953.

Cossío, José María. *Los Toros: Tratado téchnico e histórico*. 4 vols. Madrid, 1945.

Dale, Edward E. *The Range Cattle Industry*. Norman, University of Oklahoma Press, 1930.

Davidson, H. R. *The Production and Marketing of Pigs*. 2nd ed., New York, Longmans, Green & Co., 1953.

Davies, Norman de Garis. *The Tombs of Two Officials of Thutmosis the Fourth*. London, Egypt Exploration Society, 1923.

Dobie, J. Frank. *The Vaquero of the Brush Country*. Dallas, The Southwest Press, 1929.

Driggs, Howard R. *Westward America*. New York, G. P. Putnam, 1942.

Edmund. *Maître Pierre*. 9th ed., 1862. (French horse brands.)

Emrich, Duncan. *It's an Old Wild West Custom*. Kingswood, Surrey, the World's Work (1913) Ltd., 1951.

Engelhardt, O. F. M. *Father Zephrin, History of the Province of Saint Barbara*. San Francisco, James H. Barry Co., 1923.

Ensminger, M. E. *The Stockman's Handbook*. Danville, Illinois, The Interstate Printers and Publishers, Inc., 1959.

Evans, Edna Hoffman. *Written With Fire, The Story of Cattle Brands*. New York, Holt, Rinehart and Winston, 1962.

Fletcher, Sidney E. *The Cowboy and His Horse*. New York, Grossett & Dunlap, 1951.

Foster-Harris. *The Look of the Old West*. New York, Viking Press, 1955.

296

Friedli, E. *Bärndütsch*. 1908. (Swiss livestock brands.)

Gosset, A. L. J. *Shepherds of Britain*. London, Constable & Co., 1911.

Grant, Bruce. *The Cowboy Encyclopedia*. Chicago, Rand McNally & Co., 1956.

Haley, J. Evetts. *Charles Goodnight, Cowman and Plainsman*. Boston, Houghton Mifflin Co., 1936.

———. *The Heraldry of the Range; Some Southwestern Brands*. Canyon, Texas, Panhandle Plains Historical Society, 1949.

———. *XIT Ranch*. Chicago, Lakeside Press, 1929.

Heckscher. *Die Volkskunde des germanischen Kulturkreises*. Hamburg, 1925 (German livestock brands; earmarks as signs of healing, Isle of Rügen.)

Homeyer, Carl Gustav. *Die Haus-und Hofmarken*. Berlin, 1870, new ed. 1890. (The most comprehensive study of house and farm marks, including livestock marks, of northern and central Europe.)

Jackson, W. H., and Long, S. A. *Texas Stock Directory; or, Book of Marks and Brands*. (Cumulative Index 1949–52) Cliffside Park, N. J., W. F. Kelleher (reprint of volume published originally in San Antonio in 1865).

Klebs, Luise. *Die Reliefs und Malereien des Neuen Reiches*. Heidelberg, Carl Winters Verlagsbuchhandlung, 1934.

Koch, Rudolf. *The Book of Signs*. London, Dover Publications, Inc., Republication of First Edition Club, 1930.

Kolmodin. *Några renmärken från Sorsele*. Fataburen, 1917–18. (Reindeer marks in Sweden.)

Künssberg, Eberhardt Freiherr von. *Rechtsbrand und Volksbrand. Handbuch der deutschen Volkskunde*. Herausgeber W. Pessler, n.d. (German livestock brands.)

Lee, Tom. *The King Ranch*. Boston, Little, Brown and Co., 1957.

Markaskrá: *Suthur-Thingeyjasýslu og Keluneschrepps, Endurkothhuth, 1944*. Akureyri, Odds Björnssonar, 1944. List of property marks in Akureyri, Iceland, comprised of brands and ear marks for sheep. These marks are not listed by the commonly known and used method of arranging them by the design of the mark, but instead by the name of the design, by the proprietors of the marks, by farms, and by residences.)

Mora, Jo. *Trail Dust and Saddle Leather*. New York, Charles Scribner's Sons, 1946.

Nissen, K. *Sylappiske renmerker*. Fataburen (Nordiska Museets och Skansens Aarsbok), 1917 (18). (South Lappish reindeer marks in Finland.)

Older, Mrs. Fremont. *California Missions and Their Romances*. New York, Coward-McCann, Inc., 1938.

Osenbrüggen. *Wanderstudien aus der Schweiz*. Schaffhausen, 1867. (Earmarks for sheep near Churwaldens, Switzerland).

———. *Alemanisches Strafrecht*. n.d. (Legal dissertation on livestock brands and marks in Switzerland.)

Osgood, Ernest S. *The Day of the Cattleman*. Chicago, University of Chicago Press, 1929.

Peake, Dr. Ora B. *The Colorado Range Cattle Industry*. Glendale, California, The Arthur H. Clark Co., 1937.

Pelzer, Louis. *The Cattleman's Frontier*. Glendale, California, The Arthur H. Clark Co., 1936.

Rollins, Philip A. *The Cowboy*. New York, Charles Scribner's Sons, 1936.

Russwurm, C. *Eibefolke, oder die Schweden an den Küsten Esthlands*. n.d. (Earmarks for sheep, marks on the webs of goose feet, etc., as practiced by the Swedish inhabitants on the islands off the coast of Estonia: in Roiks and Kertel, Isle of Dagö [Khiuma]; isles of Worms [Vormsi], Runö [Ruhma], Odinsholm, Nuckö, and Nargö.)

Sandoz, Mari. *The Cattlemen*. New York, Hastings House, 1958.

Schmidt, Rudolf. *Volkskundliches an dem Oderbruch. Das Oderbruch*. Herausgeber P. F. Mengel, 2 vols. Eberswalde, Verlag R. Muller G.m.b.H., 1934. (Livestock brands in the marshlands of the Oder River, Brandenburg.)

Solem, E. *Lappiske Rettstudier*. 1933. (Brands used by the Lapps in Finland.)

298

Spruth, Dr. Herbert. *Die Hausmarke. Wesen und Bibliographie.* Herausgegeben von der Deutschen Arbeitsgemeinschaft genealogischer Verbande. Heft 4/5. Neustadt an der Aisch, Verlag Degener & Co., Inhaber Gerhard Gessner, 1960. (Valuable bibliography on all varieties of identification marks, including livestock marks.)

Tannenbaum, Frank. *Mexico.* New York, Alfred A. Knopf, 1951.

Tarkany Szücs, Ernö. *Eingebrannte Eigentumsmarken des Viehs in Ungarn.* Acta Ethnographica Scientarium Hungarica, Tomus 17 (3–4), Budapest, 1968. (Branded property marks on livestock in Hungary.)

Towne, Charles W., and Edward N. Wentworth. *Cattle and Men.* Norman, University of Oklahoma Press, 1955.

———. *Shepherd's Empire.* Norman, University of Oklahoma, Press, 1946.

Truett, Velma Stevens. *On the Hoof In Nevada.* Los Angeles, Gehrett-Truett-Hall, 1950.

Wallace, R., and J. A. S. Watson. *Farm Livestock of Great Britain.* 5th ed. Edinburgh, Oliver & Boyd, 1923.

Ward, Faye E. *The Cowboy At Work.* New York, Hastings House, 1958.

Ward, Hortense W. *Cattlebrands and Cowhides.* Dallas, Story Book Press, 1953.

Webb, Edith Buckland. *Indian Life At the Old Missions.* Los Angeles, Warren F. Lewis, Publishers, 1952.

Webb, Walter Prescott. *The Great Plains.* New York, Ginn & Co., 1931.

Wellman, Paul I. *The Trampling Herd.* Garden City, N.Y., Doubleday & Co., Inc., 1951.

Wennersten. *Gotlands färmärken.* Medd. NM, 1898. (Livestock brands on the Isle of Gotland, Sweden.)

Westerners, The, Los Angeles Corral. *Westerners' Brand Book,* 1950. Article by Don Percival, "Names on Cows." Los Angeles, The Arthur H. Clark Co., 1950.

Wreszinski, Walter. *Atlas zur Altägyptischen Kulturgeschichte.* Leipzig, J. C. Hinrichs, 1914.

Encyclopedias and Directories

Canadian Almanac & Directory for 1958. Toronto, Copp Clark Publishing Co., Ltd., 1958.

Collier's Encyclopedia, Vol. IV, 21–23, New York, P. F. Collier & Son Corp., 1955.

Dobie, J. Frank. "Cattle Brands," *Dictionary of American History,* Vol. I, 2nd ed., rev. Ed. by James Truslow Adams. New York, Charles Scribner's Sons, 1940.

The American People's Encyclopedia, Vol. IV, 1018. Chicago, The Spencer Press, Inc., 1953.

Der Grosse Brockhaus, Vol. IX, 121, Wiesbaden, F. A. Brockhaus, 1956.

Encyclopedia Britannica, Vol. IV, 34–35, Chicago, Encyclopedia Britannica, Inc., 1958.

Brochures

Arnold, Oren, and John P. Hale. *Levi's Stories of Western Brands and What They Mean.* San Francisco, Levi Strauss & Co., n.d.

Cattle Brands of Texas. Dallas, First National Bank in Dallas, n.d.

Proceedings, Freeze-Brand Seminar, May 17, 1966. Cooperation Extension Service, College of Agriculture, Washington State University.

The History of Cattle Brands and How To Read Them. Carter Oil Co., 1955.

Government Publications

United States Department of Agriculture, "Dehorning, Castrating, Branding, and Marking Beef Cattle." *Farmers' Bulletin No. 1600.* Washington, D.C., U.S. Government Printing Office, 1950.

United States Department of Agriculture, "Beef Cattle: Dehorning, Castrating, and Marketing Beef Cattle." *Farmers' Bulletin No. 2141.* Washington, D.C., U.S. Government Printing Office, 1959.

United States Department of Agriculture, "The Inspection Stamp as a Guide to Wholesome Meat." *Agriculture Information Bulletin No. 92* (Formerly *Miscellaneous Circular No. 63.*) Washington, D.C. U.S. Government Printing Office, 1952.

United States Department of Agriculture, "Beef Cattle for Breeding Purposes." *Farmers' Bulletin No. 1916.* Slightly rev. ed. Washington, D.C., U.S. Government Printing Office, February, 1957.

United States Department of Agriculture, "U.S. Grades for Beef." *Leaflet No. 310.* Washington, D.C., U.S. Government Printing Office, 1957.

United States Department of Agriculture, "Dairy Cattle Breeds." *Farmers' Bulletin No. 1443.* Rev. ed. Washington, D.C., U.S. Government Printing Office, April, 1958.

United States Department of Agriculture, "Beef Cattle Breeds for Beef and for Beef and Milk." *Farmers' Bulletin No. 1779.* Slightly rev. ed. Washington, D.C., U.S. Government Printing Office, March, 1958.

United States Department of Agriculture, "Breeds of Swine." *Farmers' Bulletin No. 1263.* Slightly rev. ed. Washington, D.C., U.S. Government Printing Office, July, 1958.

United States Department of Agriculture, "Marking and Labeling Program of the Meat Inspection Division, U.S. Department of Agriculture," *Agriculture Handbook No. 190.* Washington, D.C., U.S. Government Printing Office, 1960.

United States Department of Agriculture, "U.S. Grades of Beef." *Market Bulletin No. 15.* (This bulletin supersedes *Leaflet No. 310* of the same title.) Washington, D.C., U.S. Government Printing Office, 1960.

Secretary of State of Canada, "Organization of the Government of Canada," Ottawa, Canada, The Queen's Printer, 1958.

Catalogs

Catalog No. 60. San Francisco, California Stockmen's Supply Co., 1966–67.

Catalog No. 95. Hyde Park, Vt., C. H. Dana Co., Inc., 1957.

Catalog No. 59. Denver, O. M. Franklin Serum Co., n.d.

Catalog No. 103. Fort Atkinson, Wisc., National Agricultural Supply Co., 1968.

Ford, Gus L., "Texas Cattle Brands." *Texas Centennial Exposition; Catalog of Exhibit.* Dallas, Clyde C. Cockrell Co., 1936.

Periodicals

"Branded." *Nebraskaland,* Vol. 44, No. 3 (1966).

"Branded." *Wildlife Review,* Vol. IV, No. 7 (1967).

"Branding In the Open." *The Cattleman* (Fort Worth), Vol. XIX, No. 10 (March, 1933).

Burckhardt, Felix. "Viehzollmarken in Basel um 1512," *Schweizer Münzblatt 8,* 1958 (504) (Baseler Bibliographie, 1958). (Livestock custom stamps in Bâle, Switzerland, about 1512.)

Dunlop, Eugene. "Brands and Irons." *Mainliner,* Vol. 7, No. 1 (January, 1963).

Editorials. *The Cattleman* (Fort Worth), (November, 1942), (November, 1946), (December, 1950), (March, 1956), and (December, 1956).

Ernst. "Verhandlungen der Berliner Gesellschaft für Anthropologie," *Zeitschrift für Ethnologie* (1878). (Branding irons with designs or initials and their legal registration in Venezuela.)

Farrell, R. Keith. "Cryo-branding." Washington State University *Animal Health Notes,* Vol. 6, No. 1, n.d.

Farrell, R. K., Koger, L. M., and Winward, L. D. "Freeze-Branding of Cattle, Dogs and Cats for Identification." *The Journal of American Veterinary Medical Association,* Vol. 149, No. 6 (September 15, 1966).

Farrell, R. Keith, George A. Laisner, and Thomas S. Russel, "An International Freeze-Mark Animal Identification System." *The Journal of the American Veterinary Medical Association,* Vol. 154, No. 12 (June 15, 1969).

302

"Frontier Symbolism." *Steelways,* Vol. 21, No. 2 (March–April, 1965).

"Hofmarken, Viehzeichen bis 1800 in Land Jerichow, Rosasen, Rossdorf," *Ahnen und Sippen, Beilager Anhalter Kurier, Bernburger Land,* Vol. 28, No. 2, (February 28, 1941). (House marks and livestock marks in Jerichow, Rosasen, and in the community of Rossdorf, county of Jerichow II, in the former state of Anhalt, Germany.)

Kambitsch, Loren, Marvin Wittman, and Morris Hemstrom, "Freeze-Branding: Equipment and Methods." *Current Information Series, No. 100* (April, 1969). Agricultural Experimental Station, Agricultural Extension Service, College of Agriculture, University of Idaho.

Kahn, Roger. "We Keep the Crooks Out of Racing." *True,* Vol. 41, No. 277 (June, 1960).

Kopf, Ernst. "Siebenbürgische Viehbrandzeichen," *Odal, Jahrgang 8* (1939). (Livestock brands in Siebenbürgen, Hungary.)

Lucht, Alfred. "Gänsemarken aus Kamp, Kreis Greifenberg," *Monatsblatt der Gesellschaft für Pommersche Geschichte* (1937). (Goose marks in Kamp, County of Greifenberg, Pomerania.)

———. "Schafmarken von Dannenberg auf Wollin," *Monatsblatt der Gesellschaft für Pommersche Geschichte* (1942). (Sheep marks in Dannenberg, Isle of Wollin, Pomerania.)

———. "Schafmarken," *Heimatklänge,* (1938). (Pomeranian sheep marks.)

———. "Über Gänsezucht und Gänsemarken aus Robe," *Heimatklänge.* (1938). (On goose breeding and marks in Robe, Pomerania.)

McDonald, Angus M. "Wild West in Stornoway." *Scottish Field,* Vol. CVI, No. 680 (August, 1959).

Ol' Waddy. "Brands." *The Western Horseman,* Vol. XXII, No. 4 (April, 1957).

Pfalser, I. L. "Ear Marks of the West." *Relics,* Vol. 2, No. 4 (Spring, 1969).

"Picking a Sleeper." *The Cattleman* (Fort Worth), Vol. XIX, No. 10 (March, 1933).

Raben, J. "Viehmarken und Botenstock der Weidegenossenschaft Schauby-Fielby," *Die Sippe der Nordmark,* Vol. 5–6 (1941–42). (Livestock marks and messenger canes of the pasture cooperative Schauby-Fielby in Schleswig-Holstein.)

Riviers, Alphons. "Haus- und Hofmarken," *Anzeiger für Schweizerische Altertumskunde 2,* (1866). (Livestock and other marks in Graubünden, Switzerland.)

Schaller. "Hölzer- und Viehzeichen," *Schweizer Holzkunde 18,* (1928). (Swiss log and livestock brands.)

Speck, Frank G. "Earmarks of Livestock of the Settlers of Woodbridge, New Jersey, 1716–1799." *The General Magazine and Historical Chronicle,* (October, 1938).

Spencer, Dick, III. "Branding Horses." *The Western Horseman,* Vol. XXIV, No. 12 (December, 1959).

"Verzeichnisse Isländischer Viehmarken." *Monatsblatt der Berliner Akademie der Wissenschaften,* (1868). (Index of Icelandic brands for several *syssels,* or districts.)

References

Offices, Agencies and Officials Consulted

1. United States Government.
   a) Department of the Army.
      The Adjutant, U.S. Army Quartermaster School, Fort Lee, Virginia.
      The Chief, Maintenance and Manufacturing Branch Installations Division, Office of the Quartermaster General, Headquarters, Department of the Army, Washington, D.C.
      The Director, West Point Museum Headquarters, United States Military Academy, West Point, New York.
   b) Department of the Interior.
      The Commissioner, Bureau of Indian Affairs, Department of the Interior, Washington, D.C.
      The Ranch Manager, Indian Agency Office, Department of the Interior, Window Rock, Arizona.
      The Chief, Division of Ranger Activities, National Park Service, Department of the Interior, Washington, D.C.
      The Superintendent, Sequoia and Kings Canyon National Park, National Park Service, Three Rivers, California.
      The Superintendent, Rocky Mountain National Park, National Park Service, Department of the Interior, Estes Park, Colorado.
      The Superintendent, Lassen Volcanic National Park, National Park Service, Department of the Interior, Mineral, California.

The Superintendent, Yosemite National Park, National Park Service, Department of the Interior, Yosemite National Park, California.

The Superintendent, Yellowstone National Park, National Park Service, Department of the Interior, Yellowstone Park, Wyoming.

The Superintendent, Grand Teton National Park, National Park Service, Department of the Interior, Moose, Wyoming.

The Superintendent, Glacier National Park, National Park Service, Department of the Interior, West Glacier, Montana.

c) Department of Agriculture.

The Director, Division of Range Management, Forest Service, Department of Agriculture, Washington, D.C.

The Regional Forester, Region 1, Northern Region Forest Service, Department of Agriculture, Federal Building, Missoula, Montana.

The Regional Forester, Region 2, Rocky Mountain Region, Forest Service, Department of Agriculture, Federal Center, Denver, Colo.

The Regional Forester, Region 3, Southwestern Region, Forest Service, Department of Agriculture, Albuquerque, New Mexico.

The Regional Forester, Region 4, Intermountain Region, Forest Service, Department of Agriculture, Forest Service Building, Ogden, Utah.

The Regional Forester, Region 5, California Region, Forest Service, Department of Agriculture, San Francisco, California.

The Regional Forester, Region 6, Pacific Northwest Region, Forest Service, Department of Agriculture, Portland, Oregon.

The Director, Animal Disease Eradication Division, Agricultural Research Service, Department of Agriculture, Washington, D.C.

The Director, Meat Inspection Division. Agricultural Research Service, Department of Agriculture, Washington, D.C.

The Chief, Dairy Cattle Research Branch, Animal Husbandry Research Division, Agricultural Research Service, Department of Agriculture, Washington, D.C.

The Chief, Meat Grading Branch, Livestock Division, Agricultural Marketing Service, Department of Agriculture, Washington, D.C.

The Chief, Rates and Registrations Branch, Packers and Stockyards Division, Agricultural Marketing Service, Department of Agriculture, Washington, D.C.

d) Atomic Energy Commission.

The Veterinary Officer, Las Vegas Branch Office, Atomic Energy Commission, Las Vegas, Nevada.

2. States of the Union.

a) States with State Registration of Brands and State Brand Recorders.

The Secretary, Livestock Brand Office, Division of Stockyards and Brands and Livestock Theft Investigation, Department of Agriculture and Industries, State of Alabama, Montgomery, Ala.

The Director, Division of Agriculture, Department of Natural Resources, State of Alaska, Palmer, Alaska.

The Secretary, Livestock Sanitary Board, State of Arizona, Phoenix, Arizona.

The Director, Division of Brand Registry, Livestock Sanitary Board, State of Arkansas, Little Rock, Arkansas.

The Chief, Bureau of Livestock Identification, Department of Agriculture, State of California, Sacramento, California.

The Brand Commissioner, Board of Stock Inspection Commissioners, State of Colorado, Denver, Colorado.

The Director, Marks and Brands Division, Inspection Bureau, Department of Agriculture, State of Florida, Gainesville, Florida.

The Commissioner of Agriculture, Marks and Brands Division, Department of Agriculture, State of Georgia, Atlanta, Georgia.

The President, Board of Commissioners of Agriculture and Forestry, State of Hawaii, Honolulu, Hawaii.

The State Brand Inspector, State of Idaho, Boise, Idaho.

The Livestock Brand Commissioner, Livestock Brand Commission, State of Kansas, Topeka, Kansas.

The Executive Secretary, Livestock Brand Commission, Department of Agriculture and Immigration, State of Louisiana, Baton Rouge, La.

The Supervisor of Brands, Livestock Theft Bureau, Department of Public Safety, State of Mississippi, Jackson, Mississippi.

The General Recorder of Marks and Brands, Livestock Commission, State of Montana, Helena, Montana.

The Secretary and Chief Inspector, Brand Committee Division, Department of State, State of Nebraska, Alliance, Nebraska.

The Director, Division of Animal Industry, Department of Agriculture, State of Nevada, Reno, Nevada.

The Secretary, Cattle Sanitary Board, state of New Mexico, Albuquerque, New Mexico.

The State Recorder of Marks and Brands, Department of Agriculture, State of North Carolina, Raleigh, North Carolina.

The Livestock Brand Recorder, Livestock Brand Department, Department of Agriculture and Labor, State of North Dakota, Bismarck, North Dakota.

The Director, Division of Brand Registry, Board of Agriculture, State of Oklahoma, Oklahoma City, Oklahoma.

The Director, Division of Animal Husbandry, Department of Agriculture, State of Oregon, Salem, Oregon.

The Secretary, State Brand Board, State of South Dakota, Pierre, South Dakota.

The State Brand Recorder, Department of Agriculture, State of Utah, Salt Lake City, Utah.

The Registrar of Livestock Brands, Office of Brand Recording, Department of Agriculture, State of Washington, Olympia, Washington.

The Executive Officer, the Live Stock and Sanitary Board, State of Wyoming, Cheyenne, Wyoming.

b) States with County Registration of Brands.

The Superintendent, Division of Livestock Industry, Department of Agriculture, State of Illinois, Springfield, Illinois.

The State Veterinarian, Livestock Disease Control Division, Department of Agriculture, State of Michigan, Lansing, Michigan.

The Secretary, the Livestock Sanitary Board, State of Minnesota, Saint Paul, Minnesota.

The Director, Livestock Division, Department of Agriculture, State of Missouri, Jefferson City, Missouri.

The Executive Director, Livestock Sanitary Commission, State of Texas, Fort Worth, Texas.

The Veterinary Supervisor, State-Federal Cooperative Program, Department of Agriculture, Madison, Wisconsin.

c) States Without Registration of Brands.

The State Veterinarian, Department of Agriculture, State of Connecticut, Hartford, Connecticut.

The Director, Department of Poultry and Animal Health, the Board of Agriculture, State of Delaware, Dover, Delaware.

The State Veterinarian, the Livestock Sanitary Board, State of Indiana, Indianapolis, Indiana.

309

The Director, Division of Animal Industry, State of Iowa, Des Moines, Iowa.

The State Veterinarian, Division of Livestock Sanitation, Department of Agriculture, Commonwealth of Kentucky, Frankfort, Kentucky.

The Chief, Division of Animal Industry, Department of Agriculture, State of Maine, Augusta, Maine.

The State Veterinarian, Department of Agriculture, State of Maryland, Annapolis, Maryland.

The Chief Veterinary Health Officer, Division of Livestock Disease Control, Department of Agriculture, Commonwealth of Massachusetts, Boston, Massachusetts.

The State Veterinarian, Division of Animal Industry, Department of Agriculture, State of New Hampshire, Concord, New Hampshire.

The Chief, Bureau of Livestock Disease Control, Division of Animal Industry, Department of Agriculture, State of New Jersey, Trenton, New Jersey.

The Director, Division of Animal Industry, Department of Agriculture and Markets, State of New York, Albany, New York.

The Chief, Division of Animal Industry, Department of Agriculture, State of Ohio, Columbus, Ohio.

The Director, Bureau of Animal Industry, Department of Agriculture, Commonwealth of Pennsylvania, Harrisburg, Pennsylvania.

The Chief of Division, Division of Animal Industry, Department of Agriculture and Providence Plantations, Providence, Rhode Island.

The Director, State-Federal Livestock Disease Eradication Program, State of South Carolina, Columbia, South Carolina.

The State Veterinarian, Division of Animal Industries, State of Tennessee, Nashville, Tennessee.

The State Veterinarian, Department of Agriculture, State of Vermont, Montpelier, Vermont.

The State Veterinarian, Division of Animal and Dairy Industry, Department of Agriculture, Commonwealth of Virginia, Richmond, Virginia.

The Commissioner of Agriculture, Department of Agriculture, State of West Virginia, Charleston, West Virginia.

3. Associations, Institutions, and Private Sources.

The Director of Information, American National Cattlemen's Association, Denver, Colorado.

The Secretary, Texas and Southwestern Cattle Raisers' Association, Fort Worth, Texas.

The Secretary-Treasurer, United States Livestock Sanitary Association, Trenton, New Jersey.

The Docent, the Oriental Institute, University of Chicago, Chicago, Illinois.

The Resident Director, the Mount Vernon Ladies' Association of the Union, Mount Vernon, Virginia.

The President, Staten Island Historical Society, Richmondtown, Staten Island, New York.

Brother Giles Collins, O.F.M., San Miguel Parish, Old Mission San Miguel, San Miguel, California.

The Secretary-Treasurer, National Livestock Brand Conference, State Livestock Commission, Helena, Montana.

The Secretary-Treasurer, National Livestock Brand Conference, Denver, Colorado.

4. Foreign Sources.

a) Dominion of Canada.

The Recorder of Brands, Live Stock Branch, Department of Agriculture, Province of Alberta, Edmonton, Alberta.

The Recorder of Brands, Live Stock Branch, Department

311

of Agriculture, Province of British Columbia, Victoria, British Columbia.

The Livestock Commissioner, Livestock Branch, Department of Agriculture and Conservation, Province of Manitoba, Winnipeg, Manitoba.

The Livestock Commissioner, Recorder of Brands, Live Stock Branch, Department of Agriculture, Province of Ontario, Toronto, Ontario.

The Director, Canadian National Live Stock Records, Ottawa, Ontario.

The Veterinary Director General, Health of Animals Division, Production and Marketing Branch, Canada Department of Agriculture, Ottawa, Ontario.

The Director, Livestock Branch, Department of Agriculture, Province of Quebec, Quebec, Quebec.

The Recorder of Brands, Animal Industries Branch, Department of Agriculture, Province of Saskatchewan, Regina, Saskatchewan.

b) United Kingdom.

The Librarian, Library Ministry of Agriculture, Fisheries and Food, London, England.

The Secretary, Department of Agriculture for Scotland, Edinburgh, Scotland.

The Keeper, the University of Reading, Museum of English Rural Life, Reading, England.

The National Breeders' Association, Chesham, Buckinghamshire, England.

The National Sheep Breeders' Association, Radlett, Herefordshire, England.

The National Pig Breeders' Association, Watford, Herefordshire, England.

The Factor, Estate Office, Inverlochy Castle, Fort William, Inverness-shire, Scotland.

312

c) Federal Republic of Germany.
Der Bundesminister für Ernährung, Landwirtschaft und Forsten, Bonn.
d) United Arab Republic.
Le Directeur Général, Service des Antiquités, Cairo, Egypt.
e) Thailand.
The Director General, Department of Livestock Development, Bangkok.

Index of Plates and Figures

PLATE I. Egyptian Tomb Paintings

Fig. 1. Tomb of Khemuheted
2. Tomb of Nebanun
3. Tomb of Nebanun

PLATE II. Historical Brands

Fig. 4. Solingen
5. Tomb of Khemuheted
6. Broad Arrow
7. Hernán Cortés
8. Cabeza de Vaca
9. Wm. Macklane
10. Pancho Villa
11. Henry Holland
12. Stephen Austin
13. John Veghte
14. Nicolas Saez
15. Joseph Glidden
16. Richard Chisholm
17. Luis Terrazas
18. Jacob Haish
19. Henrietta King
20. Richard King—Ere Flecha
21. Richard King—Rancho Brand
22. Richard King—James Wallworth
23. Richard King—Running W

PLATE III. Cattle Trails

PLATE IV. Miscellaneous Brands

Fig. 24. George Washington
24a. Lyndon B. Johnson
25. Dwight D. Eisenhower
26. Theodore Roosevelt—Maltese Cross
27. Theodore Roosevelt—Triangle
28. Theodore Roosevelt—Elkhorn
29. Duke of Windsor—Quarter Circle EP
30. Duke of Windsor—Three Feathers
31. Buffalo Bill
32. Yomba Shoshone
33. Cudahy Packing Co., Idaho
34. Union Pacific Railroad Co., Idaho
35. Union Pacific Railroad Co., Idaho (Sun Valley)
36. Dave Beck
37. Swift & Co., Idaho
38. Swift & Co., Idaho
39. Swift & Co., Idaho
40. Swift & Co., Washington
41. Swift & Co., Washington
42. Armour & Co., Washington
43. Armour & Co., Nevada
44. Armour & Co., Idaho
45. Armour & Co., Washington
46. Armour & Co., Washington
47. Colonel Maverick
48. Thoroughbred Racing Protective Bureau
49. Matador V

PLATE V. Similarity of Symbols.

Fig. 50. Bend Sinister
51. Slash
52. Chevron
53. Rafter
54. Cross

316

55. Cross
56. Lozenge
57. Diamond
58. Mullet
59. Rowel
60. Buckle
61. Male
62. Pigpen Circle
63. Urine
64. Old Woman
65. Stone Mason
66. Steer Skull
67. Taurus
68. Rails
69. Holding Mark
70. Four Hearts
71. Shipping Mark—John and James Charlié

PLATE VI. Cadency

Fig. 72. John French
73. Mrs. John French
74. Ney French
75. Nina French
76. Homer French
77. Lonnie French
78. Burton French
79. Vent brand
80. Don Miguel
81. Carlos
82. Luis
83. José
84. Mario
85. Founder
86. Second Grandson
87. Second Son of Second Grandson

88. Third Son of Second Grandson
89. Banu Sokhr Clan of Banu Sokhr Tribe
90. Banu Sokhr Clan of Banu Sokhr Tribe
91. Banu Sokhr Clan of Banu Sokhr Tribe
92. Khurshân Clan of Banu Sokhr Tribe
93. Khurshân Clan of Banu Sokhr Tribe
94. Khurshân Clan of Banu Sokhr Tribe

PLATE VII. Fig. 95. Regions and Points of Cattle

PLATE VIII. Fig. 96. Regions and Points of the Horse

PLATE IX. Fig. 97. Regions and Points of Sheep

PLATE X. Fig. 98. Regions and Points of Swine

PLATE XI. Blotting of Brands

Fig. 99. Bar T
100. Curry Comb
101. Eleven Quarter Circle
102. Rocking Chair
103. XIT
104. Star Cross
105. Circle
106. Chain
107. Circle
108. Buckle
109. Bar S
110. Forty-Eight
111. Hell
112. Triple K Connected
113. Circle Two Step
114. Quien Sabe
115. Lazy Flying E
116. Two Lazy Two P

PLATE XII. Types of Running Irons

Fig. 117. Running Iron

118. Wooden Handle

119. Cinch Ring

120. Saddle Iron

121. Fishhook End

122. Hook End

123. Eyebolt End

PLATE XIII. Working Drawing of Stamp Iron

PLATE XIV. Rules of Reading Brands

Fig. 124. A Bar X

125. R Lazy Two

126. O Bar O

127. Slash Connected E Connected Slash

128. Lapped Circles

129. Open A Half Box Connected

130. Circle A

131. J Slash Diamond

132. Double O

133. Slash Connected E Connected Slash

134. Diamond and A Half

135. Open A Connected Broken Bar

136. 4 Bar X

137. R Lazy 2

138. O Bar O

139. Diamond T

140. Circle A

141. J Slash Diamond

142. Three O Rail

143. Diamond and A Half

144. Circle A

145. Circle Bar

146. Double Circle (Doughnut)

147. Diamond T

148. One O One

149. Nine O Nine

150. Four Sixes
151. Circle A
152. Circle A
153. Rafter O
154. One O One
155. Half Diamond O
156. Quarter Circle O
157. O Quarter Circle
158. A
159. Quarter Circle O Connected
160. Cross
161. Open A O
162. Swinging O
163. Rocking O
164. Open A
165. Y Four Connected
166. X (Ten)

PLATE xv. Brand Dimensions

Fig. 167. Double Bar
168. Stripes
169. Bar after Character
170. Bar between Characters
171. Letter
172. Circular Boxed Brand
173. Square Boxed Brand
174. Dot
175. Slash and Character
176. Bench
177. Letter with Return of Projection
178. Letter with Projection
179. Double Letters (Vertical Arrangement)

PLATE xvi. Single and Connected Alphabets

Fig. 180. Triple Letters
181. Triple Letters Connected

PLATE XVII. Standard and Flying Alphabets

Fig. 182. Standard Alphabet
     183. Flying Alphabet

     PLATE XVIII. Running and Long Alphabets

Fig. 184. Running Alphabet
     185. Open Running A
     186. Roundtop A
     187. Mustache A
     188. Long Alphabet

     PLATE XIX. Hooked and Bradded Alphabets

Fig. 189. Hooked Alphabet
     190. Bradded Alphabet

     PLATE XX. Forked and Barbed Alphabets

Fig. 191. Forked Alphabet
     192. Barbed Alphabet

     PLATE XXI. Dragging and Walking Alphabets

Fig. 193. Dragging Alphabet
     194. Walking Alphabet

     PLATE XXII. Swinging and Rocking Alphabets

Fig. 195. Swinging Alphabet
     196. Rocking Alphabet

     PLATE XXIII. Crazy and Backward Alphabets

Fig. 197. Crazy (Inverted) Alphabet
     198. Backward (Inverted) Alphabet
     199. Crazy-Backward (Inverted-Reverse) Alphabet

     PLATE XXIV. Lazy Down Alphabets

Fig. 200. Lazy Left Down Alphabet
     201. Lazy Right Down Alphabet

     PLATE XXV. Lazy Up Alphabets

Fig. 202. Lazy Left Up Alphabet
     203. Lazy Right Up Alphabet

PLATE XXVI. Tumbling Alphabets

Fig. 204. Tumbling Left Alphabet
205. Tumbling Right Alphabet

PLATE XXVII. Single and Connected Numbers

Fig. 206. Triple Numerals
207. Triple Numerals Connected

PLATE XXVIII. Bars

Fig. 208. Bar
209. Bar (ahead of character)
210. Bar (behind character)
211. Over Bar
212. Through Bar
213. Under Bar
214. Double Bar
215. Double Bar (ahead of character)
216. Double Bar (behind character)
217. Double Over Bar
218. Double Through Bar
219. Double Under Bar
220. Rail
221. Rail (ahead of character)
222. Rail (behind character)
223. Over Rail
224. Through Rail
225. Under Rail
226. Double Rail
227. Double Rail (ahead of character)
228. Double Rail (behind character)
229. Double Over Rail
230. Double Through Rail
231. Double Under Rail
232. Stripes

233. Stripes (ahead of character)
234. Stripes (behind character)
235. Over Stripes
236. Through Stripes
237. Under Stripes
238. Broken Bar
239. Broken Bar (ahead of character)
240. Broken Bar (behind character)
241. Broken Over Bar
242. Broken Through Bar
243. Broken Under Bar

PLATE XXIX. Slashes and Triangles

Fig. 244. Slash or Cut
245. Slash (ahead of character)
246. Slash (behind character)
247. Broken Slash or Broken Cut
248. Broken Slash (ahead of character)
249. Broken Slash (behind character)
250. Reverse Slash or Reverse Cut
251. Reverse Slash (ahead of character)
252. Reverse Slash (behind character)
253. Broken Reverse Slash or Broken Reverse Cut
254. Broken Reverse Slash (ahead of character)
255. Broken Reverse Slash (behind character)
256. Triangle
257. Triangle (ahead of character)
258. Triangle (behind character)
259. Triangle (above character)
260. Triangle (below character)
261. Triangle (around character)
262. Inverted Triangle
263. Inverted Trangle (ahead of character)
264. Inverted Triangle (behind character)

265. Inverted Triangle (above character)
266. Inverted Triangle (below character)
267. Inverted Triangle (around character)

PLATE XXX. Diamonds

Fig. 268. Half Diamond
269. Half Diamond (ahead of character)
270. Half Diamond (behind character)
271. Half Diamond (above character)
272. Half Diamond (below character)
273. Reverse Half Diamond
274. Reverse Half Diamond (ahead of character)
275. Reverse Half Diamond (behind character)
276. Reverse Half Diamond (above character)
277. Reverse Half Diamond (below character)
278. Diamond
279. Diamond (ahead of character)
280. Diamond (behind character)
281. Diamond (above character)
282. Diamond (below character)
283. Diamond (around character)
284. Diamond and A Half
285. Two Diamonds
286. Five Diamonds

PLATE XXXI. Boxes

Fig. 287. Open Box
288. Open Box (ahead of character)
289. Open Box (behind character)
290. Open Box (above character)
291. Open Box (below character)
292. Reversed Open Box
293. Reversed Open Box (ahead of character)
294. Reversed Open Box (behind character)
295. Reversed Open Box (above character)

296. Reversed Open Box (below character)

297. Box

298. Box (ahead of character)

299. Box (behind character)

300. Box (above character)

301. Box (below character)

302. Box (around character)

PLATE XXXII. Circles

Fig. 303. Quarter Circle

304. Quarter Circle (ahead of character)

305. Quarter Circle (behind character)

306. Quarter Circle (above character)

307. Quarter Circle (below character)

308. Reverse Quarter Circle

309. Reverse Quarter Circle (ahead of character)

310. Reverse Quarter Circle (behind character)

311. Reverse Quarter Circle (above character)

312. Reverse Quarter Circle (below character)

313. Half Circle

314. Half Circle (ahead of character)

315. Half Circle (behind character)

316. Half Circle (above character)

317. Half Circle (below character)

318. Reverse Half Circle

319. Reverse Half Circle (ahead of character)

320. Reverse Half Circle (behind character)

321. Reverse Half Circle (above character)

322. Reverse Half Circle (below character)

323. Circle

324. Circle (ahead of character)

325. Circle (behind character)

326. Circle (above character)

327. Circle (below character)

328. Circle (around character)

329. Double Circle or Doughnut
330. Two Links
331. Lapped Circles
332. Broken Links
333. Goose Egg or Mashed O

PLATE XXXIII. Common Picture Brands

Fig. 334. Anchor
335. Tumbling Anchor
336. Andiron
337. Anvil
338. Arrow
339. Broken Arrow
340. Barrel
341. Bench
342. Bit (bridle)
343. Bit (Spanish)
344. Boot
345. Bottle
346. Bow and Arrow
347. Buckle
348. Buckle (cinch)
349. Chair
350. Rocking Chair
351. Lamp Chimney
352. Meat Cleaver
353. Curry Comb
354. Crescent
355. Cross
356. Crutch
357. Dollar Sign
358. Flag
359. Fleur-de-Lis
360. Hatchet
361. Heart

326

362. Broken Heart
363. Crazy Heart
364. Flying Heart
365. Split Heart
366. Two Hearts
367. Fish Hook
368. Hay Hook
369. Key

PLATE XXXIV. Common Picture Brands

Fig. 370. Key Hole
371. Hash Knife
372. Ladder
373. Lazy Ladder
374. Tumbling Ladder
375. Clover Leaf
376. Lightning
377. Moon
378. Frying Pan
379. Pig Pen
380. Rolling Pin
381. Pipe
382. Pitch Fork
383. Plough
384. Question Mark
385. Rafter
386. Rake
387. Scissors
388. Shield
389. Shovel
390. Sled
391. Square and Compass
392. Rowel
393. Star
394. Stirrup

395. Sun
396. Sunrise
397. S-Wrench
398. Horse Track
399. Turkey Track
400. Tree
401. Wind Vane
402. Wine Glass
403. Oxen Yoke

PLATE xxxv. Army Brands and Branding Irons

Fig. 404. U.S. Army Alphabet
405. Preston Brand
406. U.S. Army Brand
407. U.S. Army Surplus Brand
408. U.S. Army Inspected and Condemned Brand
409. Dimensional Preston Brand
410. U.S. Army Branding Iron (1944)
411. 7th Cavalry Regiment Branding Iron
412. Cross Section Through U.S. Army Stamp Iron (1925)

PLATE xxxvi. The West Point Iron

Fig. 413. Fastening Detail (West Point Iron)
414. Top View (West Point Iron)
415. Side View (West Point Iron)
416. Front View (West Point Iron)

PLATE xxxvii. United States Government Brands

Fig. 417. Crossed Arrows—Pine Ridge Agency
418. Interior Department—Pine Ridge Agency
419. Triangle—Pine Ridge Agency
420. Indian Symbol—Pine Ridge Agency
421. Interior Department—Fort Duchesne
422. Navaho Reservation
423. Navaho Tribe
424. Unitah and Ouray Agency

425. Cheyenne River Agency
426. Lower Brule Agency
427. Rosebud Agency
428. Sisseton Agency
429. Crow Creek Agency
430. Pine Ridge Agency
431. Yankton Agency
432. Standing Rock Agency
433. Atomic Energy Agency
434. Rocky Mountain National Park;
  National Forest Regions 2, 3, 4, 5, and 6;
  War Relocation Authority
435. Sequoia and Kings Canyon National Park;
  Yellowstone National Park;
  Grand Teton National Park
436. Glacier National Park
437. Sequoia and Kings National Park;
  Yosemite National Park
438. Lassen Volcanic National Park;
  Yellowstone National Park
439. Yosemite National Park
440. Glacier National Park;
  National Forest Region 1
441. Tuberculosis Reactor
442. National Vaccinate Tattoo
443. Brucellosis Reactor

PLATE XXXVIII. Old Navaho Brands

Fig. 444. to
Fig. 461. Old Navaho Brands

PLATE XXXIX. Federal Carcass Brands

Fig. 462. Institutional Brand (USDA)
  463. Institutional Brand (USDA)
  464. Institutional Brand (USDA)

465. Institutional Brand (USDA)
466. Inspected and Passed (USDA)
467. USDA Prime Beef or Lamb
468. USDA Choice Calf
469. USDA Good Yearling Mutton
470. USDA Standard Veal
471. USDA Commercial Beef
472. USDA Utility Mutton
473. USDA Cutter Bull
474. USDA Canner Stag
475. USDA Good Beef (roller)

PLATE XL. State Government Brands

Fig. 476. Tuberculosis Reactor
477. Brucellosis Reactor
478. Spayed Heifer—Alaska
479. Official Vaccinate
480. Estray—Idaho
481. Adult Vaccinate
482. Mastitis
483. Feeder
484. Livestock Commission—Montana
485. Board of Stock Inspection Commissioners—Colorado
486. Will Rogers—Oklahoma
487. Fish and Game Department—Idaho
488. Fish and Game Commission—Nevada
489. Game and Fish Department—Colorado
490. University—Idaho
491. University Agricultural Experimental Station—Nevada
492. State College—Colorado
493. State Hospital South—Idaho
494. State Hospital—Colorado
495. Northern State Hospital—Washington

496. State School for the Deaf and Blind—Idaho
497. State School and Colony—Idaho
498. State Training School—Utah
499. State Home for Dependent Children—Colorado
500. State Soldiers' and Sailors' Home—Colorado
501. State Welfare Farm—Idaho
502. State Children's Home—Nevada
503. State Penitentiary—Idaho
504. State Reformatory—Colorado
505. Department of Institutions—Hawaii
506. Division of Training Schools—Hawaii
507. Territorial Hospital—Hawaii
508. Territorial Hospital—Hawaii
509. Prison System—Texas

PLATE XLI. Earmarks

Fig. 510. Button Tip (Pennant)
511. Point Tip
512. Slick Ear (Full Ear)
513. Over Half Tip
514. Under Half Tip
515. Tip
516. Over Half Crop
517. Over Quarter Crop
518. Under Quarter Crop
519. Under Half Crop
520. Overslope Half Crop
521. Three-quarter Over One-quarter Crop (Over Step)
522. Three-quarter Under One-quarter Crop (Under Step)
523. Underslope Half Crop
524. V Over Half Crop
525. Over Straight (Lop)
526. Under Straight
527. V Under Half Crop

331

528. Dutch Over Half Crop
529. Roundtop Over Half Crop
530. Roundtop Under Half Crop
531. Dutch Under Half Crop
532. Flicker Over Half Crop
533. Key Over Half Crop
534. Key Under Half Crop
535. Flicker Under Half Crop

PLATE XLII. Earmarks

Fig. 536. Crop
537. Button Crop
538. Point Crop
539. Round Crop
540. Overslope Crop
541. Button Overslope Crop
542. Point Overslope Crop
543. S Crop
544. Under Slope Crop
545. Button Under Slope Crop
546. Point Under Slope Crop
547. Ching-whala Crop
548. Half Over Slope Crop
549. Tip Hook Crop
550. Chihuahua Crop
551. Lightning Crop
552. Half Under Slope Crop
553. Under Round
554. Over Round
555. Reverse Lightning Crop
556. Three-quarter Over Crop
557. Punch
558. Grub
559. Three-quarter Under Crop

PLATE XLIII. Earmarks

Fig. 560. Half V Over Bit
    561. V Over Bit (Peak)
    562. V Under Bit
    563. Half V Under Bit
    564. Bench Over Bit
    565. Double V Over Bit
    566. Double V Under Bit (M-Punch)
    567. Bench Under Bit
    568. Key Over Bit
    569. U Over Bit
    570. U Under Bit
    571. Key Under Bit (Keyhole)
    572. Dutch Over Bit
    573. Square Over Bit
    574. Square Under Bit
    575. Dutch Under Bit
    576. Quien Sabe Over Bit
    577. 7 Over Bit
    578. 7 Under Bit
    579. Quien Sabe Under Bit
    580. Kitchen Split
    581. Reverse 7 Over Bit
    582. Reverse 7 Under Bit
    583. Chihuahua Under Bit

PLATE XLIV. Earmarks

Fig. 584. Over Slope
    585. Key Over Slope
    586. Key Under Slope
    587. Under Slope
    588. Rimmed Over Slope
    589. Drop Over Slope
    590. Drop Under Slope

591. Rimmed Under Slope
592. S Over Slope
593. Point Over Slope
594. Point Under Slope
595. S Under Slope
596. Over and Under Quarter Crop
 (Fingermark, Fingerprint, Thumbprint)
597. Key Swallow Fork
598. Quien Sabe Swallow Fork
599. Square Swallow Fork
600. Swallow Fork
601. Full Over Half Swallow Fork
602. Over Slope Swallow Fork
603. Pelow Swallow Fork
604. Double Swallow Fork (Sawtooth, Saw)
605. Full Under Half Swallow Fork
606. Under Slope Swallow Fork
607. Reverse Pelow Swallow Fork

PLATE XLV. Earmarks

Fig. 608. Over Half Swallow Fork
609. Quedow
610. Reverse Quedow
611. Under Half Swallow Fork
612. Over Sharp
613. Under Sharp
614. Sharp
615. Dutch Point
616. X Split Swallow Fork
617. Dutch Split
618. Steeple Fork
619. Pelow Crop
620. Over Half Crop and Tip (Step, Stair)
621. Over and Under Quarter Crop
 (Fingermark, Fingerprint, Thumbprint)

334

622. Over Straight and Tip
623. Reverse 7 Over Bit and Under Slope Crop
624. Reverse 7 over Bit and Tip
625. Over Round and Under Round
626. Three-quarter Over Crop and Tip
627. Three-quarter Under Crop and Tip
628. Over Slope and Crop
629. Over Slope and Under Half Crop
630. Tip and Under Slope
631. Half V Over and Under Bit
632. Reverse 7 Over and Reverse 7 Under Bit
    (Paddle, Double Figure 7)
633. Over Half Crop and Under Slope
634. Under Slope and V Under Bit
635. Over and Under Straight

PLATE XLVI. Earmarks

Fig. 636. Slit
637. Key Slit
638. Double Slit
639. Over Half Key Slit
640. Under Half Key Slit
641. Hack
642. Over Hack
643. Under Hack
644. Slash Over Hack
645. L Over Hack
646. L Under Hack
647. Slash Under Hack
648. Over Split
649. Under Split
650. Tipped L Over Split
651. L Over Split
652. L Under Split
653. Tipped L Under Split

PLATE XLVII. Earmarks

Fig. 654. Drag Over Split (Stovepipe)
655. Barbed Over Split
656. Barbed Under Split
657. Drag Under Split
658. Sloped Over Split
659. Y Over Split
660. Y Under Split
661. Sloped Under Split
662. Key Over Split
663. Pelow Over Split
664. Pelow Under Split
665. Key Under Split
666. Comet Over Split
667. Curved Over Split (Bent Over Split)
668. Curved Under Split (Bent Under Split)
669. Comet Under Split
670. Over Slope Key Split
671. Curl Over Split
672. Curl Under Split
673. Under Slope Key Split
674. Half Key Over Split
675. Hooked Over Split
676. Hooked Under Split
677. Half Key Under Split

PLATE XLVIII. Earmarks

Fig. 678. Fanned Over Split
679. Cross Over Split
680. Cross Under Split
681. Fanned Under Split
682. Over Split-Split
683. X Over Bit Split
684. X Under Bit Split
685. Under Split-Split

686. Split
687. Full Split
688. Double Split
689. Finger Split
690. Hack Split
691. Double Hack Split
692. Flickertail Split
693. Fantail Split (Cloverleaf)
694. Raised Barb Split
695. Dropped Barb Split
696. Y Split
697. Rocker Split (Shoestring)
698. L Split
699. Dropped L Split
700. S Split
701. Chin-gow Split
702. V Split
703. T Split (Split and Downfall)

PLATE XLIX. Earmarks

Fig. 704. Over Half Key Split
705. Under Half Key Split
706. Key Split
707. Slash Split
708. Over Slope Split
709. Double Over Slope Split
710. Double Under Slope Split
711. Under Slope Split
712. Over Jigger
713. Under Jigger
714. Over Slash
715. Curved Over Slash
716. Curved Under Slash (Reef, Hatchet)
717. Under Slash
718. Tip Flicker

719. Over Flicker
720. Under Flicker
721. Half Jinglebob
722. Jinglebob
723. Full Curved Jinglebob
724. Chin-gow Jinglebob

PLATE L. Earmarks

Fig. 725. Over Slash Jinglebob
726. Rocker Split Jinglebob
727. Flickerbob
728. Under Slope Flickerbob
729. Chihuahua Jinglebob
730. Sonora Jinglebob (Holy Split)
731. Tip and Split
732. Tip and Double Split
733. Tip and V Split
734. Swallow Fork and Split
735. Tip and Over Slash
736. Over Slope and Split
737. Under Slope and Split
738. Swallow Fork and Slash Over and Under Hack
739. Tip and Over and Under Slash Hack
740. Over Slope and Under Slash Hack
741. Under Slope and Over Slash Hack
742. Round Swallow Fork and Split
743. Tip and Double Under Slope Split
744. Over Slope and Over Slash
745. Under Slope and Under Slash
746. Tip and Over and Under L Hack

PLATE LI. Earmarking

Fig. 747. Rimmed Over Slope and Over Slope Hack
748. Rimmed Under Slope and Under Slope Hack
749. Reverse Under Slash and Under Bit

338

750. Under Rim and Under Slope Hack
751. Over Half Tip and Split
752. Over Slope Crop and Under Slope Hack
753. Over Slope and Rocker Split
754. Curved Under Slope Split and Under Bit
755. V Over Bit and Slash
756. Over Three-quarter Crop and Hack
757. Half Under Slope Crop and Hack
758. Chingadero Jinglebob
759. Over Round and Hack
760. Crop and Split
761. Under Round and Hack
762. Over and Under Slash Hack
763. Over and Under L Hack
764. L Over Split and Under Flicker
765. Over and Under Hack and Split
766. Over Flicker and Half Jinglebob
767. L Over Hack and Split

PLATE LII. Earmarking System for Sheep

(R—Right Ear; L—Left Ear)

Fig.	Number	Ear
768.	10	R
769.	1	L
770.	20	R
771.	2	L
772.	30	R
773.	3	L
774.	40	R
775.	4	L
776.	50	R
777.	5	L
778.	60	R
779.	6	L
780.	70	R
781.	7	L

782.	80	R
783.	8	L
784.	90	R
785.	9	L
786.	200	R
787.	100	L
788.	300	R and L
789.	400	R and L
790.	500	R and L
791.	600	R and L
792.	700	R and L
793.	800	R and L
794.	900	R and L
795.	1000	R and L
796.	1073	R and L

PLATE. LIII. Earmarking Systems for Swine and Goats

Fig. 797. Angora System (Goats)
798. Hampshire System (Swine)
799. Tamworth System (Swine)
800. Beltsville System (Swine)

PLATE LIV. Earmarking System for Swine

(R—Right Ear; L—Left Ear)

Fig. 801.	Number 10	Ear R
802.	1	L
803.	20	R
804.	2	L
805.	30	R
806.	3	L
807.	40	R
808.	4	L
809.	50	R
810.	5	L
811.	60	R

812.	6	L
813.	70	R
814.	7	L
815.	80	R
816.	8	L
817.	90	R
818.	9	L
819.	100	R and L
820.	200	L and R
821.	300	R and L
822.	400	L and R
823.	500	R and L
824.	583	R and L

PLATE LV. Dewlaps

Fig. 825. Single Dewlap Up
826. Double Dewlap Up
827. Single Dewlap Down
828. Double Dewlap Down
829. Dewlap Throat
830. Dewlap Between Front Legs
831. Necktie Dewlap

PLATE LVI. Dewlaps

Fig. 832. Bell Dewlap Throat
833. Dewlap Brisket
834. Jughandle Dewlap
835. Broken Jughandle Dewlap
836. Wire Through Dewlap
837. Notch In Dewlap

PLATE LVII. Wattles

Fig. 838. Nose Wattle (Bud, Snub)
839. Face Wattle
840. Forehead Wattle
841. Wattle Over Eye

341

842. Wattle Under Eye
843. Cheek Wattle
844. Chin Dewlap (Chin Whiskers)
845. Dewlap Jaw
846. Bell Dewlap Chin
847. Wattle Side of Neck
848. Wattle Crest of Neck

PLATE LVIII. Wattles

Fig. 849. Wattle Shoulder
850. Wattle Shank
851. Wattle Ribs
852. Wattle Hips
853. Wattle Tail
854. Wattle Stifle

PLATE LIX. California Mission Brands

Fig. 855. San Diego de Alcalá
856. San Diego de Alcalá
857. San Carlos Barromeo (Carmelo)
858. San Antonio de Padua
859. San Gabriel, Arcángel
860. San Gabriel, Arcángel
861. San Luis Obispo de Tolosa
862. San Francisco de Asis (Dolores)
863. San Juan Capistrano
864. Santa Clara de Asis
865. San Buenaventura
866. Santa Barbara
867. La Purísima Conceptión
868. Santa Cruz
869. La Soledad
870. San José
871. San Juan Bautista
872. San Miguel, Arcángel

873. San Fernando Rey
874. San Luis Rey
875. Santa Inés
876. San Rafael, Arcángel
877. San Francisco Solano (Sonoma)

PLATE LX. Canadian Federal and Provincial Brands

Abbreviations: RCMP—Royal Canadian Mounted Police; CDA —Canadian Department of Agriculture; PFRA—Prairie Farm Rehabilitation Administration; CDCI—Canada Department of Citizenship and Immigration. Name of province following brand identification indicates recordation of brand therein.

Fig. 878. RCMP—Alberta, British Columbia, and Saskatchewan
879. RCMP Vent Brand—Alberta
880. RCMP Vent Brand—British Columbia
881. Brucellosis Reactor, CDA—Alberta
882. Tuberculosis Reactor, CDA—Alberta
883. Production Service, CDA—Alberta and Saskatchewan
884. Dominion Range Experimental Station, CDA—Alberta
885. Dominion Range Experimental Station, CDA—British Columbia
886. Dominion Experimental Farm, CDA—Alberta
887. Production Service, CDA—Alberta and Manitoba (used but not recorded)
888. Production Service, CDA—British Columbia (used but not recorded)
889. PFRA, CDA—Saskatchewan
890. PFRA, CDA—Saskatchewan
891. PFRA, CDA—Saskatchewan
892. PFRA, CDA—Saskatchewan
893. PFRA, CDA—Saskatchewan
894. PFRA, CDA—Saskatchewan

343

895. PFRA, CDA—Saskatchewan
896. Indian Affairs Branch, CDCI—Alberta and Saskatchewan
897. Indian Affairs Branch, CDCI, Vent Brand—Alberta
898. Indian Affairs Branch, CDCI—British Columbia
899. Canada Department of Mines and Technical Surveys—Alberta and British Columbia
900. Banff National Park, Canada Department of Northern Affairs and Natural Resources—Alberta
901. St. Cyprian Indian Residential School—Alberta
902. St. Paul's Residential School—Alberta
903. Kamloops Indian Residential School—British Columbia
904. Kootenay Indian Residential School—British Columbia
905. Lejac Indian Residential School—British Columbia
906. Department of the Attorney General of Alberta and Alberta Department of Agriculture—Alberta
907. Alberta Department of Agriculture Vent Brand—Alberta
908. University of Alberta—Alberta
909. Provincial Auxiliary Mental Hospital—Alberta
910. St. Anthony's Indian Residential School—Saskatchewan
911. St. Michael's Indian Residential School—Saskatchewan
912. St. Philip's Indian Residential School—Saskatchewan
913. Saskatchewan Department of Municipal Affairs—Saskatchewan
914. Saskatchewan Department of Social Welfare and Rehabilitation—Saskatchewan
915. University of British Columbia—British Columbia

916. British Columbia Department of Agriculture—
British Columbia

PLATE LXI. Scottish Sheep Brands

Fig. 917. to
Fig. 961. Scottish Sheep Brands

NOTE: For plates and figures of German horse brands. A serial number has been assigned to each individual horse breeders' association in order to facilitate the indexing of brands. The various divisions of the associations have been annotated, if applicable, as follows: L—Light Horse Division; LH—Heavy Light Horse Section; LT—Thoroughbred Section; D—Draft Horse Division; and S—Smallhorse Division.

Where the type of horse (light or draft) is not evident in the name of the association, or where there is no division to indicate the type, the type of horse bred by the association has been given in parentheses after the name. Other references appear in full, except regional farmers' units (Landesbauernschaften) of the Reich Food Estate (Reichsnährstand), abbreviated to RFU. The sequence of serial numbers assigned generally follows the text of the manuscript.

Serial Number	Horse Breeders Association
1	Assoc. of Breeders of the Light Horse of Trakehnen Ancestry, Inc.
2	Assoc. of Hanoverian Light Horse Breeders, Inc.
3–L, 3–D, 3–S	Westphalian Horse Pedigree Book, Inc.
4	Assoc. of Breeders of the Holstein Horse, Inc. (light horse)
5	Assoc. of Breeders of the Olden-burger Horse. (light horse)
6	East Frisian Stud Book Inc. (light horse)
7–L, 7–D	Assoc. of Horse Breeders Hesse-Nassau

Serial Number	Horse Breeders Association
8–L, 8–D	Electoral-Hessian Horse Pedigree Book, Inc.
9	Assoc. of Württemberger Light Horse Breeders, Inc.
10–L (H), 10–L (R), 10–D	Regional Assoc. of Bavarian Horse Breeders, Inc. (L(H)–Light Haflinger Horse L (R)–Light Rottaler Horse)
11–L, 11–D	Badian Horse Pedigree Book, Inc.
12–L, 12–D	Regional Assoc. of Horse Breeders Pfalz
13–L, 13–D	Regional Assoc. of Horse Breeders in the Saarland, Inc.
14–L, 14–D	Assoc. of Brandenburger Horse Breeders, I
15–L, 15–D	Regional Assoc. of Mecklenburger Horse Breeders
16–L, 16–D	Former Fore-Pomeranian counties
17	Breeding Island Hanover (light horse)
18–L, 18–D	Saxonian Horse Pedigree Book
19–LH, 19–LT, 19–D	Regional Horse Breeding Assoc. Saxony-Anhalt
20–L, 20–D	Regional Assoc. of Thuringian Horse Breeders
21	East Prussian Stud Book Corporation for Light Horses of Trakehnen Ancestry Inc.; West Prussian Stud Book Corporation for Light Horses of Trakehnen Ancestry, Inc.
22	Assoc. of Pomeranian Light Horse Breeders, Inc.
23–L, 23–D	Silesian Horse Pedigree Book, Inc.
24–L, 24–D	Regional Assoc. of Horse Breeders Wartheland
25	Rhenish Horse Pedigree Book, Inc. (draft horse)

346

Serial Number	Horse Breeders Association
26	Pedigree Book for Draft Horses, Lower Saxony, Inc.
27	Pedigree Book for Rhenish-German Draft Horses in Holstein, Inc.
28	Assoc. of Schleswiger Horse Breeders' Clubs, Inc. (draft horses)
29	Assoc. of Württemberg Draft Horse Breeders, Inc.
30	Rhenish Horse Pedigree Book for Rhineland-Nassau
31	Danzig Stud Book for Heavy Work Horses, Inc.
32	East Prussian Stud Book for Heavy Work Horses, Inc.
33	Assoc. of Pomeranian Draft Horse Breeders, Inc.
34	Regional Assoc. of Pony and Smallhorse Breeders, Schleswig-Holstein
35	Assoc. of Pony and Smallhorse Breeders, Hanover
36	Assoc. of Smallhorse and Pony Breeders, Weser-Ems
37	Assoc. of Pony and Smallhorse Breeders of the North Rhine Province
38	Assoc. of Pony and Smallhorse Breeders Hesse, Inc.
39	South German Smallhorse Pedigree Book, Inc.
40	Assoc. of Smallhorse Breeders of Bavaria
41	German Smallhorse Pedigree Book

PLATE LXII. German Horse Brands

Fig. 962. Main Stud Farm Trakehnen
  963. 1, 15–L, 16–L, 17, 21, East Prussian RFU,
    Danzig RFU.
  964. 21, East Prussian RFU.
  965. 1, 21, East Prussian RFU.
  966. Württemberg Main Stud Farm, 9
  967. 9
  968. 9
  969. 29
  970. 29
  971. 29
  972. 16–L, 22
  973. Electoral Marche RFU.
  974. 16–L, 22, Pomerania RFU.
  975. Württemberg RFU.
  976. Württemberg RFU.
  977. 8–D

PLATE LXIII. German Horse Brands

Fig. 978. 2, 17
  979. 17
  980. Stud Farm Celle
  981. Main Stud Farm Graditz
  982. 2, 17, Hanover RFU.
  983. Main Stud Farm Graditz
  984. Main Stud Farm Neustadt
  985. 2
  986. Stud Farm Beberbeck
  987. 14–L
  988. Stud Farm Altefeld
  989. 24–L

PLATE LXIV. German Horse Brands

Fig. 990. 20–D

348

991. 38

992. Schleswig-Holstein RFU.

993. 38

994. 20–D

995. 39

996. 39

997. 39

998. 40

999. 40

1,000. 38

1,001. 8–L

1,002. 8–L

1,003. 41

1,004. 41

1,005. 41

1,006. 10–D

1,007. 10–D (H)

1,008. 41

1,009. 34, 35, 36

1,010. 32

1,011. 32, East Prussian RFU.

1,012. 34, 35, 36, 37, 3–S

PLATE LXV. German Horse Brands

Fig. 1,013. 3–L, 3–D, Westphalian RFU.

1,014. 3–L, 3–D

1,015. 23–L, 23–D

1,016. 23–L, 23–D, Silesian RFU.

1,017. 14–D

1,018. 16–L, 22

1,019. 16–D, 33

1,020. 27

1,021. 27

1,022. 27

1,023. Stud Book West Prussia

1,024. 4
1,025. 23–L, 23–D
1,026. Pedigree Stud Farm Zweibrücken
1,027. 12–L
1,028. 12–L
1,029. 12–L

PLATE LXVI. German Horse Brands

Fig. 1,030. 11–D
1,031. 11–D, Badian RFU.
1,032. 11–L
1,033. 11–L, Badian RFU.
1,034. 14–D, Electoral Marche RFU.
1,035. 14–D
1,036. 16–D, 33
1,037. 16–D, 33
1,038. 4
1,039. Brunswick RFU.
1,040. 19–LT
1,041. 19–LT
1,042. 12–D, Saar Palatinate RFU.
1,043. 12–D
1,044. 15–D
1,045. 2, Hanover RFU.
1,046. 26
1,047. 26
1,048. 8–D

PLATE LXVII. German Horse Brands

Fig. 1,049. Stud Farm Braunsberg
1,050. 20–L, 20–D
1,051. 13–L
1,052. 13–D
1,053. 19–D
1,054. 19–D

1,055. 19–D
1,056. 19–D
1,057. 18–L, 18–D
1,058. 18–L, 18–D, Saxony RFU.
1,059. 19–LH
1,060. 19–LH
1,061. 20–L
1,062. 20–L
1,063. 20–L
1,064. 20–L
1,065. 28
1,066. Saxony-Anhalt RFU.
1,067. East Frisian RFU.
1,068. 28, Schleswig-Holstein RFU.
1,069. 26

PLATE LXVIII. German Horse Brands

Fig. 1,070. 2
1,071. 15–L
1,072. Bavarian Pedigree Stud Farm Achselschwang
1,073. 14–L
1,074. 14–L
1,075. 14–L
1,076. 6
1,077. 31
1,078. 31
1,079. 7–L, 7–D
1,080. 7–D
1,081. 7–L, 7–D
1,082. 7–D
1,083. 8–L, 8–D
1,084. Württemberg Main Stud Farm Marbach,
         Württemberg RFU.
1,085. 15–L, Mecklenburg RFU.
1,086. 15–L

1,087. 15–D

1,088. 5, Oldenburg RFU.

1,089. 6

1,090. 15–D

1,091. 32, East Prussian RFU.

1,092. 5

1,093. 5

1,094. 6

PLATE LXIX German Horse Brands

Fig. 1,095. 12–D

1,096. Saxony-Anhalt RFU.

1,097. Lower Bavaria RFU.

1,098. 15–L, 15–D, 16–D

1,099. 25, 30

1,100. 25, 30, Rhineland RFU.

1,101. 10–L (R)

1,102. Pedigree Stud Farm Schwaiganger

1,103. 11–D

1,104. 3–L, 9, 10–L (H), 19–LH, 19–LT, 23–L, 3–D, 8–D, 28, 10–D, 29, 19–D, 23–D, 3–S

1,105. 26

1,106. 20–L, 20–D

1,107. 3–D, 31

1,108. 11–L

1,109. 15–L

1,110. 32

1,111. 7–L, 8–L

1,112. 3–L, 3–D

1,113. Saar Palatinate RFU.

1,114. Schleswig-Holstein RFU.

1,115. 24–D

1,116. Upper Bavarian RFU.

1,117. 24–D

PLATE LXX. Mexican Bull Ranches

Fig. 1,118. Atenco
1,119. Ayala
1,120. Coaxamalucan
1,121. Pasteje
1,122. La Punta
1,123. La Laguna
1,124. Peñuelas
1,125. Piedras Negras
1,126. Xajay
1,127. Rancho Seco
1,128. (San Diego de) los Padres
1,129. San Mateo
1,130. Zacatepec
1,131. Zotoluca

PLATE LXXI. Hungarian State Stud Farms

Fig. 1,132. Radautz
1,133. Piber
1,134. Kísber
1,135. Babolna
1,136. Mezö-Hegyes
1,137. Fogaras

PLATE LXXII. Lewis and Clark Branding Iron

PLATE LXXIII. Perspective View of Lewis and Clark
Branding Iron

PLATE LXXIV. An Example of Cryo-branding

Plates and Figures

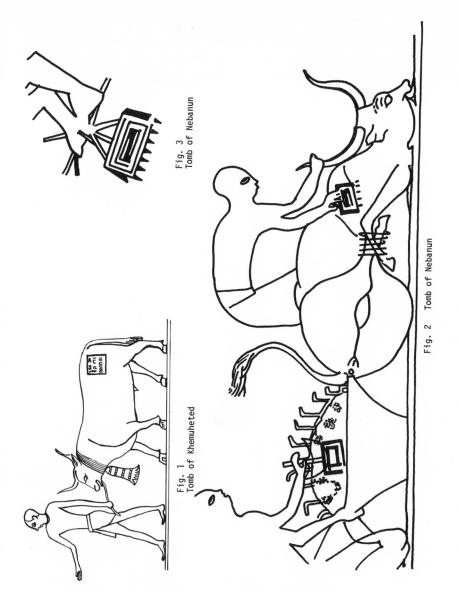

Fig. 3
Tomb of Nebanun

Fig. 2   Tomb of Nebanun

Fig. 1
Tomb of Khemuheted

PLATE I. EGYPTIAN TOMB PAINTINGS

Fig. 4
Solingen

Fig. 5
Tomb of Khemuheted

Fig. 6
Broad Arrow

Fig. 7
Cortés

Fig. 8
Cabeza de Vaca

Fig. 9
Wm Macklane

Fig. 11
Henry Holland

Fig. 12
Stephen Austin

H.C.

Fig. 16
Richard Chisholm

Fig. 10
Pancho Villa

Fig. 14
Nicolas Saez

Fig. 17
Luis Terrazas

Fig. 15
Joseph Glidden

Fig. 13
John Veghte

Fig. 18
Jacob Haish

Fig. 19
Henrietta King

Fig. 20
Richard King
Ere Flecha

Fig. 21
Richard King
Rancho Brand

Fig. 22
King-Wallworth

Fig. 23
Richard King
Running W

PLATE II. HISTORICAL BRANDS

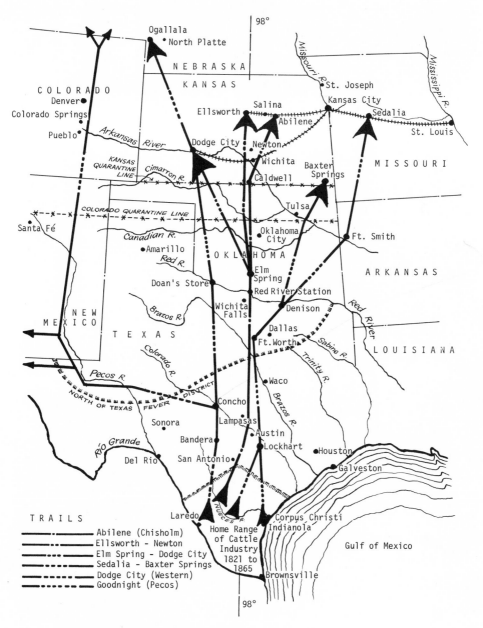

98°

Ogallala
• North Platte

NEBRASKA

KANSAS

COLORADO
Denver •
Colorado Springs •
Pueblo •

Arkansas River

Missouri R.

Mississippi R.

• St. Joseph

Kansas City

Salina
Ellsworth   Abilene
                                        Sedalia
                                    St. Louis

KANSAS
QUARANTINE
LINE   Cimarron R.

Dodge City   Newton

Wichita   Baxter
Caldwell   Springs

MISSOURI

Santa Fé

COLORADO QUARANTINE LINE

Canadian R.

• Amarillo

Red R.

OKLAHOMA

Tulsa

Oklahoma
City   Ft. Smith

ARKANSAS

NEW
MEXICO

TEXAS

Doan's Store

Brazos R.

Elm
Spring
Red River Station

Wichita
Falls   Denison

Red River

Dallas
Ft. Worth

Colorado R.

Pecos R.

NORTH OF TEXAS FEVER

DISTRICT

• Waco

Sabine R.

Trinity R.

LOUISIANA

Brazos R.

Concho

Sonora

Lampasas

Bandera

Rio Grande

Del Rio

San Antonio •

Austin
Lockhart

• Houston

Galveston

TRAILS

———•——— Abilene (Chisholm)
———••——— Ellsworth - Newton
———•••——— Elm Spring - Dodge City
————————— Sedalia - Baxter Springs
———•——— Dodge City (Western)
———••——— Goodnight (Pecos)

Laredo

NUECES R.

Home Range
of Cattle
Industry
1821 to
1865

Corpus Christi
Indianola

Gulf of Mexico

Brownsville

98°

PLATE III. CATTLE TRAILS

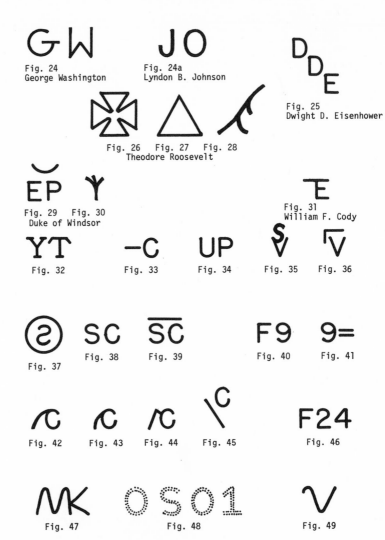

Fig. 24
George Washington

Fig. 24a
Lyndon B. Johnson

Fig. 25
Dwight D. Eisenhower

Fig. 26   Fig. 27   Fig. 28
Theodore Roosevelt

Fig. 29   Fig. 30
Duke of Windsor

Fig. 31
William F. Cody

Fig. 32   Fig. 33   Fig. 34   Fig. 35   Fig. 36

Fig. 37   Fig. 38   Fig. 39   Fig. 40   Fig. 41

Fig. 42   Fig. 43   Fig. 44   Fig. 45   Fig. 46

Fig. 47   Fig. 48   Fig. 49

PLATE IV. MISCELLANEOUS BRANDS

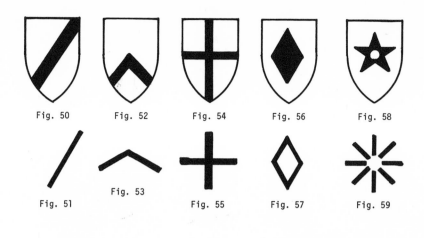

Fig. 50   Fig. 52   Fig. 54   Fig. 56   Fig. 58

Fig. 53

Fig. 51   Fig. 55   Fig. 57   Fig. 59

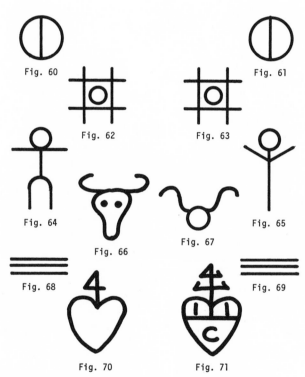

Fig. 60   Fig. 61

Fig. 62   Fig. 63

Fig. 64   Fig. 65

Fig. 67

Fig. 66

Fig. 68   Fig. 69

Fig. 70   Fig. 71

PLATE v. SIMILARITY OF SYMBOLS

H 5 2 Y

Fig. 72
John French

H 5 2 Y

Fig. 73
Mrs. John French

H 5 2 Y

Fig. 74
Ney

H 5 2 Y

Fig. 75
Nina

H 5 2 Y

Fig. 76
Homer

H 5 2 Y

Fig. 77
Lonnie

H 5 2 Y

Fig. 78
Burton

H 5 2 Y

Fig. 79
Vent Brand

Fig. 80
Don Miguel

Fig. 81
Carlos

Fig. 82
Luis

Fig. 83
José

Fig. 84
Mario

N

Fig. 85
Founder

N

Fig. 86
Second Grandson

N

Fig. 87
Second Grandson of
Second Grandson

N

Fig. 88
Third Grandson of
Second Grandson

Banu Sokhr Tribe

Fig. 89    Fig. 90    Fig. 91
        Banu Sokhr Clan

Fig. 92    Fig. 93    Fig. 94
        Khurshân Clan

PLATE VI. CADENCY

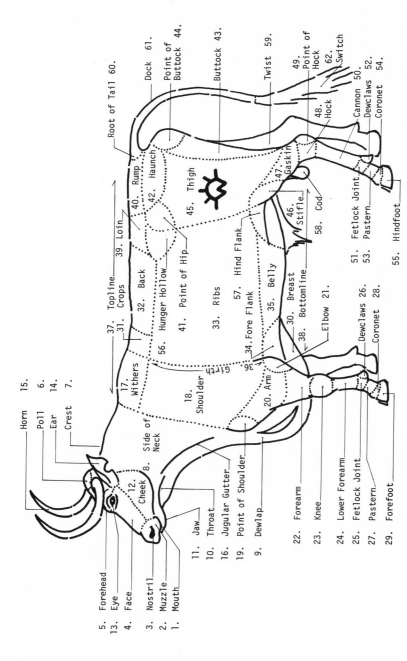

5. Forehead
13. Eye
4. Face
3. Nostril
2. Muzzle
1. Mouth

15. Horn
6. Poll
14. Ear
7. Crest

12. Cheek
8. Side of Neck

11. Jaw
10. Throat
16. Jugular Gutter
19. Point of Shoulder
9. Dewlap

17. Withers
18. Shoulder
56. Girth

37. Topline
31. Crops
32. Back
39. Loin
40. Rump
42. Haunch

Root of Tail 60.
Dock 61.
Point of Buttock 44.
Buttock 43.
Twist 59.

45. Thigh
41. Point of Hip
33. Ribs
57. Hind Flank
35. Belly
34. Fore Flank
30. Breast
38. Bottomline

46. Stifle
47. Gaskin
58. Cod
49. Point of Hock
48. Hock
62. Switch
50. Cannon
52. Dewclaws
54. Coronet

51. Fetlock Joint
53. Pastern
55. Hindfoot

36. Hunger Hollow

20. Arm
21. Elbow

22. Forearm
23. Knee
24. Lower Forearm
25. Fetlock Joint
27. Pastern
29. Forefoot

26. Dewclaws
28. Coronet

Fig. 95

PLATE VII. POINTS AND REGIONS OF CATTLE

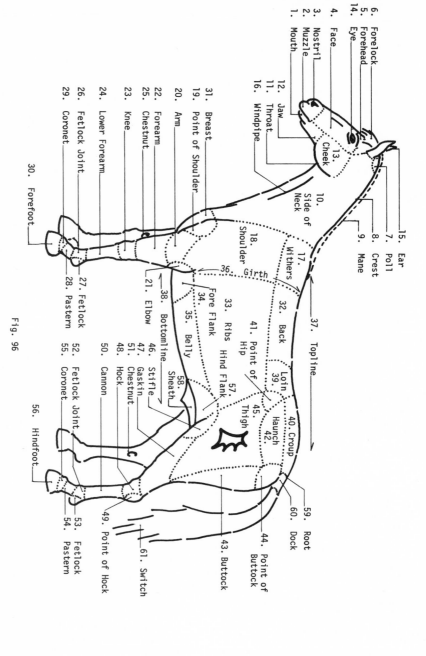

6. Forelock
5. Forehead
14. Eye
4. Face
3. Nostril
2. Muzzle
1. Mouth
15. Ear
7. Poll
8. Crest
9. Mane
13. Cheek
12. Jaw
11. Throat
16. Windpipe
10. Side of Neck
31. Breast
19. Point of Shoulder
20. Arm
22. Forearm
25. Chestnut
23. Knee
24. Lower Forearm
26. Fetlock Joint
29. Coronet
30. Forefoot
18. Shoulder
17. Withers
36. Girth
21. Elbow
38. Bottomline
34. Fore Flank
35. Belly
33. Ribs
32. Back
37. Topline
41. Point of Hip
39. Loin
40. Croup
42. Haunch
45. Thigh
57. Hind Flank
58. Sheath
59. Root
60. Dock
44. Point of Buttock
43. Buttock
46. Stifle
47. Gaskin
51. Chestnut
48. Hock
50. Cannon
52. Fetlock Joint
55. Coronet
49. Point of Hock
61. Switch
53. Fetlock
54. Pastern
27. Fetlock
28. Pastern
56. Hindfoot

PLATE VIII. POINTS AND REGIONS OF HORSES

Fig. 96

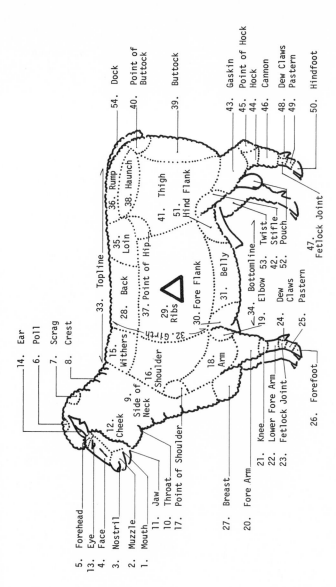

5. Forehead
13. Eye
4. Face
3. Nostril
2. Muzzle
1. Mouth

14. Ear
6. Poll
7. Scrag
8. Crest

11. Jaw
10. Throat
17. Point of Shoulder
12. Cheek
9. Side of Neck
16. Shoulder
15. Withers
33. Topline

27. Breast

20. Fore Arm
21. Knee
22. Lower Fore Arm
23. Fetlock Joint

26. Forefoot

18. Arm
28. Back
37. Point of Hip
29. Ribs
32. Girth
30. Fore Flank
31. Belly
34. Bottomline
19. Elbow
24. Dew Claws
25. Pastern

35. Loin
36. Rump
38. Haunch
41. Thigh
51. Hind Flank
53. Twist
42. Stifle
52. Pouch
47. Fetlock Joint

54. Dock
40. Point of Buttock
39. Buttock
43. Gaskin
45. Point of Hock
44. Hock
46. Cannon
48. Dew Claws
49. Pastern
50. Hindfoot

Fig. 97

PLATE IX. POINTS AND REGIONS OF SHEEP

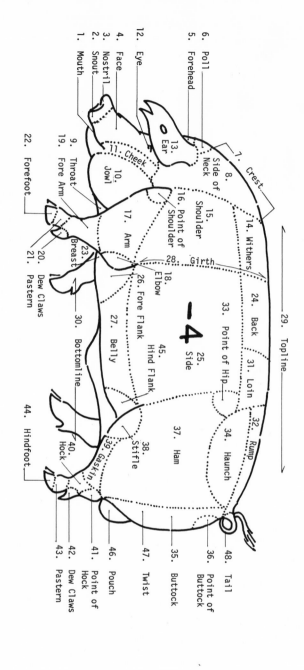

PLATE X. POINTS AND REGIONS OF SWINE

Fig. 98

1. Mouth
2. Snout
3. Nostril
4. Face
5. Forehead
6. Poll
7. Crest
8. Side of Neck
9. Throat
10. Jowl
11. Cheek
12. Eye
13. Ear
14. Withers
15. Shoulder
16. Point of Shoulder
17. Arm
18. Elbow
19. Fore Arm
20. Dew Claws
21. Pastern
22. Forefoot
23. Breast
24. Back
25. Side
26. Fore Flank
27. Belly
28. Girth
29. Topline
30. Bottomline
31. Loin
32. Rump
33. Point of Hip
34. Haunch
35. Buttock
36. Point of Buttock
37. Ham
38. Stifle
39. Gaskin
40. Hock
41. Point of Hock
42. Dew Claws
43. Pastern
44. Hindfoot
45. Hind Flank
46. Pouch
47. Twist
48. Tail

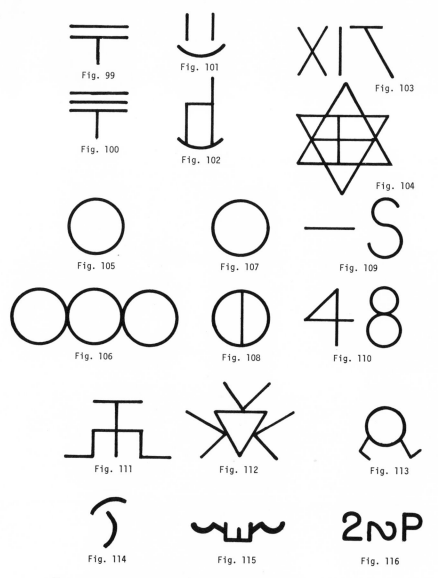

Fig. 99

Fig. 101

Fig. 103

Fig. 100

Fig. 102

Fig. 104

Fig. 105

Fig. 107

Fig. 109

Fig. 106

Fig. 108

Fig. 110

Fig. 111

Fig. 112

Fig. 113

Fig. 114

Fig. 115

Fig. 116

PLATE XI. BLOTTING OF BRANDS

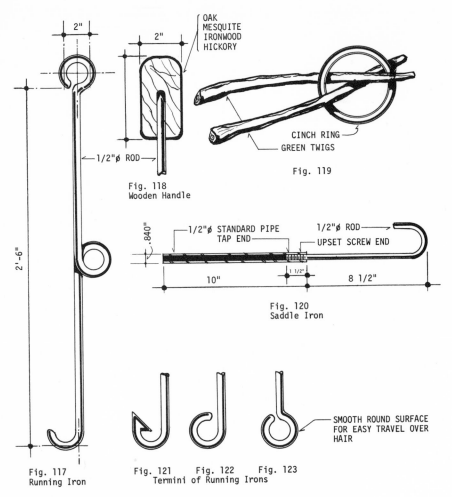

2"

2"

OAK
MESQUITE
IRONWOOD
HICKORY

1/2"ø ROD

Fig. 118
Wooden Handle

CINCH RING
GREEN TWIGS

Fig. 119

2'-6"

.840"

1/2"ø STANDARD PIPE
TAP END

1/2"ø ROD

UPSET SCREW END

10"

1 1/2"

8 1/2"

Fig. 120
Saddle Iron

SMOOTH ROUND SURFACE
FOR EASY TRAVEL OVER
HAIR

Fig. 117
Running Iron

Fig. 121   Fig. 122   Fig. 123
Termini of Running Irons

PLATE XII. TYPES OF RUNNING IRONS

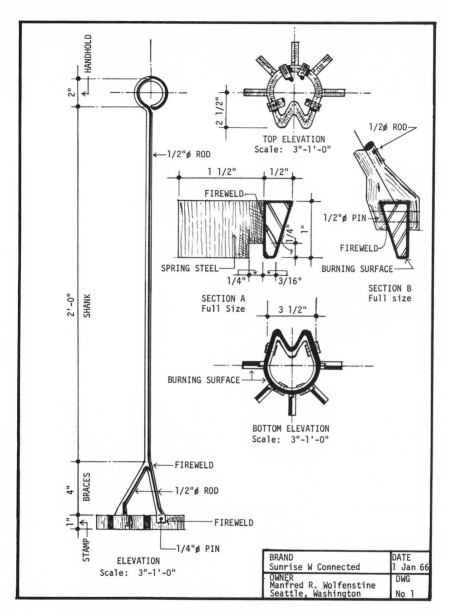

HANDHOLD

2"

1/2"∅ ROD

2'-0" SHANK

FIREWELD

1/2"∅ ROD

4" BRACES

1" FIREWELD

STAMP

1/4"∅ PIN

ELEVATION
Scale: 3"-1'-0"

2 1/2"

TOP ELEVATION
Scale: 3"-1'-0"

1 1/2"   1/2"

FIREWELD

1/4"   7"

SPRING STEEL

1/4"   3/16"

SECTION A
Full Size

1/2∅ ROD

1/2"∅ PIN

FIREWELD

BURNING SURFACE

SECTION B
Full size

3 1/2"

BURNING SURFACE

BOTTOM ELEVATION
Scale: 3"-1'-0"

BRAND Sunrise W Connected	DATE 1 Jan 66
OWNER Manfred R. Wolfenstine Seattle, Washington	DWG No 1

Plate XIII. WORKING DRAWINGS OF STAMP IRON

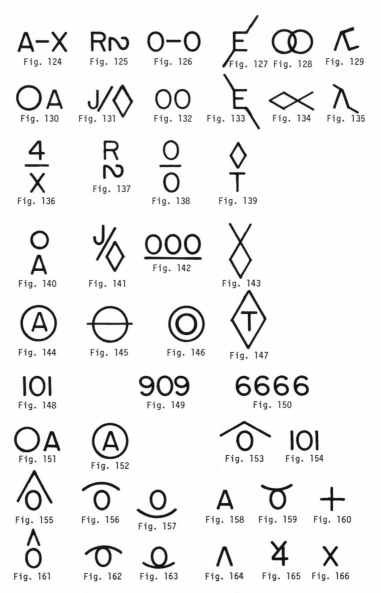

Fig. 124   Fig. 125   Fig. 126   Fig. 127   Fig. 128   Fig. 129

Fig. 130   Fig. 131   Fig. 132   Fig. 133   Fig. 134   Fig. 135

Fig. 136   Fig. 137   Fig. 138   Fig. 139

Fig. 140   Fig. 141   Fig. 142   Fig. 143

Fig. 144   Fig. 145   Fig. 146   Fig. 147

Fig. 148   Fig. 149   Fig. 150

Fig. 151   Fig. 152   Fig. 153   Fig. 154

Fig. 155   Fig. 156   Fig. 157   Fig. 158   Fig. 159   Fig. 160

Fig. 161   Fig. 162   Fig. 163   Fig. 164   Fig. 165   Fig. 166

PLATE XIV. RULES OF READING BRANDS

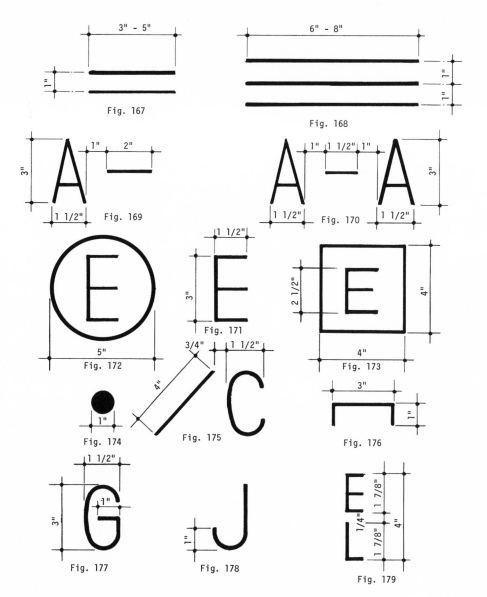

Fig. 167

Fig. 168

Fig. 169

Fig. 170

Fig. 171

Fig. 172

Fig. 173

Fig. 174

Fig. 175

Fig. 176

Fig. 177

Fig. 178

Fig. 179

PLATE xv. BRAND DIMENSIONS

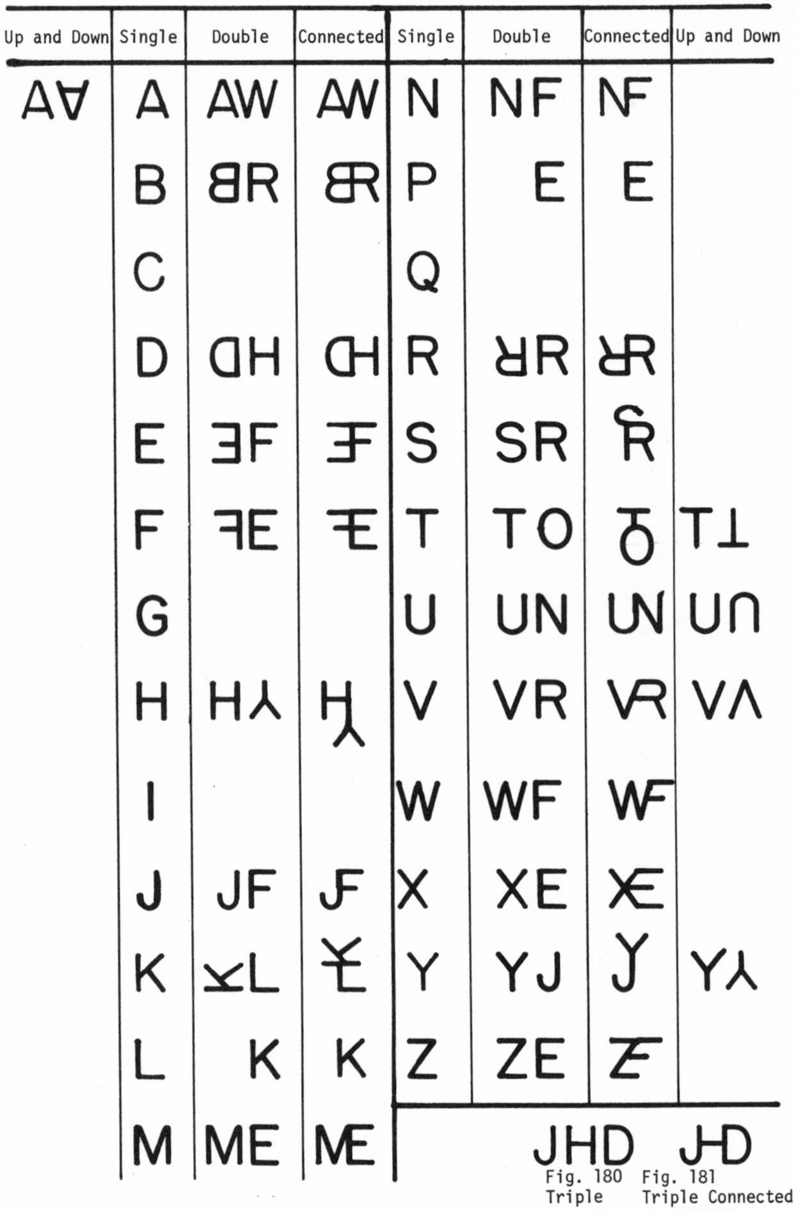

Up and Down	Single	Double	Connected	Single	Double	Connected	Up and Down
A∀	A	AW	AW	N	NF	NF	
	B	ЯR	ЯR	P	E	E	
	C			Q			
	D	HD	HD	R	ЯR	ЯR	
	E	ЭF	₣	S	SR	R̂	
	F	ЯE	Ŧ	T	TO	ᕤ	T⊥
	G			U	UN	UN	Un
	H	YH	H	V	VR	VR	VΛ
	I			W	WF	WF	
	J	JF	F	X	XE	XE	
	K	KL	Ŧ	Y	YJ	У	Y⅄
	L	K	K	Z	ZE	Ƶ	
	M	ME	ME				

JHD   J⊢D
Fig. 180   Fig. 181
Triple   Triple Connected

PLATE XVI. SINGLE AND CONNECTED ALPHABETS

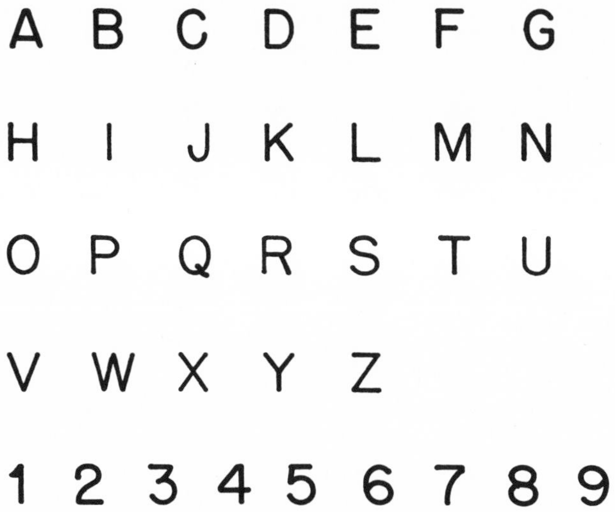
A B C D E F G
H I J K L M N
O P Q R S T U
V W X Y Z
1 2 3 4 5 6 7 8 9

Fig. 182
Standard Alphabet

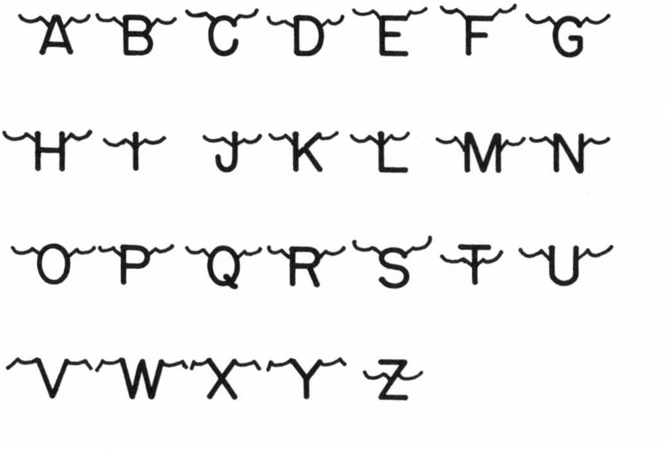
A B C D E F G
H I J K L M N
O P Q R S T U
V W X Y Z
1 2 3 4 5 6 7 8 9

Fig. 183
Flying Alphabet

PLATE XVII. STANDARD AND FLYING ALPHABETS

Fig. 185 Fig. 186 Fig. 187

Fig. 184
Running Alphabet

Fig. 188
Long Alphabet

PLATE XVIII. RUNNING AND LONG ALPHABETS

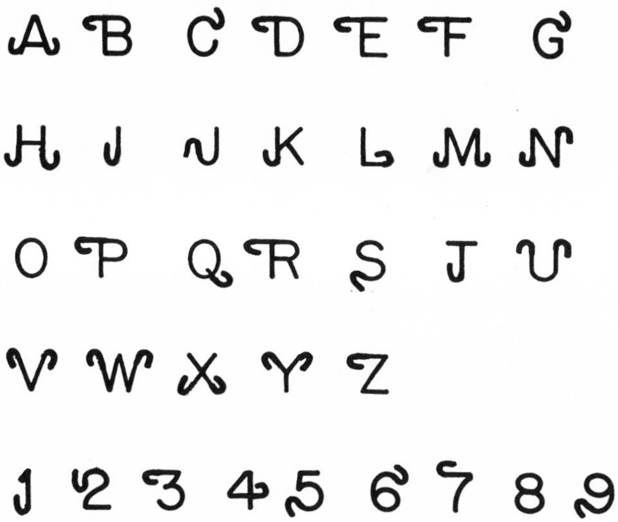

A B C D E F G

H J J K L M N

O P Q R S J U

V W X Y Z

1 2 3 4 5 6 7 8 9

Fig. 189
Hooked Alphabet

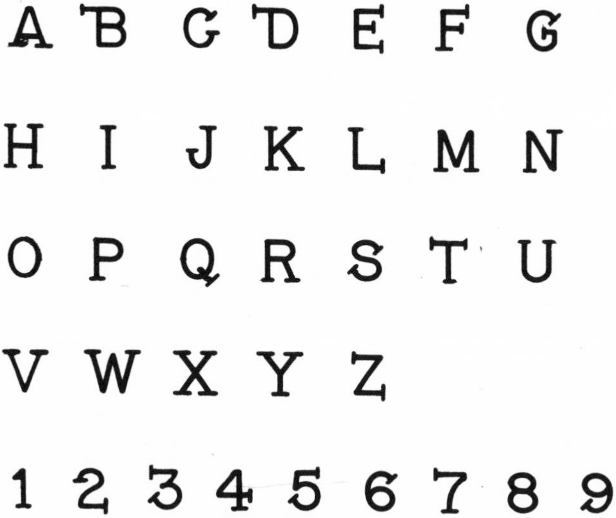

A B C D E F G

H I J K L M N

O P Q R S T U

V W X Y Z

1 2 3 4 5 6 7 8 9

Fig. 190
Bradded Alphabet

PLATE XIX. HOOKED AND BRADDED ALPHABETS

Fig. 191
Forked Alphabet

Fig. 192
Barbed Alphabet

PLATE XX. FORKED AND BARBED ALPHABETS

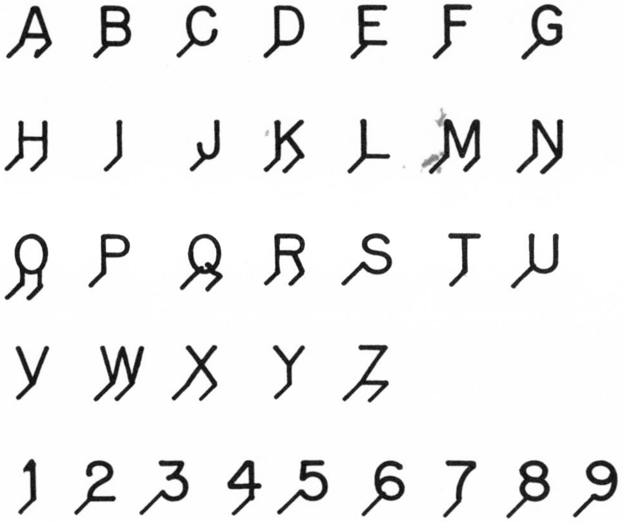

A B C D E F G
H J J K L M N
Ꝺ P Ꝺ ꝶ S T U
У Ɯ X Y Z

1 2 3 4 5 6 7 8 9

Fig. 193
Dragging Alphabet

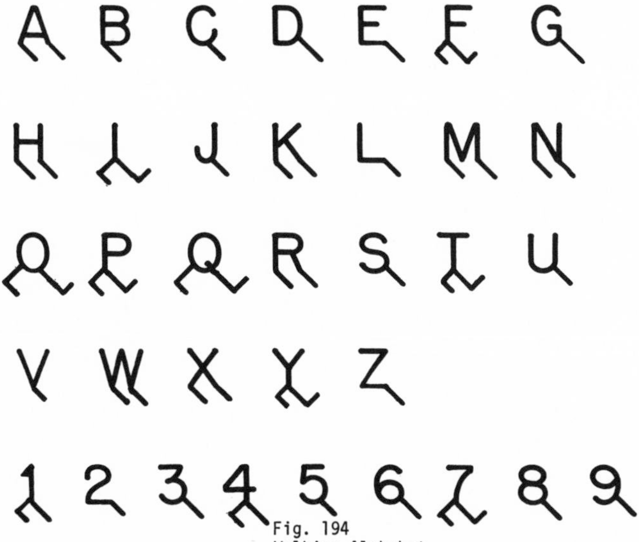

A B C D E F G
H I J K L M N
A P A R S T U
V W X Z

1 2 3 4 5 6 7 8 9

Fig. 194
Walking Alphabet

PLATE XXI. DRAGGING AND WALKING ALPHABETS

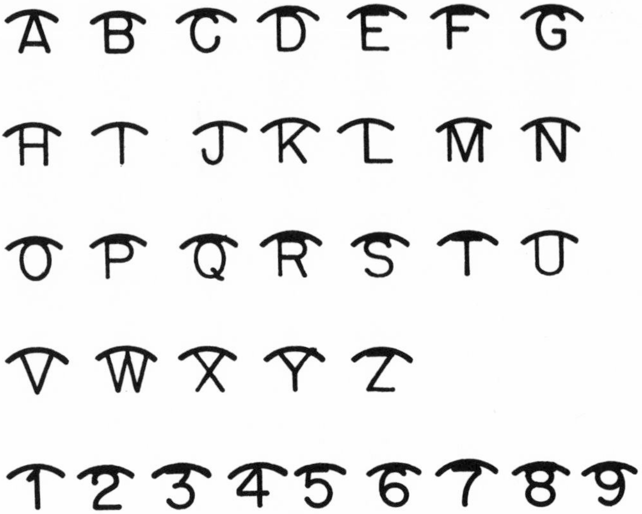

Fig. 195
Swinging Alphabet

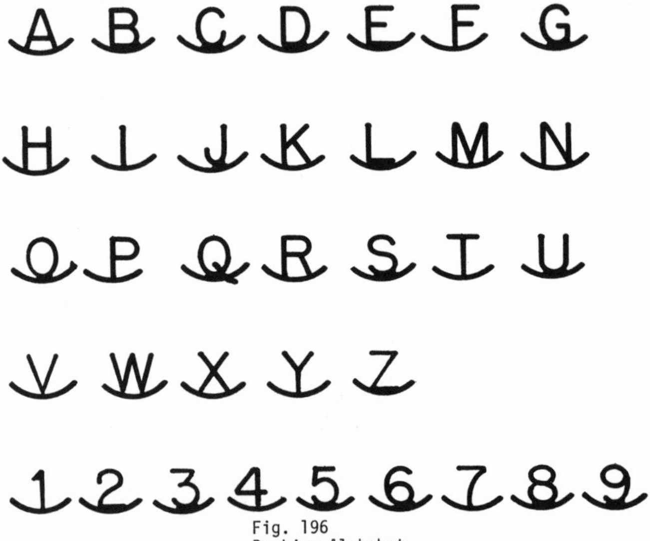

Fig. 196
Rocking Alphabet

PLATE XXII. SWINGING AND ROCKING ALPHABETS

Fig. 197
Crazy (Inverted) Alphabet

Fig. 198
Reverse (Backward) Alphabet

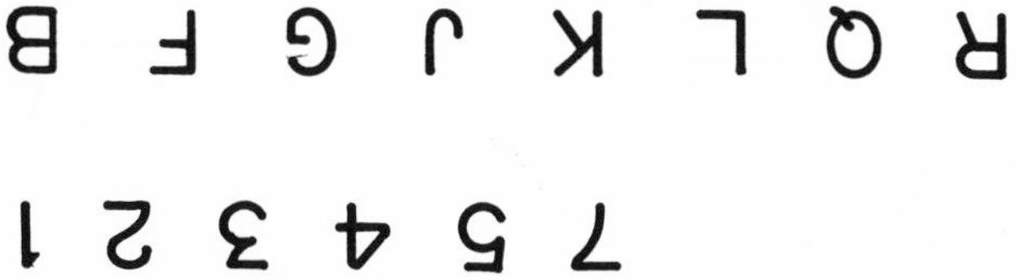

Fig. 199
Crazy-Reverse (Inverted-Backward) Alphabet

PLATE XXIII. CRAZY AND BACKWARD ALPHABETS

Fig. 200
Lazy Left Down Alphabet

Fig. 201
Lazy Right Down Alphabet

PLATE XXIV. LAZY DOWN ALPHABETS

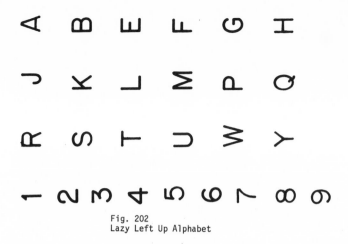

Fig. 202
Lazy Left Up Alphabet

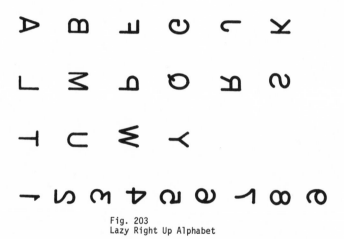

Fig. 203
Lazy Right Up Alphabet

PLATE xxv. LAZY UP ALPHABETS

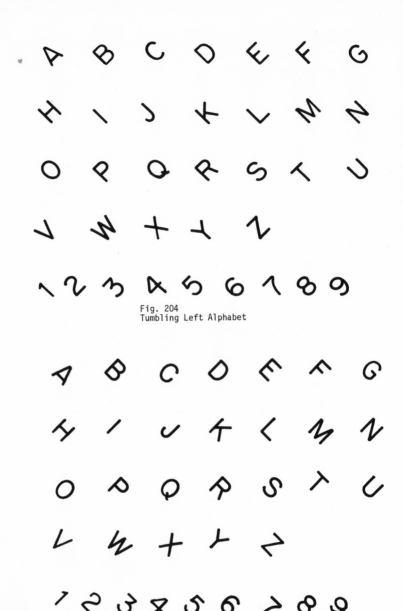

Fig. 204
Tumbling Left Alphabet

Fig. 205
Tumbling Right Alphabet

PLATE XXVI. TUMBLING ALPHABETS

Single	Double	Connected
1	15	5
2	24	4 3
3	32	2
4	47	4 7
5	52	5 2
6	63	6 3
7	76	7 6
8	89	8 9
9	96	9 6

Fig. 206
Triple **777**

Fig. 207
Triple Connected

PLATE XXVII. SINGLE AND CONNECTED NUMBERS

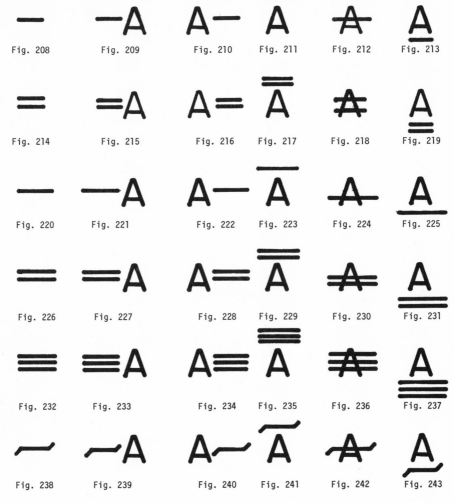

Fig. 208   Fig. 209   Fig. 210   Fig. 211   Fig. 212   Fig. 213

Fig. 214   Fig. 215   Fig. 216   Fig. 217   Fig. 218   Fig. 219

Fig. 220   Fig. 221   Fig. 222   Fig. 223   Fig. 224   Fig. 225

Fig. 226   Fig. 227   Fig. 228   Fig. 229   Fig. 230   Fig. 231

Fig. 232   Fig. 233   Fig. 234   Fig. 235   Fig. 236   Fig. 237

Fig. 238   Fig. 239   Fig. 240   Fig. 241   Fig. 242   Fig. 243

PLATE XXVIII. BARS

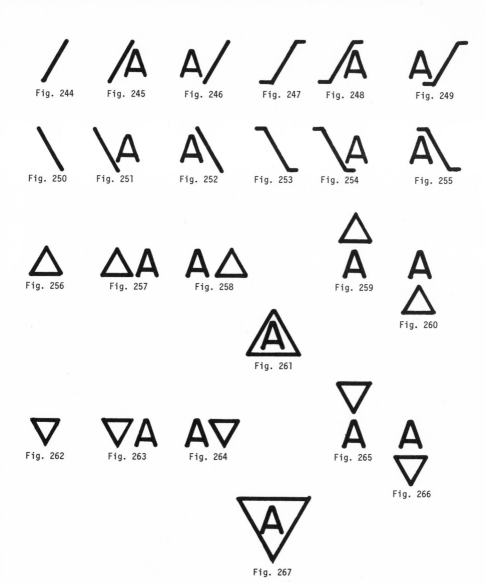

Fig. 244   Fig. 245   Fig. 246   Fig. 247   Fig. 248   Fig. 249

Fig. 250   Fig. 251   Fig. 252   Fig. 253   Fig. 254   Fig. 255

Fig. 256   Fig. 257   Fig. 258   Fig. 259   Fig. 260

Fig. 261

Fig. 262   Fig. 263   Fig. 264   Fig. 265   Fig. 266

Fig. 267

PLATE XXIX. SLASHES AND TRIANGLES

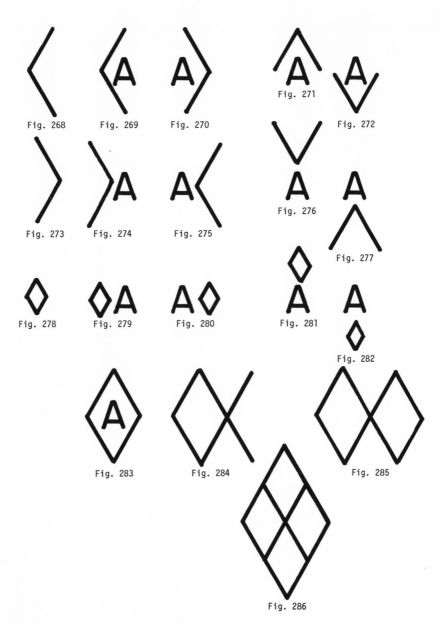

Fig. 268

Fig. 269

Fig. 270

Fig. 271

Fig. 272

Fig. 273

Fig. 274

Fig. 275

Fig. 276

Fig. 277

Fig. 278

Fig. 279

Fig. 280

Fig. 281

Fig. 282

Fig. 283

Fig. 284

Fig. 285

Fig. 286

PLATE XXX. DIAMONDS

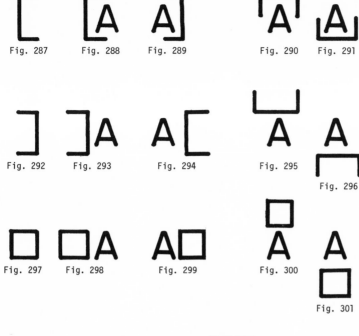

Fig. 287   Fig. 288   Fig. 289   Fig. 290   Fig. 291

Fig. 292   Fig. 293   Fig. 294   Fig. 295

Fig. 296

Fig. 297   Fig. 298   Fig. 299   Fig. 300

Fig. 301

Fig. 302

PLATE XXXI. BOXES

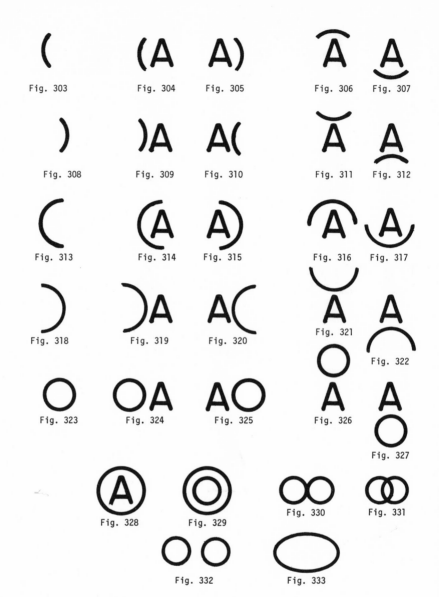

Fig. 303

Fig. 304   Fig. 305

Fig. 306   Fig. 307

Fig. 308

Fig. 309   Fig. 310

Fig. 311   Fig. 312

Fig. 313

Fig. 314   Fig. 315

Fig. 316   Fig. 317

Fig. 318

Fig. 319   Fig. 320

Fig. 321

Fig. 322

Fig. 323

Fig. 324   Fig. 325

Fig. 326

Fig. 327

Fig. 328   Fig. 329   Fig. 330   Fig. 331

Fig. 332   Fig. 333

PLATE XXXII. CIRCLES

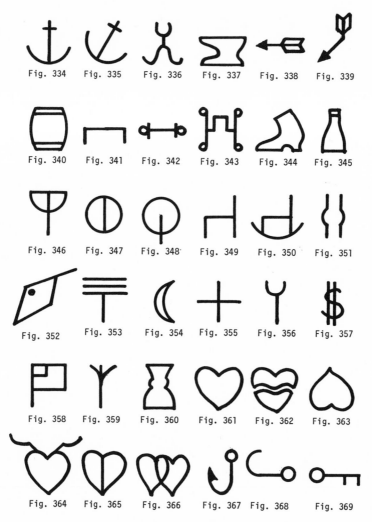

Fig. 334 Fig. 335 Fig. 336 Fig. 337 Fig. 338 Fig. 339

Fig. 340 Fig. 341 Fig. 342 Fig. 343 Fig. 344 Fig. 345

Fig. 346 Fig. 347 Fig. 348 Fig. 349 Fig. 350 Fig. 351

Fig. 352 Fig. 353 Fig. 354 Fig. 355 Fig. 356 Fig. 357

Fig. 358 Fig. 359 Fig. 360 Fig. 361 Fig. 362 Fig. 363

Fig. 364 Fig. 365 Fig. 366 Fig. 367 Fig. 368 Fig. 369

PLATE XXXIII. COMMON PICTURE BRANDS

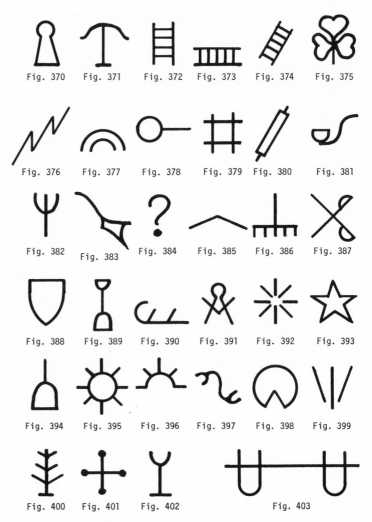

Fig. 370   Fig. 371   Fig. 372   Fig. 373   Fig. 374   Fig. 375

Fig. 376   Fig. 377   Fig. 378   Fig. 379   Fig. 380   Fig. 381

Fig. 382   Fig. 383   Fig. 384   Fig. 385   Fig. 386   Fig. 387

Fig. 388   Fig. 389   Fig. 390   Fig. 391   Fig. 392   Fig. 393

Fig. 394   Fig. 395   Fig. 396   Fig. 397   Fig. 398   Fig. 399

Fig. 400   Fig. 401   Fig. 402   Fig. 403

PLATE XXXIV. COMMON PICTURE BRANDS

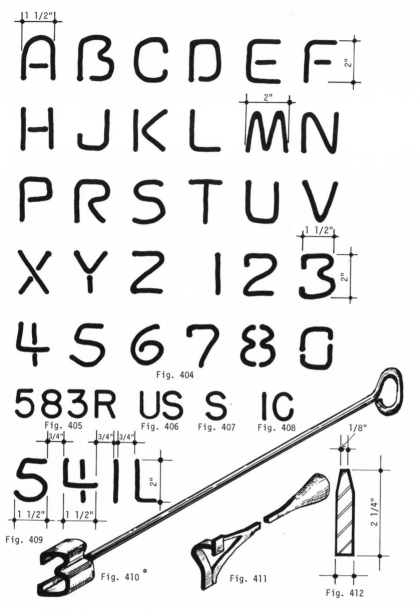

Fig. 404

Fig. 405 Fig. 406 Fig. 407 Fig. 408

Fig. 409

Fig. 410 *

Fig. 411

Fig. 412

PLATE XXXV. ARMY BRANDS AND BRANDING IRONS

* Note that the stamp on the handle is reversed and therefore would brand a re-versed 3. However, this drawing was made from a photograph in an official U.S. Army Quartermaster Supply Catalog, QM 3–3, dated June 15, 1944.

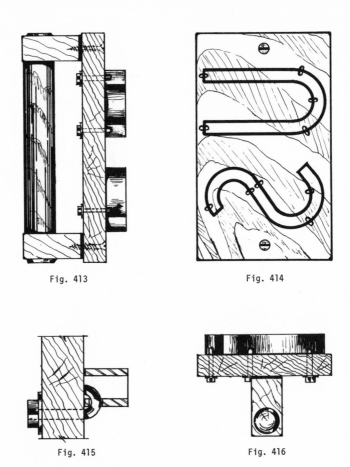

Fig. 413

Fig. 414

Fig. 415

Fig. 416

PLATE XXXVI. THE WEST POINT IRON

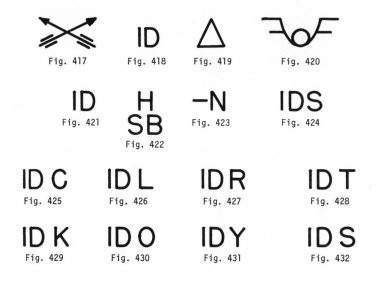

Fig. 417   Fig. 418   Fig. 419   Fig. 420

Fig. 421   Fig. 422   Fig. 423   Fig. 424

Fig. 425   Fig. 426   Fig. 427   Fig. 428

Fig. 429   Fig. 430   Fig. 431   Fig. 432

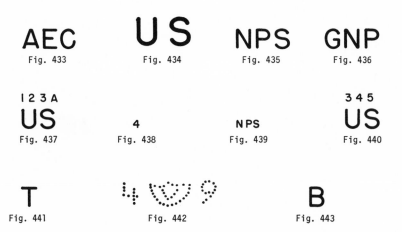

Fig. 433   Fig. 434   Fig. 435   Fig. 436

Fig. 437   Fig. 438   Fig. 439   Fig. 440

Fig. 441   Fig. 442   Fig. 443

PLATE XXXVII. U.S. GOVERNMENT BRANDS

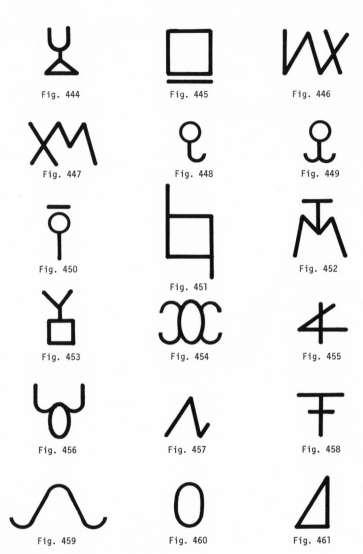

Fig. 444

Fig. 445

Fig. 446

Fig. 447

Fig. 448

Fig. 449

Fig. 450

Fig. 451

Fig. 452

Fig. 453

Fig. 454

Fig. 455

Fig. 456

Fig. 457

Fig. 458

Fig. 459

Fig. 460

Fig. 461

PLATE XXXVIII. OLD NAVAHO BRANDS

Fig. 462

Fig. 463

Fig. 464

Fig. 465

Fig. 466

Fig. 467

CALF YRLING VEAL

Fig. 468   Fig. 469   Fig. 470

Fig. 471

MUTTON BULL STAG

Fig. 472   Fig. 473   Fig. 474

Fig. 475

PLATE xxxix. CARCASS BRANDS

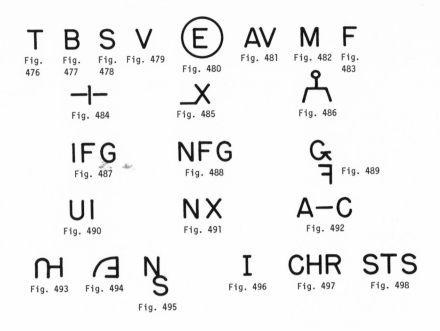

T B S V (E) AV M F
Fig. Fig. Fig. Fig. 479 Fig. 480 Fig. 481 Fig. 482 Fig.
476 477 478 483

—I— ⅄ ⺗
Fig. 484 Fig. 485 Fig. 486

IFG NFG G⅂
Fig. 487 Fig. 488 Fig. 489

UI NX A—C
Fig. 490 Fig. 491 Fig. 492

⋔ ⊿ N̩
Fig. 493 Fig. 494 S
Fig. 495

I CHR STS
Fig. 496 Fig. 497 Fig. 498

S⌒ /H7 ⅃ NH
Fig. 499 Fig. 500 Fig. 501 Fig. 502

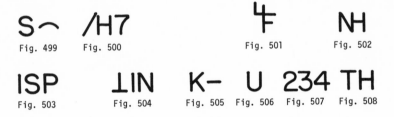

ISP ⊥IN K— U 234 TH
Fig. 503 Fig. 504 Fig. 505 Fig. 506 Fig. 507 Fig. 508

☆
Fig. 509

PLATE XL. STATE GOVERNMENT BRANDS

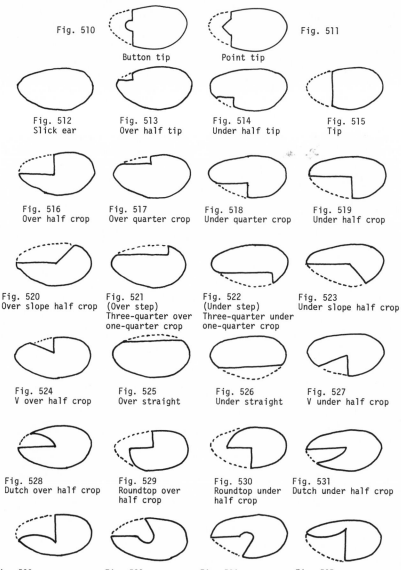

Fig. 510

Button tip

Fig. 511

Point tip

Fig. 512
Slick ear

Fig. 513
Over half tip

Fig. 514
Under half tip

Fig. 515
Tip

Fig. 516
Over half crop

Fig. 517
Over quarter crop

Fig. 518
Under quarter crop

Fig. 519
Under half crop

Fig. 520
Over slope half crop

Fig. 521
(Over step)
Three-quarter over
one-quarter crop

Fig. 522
(Under step)
Three-quarter under
one-quarter crop

Fig. 523
Under slope half crop

Fig. 524
V over half crop

Fig. 525
Over straight

Fig. 526
Under straight

Fig. 527
V under half crop

Fig. 528
Dutch over half crop

Fig. 529
Roundtop over
half crop

Fig. 530
Roundtop under
half crop

Fig. 531
Dutch under half crop

Fig. 532
Flicker over half crop

Fig. 533
Key over half crop

Fig. 534
Key under half crop

Fig. 535
Flicker under half crop

PLATE xli. EARMARKS

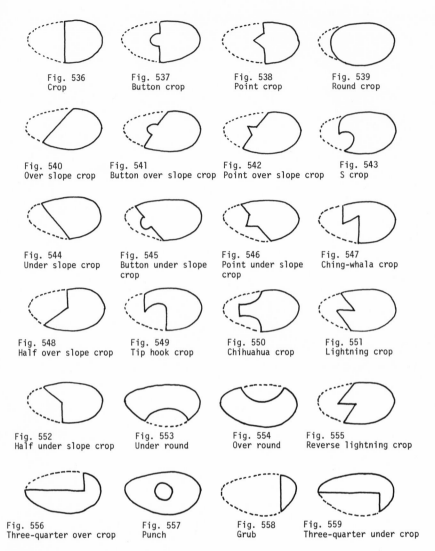

Fig. 536
Crop

Fig. 537
Button crop

Fig. 538
Point crop

Fig. 539
Round crop

Fig. 540
Over slope crop

Fig. 541
Button over slope crop

Fig. 542
Point over slope crop

Fig. 543
S crop

Fig. 544
Under slope crop

Fig. 545
Button under slope
crop

Fig. 546
Point under slope
crop

Fig. 547
Ching-whala crop

Fig. 548
Half over slope crop

Fig. 549
Tip hook crop

Fig. 550
Chihuahua crop

Fig. 551
Lightning crop

Fig. 552
Half under slope crop

Fig. 553
Under round

Fig. 554
Over round

Fig. 555
Reverse lightning crop

Fig. 556
Three-quarter over crop

Fig. 557
Punch

Fig. 558
Grub

Fig. 559
Three-quarter under crop

PLATE XLII. EARMARKS

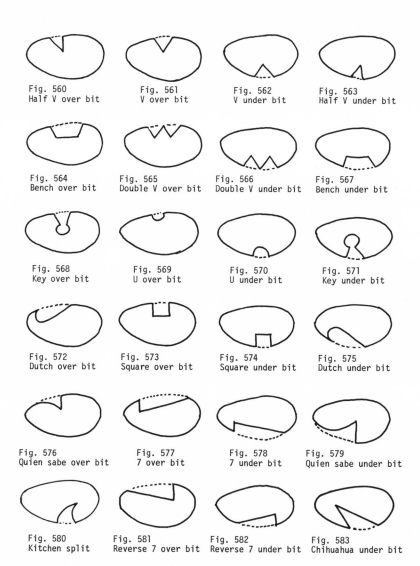

Fig. 560
Half V over bit

Fig. 561
V over bit

Fig. 562
V under bit

Fig. 563
Half V under bit

Fig. 564
Bench over bit

Fig. 565
Double V over bit

Fig. 566
Double V under bit

Fig. 567
Bench under bit

Fig. 568
Key over bit

Fig. 569
U over bit

Fig. 570
U under bit

Fig. 571
Key under bit

Fig. 572
Dutch over bit

Fig. 573
Square over bit

Fig. 574
Square under bit

Fig. 575
Dutch under bit

Fig. 576
Quien sabe over bit

Fig. 577
7 over bit

Fig. 578
7 under bit

Fig. 579
Quien sabe under bit

Fig. 580
Kitchen split

Fig. 581
Reverse 7 over bit

Fig. 582
Reverse 7 under bit

Fig. 583
Chihuahua under bit

PLATE XLIII. EARMARKS

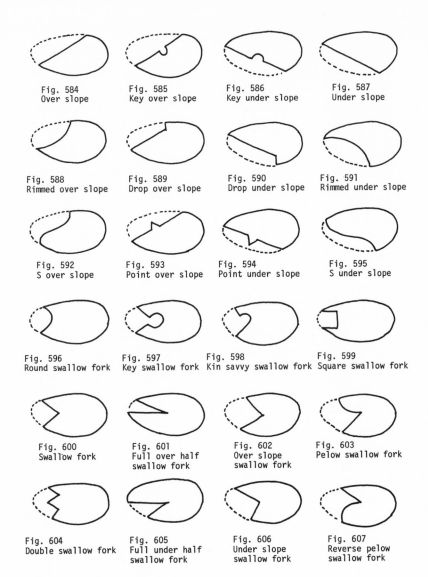

Fig. 584
Over slope

Fig. 585
Key over slope

Fig. 586
Key under slope

Fig. 587
Under slope

Fig. 588
Rimmed over slope

Fig. 589
Drop over slope

Fig. 590
Drop under slope

Fig. 591
Rimmed under slope

Fig. 592
S over slope

Fig. 593
Point over slope

Fig. 594
Point under slope

Fig. 595
S under slope

Fig. 596
Round swallow fork

Fig. 597
Key swallow fork

Fig. 598
Kin savvy swallow fork

Fig. 599
Square swallow fork

Fig. 600
Swallow fork

Fig. 601
Full over half
swallow fork

Fig. 602
Over slope
swallow fork

Fig. 603
Pelow swallow fork

Fig. 604
Double swallow fork

Fig. 605
Full under half
swallow fork

Fig. 606
Under slope
swallow fork

Fig. 607
Reverse pelow
swallow fork

PLATE XLIV. EARMARKS

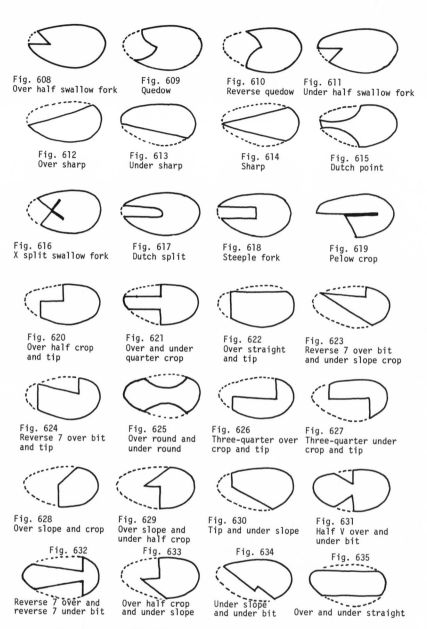

Fig. 608
Over half swallow fork

Fig. 609
Quedow

Fig. 610
Reverse quedow

Fig. 611
Under half swallow fork

Fig. 612
Over sharp

Fig. 613
Under sharp

Fig. 614
Sharp

Fig. 615
Dutch point

Fig. 616
X split swallow fork

Fig. 617
Dutch split

Fig. 618
Steeple fork

Fig. 619
Pelow crop

Fig. 620
Over half crop
and tip

Fig. 621
Over and under
quarter crop

Fig. 622
Over straight
and tip

Fig. 623
Reverse 7 over bit
and under slope crop

Fig. 624
Reverse 7 over bit
and tip

Fig. 625
Over round and
under round

Fig. 626
Three-quarter over
crop and tip

Fig. 627
Three-quarter under
crop and tip

Fig. 628
Over slope and crop

Fig. 629
Over slope and
under half crop

Fig. 630
Tip and under slope

Fig. 631
Half V over and
under bit

Fig. 632
Reverse 7 over and
reverse 7 under bit

Fig. 633
Over half crop
and under slope

Fig. 634
Under slope
and under bit

Fig. 635
Over and under straight

PLATE XLV. EARMARKS

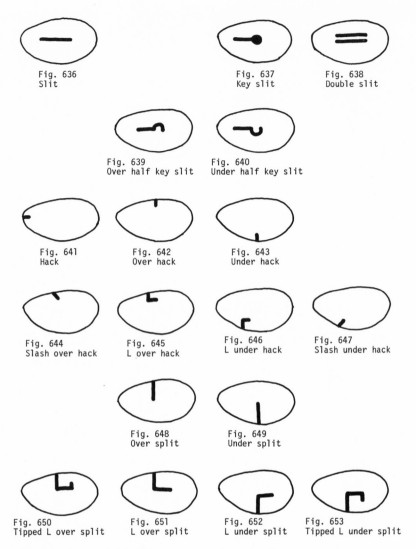

Fig. 636
Slit

Fig. 637
Key slit

Fig. 638
Double slit

Fig. 639
Over half key slit

Fig. 640
Under half key slit

Fig. 641
Hack

Fig. 642
Over hack

Fig. 643
Under hack

Fig. 644
Slash over hack

Fig. 645
L over hack

Fig. 646
L under hack

Fig. 647
Slash under hack

Fig. 648
Over split

Fig. 649
Under split

Fig. 650
Tipped L over split

Fig. 651
L over split

Fig. 652
L under split

Fig. 653
Tipped L under split

PLATE XLVI. EARMARKS

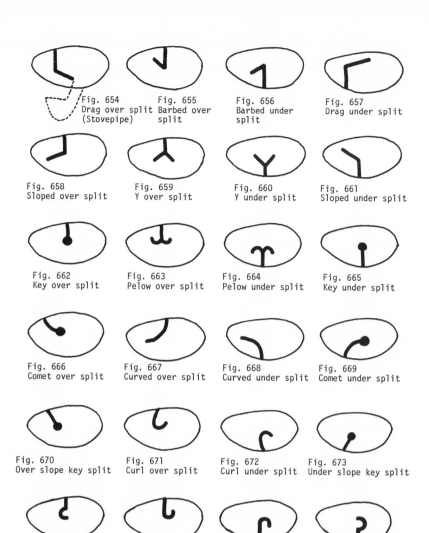

Fig. 654
Drag over split
(Stovepipe)

Fig. 655
Barbed over
split

Fig. 656
Barbed under
split

Fig. 657
Drag under split

Fig. 658
Sloped over split

Fig. 659
Y over split

Fig. 660
Y under split

Fig. 661
Sloped under split

Fig. 662
Key over split

Fig. 663
Pelow over split

Fig. 664
Pelow under split

Fig. 665
Key under split

Fig. 666
Comet over split

Fig. 667
Curved over split

Fig. 668
Curved under split

Fig. 669
Comet under split

Fig. 670
Over slope key split

Fig. 671
Curl over split

Fig. 672
Curl under split

Fig. 673
Under slope key split

Fig. 674
Half key over split

Fig. 675
Hooked over split

Fig. 676
Hooked under split

Fig. 677
Half key under split

PLATE XLVII. EARMARKS

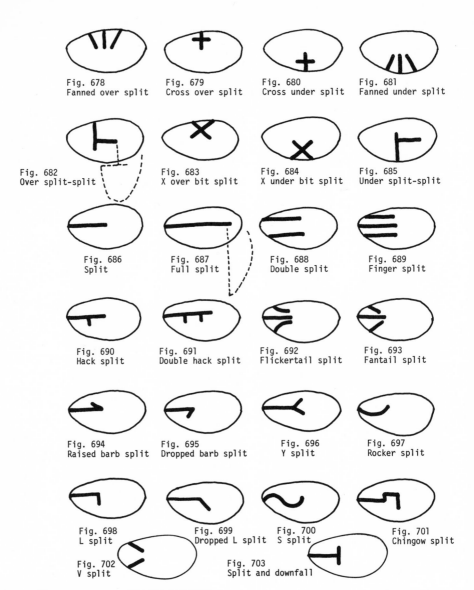

Fig. 678
Fanned over split

Fig. 679
Cross over split

Fig. 680
Cross under split

Fig. 681
Fanned under split

Fig. 682
Over split-split

Fig. 683
X over bit split

Fig. 684
X under bit split

Fig. 685
Under split-split

Fig. 686
Split

Fig. 687
Full split

Fig. 688
Double split

Fig. 689
Finger split

Fig. 690
Hack split

Fig. 691
Double hack split

Fig. 692
Flickertail split

Fig. 693
Fantail split

Fig. 694
Raised barb split

Fig. 695
Dropped barb split

Fig. 696
Y split

Fig. 697
Rocker split

Fig. 698
L split

Fig. 699
Dropped L split

Fig. 700
S split

Fig. 701
Chingow split

Fig. 702
V split

Fig. 703
Split and downfall

PLATE XLVIII. EARMARKS

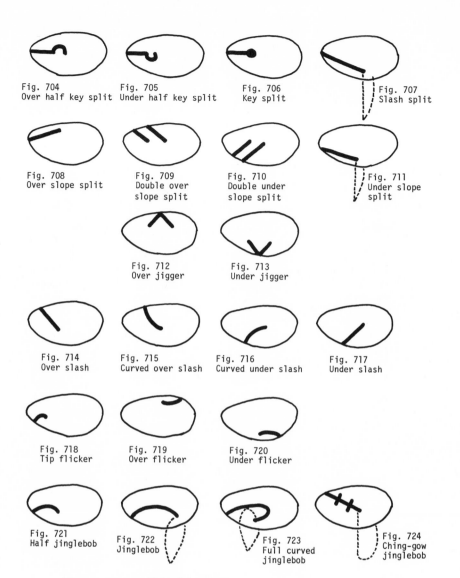

Fig. 704
Over half key split

Fig. 705
Under half key split

Fig. 706
Key split

Fig. 707
Slash split

Fig. 708
Over slope split

Fig. 709
Double over
slope split

Fig. 710
Double under
slope split

Fig. 711
Under slope
split

Fig. 712
Over jigger

Fig. 713
Under jigger

Fig. 714
Over slash

Fig. 715
Curved over slash

Fig. 716
Curved under slash

Fig. 717
Under slash

Fig. 718
Tip flicker

Fig. 719
Over flicker

Fig. 720
Under flicker

Fig. 721
Half jinglebob

Fig. 722
Jinglebob

Fig. 723
Full curved
jinglebob

Fig. 724
Ching-gow
jinglebob

PLATE XLIX. EARMARKS

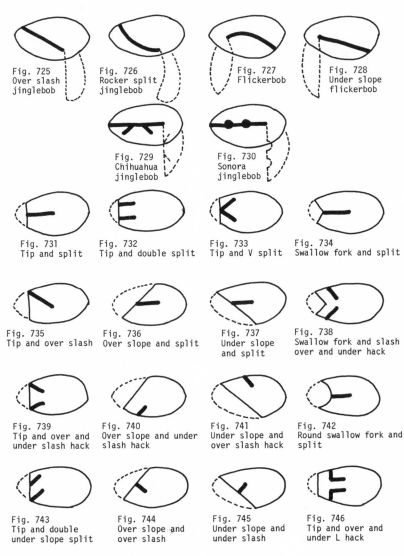

Fig. 725
Over slash
jinglebob

Fig. 726
Rocker split
jinglebob

Fig. 727
Flickerbob

Fig. 728
Under slope
flickerbob

Fig. 729
Chihuahua
jinglebob

Fig. 730
Sonora
jinglebob

Fig. 731
Tip and split

Fig. 732
Tip and double split

Fig. 733
Tip and V split

Fig. 734
Swallow fork and split

Fig. 735
Tip and over slash

Fig. 736
Over slope and split

Fig. 737
Under slope
and split

Fig. 738
Swallow fork and slash
over and under hack

Fig. 739
Tip and over and
under slash hack

Fig. 740
Over slope and under
slash hack

Fig. 741
Under slope and
over slash hack

Fig. 742
Round swallow fork and
split

Fig. 743
Tip and double
under slope split

Fig. 744
Over slope and
over slash

Fig. 745
Under slope and
under slash

Fig. 746
Tip and over and
under L hack

PLATE L. EARMARKS

Fig. 747
Rimmed over slope
and over slope hack

Fig. 748
Rimmed under slope
and under slope hack

Fig. 749
Reverse under slash
and under bit

Fig. 750
Under rim and
under slope hack

Fig. 751
Over half tip and
split

Fig. 752
Over slope crop
and under slope
hack

Fig. 753
Over slope and
rocker split

Fig. 754
Curved under slope split
and under bit

Fig. 755
V over bit and
slash

Fig. 756
Over three-quarter
crop and hack

Fig. 757
Half under slope
crop and hack

Fig. 758
Chingadero
jinglebob

Fig. 759
Over round and hack

Fig. 760
Crop and split

Fig. 761
Under round and hack

Fig. 762
Over and under
slash hack

Fig. 763
Over and under
L hack

Fig. 764
L over split and
under flicker

Fig. 765
Over and under
hack and split

Fig. 766
Over flicker and
half jinglebob

Fig. 767
L over hack
and split

Plate li. EARMARKS

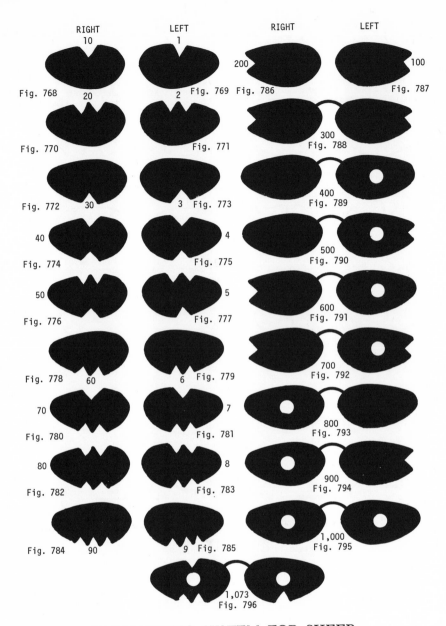

PLATE LII. EARMARKING SYSTEM FOR SHEEP

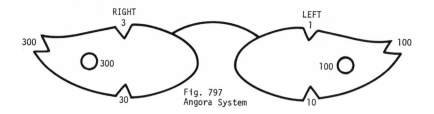

RIGHT 3
LEFT 1
300
100
300
100
30
10

Fig. 797
Angora System

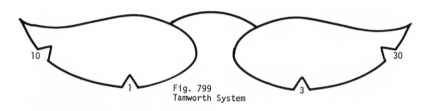

81
9
27
9
3
3
1
1

Fig. 798
Hampshire System

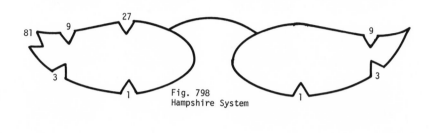

10
30
1
3

Fig. 799
Tamworth System

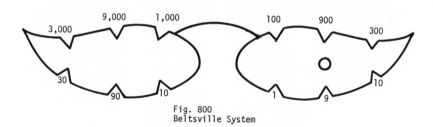

3,000
9,000
1,000
100
900
300
30
10
90
10
1
9

Fig. 800
Beltsville System

PLATE LIII. EARMARKING SYSTEM
FOR SWINE AND GOATS

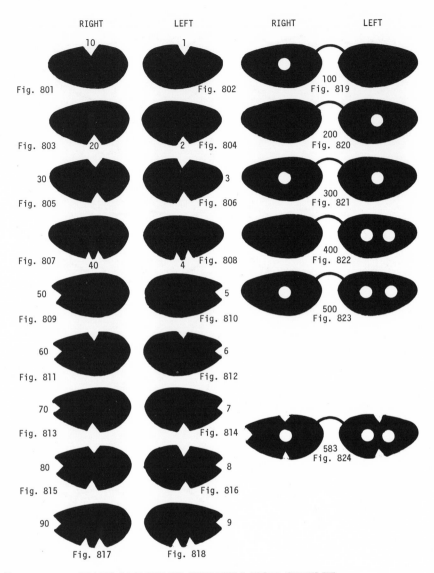

PLATE LIV. EARMARKING SYSTEM FOR SWINE

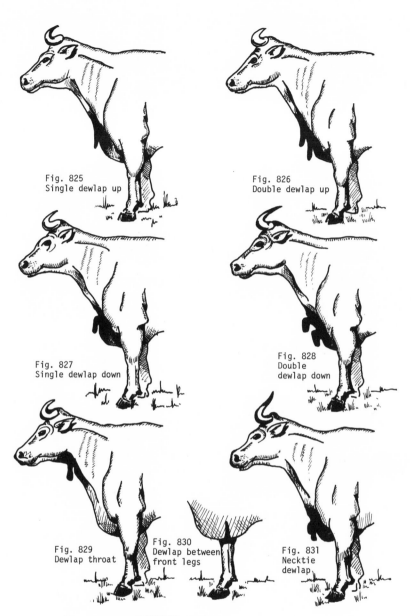

Fig. 825
Single dewlap up

Fig. 826
Double dewlap up

Fig. 827
Single dewlap down

Fig. 828
Double
dewlap down

Fig. 829
Dewlap throat

Fig. 830
Dewlap between
front legs

Fig. 831
Necktie
dewlap

PLATE LV. DEWLAPS

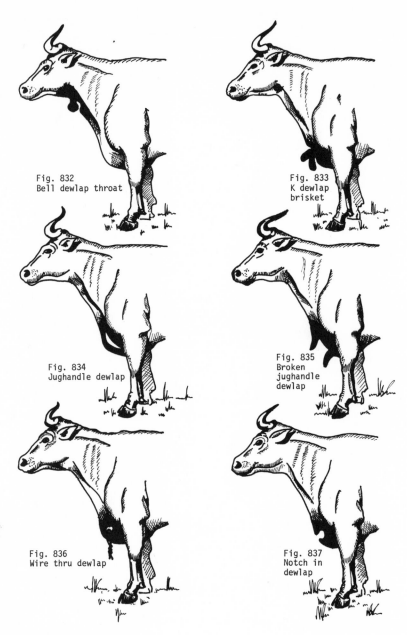

Fig. 832
Bell dewlap throat

Fig. 833
K dewlap
brisket

Fig. 834
Jughandle dewlap

Fig. 835
Broken
jughandle
dewlap

Fig. 836
Wire thru dewlap

Fig. 837
Notch in
dewlap

PLATE LVI. DEWLAPS

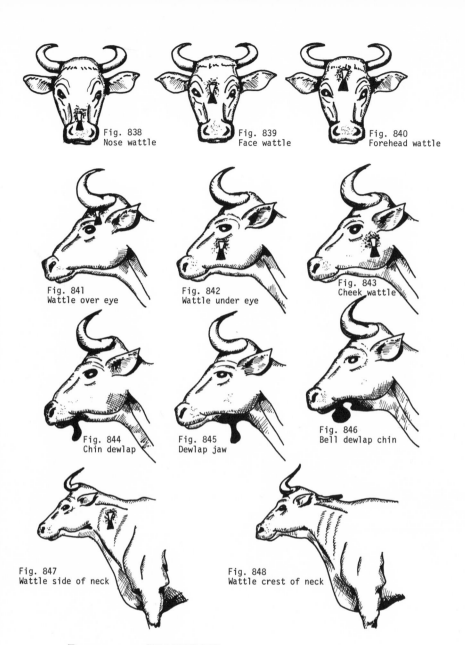

Fig. 838
Nose wattle

Fig. 839
Face wattle

Fig. 840
Forehead wattle

Fig. 841
Wattle over eye

Fig. 842
Wattle under eye

Fig. 843
Cheek wattle

Fig. 844
Chin dewlap

Fig. 845
Dewlap jaw

Fig. 846
Bell dewlap chin

Fig. 847
Wattle side of neck

Fig. 848
Wattle crest of neck

Plate lvii. WATTLES

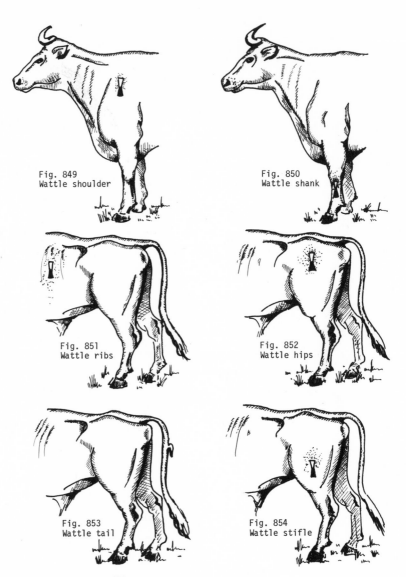

Fig. 849
Wattle shoulder

Fig. 850
Wattle shank

Fig. 851
Wattle ribs

Fig. 852
Wattle hips

Fig. 853
Wattle tail

Fig. 854
Wattle stifle

PLATE LVIII. WATTLES

Fig. 855

Fig. 856

San Diego de Alcalá

Fig. 857
San Carlos Borromeo
(Carmelo)

Fig. 858
San Antonio de Padua

Fig. 859

Fig. 860

San Gabriel, Arcángel

Fig. 861
San Luis Obispo
de Tolosa

Fig. 862
San Francisco de Asis
(Dolores)

Fig. 863
San Juan Capistrano

Fig. 864
Santa Clara
de Asis

Fig. 865
San Buenaventura

Fig. 866
Santa Barbara

Fig. 867
La Purísima Conceptión

Fig. 868
Santa Cruz

Fig. 869
La Soledad

Fig. 870
San José

Fig. 871
San Juan Bautista

Fig. 872
San Miguel, Arcángel

Fig. 873
San Fernando Rey

Fig. 874
San Luis Rey

Fig. 875
Santa Inés

Fig. 876
San Rafael, Arcángel

Fig. 877
San Francisco Solano
(Sonoma)

PLATE LIX. CALIFORNIA MISSION BRANDS

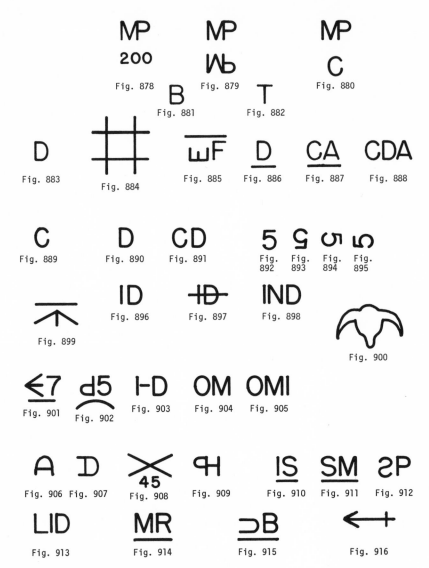

MP
200

Fig. 878

MP
Wb

Fig. 879

MP
C

Fig. 880

B

Fig. 881

T

Fig. 882

D

Fig. 883

Fig. 884

wF

Fig. 885

D

Fig. 886

CA

Fig. 887

CDA

Fig. 888

C

Fig. 889

D

Fig. 890

CD

Fig. 891

5

Fig. 892

5

Fig. 893

5

Fig. 894

5

Fig. 895

Fig. 899

ID

Fig. 896

D

Fig. 897

IND

Fig. 898

Fig. 900

7

Fig. 901

d5

Fig. 902

I-D

Fig. 903

OM

Fig. 904

OMI

Fig. 905

A

Fig. 906

D

Fig. 907

45

Fig. 908

CH

Fig. 909

IS

Fig. 910

SM

Fig. 911

SP

Fig. 912

LID

Fig. 913

MR

Fig. 914

DB

Fig. 915

Fig. 916

PLATE LX. CANADIAN FEDERAL
AND PROVINCIAL BRANDS

P5CU Fig. 917	44R Fig. 928	I2KB Fig. 938	MLU Fig. 948
I2L Fig. 918	39LB Fig. 929	BRUE Fig. 939	DMIL^{TD} Fig. 949
AMD Fig. 919	IIBU Fig. 930	32SN Fig. 940	I6SB Fig. 950
IINV Fig. 920	CB Fig. 931	27M Fig. 941	36NS Fig. 951
6BCY Fig. 921	23SP Fig. 932	LMT Fig. 942	39BL Fig. 952
9R Fig. 922	W.C.S. Fig. 933	6SP Fig. 943	LXY Fig. 953
28RL Fig. 923	MJM Fig. 934	I7BY Fig. 944	29 Fig. 954
54BC Fig. 924	SY29 Fig. 935	9V Fig. 945	6BCY Fig. 955
I3CU Fig. 925	2ML Fig. 936	74 Fig. 946	ISH Fig. 956
MJMA Fig. 926	38CY Fig. 937	34BL Fig. 947	BACK Fig. 957
37CN Fig. 927	AMKPV Fig. 959		J.IL Fig. 958

22LCY
Fig. 960

5ELBY
Fig. 961

PLATE LXI. SCOTTISH SHEEP BRANDS

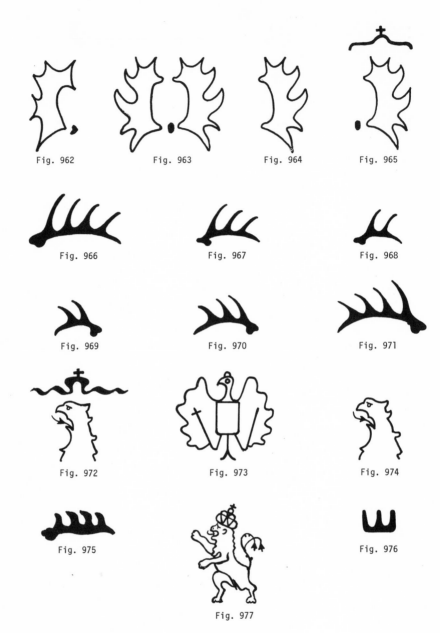

Fig. 962   Fig. 963   Fig. 964   Fig. 965

Fig. 966   Fig. 967   Fig. 968

Fig. 969   Fig. 970   Fig. 971

Fig. 972   Fig. 973   Fig. 974

Fig. 975   Fig. 976

Fig. 977

PLATE LXII. GERMAN HORSE BRANDS

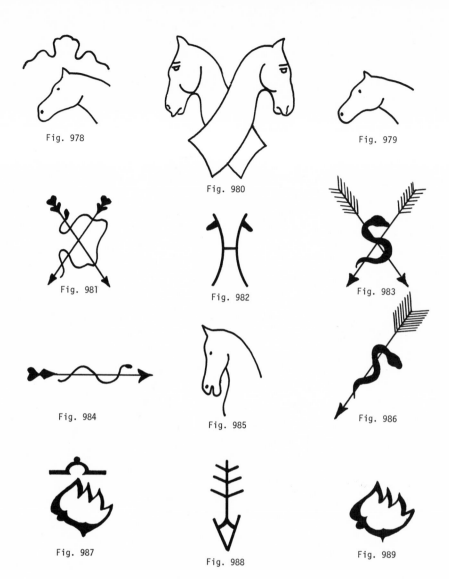

Fig. 978

Fig. 979

Fig. 980

Fig. 981

Fig. 982

Fig. 983

Fig. 984

Fig. 985

Fig. 986

Fig. 987

Fig. 988

Fig. 989

Plate LXIII. GERMAN HORSE BRANDS

Fig. 990

Fig. 991

Fig. 992

Fig. 993

Fig. 994

Fig. 995

Fig. 996

Fig. 997

Fig. 998

Fig. 999

Fig. 1000

Fig. 1001

Fig. 1002

Fig. 1003

Fig. 1004

Fig. 1005

Fig. 1006

Fig. 1007

Fig. 1008

Fig. 1009

Fig. 1010

Fig. 1011

Fig. 1012

PLATE LXIV. GERMAN HORSE BRANDS

Fig. 1013

Fig. 1014

Fig. 1015

Fig. 1016

Fig. 1017

Fig. 1018

Fig. 1019

Fig. 1020

Fig. 1021

Fig. 1022

Fig. 1023

Fig. 1024

Fig. 1025

Fig. 1026

Fig. 1027

Fig. 1028

Fig. 1029

PLATE LXV. GERMAN HORSE BRANDS

Fig. 1030

Fig. 1031

Fig. 1032

Fig. 1033

Fig. 1034

Fig. 1035

Fig. 1036

Fig. 1037

Fig. 1038

Fig. 1039

Fig. 1040

Fig. 1041

Fig. 1042

Fig. 1043

Fig. 1044

Fig. 1045

Fig. 1046

Fig. 1047

Fig. 1048

PLATE LXVI. GERMAN HORSE BRANDS

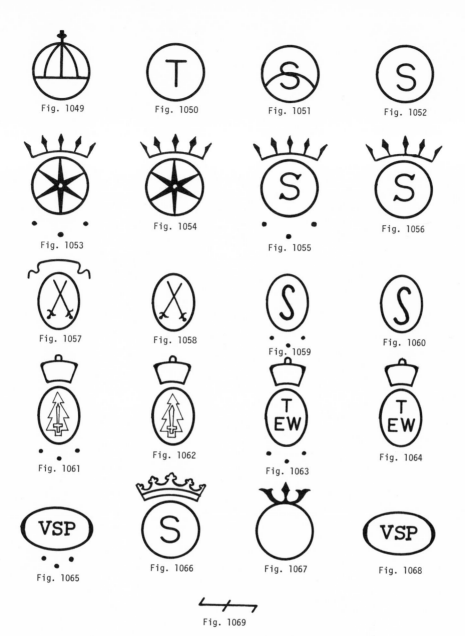

Fig. 1049

Fig. 1050

Fig. 1051

Fig. 1052

Fig. 1053

Fig. 1054

Fig. 1055

Fig. 1056

Fig. 1057

Fig. 1058

Fig. 1059

Fig. 1060

Fig. 1061

Fig. 1062

Fig. 1063

Fig. 1064

Fig. 1065

Fig. 1066

Fig. 1067

Fig. 1068

Fig. 1069

PLATE LXVII. GERMAN HORSE BRANDS

Fig. 1070   Fig. 1071   Fig. 1072   Fig. 1073 Fig. 1074   Fig. 1075

Fig. 1076

Fig. 1077

Fig. 1078

Fig. 1079

Fig. 1080   Fig. 1081   Fig. 1082   Fig. 1083

Fig. 1084   Fig. 1085   Fig. 1086   Fig. 1087

Fig. 1088   Fig. 1089   Fig. 1090   Fig. 1091   Fig. 1092

Fig. 1093   Fig. 1094

PLATE LXVIII. GERMAN HORSE BRANDS

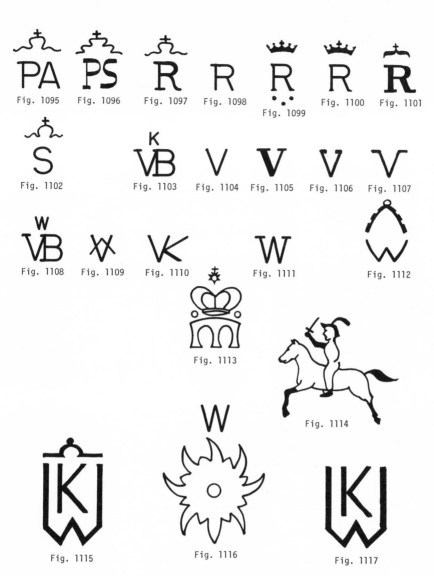

Fig. 1095 Fig. 1096 Fig. 1097 Fig. 1098 Fig. 1099 Fig. 1100 Fig. 1101

Fig. 1102 Fig. 1103 Fig. 1104 Fig. 1105 Fig. 1106 Fig. 1107

Fig. 1108 Fig. 1109 Fig. 1110 Fig. 1111 Fig. 1112

Fig. 1113

Fig. 1114

Fig. 1115 Fig. 1116 Fig. 1117

PLATE LXIX. GERMAN HORSE BRANDS

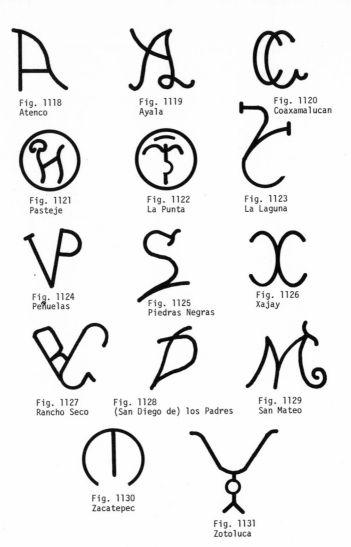

Fig. 1118
Atenco

Fig. 1119
Ayala

Fig. 1120
Coaxamalucan

Fig. 1121
Pasteje

Fig. 1122
La Punta

Fig. 1123
La Laguna

Fig. 1124
Peñuelas

Fig. 1125
Piedras Negras

Fig. 1126
Xajay

Fig. 1127
Rancho Seco

Fig. 1128
(San Diego de) los Padres

Fig. 1129
San Mateo

Fig. 1130
Zacatepec

Fig. 1131
Zotoluca

PLATE LXX. MEXICAN BULL RANCH BRANDS

Fig. 1132
Radautz

Fig. 1133
Píber

Fig. 1134
Kisber

Fig. 1135
Babolna

Fig. 1136
Mezö-Hegyes

Fig. 1137
Fogaras

PLATE LXXI. HUNGARIAN STATE STUD FARM BRANDS

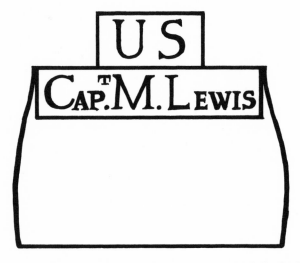

PLATE LXXII. LEWIS AND CLARK BRANDING IRON
(Meriwether Lewis, Captain, 1st Regiment, U.S. Infantry)

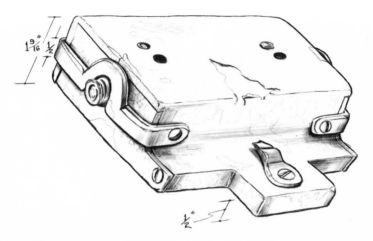

PLATE LXXIII. LEWIS AND CLARK
BRANDING IRON IN PERSPECTIVE

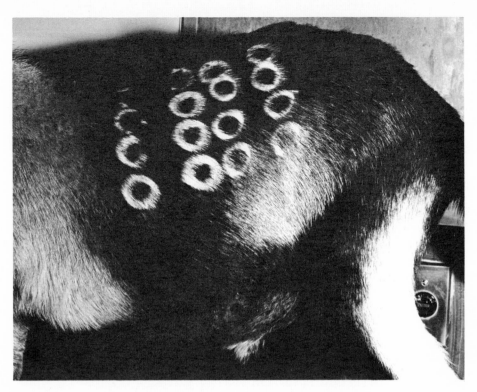

PLATE LXXIV. AN EXAMPLE OF CRYO-BRANDING

General Index

Abilene, Kansas: 7
Alabama: 184–85
Alaska: 184–85
Alberta: 237–40
Amenophis II, King: 4
Animals, regions and parts of cattle, horses, sheep, and swine: 41
Animals, taxonomical groupings: 36–41
Aphrodite, Goddess: 4
Arizona: 8, 185–86
Arkansas: 186–87
Armour and Company: 30
Austin, Stephen F. (Texas cattle baron): 6

Baden, Germany: 255
Banu Sokhr (Arab tribe): 34
Barbed wire: 13
Barrios Junco, Don Pedro de (Spanish Governor of Texas): 6
Bavaria, Germany: 251
Beck, Dave (labor leader): 30
Beni Hassan, Egypt: 3
Blotting: 17–18
Boston, Massachusetts: 9
Brand books: 165–66
Brand inspectors: 176–78
Brand laws: 164–65
Brand recorders: 167
Brand recording (application blank forms, recording fees, transfer forms, brand certificates): 173–75
Brand registration, Staten Island, New York: 162
Branding alphabets: 70–73
Branding characters and symbols: 75–81
Branding chemicals: 48
Branding chutes: 47–48

Branding heaters: 47
Branding irons: classification of, 42–45; U.S. Army stock numbers, 98–100; U.S. Military Academy, West Point, New York, 101–102; Lewis and Clark, 102–103
Branding liquid: 49
Branding method: Egyptian, 50; Texas, 50–51; California, 51; corral, 51; hog tie, 51
Branding numerals: 73–75
Branding paint: 48
Branding techniques: 52–53
Brands: locations of, 34–35; types of, 36, 53; design of, 62–69
Brands, Navajo: 106–107
Brands, U.S.: 83–126
Brands, U.S. Army: 83–101
Brands, U.S. Department of Agriculture: Forest Service, 110–12; Animal Disease Eradication Division, 112–13; Animal Husbandry Research Division (Agriculture Research Center, Beltsville, Maryland), 114–15; Meat Inspection Division, 115–20; Livestock Division, Meat Grading Service: 117, 121–24
Brands, U.S. Department of the Interior: Indian Agency, 103–106; Park Service, 108–10
Brazoria (Texas county): 6
Breed registry associations: 53, 58
Breeds: of cattle, 54–55; of horses, 55; of sheep, 56–57; of goats, 57; of swine, 57–58
British Columbia: 240–42
Brownsville, Texas: 7
Brunswick, Germany: 255
Buffalo, Wyoming: 10

431

Cabeza de Vaca, Álvar Núñez (Spanish explorer): 5
Cadency marks: 33
California: 6–7, 187–90
Canadian brands: 223–48
Canadian Indians: 229–31
Canadian National Live Stock Records Board: 234
Cattle drives: 7, 18–19
Cattle Kingdom: 6, 11–13, 15
Cattlemen's associations: 25–26
Cattle trails: 19–21
Charlié, John and James (wine merchants): 33
Chisholm, Jesse (Cherokee trader, marked Chisholm Trail): xviii
Chisholm, Richard H. (Gonzales, Texas, first recorded brand): 7, 162
Chisum, John Simpson (feudal lord of the Pecos, owner of cattle branded with the Long Rail and Jingle Bob): xviii
Cody, Colonel William F. (Buffalo Bill): 29
Colorado: 8, 12, 190
Connecticut: 221
Cortés, Captain General Hernán: 5
Crécy-en-Ponthieu, France: 5
Cryo-branding (super-cold): 59–61
Cudahy Packing Company: 30

Danzig, Free City of: 256
Delaware: 221
Deshashah, Egypt: 3
Dewlaps: 150–51, 182–83
Dorantes (Spanish explorer): 5
Douglas, Arizona: 5

East Frisia, Germany: 256ff.
East Prussia, Germany: 256ff.
Earmarkers: 54
Earmarks: 53, 133–49, 182; on cattle, 135–45; on sheep, 145–46; on goats, 146; on swine, 146–49
Ear notchers: 46
Edinburgh, Scotland: 9
Edward, Prince of Wales (Duke of Windsor): 29
Egyptians: 3
Eisenhower, President Dwight D.: 27

Electoral Marche (Brandenburg), Germany: 256ff.
Enti, Tomb of: 3
Estevan ("Arab Negro from Azamor"): 5

Fleshmarks: 149–51
Florida: 190–91
French, John (American cattleman): 34

German Democratic Republic: 251, 269–70
German Federal Republic: 251ff.
German horse breeders associations: 258–70
German horse breeding: 252–55
German state stud farms: 257–58
Georgia: 191–93, 215
Glidden, Joseph F. (most successful inventor of barbed wire): 25
Gonzales (Texas county): 7
Grangers: 10

Haish, Jacob (an inventor of barbed wire): 25
Hanover, Germany: 255ff.
Hawaii: 193–94
Heraldry: 31
Hog slapper: 46
Holland, Henry: 6
Hoof brand: 181
Horn brand: 181
Horn marks: 152
Hungarian state stud farms: 271

Idaho: 194
Illinois: 215–16
Indiana: 221
Indian Territory: 8
Iowa: 221
Ishtar, Goddess: 4

Johnson County War (Wyoming): 10
Johnson, President Lyndon B.: 27–28

Kansas: 7, 12, 194–95
Kentucky: 14–15, 221
Khemuheted, tomb of: 3
Khur Shân (Arab clan): 34

King Ranch, owners and livestock: 28
Laredo, Texas: 7
Lasuén, Father Fermin Francisco
  (Franciscan missionary): 159–61
Lewis and Harris Counties, Hebrides
  Islands: 249–50
Live Oak (Texas county): 7
Louisiana: 195–97
Lower Bavaria, Germany: 255ff.

Maclane, William: 6
Maine: 221
Maldonado (Spanish explorer): 5
Manitoba: 242–43
Manufer, tomb of: 3
Marking chalk: 49
Marking crayons: 49
Marks: 133–56
Maryland: 221
Massachusetts: 221
Matador Ranch: 29
Maverick: 16
Mecklenburg, Germany: 256ff.
Mesopotamia: 4
Mexican bull ranches: 270–71
Michigan: 216–17
Minnesota: 217
Missouri: 14, 217–18
Mississippi: 197–98
Montana: 9, 11–12, 198–99

National Livestock Brand Conference:
  167–72
Nebamun, tomb of: 4
Neck chains and straps: 54
Nebraska: 10, 12, 200
Nevada: 12, 200–18
New Hampshire: 221
New Jersey: 221
New Mexico: 8, 12, 202–203
New York: 9, 221
North Carolina: 15, 203, 215, 218
North Dakota: 12, 203–204

Oldenburg, Germany: 256ff.
Old Indianola, Texas: 7
Ogallala, Nebraska: 8
Ohio: 221
Oklahoma: 12, 204–206
Ontario: 243–44

Oregon: 7, 206–207

Pennsylvania: 221–22
Pomerania, Germany: 256ff.
Preston Branding System, U.S. Army:
  88, 90–93
Production record brands: 180–81
Prussia, Germany: 251, 257ff.

Quebec: 247

Rhineland, Germany: 256ff.
Rhode Island: 222
Richmond County (Staten Island, New
  York): 6
Roosevelt, President Theodore: 27
Round-ups: 15–16
Royal Canadian Mounted Police
  (Northwest Mounted Police 1873–
  1920): 225–28, 239

Saar Palatinate, Germany: 256ff.
Saskatchewan: 244–47
San Antonio, Texas: 7
Saez, Don Nicolas (Spanish militia-
  man): 6
St. Louis, Missouri: 19
Santo Domingo: 5
Saqqâra, Egypt: 3
Saxony, Germany: 256ff.
Saxony-Anhalt: 256ff.
Scout's Rest Ranch, Nebraska: 29
Schleswig-Holstein, Germany: 256ff.
Serra, Father Junípero (Franciscan
  missionary): 157–59
Shekh abd el Gurna, Egypt: 3
Silesia, Germany: 256ff.
Snout cutter: 47
Snout marks: 151
Solingen, Germany: 5
South Carolina: 222
South Dakota: 207–208
State brands: 127–32
State disease control brands: 128–30
Stock detectives: 21
Stock inspectors: 22
Swift and Company: 30

Tattoo markers: 45–47

433

Tattoo paste: 48
Tattoos: 53, 151–56, 183; on cattle, 153–55; on horses, 155; on sheep, 155; on fur-bearing animals, 156; on goats, 156; on poultry, 156; on swine, 156
Tennessee: 14–15, 222
Terrazas, Don Luis (Mexican cattle baron): 28
Texas: 7–8, 12, 14, 214, 218–19
"Texas fever": 22–23
Thai animal identification: 271–72
Thebes, Egypt: 4
Thoroughbred Racing Protective Bureau: 31
Thutmosis IV, King: 4
Treasury Cattle Commission: 23

Union Pacific Railroad Company: 30
United Kingdom of Great Britain and Northern Ireland: 248–50
Upper Bavaria, Germany: 255ff.
U.S. Atomic Energy Commission: 125
U.S. Department of Agriculture, Bureau of Animal Industry: 23
Userhet, tomb of: 3
Utah: 12, 208–11

Valenzuela y Peralta, Don Miguel

Ascarate de la (Mexican cattleman): 34
Vasquez Coronado, Don Francisco (Spanish explorer): 5
Veghte, Justice John: 6
Vent brands: 181
Vera Cruz, Mexico: 5
Vermont: 222
Villa, General Francisco (Pancho), born Doroteo Arango: 29
Villalobos, Gregorio (cattle shipper): 5
Virginia: 15, 222

War Relocation Authority (1942–46): 125–26
Washington: 211–13
Washington, President George: 27
Wattles: 151, 182–83
West Virginia: 15, 222
Westphalia, Germany: 257ff.
Wisconsin: 220–21
Württemberg, Germany: 257ff.
Württemberg-Baden, Germany: 251ff.
Wyoming: 10, 12, 213–14

XIT Ranch: 28–29

Yomba Shoshone Indian tribe: 30